D1602966

THE INTERNATIONAL PETROCHEMICAL INDUSTRY

Evolution and Location

Keith Chapman

HD
9579
.C32
C45
1991
west

BLACKWELL
Oxford UK & Cambridge USA

Copyright © Keith Chapman 1991

Keith Chapman is hereby identified as author of this work in
accordance with Section 77 of the Copyright, Designs and Patents
Act 1988.

First published 1991

Basil Blackwell Ltd
108 Cowley Road, Oxford, OX4 1JF, UK

Basil Blackwell, Inc.
3 Cambridge Center
Cambridge, Massachusetts 02142, USA

All rights reserved. Except for the quotation of short passages for
the purposes of criticism and review, no part may be reproduced,
stored in a retrieval system, or transmitted, in any form or by any
means, electronic, mechanical, photocopying, recording or otherwise,
without the prior permission of the publisher.

Except in the United States of America, this book is sold subject to
the condition that it shall not, by way of trade or otherwise, be
lent, re-sold, hired out, or otherwise circulated without the
publisher's prior consent in any form of binding or cover other
than that in which it is published and without a similar condition
including this condition being imposed on the subsequent purchaser.

Library of Congress Cataloging in Publication Data

Chapman, Keith.
The international petrochemical industry: evolution and location/
Keith Chapman.
p.   cm.
ISBN 0-631-16098-1
1. Petroleum chemicals industry.   I. Title
HD9579.C32C45   1991   338.4'7661804—dc20   91-10435 CIP

British Library Cataloguing in Publication Data

A CIP catalogue record for this book is available from the British Library.

Typeset in 10½ on 11½ pt Baskerville
by Best-set Typesetter Ltd., Hong Kong
Printed in Great Britain by T.J. Press Ltd., Padstow, Cornwall

This book is printed on acid-free paper.

Contents

Figures

xii   *Figures*

Tables

Preface

This book reflects a continuing research interest in the petrochemical industry over a period of more than 20 years. This interest has brought me into contact with numerous individuals in industry, consultancy and government as well as academic institutions. To many of these people I have been a novelty, and I have lost count of the number of times I have been asked how, as a geographer, I developed this interest. Although I have yet to formulate an answer which convinces myself, there is little doubt that my rather unusual professional credentials have, by stimulating some curiosity, allowed me to place a foot in many doors that would otherwise have remained firmly closed.

The level of cooperation received in response to requests for information once across these corporate thresholds has varied, but has usually extended well beyond the minimal courtesies. This is especially true of Dennis Claridge of ICI Chemicals and Polymers Ltd. In many ways, this book is a consequence of a chance meeting with him. By offering me access to the information resources of Wilton Centre, he made it possible for me to consider this undertaking. His role was not only passive, in the sense of opening doors (and filing cabinets!), but also active to the extent of reading and offering constructive comments on the manuscript.

Clive Lee of the Department of Economics at the University of Aberdeen overcame the massive barriers faced by a Leeds United supporter in communicating (in terms other than abuse) with a lifelong disciple of the other United across the Pennines to provide a different and valued perspective.

A significant part of the research upon which this book is based was undertaken in Canada and the United States. The magnificent campus of the University of Texas at Austin provided a stimulating environment on several occasions, and my visits were made all the more enjoyable by the Texan hospitality. Jim McKie of the Department of Economics ensured that this hospitality was both domestic and institutional.

Preface

Christina Anderson was responsible for typing much of the manuscript, whilst Kay Leiper, Alison Sandison and Jenny Johnson prepared the maps and diagrams.

Finally, it goes without saying that those identified in these 'credits' bear no responsibility for any errors of fact or interpretation.

Keith Chapman
University of Aberdeen

Introduction

This study attempts to describe and explain the development of petrochemical manufacture from its origins as a specialized, high technology activity at the interface of established oil refining and chemical operations to its present status as a basic industry occupying a strategic position within the world economy. Emphasis is placed upon the spatial evolution of the industry, both within individual countries and at the global scale. This necessarily involves consideration of the objectives and policies of the companies and governments which are the agents of change within the industry. It also requires an understanding of the interrelationships between technology, economics and location which determine patterns of investment in the spectacular complexes which are so characteristic of petrochemical manufacture. Although the main objective of this study is to identify and interpret patterns in the evolution of the industry itself, certain characteristics of its development and distribution have had important consequences for the areas in which it is located. These consequences not only illustrate the interrelationships between the evolution of industries and regions, but also raise important policy issues with implications extending beyond the particular case of petrochemicals.

1
Life-Cycle Perspectives on the Petrochemical Industry

The recession of the 1980s has prompted a search on the part of governments in virtually all developed countries for new technologies and industries to replace those which are widely perceived to have exhausted their growth potential. The urgency of the search for new jobs at the practical or policy level has in turn encouraged renewed academic interest in the processes of long term economic growth. Some aspects of this interest are explored in this chapter, in particular the complex relationships between these processes, technical changes at industry and product levels, and shifting spatial patterns of economic activity at various geographical scales. This review provides a framework of general ideas which are subsequently applied to an interpretation of the development, especially the geographic development, of the petrochemical industry.

1.1 Innovation, Industries and Economic Growth

It is generally accepted that technical change plays an important role in economic growth. Casual observation of recent economic history suggests that such change is focused upon particular sectors which seem to serve as engines of economic growth at different periods. Innovations in cotton textiles, metallurgy and the pervasive influence of the various advances consequent upon the harnessing of steam power were, for example, characteristic of the Industrial Revolution. The steel industry and railways provided new impetus in the mid nineteenth century, and this was followed by the impact of the widespread adoption of electricity and successive but overlapping sources of innovation associated with advances in, for example, motor vehicles, synthetic materials and electronics. Several writers have attempted to link directly these advances to alleged long cycles or waves of economic development (see Schumpeter 1939; Mensch 1979; Freeman et al. 1982; van Duijn 1983). Although the existence of such phenomena is, to say the least, debatable (see Maddison 1982; Solomou 1989), there is no doubt that 'Technical progress is the most essential characteristic of modern growth' (Maddison 1982, 56). Certainly, the rate of technical change seems to have accelerated sharply when viewed over the long perspective of human history (see Rosenberg 1972; North 1981). The Industrial Revolution is conventionally regarded as the watershed in this respect (see Mantoux 1928; Landes 1968), but North (1981) has argued that the systematic application of science and technology to the creation of wealth is much more recent. Organized research and development (R and D) was pioneered by the German chemical industry in the last quarter of the nineteenth century, and the widespread adoption of this practice 'has produced an inflection change in the supply curve of new knowledge' (North 1981, 172) which has been reflected, over the last 100 years or so, in rates of economic growth which have been exceptional by historical standards.

Technical change is a complex process which embodies a wide spectrum of developments from minor improvements to fundamental advances. Rosenberg (1976) has emphasized the cumulative significance of incremental changes, but the same author also notes that certain major innovations are significant because their impact extends throughout the economy 'in a series of ever widening concentric circles' (Rosenberg 1979, 29). Schumpeter's reference to 'new combinations' of materials and productive forces expresses essentially the same idea, whilst Freeman coined the term 'technological revolution' to describe changes which 'not only lead to the emergence of new leading branches of the economy and a whole range of new product groups, [but] also have fundamental effects on many other branches of the economy by transforming their methods of production and their input cost structure' (Freeman 1987, 16). The introduction of electricity, for example, had such effects during the last quarter of the nineteenth century (Devine 1983), and the impact of the silicon chip has been equally far-reaching in more recent years (Freeman 1984). Despite the pervasive nature of such technological revolutions, they originate in changes which are focused at the industry or sector level.[1] Indeed, Mensch (1979) has suggested that the most important innovations are those which lead to the creation of entirely new industries. This criterion of significance raises the question of the relationship between long term growth trends at the macro-economic level and the life cycles of industries.

The idea that industries display characteristic patterns of growth may be traced to the work of Kuznets (1930) who asserted that, viewed over time, the output of a specific sector may be expected to increase at a diminishing rate, assuming the form of a *logistic* or S-shaped curve. Further empirical support for this proposition was assembled by Burns (1934) and van Duijn (1980), although Gold

(1964) produced contradictory evidence. Many of the contradictions are more apparent than real, resulting from the limitations of the data and from the definition of the industries selected for analysis. Whilst individual products may conform to the model, industries are usually aggregations of products, each of which may be at a different position on the growth curve. The length of time between the origin of an industry, which in theory may be traced back to the commercial exploitation of a key or basic invention, and the maturity implied by diminishing rates of growth at the upper inflexion of the curve, may also vary widely. Furthermore, what actually happens when this point is reached is not fixed. The logistic curve may be conceived as only half of a complete cycle which may be represented as a bell-shaped curve. It is possible to think of examples of industries in which output has declined and ultimately ceased altogether. On the other hand, there are several industries which have displayed such longevity that the plateau phase seems almost indefinite. Generally speaking, the first halves of industry life cycles are better documented than the second – a situation which is characteristic of evolutionary models in the economic literature as a whole (see Alonso 1980). This tradition will be maintained in this study of the petrochemical industry since, viewed at a global scale, there is no foreseeable prospect that the output of this sector will decline in accordance with the bell-shaped hypothesis, and its development conforms more closely to the S-shaped model.

The evolution of an industry may be expressed other than in terms of trends in output, and the notion of a bell-shaped curve may be more appropriate when other criteria are used. Markusen (1985) has explored the relationships between output, investment, employment and profitability. She suggests that the overall level of profitability within an industry displays the kind of temporal sequence identified in figure 1.1(a). Zero profit incorporates the period of research and development which precedes commercial production. This may be of long or short duration. In some cases, such as Du Pont's commitment to nylon (Scherer 1984), huge sums of money may be spent before there is any return on investment and some avenues of research may prove to be commercial culs-de-sac. Super profits accrue to innovating firms during an initial oligopoly phase,[2] when the lack of competition allows high prices to be maintained whilst unit costs begin to fall as manufacturing experience is gained and the transformation from batch or customized to mass production is initiated. This transformation is completed during the stage of normal profit as the technical lead of innovating firms is eroded and more and more firms are attracted to the rapidly growing industry. Increased competition places downward pressure on both costs and prices. The law of diminishing returns limits cost reductions, but price competition intensifies in what is by now a sluggish or saturated market, resulting

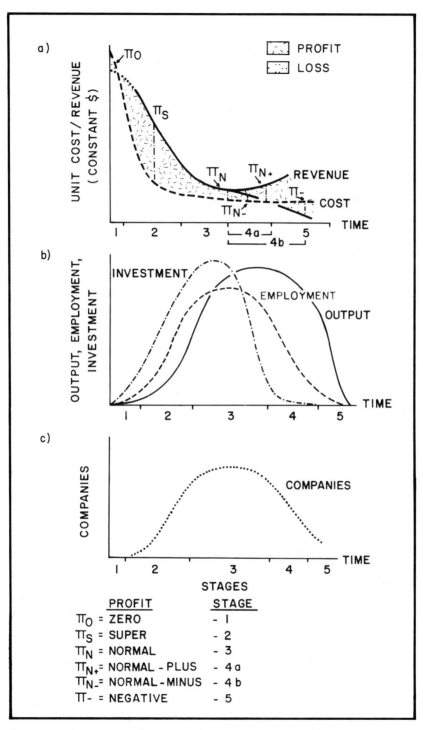

Figure 1.1 Markusen's profit-cycle model (from Markusen 1985)

in a profit squeeze. Markusen identifies two alternative scenarios at this stage. In one (normal-plus), industry reorganization enables the relatively few surviving firms to obtain control of output and prices in an oligopolistic situation; in the other (normal-minus), intense competition results in further pressure on profits and an accelerated progression to the final stage of negative profit which is associated with disinvestment and an ultimate demise of the industry.[3]

Although profitability is the central focus of Markusen's model, she notes that this parameter is associated with changes in other variables across the cycle. The vertical scale in figure 1.1(b) measures the relative level of investment, output and employment through time, and the lagged curves indicate systematic changes in the capital to labour ratio which result in higher productivity towards the end of the cycle. Changes in commercial structure are portrayed in figure 1.1(c), emphasizing the importance of oligopoly at the beginning and end of the cycle and the intervening period of intense competition associated with the phase of normal profit.[4]

Markusen's model draws together ideas from a variety of different sources. Her work is concerned with analysing the experience of *sectors* which she distinguishes from *industries*. Her sectors refer to 'a set of corporations and firms that organizes the fabrication of a particular type of product' (Markusen 1985, 20). This definition is prudent. Whilst there are formidable practical difficulties in verifying the logistic curve of industrial growth, it is relatively easy to trace the history of individual products. Marketing experience suggests that the growth in sales of a product follows a systematic path (see Levitt 1965; Cox 1967; Kluyver 1977). Initially sales are low because of customer resistance to a new and untried product. In many cases, the product never gets beyond this stage, but those which do then enter a phase of rapid and accelerating growth. Eventually demand levels off as the potential market is fully exploited, and further growth is limited to replacement and any incremental increases related to population trends. The plateau of this maturity phase may extend over a long or short period, after which sales volume gradually declines as the product loses its appeal or is replaced by something better. This market-based concept of the product life cycle has been very influential in the business literature which has emphasized its connection, through the operation of competitive strategies, with industry evolution (see Porter 1980, 156–79).

Both the industry and product life-cycle concepts have a significance which extends beyond the specification of trends in output as mediated by the operation of the market. It has been suggested that the transition from one stage to another is accompanied by characteristic developments in the technology of production (see Abernathy and Townsend 1975; Magee 1977; Thomas 1981; Utterback and Abernathy 1975). At the beginning of the product life cycle, efforts to improve product quality require frequent changes in manufacturing process and product specification. Production is labour intensive and, more specifically, skill intensive. Production runs are short and unit cost are high. During the growth stage, two sets of influences combine to encourage a switch to standardized, capital-intensive, mass production methods. On the one hand, output must be stepped up to meet rapidly growing demand; on the other hand, costs must be reduced in the face of increasing competition as patent protection lapses. Downward pressure on costs becomes even more acute in the mature stage, accentuating the trends established during the growth phase.

These patterns at product level are paralleled at the industry scale, although generalizations inevitably become more speculative. Certainly, there seems to be a progressive shift towards more capital-intensive methods of production as industries evolve. These events on the manufacturing side are accompanied by changes in the nature and significance of R and D activity. There is plenty of evidence that young industries devote a higher proportion of their resources to R and D (see Freeman 1982). This is not surprising since the opportunities for further significant technical breakthroughs must be expected to decline as an industry develops, leading to a shift in emphasis away from basic research on new products to the incremental improvement of existing products and attempts to reduce costs through process innovation. There is also an organizational aspect to the industry life cycle as emphasized by Markusen (1985) (figure 1.1(c)). Initially, constituent firms tend to be small and few in number since access to the new technology is limited. During the growth phase, know-how becomes more widely available and many new entrants leap on the bandwagon. However, the average size of firm increases as a result of the financial requirements imposed by the trend towards mass production. Finally, the scramble for static or declining markets in the mature phase tends to produce an oligopolistic structure as the industry becomes dominated by a few survivors.

1.2 Life Cycles and Location

In introducing the preceding review of the interrelationships between innovation, the evolution of industries and economic growth, reference was made to the existence of a sequence of leading sectors from the Industrial Revolution onwards. The discussion was implicitly based upon Western European and, more specifically, British experience. However, it is self-evident that there are wide variations in levels of economic development between countries. Nevertheless, it has been suggested that the nature of the manufacturing sector changes in a systematic way as economic development takes place (see Chenery 1960; Rostow 1960). Cotton textiles are typically the first 'early' industry to be established, and are followed by 'middle' and 'late' sectors such as rubber products and consumer durables respectively. These sequential relationships between industrial structure and economic growth, first associated with countries such as the United Kingdom and the United States, have also been described for countries which have industrialized later, right through from Italy and Sweden at the end of the nineteenth century to their contemporary equivalents such as Brazil and South Korea (see Rostow 1978; Beenstock 1983). The only major difference is a tendency for the process to accelerate as latecomers have been able to benefit from the pool of technology and experience accumulated by their predecessors.

The association between industrial structure and economic growth, together with the existence of wide variations in levels of development between countries, introduces a spatial dimension to the industry life cycle outlined in section 1.1. Quite clearly, the same industry may be at a very different position on the S-shaped output curve in one country as compared with another. Generalizations about the future prospects of individual sectors often neglect this obvious fact. For example, whilst the iron and steel industry of the developed market economies has passed beyond the upper inflexion of the S, it is at a much earlier stage in the newly industrializing countries. Steel production actually declined in the United States and many European countries between 1970 and 1981; average annual growth rates exceeded 10 per cent over the same period in parts of Latin America and South East Asia (Dicken 1986). This contrast emphasizes the need to incorporate the spatial dimension within the industry life-cycle concept.

Despite the size of its facilities, the iron and steel industry tends to be national rather than international in its organizational structure and its marketing strategies; this characteristic is reinforced by high levels of state ownership. In many other sectors, however, there is a clear trend towards the establishment of truly global systems of production under the control of increasingly powerful multinational corporations.[5] To the extent that these corporations serve as the principal agents for the transfer of technology between countries, their existence suggests that, in certain sectors at least, life-cycle concepts can indeed be applied at the global scale and that they may have a geographical significance which extends beyond the simple acknowledgement of differences in national levels of economic development. Such differences are themselves significant from a corporate point of view since an obvious strategy to sustain high levels of sales growth once a product has reached the mature stage of its life cycle in the domestic market is to penetrate foreign markets either by exports or by the establishment of overseas production facilities. This process of market area extension at the international scale was, for example, a major factor in the massive influx of United States manufacturing investment into Western Europe during the 1950s and 1960s (see Groo 1971; Forsyth 1972; Blackbourn 1974; Rees 1974).

The product cycle may also be used to explain an entirely different kind of overseas investment strategy which has played an important role in the changing world distribution of industries such as consumer electronics (see Ballance and Sinclair 1983; Grunwald and Flamm 1985) and textiles (see Steed 1978; Toyne et al. 1984). The manner in which the technology of production evolves in certain systematic ways during both the product and the industry life cycles has already been noted. It was Vernon (1966) who first recognized the implications of these changes for the location of industry. As products become standardized, the significance of technical inputs and skilled labour is reduced. Emphasis in the mature stage is placed upon reducing the costs of production. One way of achieving such a reduction is to shift production to lower cost locations. The greatest savings at the international scale are associated with differences in wage levels, and various writers have followed Vernon in using the product life-cycle concept to account for the dispersal of manufacturing activities controlled by multinational corporations from the developed to the newly industrializing economies (see Hirsch 1967; Wells 1972; Hymer 1979; Moran 1979; Hamilton and Linge 1981). This type of logic provides only a partial explanation, as Vernon (1979) has since acknowledged. Neverthless, the link between life-cycle concepts, which have their origin in the literature of economics and management, and industrial location is important and has attracted the attention of geographers.

Much of this interest has involved translating these concepts from the international scale at which they were first applied by Vernon (1966) to an interpretation of changes in the distribution of industry within individual countries (see Krumme and Hayter 1975; Norton and Rees 1979). In a historical context, Hekman (1980a) has argued that the dispersal of the textile industry in the United States from its original centre in New England to the South after 1880 was a consequence of developments in the technology of production. The initial clustering was encouraged by Boston's position as a source of capital, entrepreneurs and skilled mechanics associated with the embryonic machine tool industry. However, the pace of technical change gradually slowed down and experimental equipment was replaced by standardized machinery for textile production. The reliability and automatic nature of this equipment reduced the need for skilled labour for both maintenance and operating purposes, encouraging textile firms to shift their manufacturing activities to low labour cost locations in the South. Hekman (1980b) has applied similar logic to an interpretation of the geography of the US computer industry. New England and California dominate in the skill-intensive functions associated with the research, development and design of new products, but the assembly of machines and other peripherals such as terminals and printers is much more widely dispersed throughout the country. A study of trends in semiconductor manufacturing in the United States between 1950 and 1980, which described a dispersal from high to relatively low labour cost locations, is yet another illustration of the application of life-cycle ideas to the analysis of industrial location (Harrington 1985).

Such aggregate shifts at the industry scale frequently reflect the policies of large multiplant enterprises. The flexibility of multiplant operation means that such enterprises often create systems of production which are, in effect, locational hierarchies based on the product life cycle (see Massey 1984; Chapman and Walker 1991, 126–30). Thus operations associated with the mature phase are often found in peripheral or even rural locations where labour costs are low, whilst those associated with the early stages are found in core locations in close proximity to R and D facilities. There is a substantial literature exploring these ideas and, whilst there is no doubt that the product life-cycle interpretation of interregional shifts in the distribution of manufacturing within developed economies has been overenthusiastically applied (see Storper 1985; Taylor 1986), the model has provided important insights (see Erickson 1976; Massey 1979). Certainly it is relevant to an understanding of the branch plant syndrome, and it is not difficult to appreciate that, viewed from a regional perspective, an excessive dependence upon operations associated with the manufacture of products in the mature and declining phases of their life cycles is undesirable. Their growth potential is, by definition, limited and the employment they offer is typically of low skill, pay and status.

The links between the product life cycle, the spatial structure of business organizations and the development of regions have become clearer partly as a result of the evaluation of policies designed to encourage the establishment of branch plants in certain sectors to compensate for job losses in others. There are well known structural problems in old industrial areas which, as a result of their economic history, have come to rely upon sectors which, in the context of developed economies, are in the mature or declining phase of their life cycles, and several attempts have been made to use the life-cycle idea to connect the evolution of industries and regions (see Steiner 1985; Chapman and Walker 1991, 170–89). The transformation of old industrial areas by the establishment not simply of branch plants, but of integrated complexes of activities focused upon 'lead' or 'propulsive' industries in the rapid growth phase of their life cycles, is an attractive if somewhat elusive policy objective with a long pedigree (see Malecki 1983; Thomas 1985). The growth poles and growth centres which inspired many planners in the 1960s (see Darwent 1969; Moseley 1974) find their contemporary parallels in the science parks and innovation-oriented regional policies of the 1980s (see Rothwell 1982; Christy and Ironside 1987).

It is apparent that the life-cycle analogy has been translated into economic terms in several different but interrelated ways – with reference to industries, products and places (i.e. regions). Despite their temporal basis, it is also clear that these life cycles have implications for the location of economic activity at a variety of scales from international to interregional. As with all such models, however, the analogies should not be pursued too far. The technological aspects of both the industry and the product life-cycle models tend to encourage a fatalistic view of the inevitability of ultimate decline, but many studies have emphasized the technological dynamism of mature industries (see Gibbs 1987; Hayter 1987; Holmes 1987). Major innovations may occur which fundamentally change the natural technological trajectory of an industry, with important consequences for its location. For example, the US automobile industry originated in the 1890s in numerous small workshops associated with the manufacture of such items as farm machinery and horse-drawn carriages and was, therefore, widely dispersed throughout the country (Boas 1961). The introduction of Henry Ford's assembly line in Detroit in 1915 represented a fundamental departure from the craft methods previously employed. Not only did this event transform the geography of the industry, but it also amounted to a kind of rebirth in terms of its life cycle. Such rejuvenation may occur several times and there is increasing interest in the promotion of innovation in mature industries (see Abernathy et al. 1983; Piore and Sabel 1985). Indeed one of the original sponsors of the life-cycle model of product and process innovation has rejected its irreversability (Abernathy et al. 1983). Referring once again to the United States automobile industry, major innovations have occurred since the mid 1970s, including the introduction of computer-controlled machine tools, which have radically altered the nature of production (see Ayres and Steger 1985; Holmes 1987; Schoenberger 1987).

It is not only technical change which may affect the growth prospects and locational pattern of an industry. Parametric shocks which are economic or political in origin may be even more important. Governments are able, through their policy decisions, to change completely the business environment within which firms operate and, therefore, the prospects of entire industries. National frontiers often represent major discontinuities in economic as well as political terms. In these circumstances, it is very difficult to apply evolutionary models to the development of industries at the global scale. The significance of national frontiers is itself a reflection of an even more fundamental influence – the geographical dimension. Despite their implications for the location of economic activity, neither the industry nor the product life-cycle model was conceived in spatial terms.

Smith (1981) has provided a representation of the spatial evolution of a hypothetical industry by tracing through time the aggregate effect of the entry of new firms, the disappearance of some old firms and the survival of others. It is assumed that the industry is composed of single plant firms and that it is established by the more or less simultaneous birth of several firms. Their location is determined by such chance factors as the place of residence of the entrepreneurs, who are assumed (perhaps unrealistically) to acquire spontaneously the knowledge and expertise required to enter the new industry. Smith postulates the operation of a kind of economic Darwinism which ultimately results in a spatial pattern which more closely approximates an optimal distribution. These ideas have also been explored by Ellinger (1977) and White and Watts (1977). Case studies of specific industries emphasize that the optimal distribution is an elusive, moving target from the point of view of individual firms (see Lindberg 1953; Hekman 1978). The longer the period considered, the more likely it is that the key reference points in the determination of the optimum location will themselves shift as, for example, some raw material sources are exhausted and replaced by others and new markets develop in response to changing patterns of population and economic activity.

The spatial evolution of industries is not only influenced by such external geographical variables as markets and raw materials. Internal, technology-based dynamics implicit in the product-cycle concept may be expected to produce systematic spatial patterns at the industry level. Markusen (1985) suggests that an industry will initially concentrate in one or a few locations reflecting the distribution of inventors or innovations (although it is acknowledged that other factors may be decisive locational influences at this stage). Whatever the reasons for the initial concentration (see section 3.1), its attractions will be reinforced at the beginning of the life cycle. Numerous factors, such as the existence of a skilled labour pool and the development of subcontracting relationships, will draw pioneering firms together, creating the kind of agglomeration associated with the emergence of Silicon Valley in California. As the technology becomes standardized, however, the need to reduce costs results in the dispersal of the industry away from its original centre of production in search of cheaper labour. This trend may be retarded if competition has been limited by the creation of an oligopolistic commercial structure as the industry matures. The power and financial resources of the few large corporations which typically remain towards the end of the industry life cycle may ultimately result in a ruthless reduction of capacity, reversing the trend towards dispersal and concentrating production at fewer locations.

It is very difficult to provide any single unifying framework for the analysis of the development of industries, broadly conceived to include changes in production, organization and location. Indeed, there are clear dangers involved in imposing such a framework (see Walker 1985). Although the evolution of the petrochemical industry is related to the life-cycle concept in this book, the concept cannot provide a comprehensive explanation of the industry's development. An attempt is therefore made to utilize the framework where appropriate, and to draw upon other approaches to explanation, in this geographical study of one of the most important industries within the modern economy.

1.3 The Petrochemical Industry

The rapid overall rate of economic growth since the second half of the nineteenth century compared with the accumulated growth of the preceding centuries was emphasized in section 1.1. There is universal agreement amongst economists and economic historians that the period since the Second World War has been even more remarkable, and Maddison (1982) refers to the years between 1950 and 1972 as the 'golden age' of capitalist development. There is less agreement on the relative importance of the interacting factors which contributed to this uniquely favourable situation, but most observers include the effect of policies of full employment, the impetus to demand provided by post-war reconstruction, and the decline in the real price of foodstuffs, raw materials and energy (see Cornwall 1977; Aldcroft 1978; Maddison 1982; Van der Wee 1986). However, there is no doubt that the commercial exploitation of several relatively new technologies provided the impetus for the spectacular growth of certain industries which themselves stimulated further growth elsewhere in the economy. These engines of post-war growth have been variously identified to include, amongst others, computers, electrical engineering, pharmaceuticals, synthetic materials and consumer durables such as motor vehicles (see Cornwall 1977; Scammell 1980; Freeman et al. 1982; Kleinknecht 1987). Discrepancies in the lists of various authors generally reflect differing levels of disaggregation rather than any real disagreement. On a fundamental level, the inspiration for most of these developments can be traced to advances in only two broad areas of knowledge – electronics and chemistry. As far as the latter is concerned, research in many areas, including polymer science and petrochemistry, contributed to a situation in which the post-war boom in the chemical industry became

synonymous with petrochemicals. Indeed, the concept of an identifiable petrochemical 'industry' rapidly became common usage.
Strictly speaking, petrochemical manufacture is a branch of the
chemical industry, and it is defined in terms of its ultimate dependence upon petroleum-based raw materials (including natural gas)
rather than the nature of its products, many of which were known
before the industry existed when they were derived from different raw
materials. Nevertheless, the large-scale manufacture of these products
was inextricably linked to the switch to oil and natural gas as the
principal raw materials of the organic chemical industry. It is not the
petrochemicals themselves, but rather the way in which they are used
to produce other materials such as fertilizers, plastics, synthetic fibres
and rubbers, which has ensured that the petrochemical industry has
played such a key role in the post-war economy.

The notion that particular sectors have the ability to transmit
growth impulses to other branches of the economy is central to the
concept of manufacturing as the 'engine of growth' (Cornwall 1977).
The more extensive and diverse are the linkages with other sectors,
the greater is the potential for this kind of propulsive effect. The
petrochemical industry, like the chemical industry in general, is
essentially a supplier of intermediate products to other sectors. This
role has enabled it to become a vital element in a virtuous circle of
economic growth created by the mutually reinforcing effects of
changes in technology and demand. More specifically, the industry
has not only been associated with the manufacture of new products,
such as polyethylene and nylon, but has also made these products
available at declining real cost, thereby stimulating the growth of
related sectors such as plastics fabrication and certain branches of
the textile industry. These materials, ultimately derived from petrochemical products, have become almost ubiquitous, finding applications throughout the economic system. Thus the activities of the
petrochemical industry have been central to a chain of economic
events in the post-war period which seem to qualify as a technological
revolution in the Schumpeterian sense.

Whatever criteria of growth are employed, the petrochemical
industry was one of the most dynamic sectors in the developed
economies during the 1950s and 1960s. The rate of growth was not
sustained in the 1970s and 1980s, however, and, viewed over a 40
year period, the performance of the industry seems to conform to the
logistic curve originally postulated by Kuznets. The degree of this
correspondence is examined in subsequent chapters, which also
analyse the various stages in the industry's development relative
to the logistic model, placing particular emphasis upon the interrelationships between the temporal and spatial dimensions of its
development. Although the logistic model implies a consistency in
the growth patterns of industries, there are good reasons why the

position on the curve of a specific industry may vary with location (see section 1.2). This has certainly been true of the petrochemical industry, and figure 1.2 indicates a succession of curves starting at approximately ten year intervals. The diagram is very generalized, and the industry curve for petrochemicals is an aggregation of many curves for individual products with different growth histories. It also suppresses significant year to year variations related to short term economic fluctuations. On a geographical level, the curves for Western Europe and the rest of the world[6] conceal significant variations between countries. In the case of Western Europe, the sequential development of the industry, first in the United Kingdom and West Germany and then elsewhere, is analogous to the succession of waves in figure 1.2, but compressed over a shorter time-scale. The curve for the rest of the world is the least satisfactory of all, as it incorporates many nations which have become petrochemical producers for different reasons and under different circumstances.

The crude representation of figure 1.2 is based on the kind of evidence indicated in figure 1.3, which plots the rate of growth in capacity for ethylene, and in figure 1.4, which indicates the cumulative increase in the number of countries with facilities for its manufacture. Ethylene is a key petrochemical product because it is the

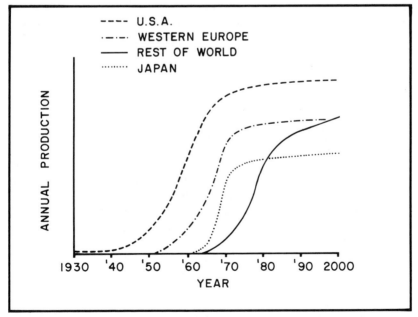

Figure 1.2 Petrochemical capacity by world region, 1930–2000 (data from ICI Chemicals and Polymers Ltd)

16 *Life-Cycle Perspectives*

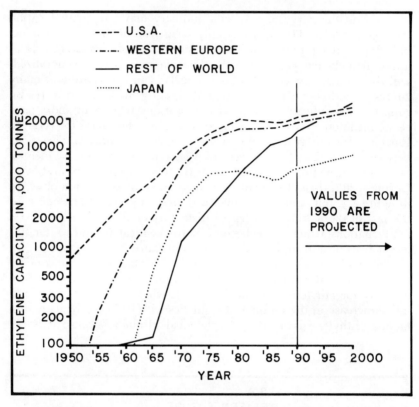

Figure 1.3 Ethylene capacity by world region, 1950–2000 (data from ICI Chemicals and Polymers Ltd)

intermediate from which many of the most important commodities, such as polyethylene and polystyrene, are derived. Ethylene capacity is therefore a reliable index of the distribution of the industry in general, and it may also be assumed that actual production broadly correlates with capacity. The implied geographical consequences of the differential rates of growth in figures 1.2 and 1.3 are made explicit in table 1.1. The decline in the dominance of the United States since 1950 is clear. Capacity in the developed economies actually fell in the first half of the 1980s and only recovered towards the end of the decade. It is evident that the changing relative positions indicated in table 1.1 are due not to the relocation of capacity, but to the establishment of petrochemical manufacture in more and more countries. The principal objective of this book is to explain the temporal and spatial patterns of development apparent in the juxta-position of figures 1.2, 1.3 and 1.4 with table 1.1.

Table 1.1 World[a] ethylene capacity, 1950–2000

	1950		1960		1970		1980		1990		2000 (estimated)	
	thousand tonnes	% share	thousand tonnes	% share	thousand tonnes	% share	thousand tonnes	% share	thousand tonnes	% share	thousand tonnes	% share
USA[b]	743	98.1	2,800	75.7	9,299	48.0	17,478	41.6	18,350	34.4	22,660	30.4
W. Europe	14	1.9	820	22.2	6,312	32.6	14,186	33.8	16,005	30.1	20,405	27.4
Japan	—	0.0	42	1.1	2,664	13.7	5,362	12.8	5,537	10.4	7,203	9.7
Others	—	0.0	34	1.0	1,100	5.7	4,954	11.8	13,367	25.1	24,177	32.5
Total	757	100.0	3,696	100.0	19,459	100.0	42,372	100.0	53,259	100.0	74,445	100.0

[a] 'World' excludes the communist bloc here and throughout this book.
[b] Including Puerto Rico.
Source: from data supplied by ICI Chemicals and Polymers Ltd

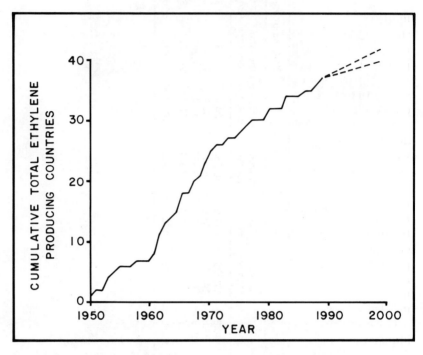

Figure 1.4 Cumulative total of ethylene producing countries, 1950–2000

1.4 The Structure of the Book

This objective is pursued in subsequent chapters, each of which
identifies and evaluates the significance of key variables affecting the
industry's development. Before considering these variables, however,
it is desirable to provide background information on the technology,
economics and location of the industry. The petrochemical industry
is notoriously difficult to define, and chapter 2 establishes the boundaries of the study by tackling this problem. It also includes a
simplified review of some of the principal petrochemical products and
processes and a summary of the industry's commercial structure.
Such information is necessary since an awareness of the technology of
an industry and an appreciation of the organizational context in
which investment decisions are made are both prerequisites to an
understanding of its evolution.

Innovation and technical change are central to the concept of
industry and product life cycles. The proposition that certain innovations may create entirely new industries may be extended to
suggest that the distribution of such industries is initially determined
by access to technical knowledge. Chapter 3 examines the multiple
and geographically diverse scientific origins of the petrochemical

industry, emphasizing that its creation cannot be ascribed to any single flash of inspiration. Reference to the early development of the industry reveals that, although technical advances had created the potential for the post-war growth of the industry, many other factors were important in allowing this potential to be fulfilled and in ensuring that the United States obtained a head start. These factors are examined in chapter 4.

Innovation is not only important at the beginning of an industry's development; the interrelationships of product and process innovation with demand growth are fundamental to the accelerating momentum associated with the middle section of the logistic curve. These interrelationships are explored in chapter 5 with particular reference to the rapid rise of the industry in the United States and Western Europe during the 1950s and 1960s. The implications of these interrelationships for the distribution of the industry within these early centres of production are explored in chapter 6, before the book proceeds in the next three chapters to a discussion of the various factors contributing to the industry's subsequent establishment in more and more countries outside these centres, beginning with Japan in 1958.

Governments have taken a great interest in the petrochemical industry and have contributed significantly to its internationalization. The benefits of import substitution and its widely perceived attractions as a growth sector have encouraged state promotion of national petrochemical industries. This strategy has been made easier as the proprietary technologies associated with the early development of the industry have become more widely available with the onset of maturity. The significance of government-sponsored import substitution policies in stimulating petrochemical development is examined in chapter 7, but the focus shifts to export-oriented investments in chapter 8. It has already been noted that the evolution of an industry cannot be explained in technological terms alone and that external shocks may radically alter its pattern of development (see section 1.2). The sharp rise in the price of oil in 1973–4 and in 1979, which was itself politically motivated, had a profound effect on the economics of petrochemical manufacture. Raw materials replaced capital charges as the dominant element in cost structures, encouraging several oil-rich countries, notably Saudi Arabia, to make petrochemical manufacture the focus of their development strategies. This is reflected in table 1.1 in the significant increase in the share of other producers from 11.8 to 25.1 per cent of world ethylene capacity between 1980 and 1990. Whilst chapters 7 and 8 emphasize the role of governments as agents of change in the petrochemical industry, the multinational oil and chemical corporations based in the core economies have also shaped its spatial evolution at the global scale by foreign direct investment. Chapter 9 examines these corporate strategies and their relationships to the economic development aspirations of governments.

The experience of the industry to the late 1970s was essentially a story of continuous growth. However, at the same time that massive petrochemical investments were being made in a number of oil-rich countries, capacity actually declined in the United States, Western Europe and especially Japan. The contrasting experiences are related to the extent that the threat of competition from new export-oriented producers accelerated rationalization in the core economies. There is, however, another explanation. The effects of the oil price shocks and the recession in the world economy have reinforced the view that the industry has reached the mature stage of its life cycle, corresponding to the upper plateau of the logistic curve (figure 1.1). The evidence for this conclusion, and the nature of the changes taking place within the industry, are assessed in chapter 10.

Most of this book is concerned with interpreting patterns of industrial development at the international and national scales. The perspective shifts to the regional level in chapter 11. Petrochemical operations are typically concentrated in spectacular agglomerations of interrelated plants. This characteristic ensures that the industry occupies a major role in the economies of the communities and regions in which it is located. Many of the issues surrounding the link between the evolution of industries and economies at the national scale are echoed in the literature of regional development. For example, just as propulsive industries have been seen to drive the macro-economic system, so the same logic has been applied at the regional level in the formulation of growth centre policies. Petrochemical complexes have frequently been identified as the focus of such policies. Conversely, the negative economic consequences of the industry's maturity in traditional centres of production have become a major concern during the 1980s. The prospects for such regional economies are directly linked to those of the industry itself. These are assessed in the final chapter, which also evaluates the usefulness and validity of the various life-cycle concepts when applied to the petrochemical industry. Such an evaluation is not simply of academic interest. Much of the ground covered in this case study is relevant to important policy questions in such areas as science and technology, industry, trade and regional development.

Notes

1 The terms 'sector' and 'industry' are regarded as synonymous and are used interchangeably in the following discussion.
2 At the product level it is possible to identify a single innovating firm which may enjoy a period of monopoly protected by patent. At the sector and

industry levels, it is more realistic to think in terms of a small group of such firms.

3 Markusen's model was developed in the context of an empirical study of the evolution of various industries in the United States. Although she regards it as portraying 'a universal aspect of capitalist dynamics' (Markusen 1985, 60), she acknowledges that the cycle is sensitive to territorial scale and that the cycle for an industry in the United States will not be synchronous with that of the same industry in, for example, a developing country.

4 It is apparent in figure 1.1(b) that Markusen's model extends the life cycle to the ultimate death of an industry as indicated by the bell-shaped output curve. As previously noted, the experience of many industries more closely corresponds to an S-shaped curve with a protracted plateau at the upper inflexion of the curve.

5 The term 'multinational corporation' will be used throughout this book in preference to the United Nations's officially adopted nomenclature 'transnational corporation'. This is because most of the enterprises involved in the petrochemical industry are truly multinational in the sense that they operate in many countries, whereas a transnational corporation may operate in only two countries to fall within the official definition.

6 'Rest of world' in figure 1.2 excludes the countries of the communist bloc and the book makes no reference to the industry's development in these countries. The kind of data sources upon which the book is based usually contain limited information on the USSR, China and Eastern Europe. A specialized knowledge of the appropriate languages and sources would be required to achieve a truly global perspective. Furthermore, the ideas regarding the evolution of economies and industries which provide the framework for this study were developed in relation to the non-communist system. The most detailed economic analysis of the petrochemical industry in the communist world is that of Rajana (1975).

2
Technology and Economics of the Petrochemical Industry

The significance of this chapter will vary from one reader to another. For those familiar with the technology and economics of the petrochemical industry, it will be superfluous; for those lacking such knowledge, it will be important. On the assumption that many will approach this book from backgrounds in academic disciplines such as economics and geography rather than from direct experience of the industry, it seems appropriate to provide factual information essential to an understanding of subsequent chapters. In particular, an attempt is made to define the boundaries of the petrochemical industry for the purposes of this study, to outline its technical basis and to describe its commercial structures.

2.1 Defining the Industry

The petrochemical industry is notoriously difficult to define because of the complexity of its operations and the diversity of its products. This is reflected in the fact that, despite its existence in common usage, 'the petrochemical industry' is not an identifiable category in national and international industrial classifications. The broadest definition of the industry is, as noted in chapter 1, in terms of its raw material basis. Thus 'petrochemicals' are those chemicals that are manufactured from feedstocks obtained from oil or natural gas,[1] and the industry is therefore a part of the wider constellation of activities which constitute 'the chemical industry'. This definition is pragmatic rather than scientific, however, since many 'petrochemicals' can also be obtained from other organic raw materials such as coal or vegetable matter. In these circumstances, it is not possible to unambiguously define a petrochemical product in the same way as a motor vehicle or a computer, but rather it is necessary to estimate what proportion of the output of the various sectors typically identified, at varying levels of disaggregation, in industrial classification schemes is actually derived from petroleum sources. This may be difficult in some cases, but there are sectors which are both common to such schemes and also universally regarded as exclusively petrochemical in character. The precise terminology used to described these sectors may vary from one set of national statistics to another, but they generally include plastics and resins, synthetic fibres and organic chemicals. These sectors themselves embrace a multiplicity of products. Indeed, it has been estimated that approximately 14,000 different petrochemicals have achieved commercial status (US International Trade Commission 1987, 1–4).

The problem of identifying the key operations of the petrochemical industry is not as great as the diversity of its products might suggest. In fact, most of these products may be traced to relatively few base chemicals or 'building blocks'. Approximately 85 per cent are ultimately derived from just two groups of base chemicals – the *olefins* and the *aromatics* (Shell International Chemical Co. 1988, 20). The olefins include ethylene, propylene, butylenes and butadiene;[2] the major aromatics are benzene, toluene and xylenes. Figure 2.1 is a simplified representation of the principal petrochemicals and their applications. Ethylene is the most important base chemical in terms of the volume of production, followed by propylene and benzene.

Figure 2.1 emphasizes that the operations of the industry typically involve linked and sequential processes which make it possible to distinguish between primary or base chemicals, such as the olefins and aromatics, petrochemical intermediates and petrochemical products. The manufacture of base chemicals is the first stage in the conversion of raw materials to petrochemical products. Although some of these products, such as polyethylene and polypropylene, are derived directly from the base chemicals, many others require intervening stages, such as the production of ethyl benzene and styrene (leading to polystyrene). Generally speaking, base chemicals and intermediates are associated with transactions that are internal to the industry, whilst petrochemical products are sold to, and define its boundary with, other sectors. As already noted, the range of products is vast (figure 2.1), but the total volume of output is dominated by relatively few. These products are generally better known for their properties and applications than their chemical formulas. Table 2.1 emphasizes the importance of plastics and resins. It is not comprehensive, but well over half of the total output by weight of the world petrochemical industry[3] is in the form of plastics and resins (mainly derived from ethylene and propylene) and more than three-quarters is accounted for by this broad group together with synthetic fibres and synthetic rubbers.

The petrochemical industry is set within a vertical processing chain between raw materials and consumers. Figure 2.2 represents this chain and the wider relationships of the industry to the rest of

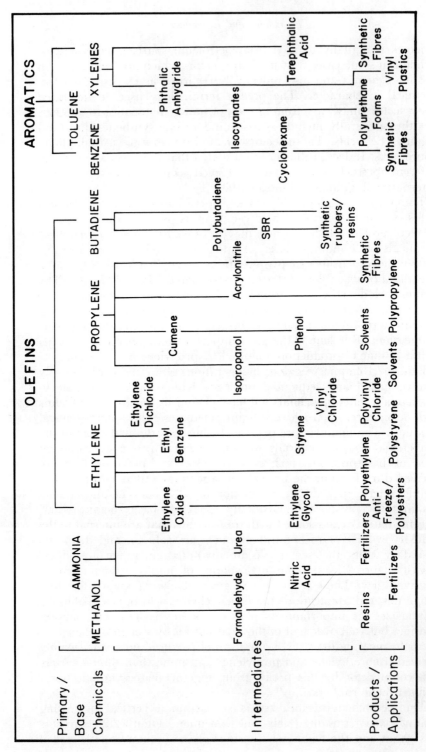

Figure 2.1 Principal petrochemicals and their applications

Table 2.1 World output of principal organic petrochemical product groups, 1986

Product group	Output (million tonnes)	Major applications
Plastics and resins	58.5	Packaging, piping, construction, cars
Synthetic rubbers	5.4	Synthetics account for about two-thirds of world consumption of rubbers
Synthetic fibres (excluding cellulosics)	11.4	Synthetics represent around 35% of fibre needs
Synthetic detergents	16.0[a]	Synthetics meet about two-thirds of detergent needs
Chemical solvents	7.0[b]	Paint, adhesives, pharmaceuticals

[a] Active matter content 3.4 million tonnes.
[b] Excludes large quantities of hydrocarbon solvents such as white spirits extracted from various refinery fractions and not included in chemical industry statistics.
Source: Shell International Chemical Co. 1988, 28

the chemical industry and also to other sectors of the economy. At the upstream end, it obtains its feedstocks from the natural gas and oil refining industries. At the downstream end, most of its products are sold to other industries. Some of these, such as plastics fabrication, are totally dependent upon the petrochemcial industry for their inputs; others, such as motor vehicles, are only partly dependent upon it, often acquiring petrochemical products indirectly in the form of, for example, tyres and plastic components from other industries. The distinction between the petrochemical industry and other sectors at the downstream end of the processing chain is not always clear, and the activities of the various chemical process industries identified in figure 2.2 are sometimes included within definitions of the petrochemical industry. They are excluded for the purposes of this study, not least because their location tends to be influenced by a set of factors different from those affecting upstream operations.[4]

2.2 Technical Basis

It has already been noted that the identity of petrochemicals rests upon the fact that they are manufactured from petroleum feedstocks.[5] Despite their common generic origin, these feedstocks vary considerably in specification. Figure 2.3 indicates some of the principal sources of feedstock for the manufacture of the olefins and aromatics which are the key building blocks of the organic petrochemical industry (i.e. excluding inorganic ammonia). The most important distinction in figure 2.3 is between those feedstocks obtained directly from natural gas and those obtained by the refining of crude oil. The principal constituent of natural gas is methane, but other components may be

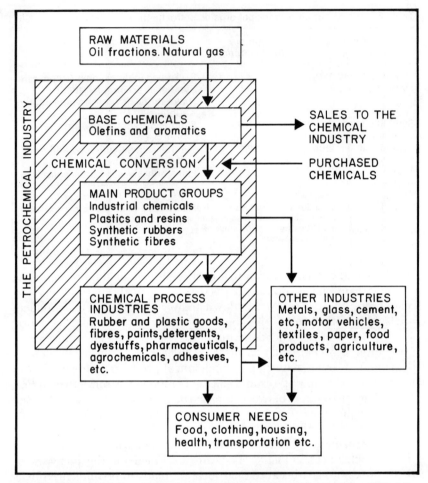

Figure 2.2 The petrochemical industry (Shell International Chemical Co. 1988, 21)

isolated by liquefaction. The natural gas liquids (NGLs) consist of ethane, propane and butane as well as condensate and natural gasoline which are present in liquid form at atmospheric temperature and pressure. All of these NGLs may be used to manufacture the olefins. The olefins may also be obtained directly from certain oil refining operations and, much more importantly, by the conversion of various refinery products ranging from liquefied petroleum gases (i.e. propane and butane) through various liquid petroleum fractions from naphtha, which is blended into gasoline, to heavier (i.e. higher boiling point) materials such as kerosene, gas oil and vacuum distillate. Unlike the olefins, the aromatics are not derived from natural gas and, with the exception of coal-based production which accounts

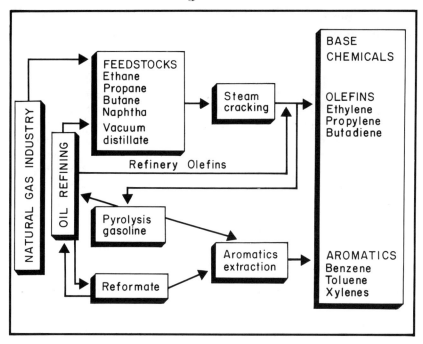

Figure 2.3 Manufacture of olefins and aromatics (adapted from Shell International Chemical Co. 1988, 22)

for only 5 per cent of the world total outside the centrally planned economies (Shell International Chemical Co. 1988, 25), they depend exclusively upon oil refinery feedstocks. These feedstocks are often similar to those used to produce the olefins. Thus the reformate in figure 2.3 is itself a derivative of naphtha in the sense that most naphtha is processed within refineries to motor gasoline, generally by catalytic reforming. The reformate resulting from this operation is a high octane gasoline component from which aromatics can also be extracted. Pyrolysis gasoline provides a link between the production of the olefins and the aromatics. It is a liquid by-product of the cracking process used to convert the various feedstocks indicated in figure 2.3 to the olefins. Like reformate, pyrolysis gasoline is rich in aromatics and can be used as a source of benzene, toluene and xylenes or as a contribution to the gasoline pool.

It is apparent from this discussion and from figure 2.3 that very close links exist between oil refining and the manufacture of base chemicals. Both the olefins and the aromatics may be obtained from similar petroleum fractions and also compete for these same materials with the requirements of the oil refining industry. The technical and commercial distinctions between oil refining and petrochemical operations are especially blurred in the case of the aromatics. A substantial proportion of aromatics production is derived from facilities that are both functionally and geographically indistinguishable from oil refineries. Considerable advantages may be gained from a similar integration of oil refining and olefin manufacture, but this association is less overwhelming, especially where feedstocks are derived from natural gas. Thus whilst the production of aromatics lies firmly within any conventional definition of the petrochemical industry, the olefin segment of the industry has a clearer, activity-based identity. This is especially relevant to a study concerned with explaining the *location* of the petrochemical industry since the distribution of most aromatics facilities is controlled by the distribution of oil refineries. Consequently the aromatics receive little attention in this book, which might be more accurately described as a study of the olefin rather than the petrochemical industry.

The key operation in this industry is the conversion of petroleum

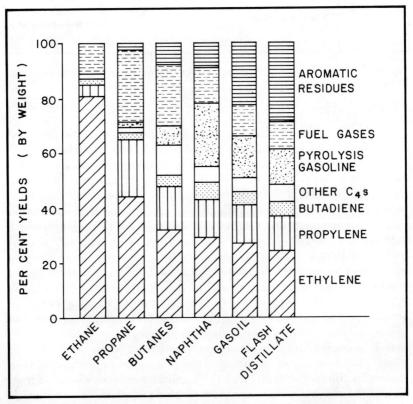

Figure 2.4 Pecentage yields by weight of ethylene and coproducts from steam cracking (Shell International Chemical Co. 1988, 24)

feedstocks to the olefins (figure 2.3). This is achieved by 'cracking' either refinery fractions or NGLs in the presence of steam under varying conditions of temperature and pressure (i.e. severity). Cracking results in the thermal decomposition of the feedstocks to yield a combination of liquid and gaseous coproducts. Figure 2.4 emphasizes the importance of feedstock type as an influence upon the output pattern, indicating that the share of ethylene declines as heavier feedstocks are used. Some limited alterations to the yield patterns for specific feedstocks indicated in figure 2.4 may be achieved by modifying reaction conditions, principally temperature, pressure and the residence time of feedstock within the reactor.

Although steam cracking is normally intended to maximize the output of ethylene, the remaining liquids and gases cannot be ignored since their utilization significantly affects the economics of ethylene production. Essentially, the unit costs of ethylene rise as the proportion of coproducts diverted to works fuel increases. It is, therefore, important to find alternative commercial outlets for the other olefins (i.e. propylene and butylenes) and butadiene. This provides a considerable economic incentive to develop and market downstream derivatives from these coproducts. This has in turn encouraged the development of integrated complexes focused upon the cracking operation. As pressure to exploit economies of scale led to an increase in the size of cracking units, especially during the 1960s, the connection between the imperative to maximize the utilization of coproducts and the physical expansion of massive industrial complexes was reinforced (see chapter 6). This connection did not rest only upon linkages with downstream operations associated with the manufacture of the various olefin derivatives. Where cracking is based upon liquid feedstocks such as naphtha and gas oil, it is often linked to an adjacent oil refinery both as a source of inputs and as an outlet for such products as pyrolysis gasoline and aromatic residues (figure 2.3). These may be incorporated within the refinery processing scheme, with the lighter fractions blended into gasoline and the heavier materials into fuel and lubricating oils.

It is clear that the type of feedstock is a major influence upon the economics of olefin production. This is apparent in both capital costs, which are higher for liquid-based crackers, and operating costs, which are closely related to the problem of coproduct utilization. There is an important geographical dimension to these issues because of the very different raw material roots of the US as compared with the Western European and Japanese industries. This is apparent in figure 2.5, which emphasizes the much greater importance of gas-based feedstocks in the United States. These differences may be traced to circumstances surrounding the early development of the industry. These origins are explored in detail in subsequent chapters, but a brief summary is necessary at this stage to account for the

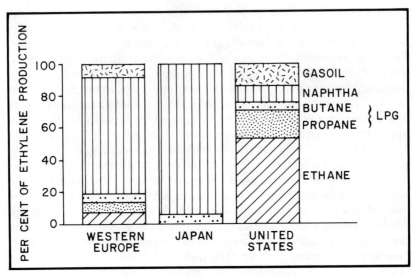

Figure 2.5 Feedstocks for ethylene production in Western Europe, Japan and the United States, 1986 (Shell International Chemical Co. 1988, 25)

pattern indicated in figure 2.5. Maximizing the output of gasolines has traditionally been the principal objective of the US oil refining industry. By-product gases were generated as a result of various refining operations, notably catalytic cracking, geared towards the achievement of this objective. The availability of these gases, which could be used as feedstocks for petrochemical manufacture, encouraged a number of oil companies to move into this new area at a very early stage. Nevertheless, this supply was inadequate to sustain the development of the new industry and attention shifted towards natural gas, especially the abundant reserves of Texas and Louisiana. The emphasis upon gas-based feedstocks in the United States was due not only to their availability, but also to the limited availability of the naphtha fractions which were the principal alternative. The high demand for gasoline ensured that most of these fractions contributed to the gasoline pool within individual refineries. This dominating influence of gasoline in US refining schedules was further reinforced in an indirect way by the rise of natural gas as an energy source after World War II. By serving markets that might otherwise have been supplied by fuel oil, natural gas has contributed to the emphasis upon the lighter ends of the barrel that is characteristic of the operations of the US refining industry.

In contrast to the United States, Western Europe and Japan did not have large quantities of indigenous natural gas available when their petrochemical industries were established in the 1950s and

1960s respectively. The output pattern of their refining industries was also very different. Fuel oil was the most important single product and refining schedules were planned accordingly. Demand for gasolines was limited because of lower levels of car ownership. This reversal of the role of gasolines and fuel oils as the motors of the refining system meant that light distillates such as naphtha were often surplus to fuel requirements in Western Europe and Japan and were, therefore, available for use as petrochemical feedstocks. This availability encouraged the early development of the industry and led to the contrasting feedstock patterns apparent in figure 2.5.

There has been some convergence in these patterns. Several manufacturers in the United States built cracking plants based on naphtha and gas oil during the 1970s because they believed that domestic natural gas production was reaching its peak and that the supply of NGLs would subsequently decline. These decisions were also influenced by an anticipated shortage of propylene, which, as already emphasized in figure 2.4, is produced in larger quantities from the cracking of heavier feedstocks. Concurrent with these trends in the United States, events in the North Sea were making substantial quantities of NGLs suitable for petrochemical manufacture available for the first time in Western Europe. Another development which was initiated during the 1970s was the construction of new, or the modification of existing, cracking plants to allow them to use a wider range of feedstocks. Theoretically it is possible to design facilities capable of accepting all types of feedstocks from ethane to heavy fuel oil, but in practice their flexibility is usually constrained to combinations of naphtha with gas oil and naphtha with NGLs. The search for greater flexibility has been driven by operational considerations and is intended to allow producers to respond to increasingly volatile feedstock price movements. Despite these trends, however, the difference in the raw material basis of the industry in the United States compared with Western Europe and Japan has been and remains important, not least because it has meant that changing feedstock costs, especially since the first and second oil price shocks, have had complex and differential effects upon comparative advantage at the international scale (see chapter 8).

2.3 Commercial Structure

The petrochemical industry has always been dominated by large companies. Its commercial origins may be traced to the research activities of companies in the oil and chemical industries, and there have been few opportunities for independent entrepreneurs and small firms. This has ensured that the industry's development has been shaped from the very beginning by the spatial and organizational

structure of some of the world's largest companies. Table 2.2 lists the
top 20 producers of petrochemicals and plastics in 1989 ranked in
terms of the value of their sales. The size of these companies is
emphasized by the inclusion of their overall ranking in the corresponding *Fortune* listings. The lowest position of any of the companies
identified in table 2.2 when set in this wider context is Nova, which is
placed 325th, on the basis of overall sales value, in the 1989 listing of
the top 500 global industrial corporations. It is important to stress
that table 2.2 refers to petrochemicals and plastics and not to the
entire chemical industry, which also includes such important sectors
as pharmaceuticals. Quite a different pattern emerges when petrochemicals are subsumed within this more comprehensive category.
The German 'big three' of BASF, Bayer and Hoechst occupy the
leading positions, and Ciba-Geigy, which has no involvement in the
petrochemical industry, appears in the top ten. The most significant
feature is the greater importance of the oil companies in petrochemicals and plastics (10 of the top 20 in 1989) as compared with
the chemical industry as a whole (2 of the top 20 in 1989).

The growing influence of the oil companies has been one of the

Table 2.2 Leading producers of petrochemicals and plastics, 1989

Rank	Company	Country	Sales ($ million)	Fortune Rank
1	Royal Dutch/Shell	Neth./UK	11,075[a,b]	4
2	Enimont	Italy	10,766	100
3	Exxon	US	9,210[a,b]	3
4	Dow Chemical	US	8,772	53
5	British Petroleum	UK	5,654[a]	10
6	Union Carbide	US	5,613	144
7	Atochem	France	5,398	37[e]
8	Norsk Hydro	Norway	5,289[a,d]	129
9	Hüls	W. Germany	5,287	281
10	Occidental Petroleum	US	5,204	46
11	BASF	W. Germany	5,116[c]	31
12	General Electric	US	4,896[a]	7
13	ICI	UK	4,844	40
14	Amoco	US	4,274[a,b]	34
15	Bayer	W. Germany	4,207[c]	38
16	Mobil	US	4,039[a,b]	8
17	Du Pont	US	3,432[c]	19
18	Chevron	US	3,048[a,b]	25
19	Petrofina	Belgium	2,964[a]	98
20	Nova	Canada	2,907[a]	325

[a] Chemicals only.
[b] Excludes transfers between business segments.
[c] Polymers
[d] Includes fertilizers.
[e] Ranking of Elf Aquitaine group.
Source: Chemical Insight, no. 444, 1990; *Fortune*, 30 July 1990.

most significant developments in the international chemical industry. Their interest has been inextricably linked to the importance of oil and natural gas as feedstocks for chemical manufacture. Indeed, several oil companies, notably Standard Oil (New Jersey) and Shell, played a pioneering role in promoting these feedstocks. Many others followed their lead as the potential for growth became apparent. Such moves into petrochemicals seemed a sensible form of diversification for companies with strong feedstock positions based on their traditional activities. Although this kind of forward integration was initially opportunistic and pulled as much by the prospect of rapid growth as pushed by the availability of feedstocks, the strategic advantages of their raw material position was demonstrated in the upheavals caused by the oil price shocks of 1973–4 and 1978–9. These advantages were reflected in a clear trend during the 1980s for the oil companies to increase their share of petrochemical capacity, especially in base chemicals, at the expense of the chemical companies.

These latter companies, nevertheless, have played and continue to play an important part in the development of the petrochemical industry. Companies such as Union Carbide in the United States, ICI in the United Kingdom and IG Farben (the precursor of BASF, Bayer and Hoechst) in Germany were responsible for major innovations before World War II that contributed to the post-war growth of the industry. Furthermore, they participated in this growth by switching their organic chemical manufacturing operations from coal to petroleum feedstocks. As their consumption of these feedstocks increased, many chemical companies attempted to secure their supplies by various means including backward integration into oil refining and joint ventures with, and in a few cases the acquisition of, oil companies. Despite such strategies, most chemical companies were less well placed to cope with the oil price shocks than the oil companies, for which these events were not entirely negative. Several chemical companies carried out major reappraisals of their commitments to petrochemicals. Although these were prompted by the difficulties created by the oil price shocks, they also reflected a judgement that, with the onset of maturity, the future growth of the petrochemical industry was likely to be less impressive than in the recent past and that the diversion of corporate resources into other areas of the chemical industry such as pharmaceuticals was likely to yield more attractive returns. Thus companies such as Monsanto and Hercules have largely withdrawn from the petrochemical industry and, in so doing, have contributed to the stronger overall position of the oil companies.

Although most of the participants in the petrochemical sector are firmly based in either the oil or the chemical industries, a few have entered from other directions. General Electric (12th in table 2.2) is representative of such wider interests. The petrochemical industry was, by virtue of its spectacular growth during the 1960s, a magnet to large firms seeking to diversify their activities within the core economies of North America, Western Europe and Japan. Such moves were usually driven by the desire to achieve a more balanced corporate portfolio rather than any logical connections with existing operations. In some cases, however, they represented backward integration by firms in industries such as textiles which purchased vital inputs from the petrochemical sector. Generally speaking, such diversification into petrochemicals was a characteristic of the industry's golden age, and most of those attracted to it during this period subsequently withdrew with the advent of harder times.

Sectoral origin is not the only basis for differentiating between the organizations involved in the petrochemical industry. The distinction between state-owned or -controlled and private sector enterprises is an important aspect of the industry's commercial structure. The respective national governments have major holdings in three of the companies listed in table 2.2 – Enimont (Italy), Norsk Hydro (Norway) and Atochem (France). These are the exceptions rather than the rule within the developed economies, but the pattern is reversed in Latin America, South East Asia and the Middle East where organizations such as Petrobràs (Brazil), Pemex (Mexico), Chinese Petroleum Corporation (Taiwan) and Sonatrach (Algeria) have been responsible for initiating and promoting national petrochemical industries. Viewed at a global scale, there is little doubt that the establishment of the industry would have been long delayed in many countries without the intervention of the state (see chapter 7).

2.4 Conclusions

Chemical manufacture simultaneously occupies a central role in the structure of industrial economies whilst remaining an anonymous activity in the sense that most of its products are sold to other industries rather than to final consumers at the household level. These characteristics have been maintained as petrochemicals have come to account for a growing proportion of the total output of the chemical industry.[6] Many studies have demonstrated the focal position of the petrochemical industry within the modern economy using miscellaneous production and trade statistics (Pfann 1979), input–output analysis (Little 1978) and economic programming models (Rudd et al. 1981). It follows that the chemical industry in general and, latterly, the petrochemical sector in particular are essential to the process of economic development. This is apparent in the recent economic history of North America, Western Europe and Japan, which suggests that it is not unreasonable to suggest that 'petro-chemical products . . . are key to the future industrialization of developing countries' (Vergara and Brown 1988, 1).

Notes

1 In practice, this definition is often qualified to refer to organic chemicals (i.e. containing a basic structure of carbon atoms combined with hydrogen and other elements). Many important inorganic chemicals, such as ammonia and sulphur, are produced from oil and gas. Indeed, ammonia (mainly for fertilizers) has been estimated to account for 25–30 per cent by weight of global petrochemical production (UNIDO 1978). However, ammonia and its derivatives are usually treated quite separately and this book excludes such inorganic chemicals from consideration.
2 Butadiene is more accurately described as a *diolefin*.
3 Excluding inorganic products such as ammonia.
4 There is some discussion of the linkages between petrochemical operations and downstream activities such as plastics fabrication in chapter 11 in the context of an analysis of the regional development role of the petrochemical industry.
5 The review in this section is brief and provides the minimum technical background required to follow arguments in subsequent chapters. Many books are available which provide comprehensive reviews of the technology and, to a lesser extent, the economics of the petrochemical industry (see Axtell 1986; Goldstein and Waddams 1967; Hatch and Matar 1981; List 1986; Wiseman 1986; Witcoff and Reuben 1980).
6 For example, it has been estimated, on the basis of an admittedly broad definition incorporating the chemical process industries identified in figure 2.2, that petrochemicals account for approximately 75 per cent of the total value of output by the US chemical industry (US International Trade Commission 1987, 1–4).

3

Technical and Commercial Origins

New industries are created by technical change (see chapter 1). The manner of their creation is, however, a matter of debate. On the one hand, it may be regarded as the consequence of a fundamental technical breakthrough or heroic innovation; on the other hand, it is seen as the outcome of a gradual process of incremental change (Rosenberg 1972). Closely related to these alternative views is the issue of the motivating forces driving innovation. The economic problems of the 1980s have encouraged governments to look to science and technology to provide new engines of growth (see Rothwell and Zegweld 1981). This policy concern has in turn renewed academic interest in the relative significance of what have been termed 'science-push' and 'demand-pull' theories of innovation (see Schumpeter 1934; Schmookler 1966; Mowery and Rosenberg 1979). The basis of science-push is the proposition that advances in knowledge spontaneously create economic opportunities; demand-pull essentially rests upon the familiar dictum that 'necessity is the mother of invention.' The supply-side approach of science-push is consistent with the heroic view of innovation, whereas the demand-pull mechanism tends to suggest incremental rather than radical change. In practice it may be difficult to assess the relative strength of the two stimuli, and Stobaugh (1988, 47) notes that innovation within companies often involves a kind of 'backing and forthing' as scientific and marketing considerations jointly influence the development of a new product. This observation leads to another aspect of the debate regarding the nature of innovation, focused upon the role of independent inventor/entrepreneurs as compared with institutional research carried out in goverment agencies and private sector corporations. The increasing importance of institutional research within modern economies is generally accepted, although controversy remains regarding the effectiveness of large and small firms as innovators (Freeman 1982).

3.1 Invention, Innovation and Initial Location

The sources of innovation in industry may be considered not only from a technical and organizational point of view, but also from a geographical perspective. At a global scale it is obvious that the potential for invention and innovation varies between countries, and it is possible to identify changes in technological leadership through time (Maddison 1982). New industries are most likely to emerge in these leader countries, and the manner in which new technology spreads through the world economy is an important aspect of the relationship between the developed and developing countries (see section 7.1). At a national level, the concentration of high technology industries such as electronics in particular areas has stimulated interest in the geographical circumstances surrounding the birth of new industries. Explaining why such industries appear in one area rather than another is a key problem in economic geography, not least because of the tendency for early centres of production to exercise a major influence upon an industry's subsequent pattern of development. Examples of the impact upon industries and regions of individual inventor/entrepreneurs such as Wedgwood in Stoke in eighteenth-century England and Shockley and Ternan in California in the early 1950s encourage the view that the geographical incidence of invention and innovation within countries is random, and models of the spatial evolution of industries tend to beg the question of the location of the first production facilities (see Smith 1981; Markusen 1985). Whilst there is no doubt that every case is unique, there are good reasons for supposing that the distribution of inventive activity is far from random and that certain locations are more likely to spawn new industries than others (see Feller 1975).

Patents have been used as a surrogate measure of inventive activity in various historical studies which have emphasized the dominance of urban centres (Pred 1965; 1966; Feller 1971; 1973). Just as the scientific and cultural milieux of countries affect their technological potential, so similar factors seem to have influenced the geography of invention within countries. The demand-pull hypothesis is central to many interpretations of the role of major cities as centres of technical change during the nineteenth century. Important advances were often a response to specific problems which emerged in existing centres of economic activity, and a kind of technological convergence frequently resulted in the extension or application of an idea generated in one context to a similar situation in a different industry (see Rosenberg 1963; Hekman 1980a). Such technological spin-offs are not simply of historical significance, and a similar phenomenon has frequently been described in, for example, the electronics industry (see Dorfman 1983; Hall and Markusen 1985). Reference to nineteenth-century evidence and experience is based on the implicit assumption that technical change is inspired by the activities of individuals, but the increasing importance of institutional research has prompted a growing interest in the geography of corporate R and D (see Malecki 1979; 1980; Howells 1984). Numerous location factors have been identified, including proximity to the corporate head office, research universities and government agencies as well as the preferences of scientific personnel for attractive living environments. Although R and D establishments are not necessarily located in the same urban centres that were the focus of inventive activity in the nineteenth century, their distribution is typically clustered in major metropolitan regions.

The geography of inventive activity is relevant to an understanding of industrial location to the extent that inventions are translated into the innovations responsible for the creation of new industries. Analysis of the diffusion of innovations suggests that inventions will be adopted most rapidly in their region of origin. This quicker response enhances the future competitive position of the region in which the invention occurred, setting in motion a positive feedback process involving growth, invention and innovation. Pred (1965; 1966) invokes such a mechanism in accounting for the pattern of US urban-industrial growth during the nineteenth century. However, the shifting fortunes of regions within developed economies, including the relative decline of the cities which were the centres of growth in Pred's accounts, have since emphasized that the process of cumulative causation is not irreversible. Established centres may, for example, stifle innovation through the adoption of restrictive practices and conservative attitudes (see Chapman and Walker 1991, 177–9). New industries to some extent create their own conditions for growth in new areas, as exemplified by the replacement of the former fruit orchards of Silicon Valley in California by electronics plants (Saxenian 1985). In these circumstances, new industries may 'seem to "leapfrog" in space, establishing growth centers and new growth peripheries that are relatively insulated from existing highly industrialized regions' (Storper and Walker 1989, 11–14).

Large business organizations are major agents of change in this respect, and the explanation of contemporary patterns of invention and innovation in manufacturing lies more in an appreciation of the role of corporate administrative hierarchies than in the urban hierarchies emphasized by Pred. Where inventions are made and commercially exploited by individuals there are important practical reasons associated with domestic commitments which tend to result in their introduction at or near home (see Gudgin 1978). Such constraints do not apply in a corporate context. Whilst there is some evidence that manufacturing innovations are initially applied in plants relatively close to the R and D establishments which developed them (Oakey et al. 1980), there is no overwhelming reason why this should always happen. Thus industries which have their origins in research carried out by large corporations are likely to be influenced in their initial location by factors other than those that may be traced to the inventive and entrepreneurial activities of individuals. The existing distribution of corporate production facilities is often a major influence as new products and technologies are introduced within or adjacent to an established factory. The fact that large organizations are frequently drawn into new areas as a result of pursuing lines of research which are a natural extension of their traditional pattern of activities (see Penrose 1959), such as the exploitation of by-products, reinforces this effect.

This review of ideas concerning spatial aspects of invention and innovation in manufacturing emphasizes that the technical and organizational circumstances of an industry's creation have an important bearing upon its initial location. The objective of this chapter is to analyse these circumstances as they relate to the petrochemical industry. The industry scarcely existed before 1940, when it may be visualized as lying at the beginning of its logistic curve of output growth (see section 1.1). However, its subsequent gradually accelerating expansion during the 1940s and its spectacular growth and dispersal during the 1950s and 1960s can only be understood in the context of various scientific and commercial developments which occurred during the preceding 50 years or so.[1]

3.2 Organic Chemistry in Germany before 1914

Organic compounds may be manufactured from a wide range of raw materials including vegetable matter, such as molassess, and coal, but 'The heavy organic chemical industry is nowadays virtually synonymous with the petrochemical industry' (Reuben and Burstall 1973, 196). Nevertheless, the petrochemical industry is defined not by the distinctive nature of its products, but rather by its raw material basis. Many of its key products were first manufactured from other raw materials, especially coal, and their properties were explored long before the term 'petrochemical' had acquired its contemporary significance. The pioneering work which established the scientific principles of organic chemistry is associated particularly with the efforts of Liebig in Germany, who created an impressive research laboratory at the University of Giessen in the 1820s and also inspired a succession of academic disciples who became influential in their own right (Haber 1958). Much effort was devoted to the derivation of true formulas for organic compounds, and the theoretical principles upon which organic chemistry is based were reasonably well understood by the mid 1860s (Sherwood Taylor 1957). This knowledge was crucial to the recognition that complex molecules could be synthesized by linking together simpler molecules – a recognition which in turn emphasized the vast potential of organic chemistry.

The commerical significance of these advances in the universities was first demonstrated in the manufacture of synthetic dyestuffs, which become *the* growth sector of the chemical industry during the last 30 years of the nineteenth century. The dyestuffs required by the textile industry were traditionally obtained from vegetable extracts such as indigo, but these sources were rapidly replaced by coal tar following the discovery of aniline purple in 1856. Coal tar was available as a by-product from town gas plants, and work on the chemistry of this substance in the 1840s built upon the earlier theoretical research of Liebig and others. The development of synthetic dyestuffs has been extensively studied, especially with regard to the relative significance of science-push and demand-pull factors in contributing to its rapid growth (see Walsh et al. 1979; Walsh 1984). The rise of synthetic dyes had a profound impact upon the chemical industry. It was responsible for the creation of the organic chemical industry, which scarcely existed before 1850 but has since become by far the most important branch of industrial chemistry. The commerical rewards of applying scientific methods in the context of an organized programme of research were clearly demonstrated by the successes of the German dyestuffs industry (see Beer 1959), and this provided a model for the subsequent development of the chemical industry as a whole. Finally, these successes propelled Germany to a pre-eminent position in the international chemical industry. Before 1840 England and France had been the dominant producers, but by 1913 Germany accounted for 88 per cent of world production of dyestuffs (Hayes 1987, 12) and was also far ahead of its rivals in synthetic drugs, flavours and fine chemicals (see Hohenberg 1967; Haber 1971).

The requirements of the textile industry were the principal demand-pull stimuli to synthetic dyes at mid century, but the major challenge to the chemical industry at the turn of the century was the fixation of atmospheric nitrogen to meet a perceived need for fertilizers. Fears of an impending world food shortage were aroused by Sir William Crookes in his presidential address to the British Association in 1898. He believed that a combination of limited land suitable for wheat cultivation and a rapidly growing world population necessitated significant increases in yields to avert disaster. Nitrogen fertilizers were seen as the key to improvements in productivity, but Chilean nitrates, which were the world's principal source, were expected to be exhausted in 30 years. The warning seemed especially relevant to Germany which was the world's largest importer of Chilean nitrates. The vulnerability of this extended supply line in time of war was evident to the political and military establishment in imperial Germany. Crookes called upon the chemical industry to meet the challenge of replacing the finite natural resource with a synthetic substitute. Not surprisingly, the German industry was quick to respond in view of its impressive technical achievements associated with dyestuffs and the strategic implications of continued dependence upon Chilean nitrates. Although several approaches to nitrogen fixation were developed before 1914, by far the most significant process was developed in Germany through the cooperation of Fritz Haber, a professor at Karlsruhe University, and Carl Bosch, an engineer with Badischer Anilin- und Soda-Fabrik (BASF), which had built upon its successes in dyestuffs to become Germany's largest chemical enterprise. In laboratory experiments in 1909, Haber proved the feasibility of isolating nitrogen from the atmosphere and combining it with hydrogen to form ammonia. BASF then switched its attention from other approaches to the problem and charged Bosch with the resposibility of scaling up Haber's laboratory equipment. A pilot plant was constructed in 1910 and commerical production began in 1913 at Oppau adjacent to BASF's existing Ludwigshafen complex. The outbreak of war confirmed German fears regarding Chilean nitrates and stimulated rapid expansion at Oppau and the construction of a massive new plant which came into operation at Leuna near Merseburg in 1917.

The Haber-Bosch process for the synthesis of ammonia from hydrogen and nitrogen 'represents one of the most important advances in industrial chemistry, and one that has contributed significantly to the shaping of the contemporary structure of the chemical industry' (Haber 1971, 90). By releasing ammonia production from its previous dependence upon the limited supplies available in coke-oven gas, it emphasized the lesson of synthetic dyestuffs: that the principles of chemistry could be employed to replace scarce resources with more abundant substitutes. On a technical level, the process heralded the introduction on an industrial scale of high temperature and high pressure processes which were subsequently applied in the manufacture of synthetic methanol, the hydrogenation of oil from coal, and various oil refining and petrochemical processes. Haber quickly appreciated the potential value of catalysts in improving the yields of his process, and BASF experimented with 2500 different substances between 1909 and 1912 (Haber 1971, 93). This work stimulated a wider interest in catalysis which later contributed to important advances in oil refining and petrochemical manufacture. The large-scale and continuous nature of the Haber-Bosch process was a forerunner of the kind of operations associated with petrochemical manufacture, and it encouraged the combination of chemical and engineering expertise required to construct the massive complexes characteristic of the modern industry. The increased scale of production units demanded huge capital investments which in turn reinforced the historical trend towards larger business organizations in the chemical industry, a trend which was further promoted by the development of petrochemicals.

If ammonia synthesis pioneered many of the techniques of industrial chemistry subsequently employed in petrochemical manufacture, advances in acetylene chemistry provided the basis for later work on ethylene. The first significant use of acetylene was for illumination in competition with coal gas. Commercial processes for its manufacture were developed simultaneously in France and the US in 1892, and the origins of the modern Union Carbide corporation may be traced to this discovery. However, the Germans were also interested in calcium carbide as a starting point in a process to fix atmospheric nitrogen. Considerable efforts were devoted to this problem more or less concurrently with the competing Haber-Bosch process (Haber 1971, 88–90). Both processes were important during World War I, although the Haber-Bosch route became the preferred choice after 1918. Nevertheless, the interest in acetylene generated by the fertilizer problem at the turn of the century increased the awareness of its potential for other purposes. Its high energy content meant that it was a good starting point for the manufacture of many chemicals without using high temperatures or pressures. Research begun in Germany before World War I, associated particularly with the activities of Hoechst, continued when hostilities ceased, and the displacement of the carbide-based process for the synthesis of ammonia by the Haber-Bosch technology diverted attention to other uses for acetylene which were pursued in the 1920s and 1930s.

The German domination of the international chemical industry by the outset of World War I was a remarkable achievement. It was an achievement based upon innovation. Although outstanding individuals such as Liebig and Haber played their part, the pre-eminence of the chemical industry of the newly unified German state was not a result of a fortuitous concentration of scientific talent, but rather a consequence of deliberate policies designed to foster and exploit such talent (see Beer 1959; Walsh et al. 1979; Freeman 1982). These included state support for higher education and the creation of a social climate sympathetic to industrial and applied research. This research took place in both academic institutions and the laboratories established by the German dye companies in the 1870s and 1880s. These laboratories were the forerunners of the R and D centres which have become a standard feature of the organization of contemporary industrial research. It was in such laboratories that the next series of technical advances relevant to an understanding of the origins of the petrochemical industry were made.

3.3 The Development of Synthetic Materials

The organic chemical industry has been characterized from the very beginning by a tendency towards ever larger forms of organization, and this trend was initiated in Germany (Haber 1958). By 1914, a process of amalgamation had created two large cartels which were designed to reduce competition between the six principal German chemical companies.[2] These cartels moved closer to a complete union in 1916 with the creation of a coordinated federation. This in turn became a single massive combine, comprising a core firm and more than 50 semi-autonomous dependents, on 1 January 1926. Thus IG Farbenindustrie AG (IG Farben) was born. This organization not only dominated the German chemical industry, but also engendered apprehension elsewhere. In Britain, the creation of Imperial Chemical Industries (ICI) was a direct response to the commercial threat posed by IG Farben (Reader 1975), whilst Du Pont in the US established a technical exchange agreement with ICI for similar defensive reasons (Taylor and Sudnik 1984). World War I had drawn attention to the German control of dyestuffs and its strength in the related fields of organic chemistry associated with the manufacture of fertilizers, explosives and drugs. This realization prompted government support for the chemical industry in both the United Kingdom and the US. The creation of the British Dyestuffs Corporation in 1916 was, for example, assisted by government subsidy, whilst measures to protect the US chemical industry from imports together with the massive boost in wartime demand for explosives were a major stimulus to the growth of such companies as Du Pont, Dow and Hercules. Despite these attempts to catch up on the German lead in organic chemistry and the damaging effect upon Germany of the terms of the Treaty of Versailles, especially the French occupation of the Ruhr, US chemical firms 'were far behind the Germans in crucial technical areas' (Taylor and Sudnik 1984, 106) during the 1920s, and Reader (1975, 94) reaches a similar conclusion regarding the position of ICI. The creation of IG Farben, 'an enterprise that designed itself around the imperatives of research' (Hayes 1987, 4), signalled Germany's determination to maintain its lead; this organization played a major role in the development of plastics and synthetic rubber which, together with the production of oil from coal, became the technological frontier in the inter-war years.

The work on acetylene initiated by Hoechst was continued by the new combine, which was concerned not only with the applications of acetylene but also with its production. In addition to the traditional route of hydrolysing calcium carbide derived from the high temperature processing of coke and limestone, IG Farben developed an electric arc process using coke oven gases and, later, methane from natural gas. A substantial proportion of Germany's inter-war organic chemical industry was based on acetylene which was, in many respects, to IG Farben what ethylene subsequently became to the post-war petrochemical industry. Many of the products which IG Farben made from acetylene were later made from ethylene. Indeed, the combine was not unaware of the potential of ethylene, which was contained in coke oven gases, obtained as a by-product of acetylene manufacture and deliberately synthesized in various ways (Spitz 1988, 43). Nevertheless, its uses by IG Farben remained specialized because, within the ultimately coal-based context of the German chemical industry, it was a more expensive intermediate than acetylene.

Many of IG Farben's most important acetylene derivatives, such as vinyl chloride, styrene and butadiene, were essential to the commercial development of the synthetic materials[3] which later provided the demand-led impetus to the post-war growth of the petrochemical industry. Most of these materials first entered commercial production during the 1930s (table 3.1). Many were discovered by independent researchers in university laboratories long before they became commercial products. Polystyrene, for example, was first observed in 1830 and only came into industrial production almost 100 years later.

Early plastics and man-made fibres such as Celluloid and rayon were not true synthetics since they were derived from natural materials modified by the application of chemicals. Around the turn of the century, attempts to understand the molecular structures of materials such as rubber, starch and cellulose suggested the possibility of creating similar structures in the laboratory. This possibility became a reality in 1907 when Baekeland, a Belgian chemist living in

Table 3.1 First commercial production of selected synthetic materials

	Company[a]	Country	Year[b]
Thermoplastics			
Polystyrene	IG Farben[c]	Germany	1930
PVC	IG Farben	Germany	1931
LD polyethylene[d]	ICI	UK	1939
HD polyethylene[d]	Montecatini	Italy	1954
LLD polyethylene[d]	Union Carbide	US	1977
Polypropylene	Hercules	US	1957
Synthetic fibres			
Nylon 6,6	Du Pont	US	1938
Nylon 6[e]	IG Farben	Germany	1941
Polyester	Du Pont	US	1953
Synthetic rubbers			
Styrene-butadiene	IG Farben	Germany	1934
Nitrile	IG Farben	Germany	1934
Butyl	Standard Oil (New Jersey)	US	1943
Chloroprene	Du Pont	US	1933

[a] In some cases, the innovating companies were not responsible for invention of the product.
[b] The dates of production refer to the introduction of commercial- as opposed to experimental-scale output. This distinction is not always clear and the dates differ slightly from those given in some other sources.
[c] Excludes the commercially unsuccessful plant of the Naugatuck Chemical Co.
[d] LD, low density; HD, high density; LLD, linear low density.
[e] Originally known as Perlon in Germany.

Yonkers, New York, developed the first commercial plastic by combining phenol and formaldeyhde. He started the manufacture of
Bakelite in 1910 and its success, apparent in the rapid licensing of the
technology in other countries including Germany, stimulated interest
in other polymers. Baekeland's discovery was a major breakthrough,
but it was based upon essentially empirical methods and the true
formula for Bakelite was not established until 1930. The scientific
basis of polymer chemistry, and in particular the idea that complex
organic substances are composed of long chains of simple molecules
arranged in specific repetitive patterns, were elucidated by Staudinger
at Freiburg University between 1920 and 1926. Staudinger's work
opened up the possibility of synthesizing an almost infinite variety of
organic materials from simple and readily available sources. The
implications of this were quickly appreciated by IG Farben, which
set up a polymer research laboratory in 1927 and which employed
Staudinger as a consultant throughout the inter-war period. The new
laboratory was indicative of IG Farben's commitment to synthetics,
which 'was far greater than in any other firm' (Freeman 1982, 52).
This R and D expenditure yielded results, and IG Farben was
responsible for the first commercial production of polystyrene[4] and
polyvinyl chloride (PVC), two of the most important commodity
plastics of the post-war period. The impetus to IG Farben's interest
in plastics was provided by scientific advances. The military and
strategic aspects of replacing imported raw materials with synthetic
substitutes certainly accelerated their development under the autarkic
policies of the Nazis and specific production targets were set in the
Four Year Plan of 1936, but the chronology emphasizes that IG
Farben responded to a science-push in the direction of synthetic
materials several years before Hitler came to power.

IG Farben was not the only company interested in the commercial
development of synthetic materials. Several factors encouraged Du
Pont, the largest US chemical company, to move into this field in the
1920s. Diversification from Du Pont's traditional base in explosives
was accelerated by an antitrust decision in 1913 which split the company into three parts, creating two new independent firms. Dyestuffs,
in which Du Pont became heavily involved during the First World
War as a result of the need to replace German imports, were not
regarded as a good long term prospect following a review of the
company's future strategy immediately after the war (see Taylor and
Sudnik 1984). This review concluded that diversification was necessary, and focused attention upon synthetics and especially synthetic
fibres in an effort to find alternative outlets for nitrocellulose which
was available from the company's expanded wartime capacity. This
led, through the acquisition of French technology, into rayon and
Cellophane. Accumulated profits from wartime production placed
the company in a strong position to expand by acquisition, and the

takeover of Viscoloid in 1925 was an important move into plastics. This approach to growth has been characteristic of Du Pont, and Mueller (1962) maintains that most of the company's major product innovations have been based on technology acquired from others.

This could not, however, be said of nylon. This polymer has had a massive impact upon the evolution of Du Pont, which by the 1950s had become the 'nylon company' (Taylor and Sudnik 1984, 154). 'Nylon...ranks as one of the most outstanding accomplishments of modern industrial chemistry and private-industry sponsored research' (Mueller 1962, 334). Its commercial introduction in 1938 may be traced back to Du Pont's increased commitment to basic research following a change in the presidency of the company in 1925 (Hounshell and Smith 1988, 223–48). This commitment found immediate expression in the creation of a new laboratory at corporate headquarters at Wilmington which began work on synthetic rubber in the same year. The recruitment of W. H. Carrothers from Harvard University in 1929 confirmed not only Du Pont's research orientation but also its particular interest in synthetic materials. Carrothers in the US and Staudinger in Germany are usually credited with laying the theoretical foundations of polymer chemistry. Although Carrothers insisted upon complete freedom to pursue his own lines of enquiry as a condition of his recruitment from Harvard, the activities of his team proved very profitable for Du Pont. A synthetic rubber (Neoprene) was patented in 1931 and quickly brought into production (see Smith 1985). This was in many respects superior to the equivalent German product, and in 1934 the Wehrmacht was urging the licensing of Du Pont's technology in preference to the use of IG Farben's (Hayes 1987, 138).[5] Nevertheless nylon, which was discovered in the course of Carrothers's work on the polyamides, was by far the most important product innovation in synthetic materials by a US company before World War II. It was important because the production of intermediates for use in nylon and similar materials became a significant aspect of petrochemical manufacture in the postwar years and because it played a major role in the creation of an entirely new synthetic fibre industry.

Apart from Du Pont, Dow and Union Carbide[6] probably appreciated the potential significance of synthetic materials earlier than most US chemical companies. Dow concentrated on styrene and polystyrene, partly because of its interest in the two chemical constitutents of these materials – ethylene and benzene. This interest was based on the company's activities at Midland, Michigan during World War I, where ethylene was associated with the production of mustard gas and benzene with explosives. From 1930 onwards, Dow focused its research efforts on organic chemicals and plastics (see Whitehead 1968). Polystyrene was the most significant result of these efforts before World War II and commercial production began in

1937, seven years after IG Farben. Carbide commenced research into vinyl resins in 1926, more or less concurrently with similar programmes by Du Pont and B. F. Goodrich. Its interest was partly related to the company's traditional strength in acetylene chemistry, since acetylene was the main source of vinyl chloride during the 1930s. Carbide had actually produced vinyl chloride from ethylene (via ethylene dichloride), which became the established route in the post-war period, on an experimental basis as early as 1929. Its attempts to convert this material into the polymer were unsuccessful, however, and IG Farben started commercial production of PVC in 1931, five years earlier than Carbide. By comparison with Germany, where the activities of IG Farben dominated research on synthetic materials, efforts in the US were more diffuse in an organizational sense. Du Pont, Dow and Union Carbide were the principals, but other companies were also involved. Eastman Kodak, from the film side, and GEC, through its interest in insulating materials, developed expertise in specialized areas, whilst a number of smaller companies such as Naugatuck Chemical Company and Fiberloid Corporation played a part. Monsanto, which became heavily involved in plastics and synthetic fibres after World War II, was late in the game and only began to move in this direction at the end of the 1930s (see Forrestal 1977).

Any review of the origins of the plastics industry, especially in terms of its impact upon petrochemical manufacture, would be incomplete without reference to polyethylene. This polymer was discovered neither in Germany nor in the US, but by ICI in the UK. It is a classic illustration of the potential benefits of basic research since it was first observed, in fortuitous circumstances, as a residual by-product during a series of experiments concerned with the effect of high pressures on chemical reactions (see Allen 1967; Reader 1975). ICI was slow to appreciate the significance of this discovery made in its Winnington laboratories, and the commercial production of poly-ethylene was delayed until 1939. Its full potential was not realized until after the war, when it rapidly became the most important single product of the petrochemical industry. Indeed, the commercial success of polyethylene was a major factor in the post-war growth of the new industry.

Advances in polymer chemistry led to a take-off in patenting activity in synthetic materials after 1925 (see Walsh et al. 1979; Walsh 1984). No single product or innovation was responsible for the birth of synthetic materials, but rather an accumulation of developments, each of which added to the overall potential for growth. Despite the multiplicity of these developments, the origins of the plastics, synthetic fibre and rubber industries cannot be conceived in terms of the initiatives of inventor/entrepreneurs. From the very beginning they have been dominated by large organizations, and their initial location has been determined not by the random distribution of inventor/ entrepreneurs but by the strategies of multiplant enterprises. Even where new firms were established to exploit proprietary technologies, they were often subsequently taken over by larger ones. This was especially true in the US where Union Carbide's acquisition of the assets of Baekeland's Bakelite Corporation in 1939 'climaxed a series of extensions through which the production of plastics and resins came more and more into the hands of large chemical companies' (Haynes 1954, 334). Most of the major breakthroughs in synthetic polymers were made as a result of corporate R and D. This reflected the widespread adoption of this mode of organized research in the chemical industry following the pattern established during the dyestuffs period in Germany. Key individuals such as Staudinger and Carrothers played an important part, but they were usually employees of or consultants to large companies. Thus the commercialization of their ideas and, more significantly, their translation into manufacturing plants were determined by corporate policies rather than the personal considerations which motivate inventor/ entrepreneurs.

The technical history of synthetic materials indicates the overlapping and frequently concurrent nature of lines of research within different companies and different countries. In many cases it is misleading to identify either a single institutional or a single geographical origin for an important innovation. Although ICI was responsible for the discovery of polyethylene, for example, Du Pont, Union Carbide and IG Farben very quickly established their own manufacturing facilities during World War II quite independently of ICI's expertise.[7] This is not unusual, and it is possible to calculate a technical imitation lag which measures the gap in years between the first commercial manufacture of a product anywhere in the world and its manufacture in a particular country (see section 5.2). Hufbauer (1966) estimated such national lags for a wide range of synthetic materials. The calculations are crude and depend upon several assumptions, but they emphasize that any lead obtained in a specific product by either Germany, the United States or the United Kingdom in the inter-war years was short-lived. This was partly because the major chemical companies in these countries were pursuing parallel lines of enquiry and partly because of the existence of various mechanisms for the transfer of information between them. Large private sector corporations are often pulled in two directions as far as their attitudes towards proprietary information is concerned (see section 5.2). On the one hand, there is a constant search for breakthroughs which may be protected by patent legislation and used to generate technological monopoly profits. On the other, this search is frequently accompanied by measures to guard against a competitor achieving such an advantage. The balance between offensive and defensive strategies varies between companies and industries. Cartel arrangements became a feature of the international chemical industry from the late nineteenth century onwards, and technical exchange agreements were one aspect of this structure. These agreements accelerated the temporal and spatial diffusion of technology relating to synthetic materials between Germany, the US and the UK. Du Pont, for example, had a long standing arrangement with ICI and also became involved in various deals with IG Farben towards the end of the 1930s (see Taylor and Sudnik 1984).

By 1940, most of the world's major chemical companies had appreciated the potential significance of synthetic materials for their businesses. In the US, plastics and fibres based on cellulose and phenolic resins of the type pioneered by Baekeland were fairly widely produced by 1940, but the polymers such as PVC and polystyrene, which were so important in the post-war growth of the petrochemical industry, were only just beginning to make an impact. Both output and technology were more advanced in Germany, and IG Farben accounted for more than a third of all patents in plastics materials taken out by the 30 most innovative firms in this field between 1931 and 1945 (Freeman et al. 1963; Freeman 1982). Supported by Nazi policies of self-sufficiency, German production of synthetic materials was much greater than that of the US between 1932 and 1939 (Walsh et al. 1979, 87). Du Pont, which committed more resources to the development of synthetic materials than any other US company, had less than half the number of patents of IG Farben over the 1931–45 period. Others such as Dow, Union Carbide, Hercules and Monsanto became aware at different times during the 1920s and 1930s not only of the growth prospects of plastics and resins, but also of the fact that these prospects could only be realized by producing large tonnages of the required chemical intermediates. Outside Germany and the US, ICI was the most significant contributor to the development of plastics, although its entry was 'late and hesitant' (Reader 1975, 349). However accurate their optimistic visions of the future for synthetic rubbers, fibres and plastics, few of the companies involved really made the connection, central to the post-war development of the petrochemical industry, between these new products and the use of oil and natural gas as raw materials for chemical manufacture. This was probably because many of the process innovations which brought about this change in raw materials originated in the oil rather than the chemical industry.

3.4 From Coal to Oil

By 1940, most of the new synthetic materials, like organic chemicals in general, were derived from coal. Germany's dependence on imported oil focused IG Farben's technology upon coal. In the UK, ICI regarded coal as the 'ultimate raw material' for organic chemistry and, as late as 1943, considered that 'petroleum was not of much interest' (Reader 1975, 395). The attitude of these two European companies was understandable in view of the resource base in their home countries, but Du Pont's continued faith in coal at the end of the 1930s (see Reader 1975, 321) was more surprising in the context of developments in the US oil industry. Technological pressures from both sides were bringing about a convergence in the interests and activities of the oil and chemical companies in the US, raising the prospect that members of each group might become involved in the other's traditional lines of business. A few chemical companies were quick to appreciate the possibilities of using oil and natural gas as raw materials. Union Carbide, for example, formed a subsidiary in 1920 to exploit them. For their part, the oil companies felt threatened by IG Farben's attempts to produce synthetic oil by the hydrogenation of coal and were therefore drawn into this area to defend their long term interests.

IG Farben's concern with the hydrogenation of coal was, in many ways, an inheritance from the German chemical industry's earlier commitment to nitrogen fixation (see Hughes 1969; Stranges 1984). It has already been shown in section 3.2 how fertilizer capacity increased sharply in Germany during the First World War. This expansion became a serious burden in the 1920s when increased competition and a depression in agriculture resulted in falling prices and chronic overcapacity. Hughes (1969) has argued that IG Farben's desire to find an alternative use for its surplus Haber-Bosch facilities at Leuna, and its wish to retain and take advantage of its accumulated expertise in high pressure chemistry, combined to create a 'technological momentum' which led the organization almost inevitably into its oil from coal project. This momentum was reinforced by various political and economic factors including Germany's acute shortage of foreign exchange to pay for oil imports in the aftermath of World War I. There was also concern that Germany was lagging behind the US in the introduction of automobiles. The lack of indigenous oil was a constraint to the motorization of the German economy and the production of gasoline from coal seemed an attractive substitute. The attractions of this technology acquired a more sinister aspect with the accession of Hitler, and the coal to oil project became a central plank in the autarky policies of the Third Reich in its preparation for war (see Hughes 1969; Krammer 1978; Borkin 1979; Hayes 1987).

IG Farben's interest in hydrogenation was paralleled by ICI, which faced similar problems as a result of its massive investment in synthetic fertilizers at Billingham following the formation of the company in 1926. Instead of securing the future of the new company, this investment 'was a burden for the rest of ICI to carry' (Reader

1975, 121), and 'oil-from-coal held out a prospect of saving something from the wreckage of the fertilizer project' (Reader 1975, 128). Conversion of surplus fertilizer capacity was better than scrapping it, and ICI pressed on with hydrogenation despite reservations about the future competitiveness of synthetic oil. As in Germany, strategic arguments were used to promote the project, and intensive lobbying by ICI eventually persuaded the British government to grant preferential tax treatment in 1934 to synthetic petroleum products as compared with equivalent products derived from imported oil.

The possibility of producing oil from coal might be expected to hold less attraction in the US with its large oil industry than in Western Europe. However, the 1920s 'began with the widely held view that domestic oil reserves were soon to run out' (Williamson et al. 1963, 336). This view was analogous to the fear of an impending world food shortage which, 20 years earlier, stimulated the search for a way of fixing atmospheric nitrogen. In these circumstances, several oil companies including Standard Oil of New Jersey became interested in oil from coal technology. Their interest was related partly to doubts about the long term availability of their basic raw material and partly to fears that synthetic oil might prove cheaper than the real thing. These fears were strengthened following a visit by Frank Howard, Standard's (New Jersey) senior R and D officer, to IG Farben's test facilities at Ludwigshafen in 1926. Following this visit, the two companies entered into various arrangements not only to secure their respective interests in hydrogenation, but also to cope with any future difficulties arising from their overlapping activities in coal, oil and chemicals. In 1929, IG Farben sold all but its German rights to the hydrogenation of coal and oil in return for stock in Standard Oil (New Jersey). Title to the patents was vested in a new Standard–IG Corporation. The links between them were reinforced a year later with the formation of the Joint American Study Company (JASCO) to test and license new processes, originating from either partner, for making chemical products from petroleum and natural gas. JASCO was an early recognition of the technical convergence which subsequently redefined the boundaries between the oil and chemical industries and created problems of commercial diplomacy for companies on both sides. Even before the contract was signed, falling oil prices linked to the effects of the Depression and major discoveries in East Texas had made it apparent that the hydrogenation of coal provided no threat to oil wells. Doubtless Standard (New Jersey) was relieved to find that the assumptions which motivated its initial interest in hydrogenation were too pessimistic. The experience was not wasted, however, since, in addition to their potential in making oil from coal, the principles of hydrogenation could be applied to good effect in the refinery processing of conventional oil. Preliminary work in pilot plants at Standard Oil's (New Jersey) Baton

Rouge refinery in 1928 and 1929 convinced the company's research staff 'that hydrogenation was the most important scientific development that had ever occurred in the oil industry' (Larson et al. 1971, 155). This development was itself part of a wider trend towards the 'chemicalization' of refinery processes during the 1920s, which was driven by the needs of the oil companies but which had implications for the chemical industry.

It has been shown in section 3.3 that many of the product innovations upon which the post-war growth of petrochemicals was based were made by European chemical companies, but the impetus for the process innovations in oil refining which determined the availability of raw materials to the new industry came from the US. The main objective of oil refiners before 1940 was to find ways of increasing the output of gasoline relative to other products. This reflected the rapid growth in automobile use and the sharp decline in the demand for kerosene which, prior to the advent of electricity, had been the industry's most important product. The pressure to achieve greater control over the yield of refinery products was especially strong in the Midwest, where the output of local oilfields was already declining by 1900, transport costs were high and competition from cheap coal was fierce for heavy residual fuel oil. The most promising approach to increased gasoline yields was provided by cracking, in which the large molecules of heavier oils are broken down under varying conditions of temperature and pressure into the smaller ones characteristic of lighter products. Interest in this technology was enhanced by the fact that it resulted in a better quality product than simple distillation, a consideration which became more important with the introduction of higher compression engines requiring improved octane ratings. The basic idea of cracking was known at the beginning of the century, but its translation into commercial practice occurred in two overlapping stages – the first associated with thermal cracking and the second with catalytic cracking. The history of these developments has been well documented (see Enos 1962a; 1962b; Williamson et al. 1963) and emphasis here is placed upon their significance for the petrochemical industry.

Thermal cracking had its origins in the work of William Burton at the Whiting refinery of Standard Oil of Indiana. After a series of dangerous experiments, the first commercial unit was commissioned in 1913. The process was quickly modified and improved so that by 1919 Standard Oil (Indiana) had several hundred Burton stills in operation at its Whiting and Wood River refineries. The success of this process was reflected in the widespread interest of other oil companies in licensing it. However, the stringent terms imposed by Standard Oil (Indiana) encouraged others to develop their own solutions, and the 1920s was a period of rapid process innovation in oil refining focusing on thermal cracking. A major difficulty with thermal cracking was the need to construct facilities capable of withstanding the high temperatures and pressures upon which the technique depends. Even whilst a flurry of similar thermal processes was introduced during the 1920s it was widely recognized that the use of catalysts would probably allow similar results to be achieved under less extreme operating conditions. Numerous oil companies were involved in the search for a satisfactory catalytic process, but the first breakthrough was made by a wealthy French engineer, Eugene Houdry, and he had successfully demonstrated the principle of catalytic cracking on an experimental basis by 1927. However, ten years elapsed before the process was introduced on a commercial scale. This delay was due to a combination of technical, financial and legal problems and Houdry's need to secure corporate backing. Socony-Vacuum[8] and Sun Oil provided support but, as with Burton's thermal process, licensing difficulties encouraged other companies to find a way to bypass the Houdry patents. Some measure of the significance attached to catalytic cracking was provided by the formation of Catalytic Research Associates in 1938. Initially composed of four companies, it was expanded by the addition of four more members in 1939.[9] This was a very powerful grouping which, by the end of 1942, had spent more than $15 million in a cooperative research effort directed towards the development of an alternative and better catalytic cracking process to that pioneered by Houdry (Williamson et al. 1963, 622).

The introduction of cracking processes had a major impact on the oil refining industry in the US before 1940. In 1919 only 16 per cent of gasoline output was derived from cracking units, compared with 51 per cent in 1941 (Williamson et al. 1963, 395 and 605). Thermal cracking reached its zenith on the eve of the Second World War, but was rapidly displaced by catalytic cracking as the preferred method of maximizing gasoline production. In addition to these specific effects upon the US oil refining industry, process innovations associated with cracking had broader implications for the rise of petrochemical manufacture. On a general level, they were symptomatic of a move away from the essentially empirical methods used by oil refiners in the nineteenth century towards a more scientific approach. This involved basic research into the chemistry of petroleum[10] which led the oil companies to recognize that their products could be used as more than just energy sources. Furthermore, the increasing scale of refining operations associated with the transition from batch production methods typified by the earliest thermal cracking stills, to the continuous flow approach used in catalytic cracking, promoted the development of chemical engineering. The emergence of this new branch of engineering was reflected in the laboratories of major companies and universities such as the Massachusetts Institute of Technology, and these developments 'gave American companies, for a period of time, a major advantage in the design and operation of large-scale plants for the production of a number of important hydrocarbons and chemicals' (Spitz 1988, 120). Perhaps the most significant impact of refinery cracking processes was to make available increasing quantities of chemically reactive hydrocarbons such as the olefins and aromatics. For some oil companies at least, the volumes of these materials, especially the olefin gases, were 'too large and too steady in supply to ignore' (Beaton 1957, 501).

A clear parallel may be drawn between the position of the oil companies with refineries in the 1920s and 1930s and that of the coal, steel and gas companies operating coke ovens in the 1870s and 1880s. Just as the coal tar available as a by-product from coke ovens became the key raw material of the organic chemical industry in the late nineteenth century, so gases from oil refineries were instrumental in bringing about the switch to petroleum and natural gas after the Second World War. Generally speaking, the coal tar producers failed to perceive the opportunities presented by the new organic chemical business. This was especially true in the UK which exported large quantities of coal tar to Germany. The oil companies in the US did not make the same mistake. By the mid 1920s they were collectively aware of the possibilities for using petroleum as a raw material for chemical manufacture, although there were wide variations in the speed with which these possibilities were taken up. Despite its pioneering role in the development of thermal cracking and its early commitment to research at Whiting, Standard Oil of Indiana was fairly typical in displaying only a 'desultory interest in chemicals before World War II' (Dedman 1984, 181). Standard Oil of New Jersey and Shell, however, became involved at least 20 years earlier than most other oil companies.

Standard Oil's (New Jersey) links with IG Farben have already been discussed. Its rapid appreciation of the possible implications of hydrogenation for the oil industry reflected the company's early commitment to research. A series of organizational changes, beginning with the establishment of a development department in 1919 and culminating in the formation of the Standard Oil Development Company in 1927, were designed to encourage research within the parent company and its various affiliates (see Larson et al. 1971). Although the emphasis was placed on the fuel and lubricant properties of petroleum, its potential as a raw material for chemical manufacture was an important line of enquiry within the Standard (New Jersey) organization. Indeed, the company began exploiting this potential in 1920 when it acquired a plant adjacent to its Bayway, New Jersey refinery originally established in 1917 by Carleton Ellis, an inventor/entrepreneur. Ellis developed a process to manufacture isopropyl alcohol from propylene and other olefins contained in by-product gases from Bayway. This product found extensive uses as a solvent and antifreeze. Capacity increased rapidly during the 1920s and the company found ways of producing several different types of specialized alcohols from the same raw material source. The complex of alcohol units at Bayway was the first refinery-linked petrochemical operation in the world, and it set the pattern for many similar developments which became commonplace more than 20 years later. This complex originally developed to take advantage of gases which would otherwise have been burnt as fuel or flared, but Standard (New Jersey) was quick to realize that processes could be introduced to deliberately produce feedstocks for chemicals. A propane cracker was, for example, constructed at Bayway to supply ethylene for use in the nearby tetraethyl lead plant of Ethyl Corporation. This was followed during the 1930s by experimental attempts to crack liquids such as naphtha and gas oil. These efforts paved the way for the purpose-built cracking plants which became the heart of the post-war petrochemical complexes. Standard's (New Jersey) involvement in petroleum cracking, alcohols and hydrogenation as well as its connections with IG Farben and its early work on synthetic rubber (see section 4.1) together represented a substantial commitment to petrochemicals before 1940. This commitment was concentrated in facilities at the company's largest and most sophisticated refineries at Bayway and Baton Rouge.

Shell made a strategic decision to enter the chemical business in 1927. Most of the company's research activity to that date was located in the Netherlands and little effort was directed towards possible chemical uses for oil. Both of these circumstances changed following the creation of a chemical department at head office in Amsterdam. The company identified two potential sources of raw materials – natural gas and refinery gases. Studies of the properties of cracked gases were started at the company's main laboratory at Amsterdam in the mid 1920s, but the lack of a supply of such gases was a major limitation and it was decided to establish a purpose-built research facility in the US where Shell had access to both refinery gases and natural gas. A site was chosen at Emeryville near San Francisco, and a corporate organization for the new US-based research function was established with the formation of the Shell Development Company in 1927, the same year as its Standard Oil (New Jersey) counterpart. This location reflected Shell's substantial involvement in the California oilfields and the proximity of its Martinez refinery as a source of gases. A conscious decision was taken to avoid establishing the reseach facility at Martinez or at one of Shell's other California refineries to avoid its degeneration into a testing department and to emphasize the distinctive nature of its work on chemicals (Beaton 1957, 516). Proximity to the University of California at Berkeley was also an influence upon the location decision.

Shell's first chemical manufacturing facility was actually established at IJmuiden in the Netherlands in 1929 using coke oven gas from a steel plant to produce ammonia. The company began chemical production in the US two years later when a similar plant, using natural gas as a raw material, was constructed at Shell Point a few miles to the east of its Martinez refinery. The timing of this venture, which was the first natural-gas-based fertilizer plant in the world, was disastrous. It simply added to existing overcapacity in the fertilizer business and its startup coincided with a price collapse. Nevertheless, the plant continued to operate and eventually started making money towards the end of the 1930s. Despite its pioneering use of natural gas, the Shell Point facility was essentially based upon proven technology, and Shell's research at Emeryville focused on the possibilities of using refinery gases for chemical manufacture. These investigations followed similar lines to the work of Standard Oil (New Jersey) and led Shell into the manufacture of various solvents. Some of these were familiar products such as isopropyl alcohol and acetone already manufactured by Standard Oil (New Jersey) and Union Carbide, whilst others were new commercial products such as methyl ethyl ketone. Small-scale manufacturing operations began at Martinez in 1930, but, by the end of the decade, Shell had substantial solvents capacity using by-product gases at its two principal refineries in California-Martinez (San Francisco) and Wilmington-Dominguez (Los Angeles).

The early entry of Standard Oil (New Jersey) and Shell into petrochemical manufacture from the oil side was matched from the chemical side by the activities of Union Carbide.[11] The principal strength of the corporation lay in acetylene chemistry, but it soon appreciated the possibilities offered by oil and natural gas as raw materials for the production of aliphatic chemicals. This awareness was reflected in the formation in 1920 of a subsidiary, Carbide and Carbon Chemicals Corporation, to develop the new field. It immediately embarked on a research programme which differed from the activities of Standard Oil (New Jersey) and Shell in its emphasis upon natural gas rather than refinery gases as a raw material for chemicals. This emphasis also resulted in a particular interest in ethylene, which subsequently became the key intermediate of the petrochemical industry, rather than propylene and the C_4 stream which were the main concern of the oil companies because of their relative abundance in refinery gases. Research into the production and utilization of ethylene began during World War I and was carried out in one of Carbide's own laboratories at Tonawanda, New York and in a company-sponsored programme at the Mellon Institute of Industrial Research in Pittsburgh. By the early 1920s, this work had progressed to such an extent that Carbide began looking for a greenfield site at which to concentrate its new petrochemical activities. A suitable location was found at South Charleston, West Virginia. The Kanahwa Valley not only had abundant ethane-rich natural gas to provide the key raw material, but was also well placed in relation to the markets of the East Coast. Established in 1926, the South Charleston plant expanded rapidly and was the world's first major stand-alone (as opposed to refinery-linked) petrochemical complex. The success of this operation encouraged Carbide to build a second complex in 1934 adjacent to the Standard Oil (Indiana) refinery at Whiting. This facility used both by-product gases and natural gas. The activities at South Charleston and Whiting ensured that Carbide became the 'undisputed leader' in aliphatic chemicals in the US during the 1930s (Haynes 1954, 219). The versatility of hydrocarbon gases as raw materials was emphasized by the expanding range of chemicals manufactured at these sites. These included various products which subsequently became commodity items in the post-war petrochemical industry including ethylene glycol, in which Union Carbide has retained a dominating market position, ethanol and vinyl chloride. Several aspects of Carbide's activities before 1940 foreshadowed the later development of the industry in the US. The company's use of both natural and refinery gas was important because the latter source proved inadequate to support the growth of the post-war years and, in focusing on ethylene, it successfully identified the intermediate most closely associated with that growth. It also anticipated future events by designing its South Charleston cracking plant to maximize the output of hydrocarbons for chemical use, and even considered, as early as 1927, backward integration into oil refining to achieve the same objective – a strategy followed by certain chemical companies more than 40 years later. Finally, in 1939 Carbide started planning a third manufacturing complex at Texas City on Galveston Bay, heralding the massive concentration of petrochemical capacity which emerged in the Gulf Coast region during and after the Second World War.

Although Standard Oil (New Jersey), Shell and Union Carbide were responsible for the most significant petrochmical manufacturing investments during the earliest phase of the industry's development in the US, various other companies played a part. Dow first became involved with ethylene whilst manufacturing mustard gas during World War I, but did not build upon this experience to the same extent as Union Carbide. Reference has already been made to the interest of Dow and, to a lesser extent, Monsanto in synthetic materials (section 3.3). By the mid 1930s, both of these companies had realized that many of these materials could be synthesized from petroleum hydrocarbons, but had scarcely begun to translate this realization into manufacturing facilities. Most of the earliest petrochemical plants manufactured solvents. The Sharples Solvents Corporation was incorporated in 1926 to exploit the pioneering work of its founder, P. T. Sharples, using casing-head gasoline in Texas. Full-scale manufacturing plants were established first at Belle, West Virginia and later at Wyandotte, Michigan. In Oklahoma, the Cities Service Company constructed a small solvents plant at its Muskogee refinery and the Barnsdall Corporation initiated a research programme in 1925 concerned with the production of alcohols from refinery gases. It established small manufacturing plants in association with refineries at Tiverton, Rhode Island and Barnsdall, Oklahoma before being taken over by Standard Oil (New Jersey) and merged into the new Standard Alcohol Company in 1932. Standard Oil of California was yet another oil company which entered petrochemicals as an outlet for refinery gases. It began research on the properties of these gases in the mid 1920s and started manufacturing solvents from them at its Richmond (San Francisco) refinery in 1935.

3.5 Conclusions

Life-cycle models of the evolution of industries imply that birth occurs with the first commercial manufacture of a new and important product which signifies the beginning of the logistic curve of output growth (see section 1.1). Even if birth can be unambiguously defined in this way, there is rarely any single, identifiable act of conception. The idea of 'technological momentum', originally used by Hughes (1969) to describe German efforts in the field of hydrogenation, seems an appropriate characterization of the development of industrial organic chemistry in general. With the benefit of hindsight, there appears to have been a kind of scientific inevitability underlying the various product and process innovations which created the petrochemical industry. This progression at the industry level is paralleled at the firm level as inherited expertise and capital equipment have encouraged specialization in particular products. Both IG Farben and ICI, for example, became involved in the hydrogenation of coal because of their need to find alternative commercial uses for surplus synthetic ammonia capacity. This capacity, together with the associated knowledge of high pressure chemistry which it reflected, is an illustration of the kind of technical slack which encourages corporate growth and diversification. By-products are a characteristic source of slack within the chemical industry, and attempts to find commercial uses for them have not only stimulated growth but also contributed to technological momentum. Company histories provide many examples of such by-product-based momentum (see Penrose 1960; Whitehead 1968; Reader 1975). Indeed, this philosophy was largely responsible for the entry of oil companies such as Standard Oil (New Jersey) and Shell into the chemical industry as they attempted to make use of by-product gases from their refining activities. These efforts led to some of the earliest and most significant examples of manufacturing operations which could be described as 'petrochemical'.

The role of the oil companies illustrates the place of technological convergence in the emergence of an identifiable petrochemical industry. It has been shown how advances in oil refining technology, motivated by efforts to improve the efficiency and flexibility of existing processes, led to an overlap in the interests of the oil and chemical companies. The circumstances of its creation at this point of contact between two established industries emphasize that the petrochemical industry was not *originally* defined in terms of the distinctiveness of its products. Many of the earliest petrochemical plants manufactured familiar products such as ethyl alcohol and isopropyl alcohol which were already derived from other raw materials. However, the petrochemical industry would never have achieved its rapid growth and economic significance were it not for its association with the commercial introduction of several new products, especially plastics. Many of the scientific breakthroughs in synthetic materials were made in Europe and by a coal-based chemical company in the US (i.e. Du Pont), emphasizing that this highly significant association was, nevertheless, coincidental. The chronology of the industry's development is, therefore, a reversal of the sequence usually proposed in life-cycle models in the sense that process innovations in oil refining were immediately responsible for its creation, but product innovations in synthetic materials were crucial to its subsequent growth.

The fact that the new industry developed out of two established industries was an important influence upon both the institutional and the geographical origins of these innovations. These industries were already dominated by large business organizations, and inventor/entrepreneurs have played little part in the petrochemical industry which, from the outset, was born out of corporate R and D, supported in certain cases by government. Individual scientists have made important contributions, but their ideas have invariably been translated into commercial practice by large companies. Thus, in the case of petrochemicals at least, the proposition that the birth of an industry can be traced to the inspiration of an individual inventor/entrepreneur is no more realistic than the view that it can be ascribed to a single key discovery. A corollary of the multiple origins of the industry is the diversity of the geographical sources of the various technical and corporate initiatives which contributed to its development. Several companies based in the United States, Germany, the United Kingdom and, to a lesser extent, France and Italy were involved, often working on similar problems. Indeed, the chances of any one company stealing a significant technical march on the others were often reduced in the inter-war period by various bi- and multilateral technical exchange agreements and cooperative research programmes which promoted the diffusion of scientific information. At a national level, developments in Germany and the United Kingdom were dominated by IG Farben and ICI respectively, but several companies were involved in the US where the location of research and early manufacturing facilities was strongly influenced by the existing geography of such organizations as Standard Oil (New Jersey) and Shell. Many US chemical companies, for example, set up R and D facilities immediately after World War I in New Jersey to be near their national headquarters in the New York City area (Stobaugh 1988, 53).

Despite important research contributions from Europe and especially from Germany, petrochemical manufacture was limited to the United States before 1940. This reflected the general contrast in the relative importance of coal and oil as energy sources between the United States and Western Europe and, more specifically, vastly greater refining capacity on the western side of the Atlantic. In 1940, 71 per cent of world refining capacity was located in North America (mainly the US), compared with only 7 per cent in Western Europe (J. D. Chapman 1989, 118). Oil and gas production in Europe was negligible and the US was by far the biggest producer. In these circumstances, it is hardly surprising that US companies pioneered the commercial manufacture of organic chemicals from petroleum whilst their European counterparts continued to rely on coal. It is important to emphasize, however, that the dominating role of the US in the international petrochemical industry after 1945 was more a result of its raw material advantage and its consequent expertise in oil refinery processing and chemical engineering than any general lead in organic chemistry. Indeed, US companies lagged behind IG Farben in important areas such as synthetic materials at the beginning of the Second World War.

The massive concentration of capacity in the Gulf Coast region which rapidly became a feature of the US petrochemical industry was not evident before 1940. Production facilities were widely scattered (figure 3.1). With the exception of Union Carbide's natural-gas-based operation in West Virginia, the distribution of most plants was linked to the oil refineries which supplied their raw materials. The US oil refining industry was itself more widely dispersed before the Second World War and the Gulf Coast's share of total capacity has increased from 13.8 per cent in 1916 (Pratt 1980, 66) to 38.5 per cent in 1989 (*International Petroleum Encyclopedia* 1989, 381–3). The early petrochemical plants were associated with a few large, complex refineries such as Bayway and Baton Rouge which had the cracking facilities that were the principal source of the by-product gases suitable for petrochemicals. The attraction of these refineries to petrochemical investment was often reinforced by the proximity of cor-

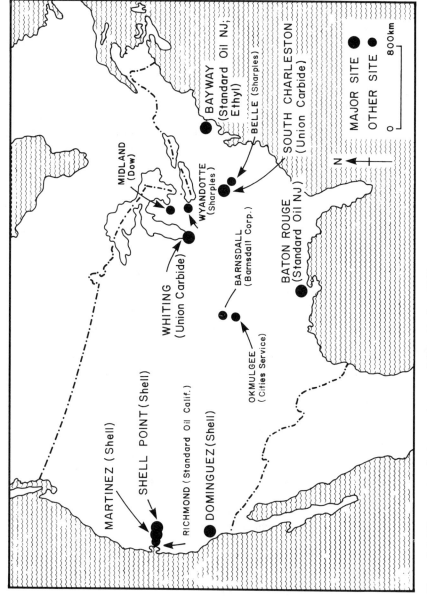

Figure 3.1 US petrochemical operations established before 1940

porate R and D establishments. Although several petrochemical plants were in operation by 1940, their aggregate output was limited. No statistics are available, but, viewed over the long perspective of industry growth represented by the logistic curve, total US production was, even after 20 years, only just beginning to register. Petroleum raw materials were important for specific groups of products such as aliphatic chemicals,[12] but these were limited in scope and significance by comparison with the explosion of petrochemical applications which developed after the war. In particular, US production of plastics was negligible and it was the combination of these relatively new products with the process innovations associated with advances in chemical engineering which led to the post-war take-off of the US petrochemical industry. The take-off was accelerated by the effect of political events in encouraging the commercial development of synthetic materials, especially rubber.

Notes

1 An excellent account of these developments, which covers the technical aspects in much more detail, may be found in Spitz (1988).
2 These companies were Badischer Anilin- und Soda-Fabrik (BASF), Friedrich Bayer and Co. (Bayer), Aktiengesellschaft fuer Anilin-Fabrikation (Agfa), Meister Lucius and Bruening (Hoechst), Leopold Cassella and Co. (Cassella) and Kalle and Co. Aktiengesellschaft.
3 The term 'synthetic materials' is used to refer collectively to synthetic plastics, synthetic rubbers and synthetic fibres. It excludes other products of the chemical industry such as dyestuffs and fertilizers which may also be regarded as synthetic in the sense that they are not derived directly from natural raw materials.
4 A polystyrene plant was built by the Naugatuck Chemical Company in Connecticut in 1925, but it was a short-lived operation owing to the adoption of a high cost process and the manufacture of an inferior product.
5 See section 4.1 for a review of the early development of synthetic rubber.
6 Most of Union Carbide's inter-war activities in petrochemicals and synthetic materials were carried out by a subsidiary called the Carbide and Carbon Chemicals Corporation.
7 Information regarding ICI's operating experience at its Wallerscote and Winnington polyethylene plants was transferred to Du Pont in 1941 under the terms of the companies' technical exchange agreement. However, Du Pont had already started work on a different process (see Allen 1967).
8 Now Mobil Oil Co.
9 The original members were M. W. Kellogg Co., IG Farben, Standard Oil (New Jersey) and Standard Oil (Indiana). The later members were Anglo-Iranian (i.e. British Petroleum), Royal Dutch–Shell, the Texas Co. (i.e. Texaco) and Universal Oil Products.

10 A special fund, administered by the American Petroleum Institute, was established for this purpose in 1926.
11 The modern corporation was originally incorporated as Union Carbide and Carbon Corporation in 1917 as a result of the union of five independent companies, although its ultimate origins may be traced to 1898 when the Union Carbide Company was formed.
12 Fermentation and wood distillation accounted for 98 per cent of US output of aliphatic chemicals in 1925. By 1930, petroleum and natural gas were the most important raw materials (Haynes 1954, 159).

4
World War II and the Establishment
of the Petrochemical Industry

The review of the technical origins of the petrochemical industry in chapter 3 emphasized the interaction of science-push and demand-pull factors in encouraging the innovations in organic chemicals, synthetic materials and oil processing which contributed to the emergence of the petrochemical industry. The balance of these influences shifted, however, immediately before and during the Second World War when military and strategic considerations, which may be regarded as a particular kind of demand-pull, exerted a major influence upon the development of the chemical and related industries in Germany and the United States. The idea that preparation for and the conduct of war may accelerate technical change is part of a wider set of questions regarding the impact of such activities upon long term trends in economic development and, more specifically, upon the fortunes of individual industries (see Milward 1977). Total economic mobilization for military purposes is comparatively recent in historical terms and first occurred during World War I. Since that time, however, the demands either of war or of maintaining an armed peace have influenced the development of existing industries within national economies and have been responsible for the creation of new ones. The need for armaments in two world wars stimulated production in a wide range of basic industries including coal, iron and steel, chemicals and engineering. In some cases, such as shipbuilding during the Second World War, wartime expansion could be regarded as a temporary boost to an industry that was already showing signs of a secular decline in output; in others, such as aircraft manufacture, it promoted the post-1945 growth of an important peacetime industry. Indeed, the origins of this industry in the United Kingdom may be traced back to the First World War when the annual production of aircraft increased from negligible levels in 1914 to more the 32,000 units four years later (Hardach 1977, 87). An obvious parallel may be drawn with the modern aerospace industry which is just one element of the so-called military-industrial complex that is directly involved with many of the high technology industries of the 1980s and 1990s (see Kaldor 1981; Gansler 1982), reinforcing the general point that wars, cold wars and war games have exerted an important influence upon the development and, in certain circumstances, the location of industries during the twentieth century.

It has been observed that 'No nation could make war without the wide co-operation of its chemical industry' (Davis 1984, 90). This became especially evident during World War I when German fears of the effect of a potential shortage of Chilean nitrates upon fertilizer and explosives production were instrumental in the rapid development of the Haber-Bosch process (see section 3.2). Similarly, British, French and American apprehension regarding German domination of dyestuffs was reflected in state-supported programmes which resulted in dramatic increases in domestic production in these countries by the end of the war. Furthermore, many large business enterprises in the belligerent nations made substantial profits during the First World War (see Hardach 1977) and the chemical companies were no exception. In the United States, for example, 'Wartime expansion provided [Du Pont] with a huge reserve of $89 million in retained earnings' (Taylor and Sudnik 1984, 67), whilst 'By 1918, Dow Chemical had become a virtual arsenal with almost all of its chemicals going to the government' (Whitehead 1968, 90). These and other chemical companies were, therefore, in a strong position to finance expansion and to pursue lines of research that had their origins in activities initiated as part of the war effort. It has already been shown in chapter 3 how strategically motivated advances in synthetic oil, plastics and rubber in Germany during the latter half of the 1930s had indirect effects upon the future development of the petrochemical industry, but US government policies following Pearl Harbor had much more immediate and direct consequences. Concern about possible shortages of rubber prompted an unprecedented level of federal government support for the development of a synthetic substitute which provided a major boost to the embryonic petrochemical industry. The nature and sigificance of this boost are discussed in the first section of this chapter. The second assesses the changing balance of technical and economic power in the international chemical industry associated with the impact of World War II upon the German industry. The final section explores the circumstances surrounding the shift from coal- to oil-based processes in Western Europe which began to gather momentum in the early 1950s.

4.1 Petrochemicals and the US War Economy

Although 20 years had passed since the establishment of the first manufacturing plants, petrochemical manufacture in the US on the eve of the Second World War could scarcely be described as an industry. Most organic chemicals continued to be produced from coal, and petroleum feedstocks had made a significant impact only in the field of aliphatic solvents. Apart from a few important exceptions (see section 3.4), most oil and chemical companies were only just beginning to appreciate the possibilities. Manufacturing plants remained widely scattered throughout the country, but a few pioneering companies were looking towards the Gulf Coast. From the very beginning, Standard Oil (New Jersey) decided to focus its petrochemical research activities at Baton Rouge rather than its New Jersey refineries because of the abundance of cheap natural gas. After concentrating its early manufacturing facilities in California, Shell switched the emphasis to its Houston refinery following a strategic review of the company's position at the end of the 1930s. This was related partly to raw material factors and partly to its recognition that the major markets for chemicals lay at the opposite side of the country to its California operations. Since the company lacked any refining facilities on the Atlantic Coast, Houston was regarded as the next best thing (Beaton 1957, 546). Dow and Union Carbide were also drawn to the Gulf Coast by the availability of raw materials, especially cheap natural gas. Dow decided in 1938 to develop a site at Freeport and Union Carbide made a similar commitment a year later to establish facilities at Texas City (figure 4.2). The actions of these pioneering companies not only pointed the way forward in terms of the use of petroleum raw materials for chemical manufacture, but also foreshadowed the future geographical concentration of the petrochemical industry in the Gulf Coast region. These incipient trends were accelerated and reinforced by events during World War II when certain petroleum-based products such as synthetic rubber, toluene and aviation gasoline were identified as strategic materials and their manufacture was promoted by government policy. Synthetic rubber was the most important of these products as far as the future development of the petrochemical industry was concerned. Before reviewing these implications, it is necessary to consider some of the technical background to the introduction of synthetic rubber.

The earliest research was carried out at the beginning of the century in Germany, where methyl rubber was produced in 1901. The next significant step was the first commercial manufacture of butadiene from coal-based acetylene by Bayer in 1906. This was important because butadiene is the key intermediate upon which the development of synthetic rubber has been based (equivalent to the role of ethylene in the production of many plastics). BASF discovered that by polymerizing this intermediate with sodium, a synthetic rubber (Buna) with better qualities than methyl rubber could be produced. Small quantities were manufactured in Germany towards the end of the First World War in an attempt to fill the gap created by acute shortages of natural rubber as a result of a naval blockade. The significance of this experience was not lost on the Nazi hierarchy, and IG Farben was encouraged after 1933 to renew the efforts of the German chemical industry to discover a satisfactory substitute for natural rubber. This search was second only to the production of oil from coal (see section 3.4) in the strategic priorities set by Hitler for the chemical industry (Hayes 1987). This political commitment was crucial since the prevailing price of natural rubber and the inferior quality of the synthetic product provided IG Farben with little commercial incentive to pursue this line of research. Ironically, Hitler's pressure on IG Farben was indirectly responsible for the creation of the US synthetic rubber industry because American companies, especially Standard Oil (New Jersey), were able to build upon German research. This research resulted in the introduction of two significant improvements upon BASF's original Buna by IG Farben during the 1930s. Copolymers of butadiene with styrene and acrylonitrile were termed Buna-S and Buna-N respectively by IG Farben. Commercial manufacture of both began in 1934. The styrene-butadiene rubber (Buna-S) was conceived as a general substitute for natural rubber, whilst the more expensive nitrile rubber (Buna-N) was regarded as a special-purpose product with qualities similar to those of Du Pont's Neoprene (see section 3.3). IG Farben had great difficulty with Buna-S in matching the properties of natural rubber and, despite considerable government support, output consistently fell behind the politically determined targets imposed both before and during the Second World War. Nevertheless, the German discovery of styrene-butadiene and nitrile rubbers was a major achievement which had important consequences in the United States.

The search before World War II for a synthetic substitute for natural rubber was not restricted to Germany and a number of advances were made in the US. Reference has already been made in section 3.3 to Du Pont's development of Neoprene, and this was preceded by the accidental discovery of another oil-resistant synthetic rubber in 1922 by a chemist in Kansas City. This was eventually marketed as Thiokol and came into production in 1930. Yet another product, butyl rubber, was actually discovered by IG Farben in 1932. However, IG could not vulcanize the polymer and details of its discovery were turned over to the Joint American Study Company (JASCO) under the terms of its technical agreement with Standard Oil (New Jersey) (see section 3.4). Further work on the American side eventually led to the manufacture of butyl rubber in 1943.

The early development of synthetic rubber in the United States followed a pattern different from events in Germany. Research was motivated by commercial rather than political considerations, and emphasis was placed upon developing products with different characteristics to natural rubber with the intention of finding specialized premium markets. Nevertheless, by virtue of its links with IG Farben (see section 3.4), Standard Oil (New Jersey) was very much aware of the possibility of producing a synthetic substitute for natural rubber. Standard (New Jersey)'s interest in its relationship with IG Farben was mainly focused on hydrogenation. However, IG Farben's principal research objective was to use this relationship to further its work on synthetic rubber. It was particularly keen to find out if an oil-based route to butadiene could be developed which would be cheaper than the coal-based operations which were the focus of attention in Germany. JASCO constructed an experimental plant at Baton Rouge in 1932 to explore this possibility. This converted refinery and natural gases to acetylene from which butadiene could be derived. The plant operated until early 1937. Although butadiene produced in this way was still too expensive for synthetic rubber to represent any real threat to natural rubber, the experience provided useful information which IG Farben was able to incorporate in the design of its own facilities, and also 'demonstrated [to Standard Oil (New Jersey)] that rubber could be produced from petroleum and focused attention on the possibility of discovering an economically feasible process' (Larson et al. 1971, 171). It is generally accepted that the information exchange aspects of Standard Oil (New Jersey)'s agreement with IG Farben were unbalanced, with the German company deriving the greater advantage (see Borkin 1979; Tuttle 1981). This was certainly not because Standard Oil (New Jersey) had more to offer, but was rather a consequence of the political pressures which meant that, even if IG Farben had wished to honour the spirit of the agreement, its ability to do so was constrained by higher authority within the Nazi administration. This situation was most apparent in the case of synthetic rubber. Despite persistent efforts, Standard Oil (New Jersey) was unable to obtain more than the basic patent information on Buna-S and Buna-N. This was belatedly secured upon the outbreak of war in Europe and excluded important data on plant design and operation. Nevertheless, the patents helped Standard Oil (New Jersey) to focus its research, and there is no doubt that the company was in a better position than any other in the United States to contribute to a crash programme of synthetic rubber development.

There were various contacts between Standard Oil (New Jersey) and the principal rubber-using companies in the US towards the end of the 1930s to explore possible applications of synthetic rubber and to arrange tests for experimental purposes. However, natural rubber prices were controlled under the terms of the International Rubber Regulation Agreement and there was no commercial incentive to develop a general-purpose rubber substitute at prevailing prices. Standard Oil (New Jersey) made several unsuccessful attempts during 1939 to obtain government assistance to support further research on such a substitute (Larson et al. 1971, 413). These efforts reflected the corporation's belief in the strategic significance of synthetic rubber. The creation in 1940 of the Rubber Reserve Company, which was a federal agency charged with the responsibility of purchasing and stockpiling natural rubber, at least indicated a growing official awareness of a potential problem. This problem became a reality following Pearl Harbor and the Japanese threat to the rubber plantations in South East Asia, with the result that by late 1942 it was generally accepted that the development of a general-purpose synthetic rubber was a strategic priority. The gradual evolution between 1940 and 1942 of plans to create a new synthetic rubber industry in the United States is a complex story of conflicting political, economic and regional interests which has been extensively studied elsewhere (see Howard 1947; Tuttle 1981; Herbert and Bisio 1985). The circumstances surrounding the formulation of the synthetic rubber programme are less relevant here than its outcome, which may be considered in terms of the choice of technology, the organization of production and the location of manufacturing facilities.

After extensive testing, the various potential producers and consumers finally agreed in 1941 that a styrene-butadiene copolymer of the Buna-S type was the most suitable for general use.[1] When the decision to proceed with a synthetic rubber programme was finally taken, attention immediately focused on sources of supply for the two key intermediates – styrene and butadiene. Styrene is generally produced by the dehydrogenation of ethyl benzene which is itself formed by the reaction of ethylene and benzene. The commercial production of styrene had become a routine operation in Germany where IG Farben introduced polystyrene in 1930. Experience in the United States was more limited. Standard Oil (New Jersey) owned the US rights to IG Farben's coal-based process, but several chemical companies were charged with the responsibility of producing styrene for the synthetic rubber programme. Dow had developed its own process and started small-scale styrene production in 1937, and other companies had also begun to show an interest immediately before the war. Despite the fact that the US chemical industry was well behind IG Farben in styrene research and manufacturing capacity, by the time a political consensus was finally reached in 1942 on the form of the synthetic rubber programme it had acquired the technical knowhow to construct and operate plants to supply one of the two key materials required to sustain the programme.

Many of the problems which delayed agreement on this programme were related to a debate regarding the best approach to supplying the other vital intermediate – butadiene. Several alternative processes were considered including a group based on a variety of petroleum fractions available from natural gas and oil refineries and a completely different approach involving the catalytic conversion of industrial (i.e. ethyl) alcohol. The alcohol could itself be derived from petroleum sources, and the ultimate raw material of the alcohol-based facility operated by Carbide and Carbon at Institute, West Virginia was natural gas. Nevertheless, the real significance of the debate over butadiene supplies was related to the fact that industrial alcohol could also be produced by the fermentation of vegetable matter. Approximately 80 per cent of US industrial alcohol was produced in this way at the beginning of the war with the balance derived from natural gas (Herbert and Bisio 1985, 85). Most was obtained by the fermentation of molasses, but grain was also used. The grain-based route offered a means of utilizing substantial agricultural surpluses and a concerted political effort was made by the farming lobby in 1941 and 1942 to promote this technology. The debate involved such matters as the relative costs of butadiene produced from petroleum and grain, the possibility of potential conflicts with other wartime programmes (see below), the reliability of the various technologies, the extent of their demands upon scarce resources such as structural steel, and the speed with which production targets could be met. In addition to these short term issues, the participants in the debate realized that synthetic rubber had enormous potential and were, therefore, anxious to secure their positions in what seemed likely to become an important sector in the nation's post-war economy.

The programme ultimately approved in late 1942 incorporated both the grain- and petroleum-based processes. The production costs of the former were higher, but output could be more quickly achieved. Thus 82 per cent of the total output of butadiene was obtained from industrial alcohol in 1943, but the proportion derived from petroleum increased as new plants came on stream to reach almost 60 per cent in 1945 (Herbert and Bisio 1985, 129). The significance of this programme is emphasized by the rapid displacement of natural by synthetic rubber (figure 4.1). This was only achieved as a result of extensive federal government intervention. Essentially, the government financed the construction and operation of the new plants required to produce synthetic rubber. This included the various facilities associated with the manufacture of the necessary raw materials, butadiene and styrene, as well as the polymerization plants where the these materials were combined and converted into synthetic rubber. Further financial support was provided for the final fabrication stage to allow companies such as Goodyear and Firestone to modify their existing equipment for the manufacture of tyres and other rubber products to cope with the slightly different processing requirements of synthetic rubber. The new plants were designed and constructed by appropriate private sector organizations. Dow was, for example, placed in overall charge of the styrene programme because of its pre-war experience of this product, although Monsanto, Union Carbide and Koppers were also involved. Butadiene produc-

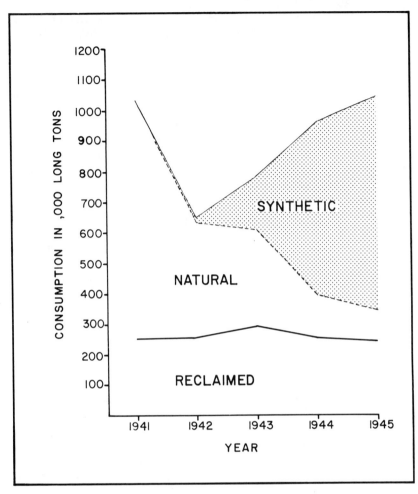

Figure 4.1 US rubber consumption by source, 1941–1945 (from data in Herbert and Bisio 1985, 127)

tion was shared between oil and chemical companies, with the former responsible for oil-based processes and the latter engaged in alcohol-based operations. Copolymerization and fabrication were carried out by the rubber companies, thus establishing the boundary, maintained after World War II, between the responsibilities of the rubber and petrochemical industries in what is essentially a linked sequence of operations. In general, the various plants were operated by the private sector on the basis of reimbursement for costs plus a management fee related to output. The plants were actually owned by the federal government under complicated financial arrangements involving the Reconstruction Finance Corporation, the Defense Plant Corporation and the Rubber Reserve Company.[2] This ownership reflected the fact that, despite some signifiant private sector investments which preceded and subsequently contributed to the synthetic rubber programme, the new industry was a creation of a government-sponsored and coordinated plan. The geographical results of this plan as it affected butadiene and styrene production are indicated in figure 4.2. Most of the facilities were located in or adjacent to existing oil refining and/or chemical complexes. This not only reflected the influence of technical linkages, but also demonstrated prudent planning on the part of the operating companies in anticipation of their eventual acquisition of these facilities from the government. The investments at Sarnia in Canada were an integral part of the synthetic rubber programme following an agreement between the governments of the two countries. These facilities, which were linked to the existing refinery of Imperial Oil, later formed the basis for the emergence of Sarnia as Canada's principal centre of petrochemical production and also provided a platform for Dow's substantial post-war commitment in Canada (see Shell Oil Co. of Canada 1956; Whitehead 1968).

The impact of wartime conditions upon the development of the petrochemical industry was most evident in the synthetic rubber programme, but several indirect effects resulted from attempts to gear the output of US oil refineries to military needs. In addition to supplying butadiene for synthetic rubber, the oil refining industry was asked to switch from its pre-war emphasis upon meeting the demands of the country's motorists towards increased outputs of fuel oil, aviation gasoline, toluene and other aromatics to serve the war effort. The problem of supplying aviation gasoline was especially acute and the ultimate requirement was consistently underestimated by the military in the early years of the war (Williamson et al. 1963, 785). By 1943, however, the need for this fuel was recognized as a top strategic priority and critical materials were made available to permit appropriate capital investments in the refineries. This equipment was needed not only to increase the output of gasoline, but also to meet the much higher octane specification of aviation fuel. In the short term this was achieved by increasing the tetraethyl lead content, but the most important result of the aviation fuel programme was to accelerate the introduction of the new technology of catalytic cracking. The background to and original purpose of this technology has already been reviewed (see section 3.4). Its ability to transform an increased proportion of the barrel into high octane blendstocks was ideally suited to the needs of the time. Without the special circumstances created by the wartime economy, catalytic cracking would have made a much more gradual appearance in the processing schemes of the refining industry, but the availability of government

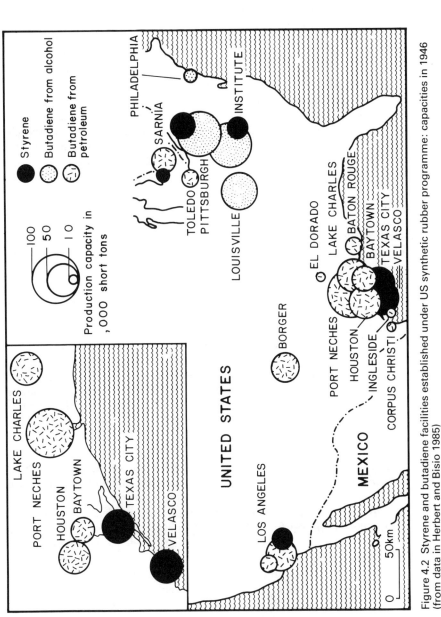

Figure 4.2 Styrene and butadiene facilities established under US synthetic rubber programme: capacities in 1946 (from data in Herbert and Bisio 1985)

funding meant that the usual constraints imposed by the need to amortize existing facilities did not apply.

Closely related to the introduction of catalytic cracking was the development of a group of similar reforming processes to convert by-product gases into liquids for use as gasoline blending components.[3] Catalytic polymerization units were introduced in a few US refineries towards the end of the 1930s to recover and utilize propylene and butylenes which had previously been flared or burnt as works fuel. The associated process of alkylation had the additional property of producing a blendstock with an especially high octane rating suitable for inclusion in aviation gasoline. Isomerization further boosted the output of these blendstocks by increasing the range of specific refinery gas components from which they could be derived. Yet another important contribution to the aviation gasoline pool was provided by Shell's process for the manufacture of a synthetic aromatic (i.e. cumene or isopropyl benzene) by combining coal-tar benzene with refinery propylene. This process was developed at Emeryville (see section 3.4) as part of a search for ways of increasing the production of aviation gasoline and was in operation at Shell's Norco, Louisiana and Wood River, Illinois refineries by mid 1942.

Toluene for the production of explosives had traditionally been derived from coal tar. Concern about the adequacy of supplies from this source in the event of war prompted a formal enquiry from the Army Ordnance Department to several oil companies in 1939 concerning its extraction and/or manufacture from petroleum. Many refineries incorporated facilities to meet this need and 81 per cent of US peak wartime output in 1944 was derived from petroleum (Williamson et al. 1963, 791). Toluene production and the aviation gasoline programme were closely linked to the extent that certain refinery processes, notably catalytic reforming, provided much of the aromatics-rich feedstock from which toluene was derived and which also contributed to the output of high octane fuel.

The most obvious impact of wartime demands upon the US oil refining industry was a 29 per cent increase in effective operating capacity between 1939 and 1945 (Williamson et al. 1963, 784). Although many companies and refineries contributed to the war effort, a substantial proportion of state-supported investment was concentrated in relatively few large and sophisticated plants. Historians of the major companies all acknowledge the significance of federally funded projects in determining the pattern of their refinery investment during the Second World War (see James 1953; Beaton 1957; Larson and Porter 1959; Larson et al. 1971; Dedman 1984). At Baton Rouge, for example, approximately half of total capital expenditure by Standard Oil (New Jersey) was supported in this way (Larson et al. 1971). Much of the effort was directed towards increasing the output of aviation gasoline and this in turn resulted in massive expenditure in the relatively new and complementary processes of catalytic cracking and catalytic reforming. These proceses were both originally conceived to increase the yield of gasolines and were both derivatives of earlier thermal processes. The introduction of the catalytic versions of these processes in the late 1930s reflected the growing sophistication of refining technology which was itself based upon the industry's increasing knowledge of petrochemistry. The significance of these two processes for the petrochemical industry lay in their production of basic intermediates suitable for chemical manufacture. It has already been shown (in section 3.4) how the availability of olefins, especially propylene and butylenes, from refinery cracking processes encouraged related petrochemical developments in the pre-war years. Catalytic reforming, which was introduced slightly later, created a similar situation after the war when the high aromatic content of the reformed naphtha produced by this process was perceived as an important new source of benzene, toluene and xylenes for chemical use. Thus the war not only promoted the technical development of refining processes which provided raw materials for chemical manufacture, but also hastened their commercial introduction. When the war finished, substantial capacity was already in place to provide the olefins and aromatics required by the petrochemical industry. This capacity was rapidly converted from its wartime orientation and, in a few cases, led the oil companies directly into chemical production. At Baytown, Texas, for example, the Ordnance Works operated by Humble Oil (a subsidiary of Standard Oil (New Jersey)) on behalf of the government was switched in 1946 to the production of aromatic solvents and gasoline blendstock when the demand for toluene declined (Larson and Porter 1959, 623). On a more general level, the wartime experience of new refining processes, such as alkylation and polymerization, which employed *chemical* principles to make fuel products, made the oil companies more aware of the possible non-energy uses of petroleum.

Although private capital made substantial contributions, state sponsorship played a major role in stimulating the development of the US oil refining and petrochemical industries during World War II. This role was all the more important in the case of petrochemicals because it came at a critical, early stage in the industry's life cycle. Its impact is most obvious in the case of synthetic rubber, and it has been variously suggested that the levels of output achieved within two years of the commencement of the government-supported programme (figure 4.1) would otherwise have taken anything from 12 (Howard 1947, 216) to 20 (Tuttle 1981, 65) years to reach under normal circumstances. One aspect of the wartime situation was the more rapid diffusion of technical information. Cooperative research and exchange of information were actively encouraged. Innovations based on government-funded research were made availabe to all interested parties through a patent pooling scheme and it was recognized that such arrangements, which are anathema to the US antitrust tradition, were essential in meeting the production targets for synthetic rubber (see Howard 1947, 169–77; Herbert and Bisio 1985, 113–24). There is clear evidence that government policy makers involved in this programme were aware of its implications for postwar industrial development. Certainly these policy makers could not fail to appreciate that the essentially state-owned synthetic rubber industry was inconsistent with the philosophy of American capitalism and, therefore, to consider the circumstances in which this anomaly could be rectified. As early as 1942, it was recognized that 'there will be a struggle amongst various groups for the control of the new [synthetic rubber] industry' (Baruch Committee, quoted in Howard 1947, 219). Furthermore, the same document noted the possible postwar economic advantages to the US in using state subsidies to establish a synthetic rubber industry capable of competing with natural rubber, and Tuttle (1981, 51) has suggested that such considerations were an important factor in the decision to commit the major proportion of state funding to producing butadiene from petroleum rather than the more proven route from industrial alcohol. It was clear that, once developed, petroleum-based processes would produce butadiene at lower cost and would, therefore, provide a more secure foundation for the establishment of an internationally competitive industry. Most government-owned manufacturing plants were sold to the private sector in the immediate post-war years, although the butadiene and copolymer plants remained in public ownership until 1953. In the case of the oil refining and petrochemical industries, most of these plants were closely associated with existing facilities; this meant that, despite a competitive bidding system, technical factors gave the operating companies an inside track when the sales were made. Not surprisingly, most of them acquired the facilities they had been responsible for. Furthermore, they acquired these facilities on very favourable terms (table 4.1) and it could be argued that, whilst the large oil and chemical companies made substantial financial and technical contributions to winning the war, they were subsequently rewarded by an initial state subsidy of inherited facilities which placed US capital in an even stronger position from which to dominate the post-war petrochemical industry.

As well as influencing the rate of growth in US petrochemical capacity, state intervention also affected the industry's location. It has already been noted that several major companies were beginning to look towards the Gulf Coast for future petrochemical sites before the outbreak of war, but the attractions of the area were reinforced by political circumstances. The Houston area in particular was regarded as less vulnerable to air attack than alternative coastal refining centres in California and the Northeast. The construction of

Table 4.1 US government styrene and butadiene facilities sold between October 1946 and December 1948

Type of plant	Location	Purchaser	Approx. plant investment at date of sale[a] ($ thousand)	Approx. purchase price ($ thousand)
Butadiene (petroleum)	Baton Rouge, LA	Esso Standard Oil Co.	1,985	325
Butadiene (petroleum)	El Dorado, AR	Lion Oil Co.	2,162	68
Butadiene (petroleum)	Ingleside, TX	Sampson Machine and Supply Co.	4,143	60
Butadiene (petroleum)	Corpus Christi, TX	Taylor Refining Co.	1,799	150
Butadiene (alcohol)	Institute, WV } Institute, WV }	Carbide and Carbon Chemical Corp.	47,483	9,350
Styrene	Texas City, TX	Monsanto Chemical Co.	19,273	9,908
Styrene	Kobuta, PA	Koppers Co., Inc.	12,242	3,265
Styrene	Velasco, TX	Dow Chemical Co.	17,828	14,518

[a] Original investment plus improvements and betterments, less retirements.
Source: Herbert and Bisio 1985, 164.

the federally funded crude oil and product pipelines from Texas to the markets of the Midwest and Northeast in 1943 reinforced the raw material advantages of the Gulf Coast and encouraged further expansion of refinery capacity. Furthermore, whatever geographical assets the Texas Gulf Coast may have possessed were exploited to the full as a result of political influence which channelled federal funds to the state. Jesse Jones, who has been described as 'a key member of the Houston business elite' (Feagin 1988, 66), was also a prominent figure in the Roosevelt administration. As head of the Reconstruction Finance Corporation and of the Rubber Reserve Company he occupied an influential position with respect to the wartime expansion of the oil refining, petrochemical and synthetic rubber industries. It has been suggested that he used this position not only to favour petroleum- over grain-based butadiene processes (Tuttle 1981, 50–1), but also to direct federal money to the Houston area (Riddell and Feagin 1987). Substantial sums were involved. Texas received more than $650 million of Defense Plant Corporation investment during the war, an amount exceeded only by Ohio and Michigan (Riddell and Feagin 1987). Over 60 per cent of the total of more than $500 million spent by all federal government agencies at or adjacent to existing oil refineries in connection with the war effort was focused on the Gulf Coast (Pratt 1980, 94). Figure 4.3 indicates the concentration of federal investment in south-east Texas associated with the synthetic rubber programme alone, and excludes government support for the production of other petrolem-based war materials such as aviation gasoline and toluene. This massive injection of federal capital not only accelerated the growth of the oil refining and petrochemical industries but, more specifically, promoted their development in the Gulf Coast region and especially in the Houston area. The Texas Gulf Coast became the dominating centre of post-war petrochemical production and, whilst it would be an exaggeration to regard this status as a direct result of state intervention, there is no doubt that it helped. This, of course, is a situation not without its irony in view of Houston's emphatic commitment to the ideology of free enterprise (see Feagin 1985; 1988).

4.2 War and the Balance of Power in the International Chemical Industry

The effect of preparations for war in stimulating German output of such materials as synthetic petrol and rubber has already been noted (see section 3.3). The same considerations which encouraged German efforts in these areas of organic chemistry, however, also ensured that they were important targets for Allied bombing; it is known that synthetic rubber production, for example, was significantly reduced

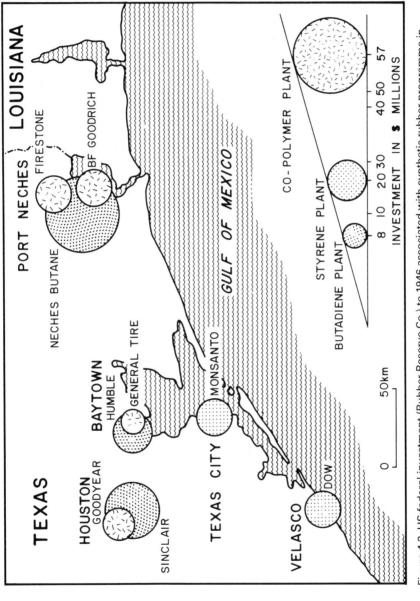

Figure 4.3 US federal investment (Rubber Reserve Co.) to 1946 associated with synthetic rubber programme in south-east Texas (from data in Riddell and Feagin 1987)

by such raids during 1944 (Herbert and Bisio 1985, 33). Nevertheless, economic historians believe that the overall effect of wartime destruction upon German industry was offset by accelerated investment during the war, so that manufacturing capacity in 1945 was equal to or greater than in 1939 (see Stolper 1967; Milward 1977; Cairncross 1986). Far more significant as far as the German chemical industry was concerned were the consequences of the post-war division of the country. A substantial proportion of its pre-war capacity was situated in what became the German Democratic Republic, partly because of the influence of such conventional location factors as the availability of raw materials and partly because of a deliberate policy immediately before and during the war of siting strategic industrial facilities in more remote and less vulnerable parts of Germany. This meant that many important chemical plants established by IG Farben, including the massive installations around Merseburg involved in the production of synthetic ammonia, rubber and petrol, were effectively lost to the Soviet Union. In many cases this was literally true as the Russians dismantled numerous facilities and transported them eastwards. This programme was viewed as part of a wider package of reparations to be imposed upon the defeated Germany. The process began before the end of the war, and it has been estimated that nearly one-third of the total value of movable industrial capacity in the eastern zone was removed before it finally stopped in 1948 (Cairncross 1986, 200). These removals included several hydrogenation facilities as well as the largest German Buna plant at Schkopau (Sutton 1973, 153). Similar dismantling and removal occurred in the western zones, but this policy was modified when it was realized that the economic impoverishment of Germany was damaging to the recovery of the rest of Western Europe, especially in the context of the deteriorating relations between the Russians and the Western Allies. A total of 667 industrial plants were removed from the western zones between the end of the war and 1951 when reparations officially ended (Balabkins 1964, 142). The synthetic oil and rubber plants in the western zones were originally regarded as priorities for removal, but were not included in the final tally of facilities actually dismantled. This was important because many of these plants in such long established centres of chemical production as Ludwigshafen and Recklinghausen were adapted to oil refining and petrochemical production in the 1950s. Overall, 'The removal of industrial equipment [from the western zones] had no appreciable effect on West German production' (Cairncross 1986, 191) so that, by 1950, new investment far exceeded such losses.

A major concern of the Allies towards the end of the war was the industrial disarmament of Germany to render it economically incapable of waging war. This objective was clearly expressed at the Potsdam Conference in 1945. The Level of Industry Plan of 1946 envisaged the elimination of certain 'prohibited industries' and severe limitations on the output of other 'restricted industries' (see Balabkins 1964; Cairncross 1986). The chemical industry straddled this classification: synthetic oil, petrol, rubber and ammonia were all prohibited, whilst the remaining areas of basic chemicals were restricted to a gross output not exceeding 40 per cent of 1936 production. These conditions were, in fact, much less severe than an earlier scheme (i.e. the Morgenthau Plan of 1944) which advocated the complete destruction of the chemical and other industries. As with the policy of reparations, however, the terms were quickly relaxed as the political and economic realities of the post-war world became apparent, and the effect upon the chemical industry was limited. A more important negative consequence of the peace settlement than plant removals and restrictions on output was the enforced breakup of IG Farben. This company was widely regarded as having played a key role in sustaining the Nazi war effort (see Borkin 1979). Its domination of the German chemical industry also conflicted with the Allies' desire to reduce levels of concentration within the post-war economy, which was motivated by a belief that big business was involved in a conspiracy supporting Hitler's ambitions. The ultimate fate of IG Farben was not resolved until 1953 when its assets were divided up between four successor companies.[4] Plans and investments were made before the Liquidation Commission reached its formal decision, but the uncertainty surrounding its future commercial structure, together with the threat of reparations and the general economic chaos during the occupation, all delayed the recovery of the German chemical industry. Nevertheless it proved remarkably resilient, as testified by the present position of Bayer, BASF and Hoechst, all of which emerged from the breakup of IG Farben, as the world's three largest chemical companies in terms of net sales (see section 2.3).[5]

The position of the German chemical industry relative to that of the United States and the other major producers was affected not only by the various restrictive measures of the post-war period, but also by the way in which the victors took advantage of the opportunity to discover its secrets. The pre-war supremacy of German technology in certain areas and the efforts of companies such as Standard Oil (New Jersey) to gain access to it have already been emphasized in chapter 3. Although this lead had disappeared in some fields, especially synthetic rubber, by the end of the war, German expertise associated with coal-based processes was often applicable to petroleum-based operations. This expertise was acquired in several ways. The direct recruitment of German chemists and engineers played some part, but numerous technical missions to captured plants and laboratories was probably more important and resulted in the removal of vast quantities of documents to Washington and, to a lesser extent, London (Krammer 1981). Details of IG

82   *War and the Establishment of the Industry*

processes for the manufacture of nylon 6, for example, were published and freed from patent restrictions by the Allied governments in 1945 (Walsh et al. 1979, 3.46). Such war booty was later reinforced by more conventional forms of technology transfer following the re-establishment of German patent rights. Anxious to capitalize on whatever areas of knowledge had not been plundered, IG Farben's successors began licensing processes to US companies. The enforced and voluntary diffusion of German technology contributed to the post-war growth of the petrochemical industry. The US was best placed to take advantage of this technology because of its over-whelming economic strength and because of its established oil, gas and refining industries. Thus the German technical lead in organic chemistry, which had been maintained in a general sense ever since the 1870s, was lost to the United States when oil and natural gas replaced coal as the principal materials.

4.3 Petrochemicals and Post-War Reconstruction in Western Europe

By 1950 half of the total US production (by weight) of organic chemicals was based on oil and natural gas, and the proportion had reached 88 per cent by 1960 (Howes 1968). The switch to petroleum feedstocks accelerated after 1945 by comparison with the gradual introduction of petrochemicals over the preceding quarter century. The changeover was even more rapid in the principal chemical producing countries of Western Europe which had relied upon coal and vegetable matter as raw materials for organic chemicals before World War II.[6] In the United Kingdom, which was the first of these countries to use petroleum feedstocks, only 9 per cent (by weight) of the total output of organic chemicals was derived from such feed-stocks in 1949, but this had increased to 63 per cent by 1962 (Hodge 1961).[7] Similar shifts were occurring elsewhere, and the average figure for Western Europe as a whole was 58 per cent in 1962 (OECD 1963a, 76). These trends in the chemical industry were related to wider changes in the relative importance of coal and oil as sources of energy which were themselves linked to strategies for the economic recovery of Western Europe.

The economic crisis of 1947 combined with the onset of the Cold War convinced the US State Department 'that a systematic pro-gramme of aid for Western Europe was in America's real interest' (Milward 1984, 56). The Marshall Plan, which operated between 1948 and 1951, was conceived in response to this assessment. The political effects of the scheme in promoting European integration were far-reaching. Its immediate economic objective was to boost levels of production with particular emphasis upon key sectors such as iron, steel and coal. One aspect of the post-war economic crisis was an acute fuel shortage, the effects of which were aggravated by the severe winter of 1946–7. War damage and the neglect of vital maintenance meant that European mines, which had supplied more than 90 per cent of the Continent's energy requirements before 1939, were in no position to meet post-war demands, and increasing quantities of expensive US coal were imported. Although the principal efforts of the Marshall Plan in the energy sector were directed towards the recovery of the coal industry, it also encouraged a substantial expansion of oil refining capacity 'as an essential requirement for the economic reconstruction and viability of Europe' (OEEC 1949, 38). Several factors contributed to the increasing interest in oil, including the growing availability of supplies from the Middle East and its favourable price relative to imported coal. Before 1939 the volume of refined product imports was approximately twice as great as crude oil, but the pressing need to conserve foreign exchange encouraged efforts to reverse this pattern by carrying out value-adding refining processes in Western Europe. This was the principal justification for increasing refinery capacity, although other economic benefits were identified including the encouragement of related petrochemical facilities (OEEC 1949, 24). The results of the US-supported refinery expansion programme were impressive, and the crude oil throughput capacity of European refineries increased from 19.5 to 103 million tons between 1948 and 1955 (OEEC 1956). In relative terms, Western Europe's share of world refining capacity rose from approximately 7 per cent in 1940 to 16 per cent in 1960 (J. D. Chapman 1989, 118). With the exception of West Germany, where refinery developments were initially more gradual, the distribution of capacity between countries broadly reflected the relative size of their economies, with almost 85 per cent of the European total in 1955 located in France, Italy and the United Kingdom (Melamid 1955). Where possible, new investment was directed towards the expansion of existing pre-war refineries, which was more cost-effective than the development of greenfield sites (Butler 1953). Most of these were located on the coast to receive imported crude oil and several of them became the focus of related petrochemical facilities.

Circumstances in the coal and oil refining industries were directly relevant to the post-war prospects of the European chemical industry. This is demonstrated by Reader's (1975) detailed account of thinking within ICI over the problem of raw materials. ICI (and, presumably, the other major European chemical companies) was well aware of events in the United States, which emphasized that oil and natural gas could be used to manufacture an expanding range of organic chemicals. Some exploratory discussions had taken place with Union Carbide and Carbon, the largest US producer of petrochemicals, and several oil companies, including Anglo-Iranian, Standard Oil (New

Jersey), Shell and Trinidad Leaseholds, had approached ICI with a view to collaboration in this field. However, petroleum feedstocks really only came under serious consideration in 1945, and this was triggered by legislative changes in the budget of that year. These eliminated taxation arrangements which had previously subsidized the production of industrial alcohol by the fermentation of molasses. Legislation was also introduced in 1945 and 1946 which exempted petroleum feedstocks used for chemical synthesis from a general duty on light hydrocarbon oils. These financial changes were, of course, specific to the UK, but there were more general influences which encouraged the use of petroleum feedstocks.

Coal shortages were a serious problem, and in 1946 the chairman of ICI suggested that the company's 'very survival is being imperilled by the lack of a vital commodity in which the country abounds' (McGowan 1946). On the other hand, the refinery expansion programme, which was partly a response to such difficulties, offered the prospect of increasing supplies of an alternative raw material. The anticipated cost as well as the availability of feedstocks was an important consideration. Whilst the coal industry was struggling to meet demand, other factors were encouraging a switch to oil in the European energy economy (see Jensen 1967). The displacement of the Western hemisphere by the Middle East, with its very low production costs, as the principal source of Western Europe's oil, together with political pressure upon the oil companies to take account of this fundamental change in the world petroleum market in their pricing policies, combined to limit the rise in oil prices (see Economic Commission for Europe 1955; Leeman 1962; Frank 1966). The managing director of Shell Chemical Company reflected the prevailing view in the industry when he observed that 'Coal as a raw material [for chemical manufacture] has the disadvantages that, in Western Europe, it is becoming increasingly costly to win and it is expensive to transport' (Williams 1960, 1011), and there is no doubt that many interrelated factors associated with economic conditions in the aftermath of the war were pointing the European chemical industry towards a petrochemical future.

It has been shown that the origins of the US petrochemical industry were associated with the utilization of natural and refinery gases (see section 3.4). The early raw material basis of the industry in Western Europe, where natural gas was an insignificant energy source and the availability of by-product gases was limited by technical differences in oil refining operations, was very different. The European refineries were designed to maximize the output of fuel oils, not gasolines as in the United States. It was the catalytic cracking units used to boost gasoline production which were the principal source of by-product gases for US petrochemical plants (see section 3.4). Although such units were installed in some European refineries, the ratio of catalytic cracking to simple distillation capacity was very much lower. It was, therefore, clear from the very beginning that refinery gases could never provide a secure foundation for the development of the industry. Nevertheless, other products suitable for this purpose were available from the new and expanded refineries. The overwhelming demand for heavy fuel oils to replace coal in such markets as electricity generation, together with the limited flexibility of contemporary refining technology in controlling yield patterns, meant that European refineries experienced some difficulty in matching their output to the structure of demand for petroleum products. Consequently, refining programmes geared to meeting the need for the heavier fractions resulted in the development of a substantial surplus of the lighter fractions such as naphtha which were automatically yielded as co-products (OEEC 1956). This surplus depressed the price of naphtha, which in turn improved the attractiveness of this fraction as a petro-chemical feedstock.

The first petrochemical operations in Western Europe were all established in the United Kingdom, and all but one were based on liquid feedstocks.[8] Refinery gases were not considered as primary feedstock at the planning stage in any of these early projects, al-though they were subsequently used by Shell to support a solvents complex linked to a new catalytic cracker at its Stanlow refinery on Merseyside in 1953. This development was modelled upon facilities at Shell's refineries in California and Texas (see section 3.4) and was followed by a similar investment at its Pernis (Rotterdam) refinery. Shell was one of several oil companies which took advantage of the increasing quantities of by-product gases that became available from their facilities following the post-war expansion of the oil refining industry, but such essentially opportunistic investments were sup-plementary to the main thrust of petrochemical development in Western Europe which was linked to the cracking of light distillates, especially naphtha. In the United Kingdom, for example, liquid fractions accounted for 91 per cent (by weight) of the total consumption of feedstocks for petrochemical purposes in 1953, with refinery gases making up the balance (OEEC 1955). The relative significance of these gases declined in subsequent years.

The expansion of refinery capacity promoted by Marshall Aid was important for the future development of the petrochemical industry not only because of its impact upon the availability and price of feedstocks, but also because it encouraged the entry of several oil companies into the European chemical industry. By the end of the 1950s, BP, Compagnie Française de Raffinage (CFR), Esso, Shell and Texaco had all become involved in petrochemical manufacture in complexes adjacent to their refining facilities at various locations in France, West Germany and the United Kingdom. Several factors encouraged such developments. The interest of Esso (i.e. Standard

Oil (New Jersey)) and Shell was a logical extension of their pioneering roles in the US. Their commitment to petrochemicals was
already established, and the expansion of their European refineries
provided an opportunity to use their experience to obtain an early
and strong position in the new European industry. Similar considerations influenced Texaco, which had entered petrochemicals in
the US immediately after the war. Like Texaco, BP was quick to
appreciate the possibilities. The company (as Anglo-Iranian) had
shown an interest in petrochemicals at the beginning of the 1930s
when it first approached ICI (Reader 1975, 322). Serious negotiations
between the two companies during the war broke down, and BP
subsequently found other partners with chemical experience to participate in ventures linked to the expansion of its refineries at Grangemouth in Scotland and at Lavera in France. The strategic interest of
these oil companies in what promised to be an important growth
sector was reinforced by the availability of feedstocks from their
refineries. The general problem of the naphtha surplus at the industry
scale was paralleled by similar difficulties within individual companies and refineries, and the diversion of this material to petrochemicals was an attractive solution. Petrochemical demands for
naphtha usually soon outstripped the supply from any single refinery,
however, and it would be misleading to suggest that the entry of the
oil companies into the European petrochemical industry was driven
simply by raw material availability. Such considerations were secondary to commercial judgements about the long term growth prospects of petrochemicals. Nevertheless, these companies were able
to use intracorporate transfers of naphtha between their various
European refineries to meet the needs of their petrochemical plants at
specific locations. Any material which could not be obtained from
internal sources could be purchased on the open market at favourable rates because of the overall supply/demand situation created by
the previously discussed interrelationships between refinery output
and the requirements of the European energy market.

   Just as the development of petrochemicals had blurred the distinction between the oil and chemical industries in the United States, so
it had a similar effect in Western Europe. Before World War II, the
chemical industry was dominated by such organizations as ICI,
IG Farben and Montecatini which could trace their commercial
origins to the earliest days of industrial chemistry. Most of the major
European chemical companies became involved in petrochemicals,
but the manufacture of the key organic chemicals and their derivatives
was no longer their exclusive preserve as more and more oil companies entered the field in the boom years of the late 1950s and the
1960s. There is no doubt that the activities of the oil companies,
based upon their expanded refinery capacity, accelerated the development of the European chemical industry. They were not tied by

the inertia of existing capital equipment to the traditional raw materials, and they had a clear commercial interest in encouraging the use of petroleum feedstocks. In several cases, such as Standard Oil's (New Jersey) process for the manufacture of butadiene from refinery gases, they served as agents for the transfer of US technology. They also had a significant effect upon the distribution of the new industry. Technical factors, associated with the interchange of raw materials and by-products, encouraged the agglomeration of oil refining and petrochemical operations in large complexes (see section 6.1), but practical considerations related to such matters as land ownership were probably equally important in promoting the geographical association of the two types of activity. In the United Kingdom, for example, the locational pattern of the earliest centres of petrochemical production established before 1960 reflects their commercial origins. Those inspired by oil companies at Fawley (Esso), Grangemouth (BP) and Stanlow (Shell) were all integrated with refineries, whilst those established by chemical companies at Carrington (Petrochemicals Ltd), Spondon (British Celanese) and Wilton (ICI) were all on independent sites (Chapman 1970). Technical factors would have ensured close functional relations between petrochemical plants and oil refineries anyway, but their geographical association in such major oil-based industrial complexes as Rotterdam and Antwerp would have been less evident had the oil companies not played such an active role in the industry's development.

4.4 Conclusions

World War II was a turning point in the evolution of the chemical industry, just as it was in broader political and economic terms. The war left the United States 'in an overwhelmingly dominant situation' (Milward 1977, 330), a situation which was reflected in the chemical industry as European, and more specifically German, leadership in output and innovation was surrendered to the United States. This shift in the balance of economic and technical power was closely associated with the rise of petrochemicals as the principal source of growth within the chemical industry. Although pre-war European research contributed significantly to this growth (see chapter 3), there is no doubt that the impetus for the switch to petroleum as the preferred raw material for organic chemicals came from the United States. This was not surprising in view of its pioneering role in the development of the modern oil industry. By the end of World War II, the United States had an acknowledged supremacy in petrochemistry that was based upon research inspired primarily by the requirements of the oil refining industry, but which had a direct bearing upon the emergence of the petrochemical industry. This supremacy was apparent in the origins of the technology employed in many of the early European petrochemical complexes. Although indigenous companies such as Hoechst, BASF, ICI and Montecatini all developed important petrochemical processes, the construction of these complexes was largely carried out by US chemical engineering contractors which acted as agents for the transatlantic transfer of technology (Freeman 1968) (see section 5.2).

Public policy associated with the conduct of the war and the management of its effects played an important role in the early development of the petrochemical industry. The Marshall Plan was an indirect influence upon its establishment in Western Europe because it supported the expansion of refinery capacity. In the United Kingdom, fiscal changes in 1945 and 1946 encouraged the chemical industry to consider seriously the possibility of making organic chemicals from petroleum rather than from coal and vegetable matter. Although Germany's defeat was an economic as well as a military setback, the attitudes of the Western Allies towards the economic recovery of West Germany changed with the advent of the Cold and Korean Wars. Despite the enforced breakup of IG Farben, the rehabilitation of the German chemical industry during the 1950s was so rapid that it became the leading European petrochemical producer by 1963 (OECD 1963b). However, it was in the United States that government policy was most influential. Whatever technical advantage its firms may have gained in petrochemistry was massively reinforced by the effects of the war. The strategically motivated synthetic rubber programme was a major factor pushing the US petrochemical industry into the accelerated growth phase of its life cycle. The substantial level of state support for this programme helped the private sector reinforce its lead in petrochemistry and establish a manufacturing base from which to dominate the post-war development of the petrochemical industry.

With a few minor exceptions, petrochemical manufacture was unique to the United States before 1950, but the industry developed rapidly in Western Europe during the 1950s. Viewed at the international scale, the new industry closely correlated with general levels of economic development and could, therefore, be regarded as market oriented in its distribution. However, the switch to petroleum feedstocks in the United States and Western Europe resulted in a new raw material orientation *within* these areas. In the United States, the Gulf Coast replaced the Manufacturing Belt as the focus of heavy chemical production. A more complex pattern was created in Western Europe as a consequence of its political fragmentation and the relative lack of indigenous oil and gas resources. However, the location of the petrochemical industry in countries such as the United Kingdom and France was strongly influenced by the distribution of oil refining capacity in the immediate post-war years. This in turn implied a significant shift in the overall distribution of organic chemical manufacture away from its traditional association with coal and steel centres towards new coastal oil-based industrial complexes, although the locational flexibility offered by pipelines has allowed long established centres of chemical production such as the Ruhr to adapt to the new circumstances. Whether associated with established chemical centres or greenfield sites, petrochemical complexes in the United States and Westen Europe experienced spectacular rates of growth in the 1950s and 1960s (as did Japan in the 1960s). The nature and sources of this growth, which was responsible for the creation of several massive agglomerations of manufacturing industry, are discussed in the next chapter.

Notes

1 This became known as GR-S or SBR rubber.
2 The Reconstruction Finance Corporation (RFC) was created in 1932 as part of Roosevelt's New Deal programme. Its purpose was to encourage the economic recovery of the US by issuing various types of loan to industry and private citizens. Several subsidiary agencies of the RFC were established in 1940 to finance industrial investments related to the war effort. The Rubber Reserve Company and the Defense Plant Corporation were two such agencies.
3 Whereas cracking involves the breakdown of larger, heavier hydrocarbon molecules into lighter, smaller ones, reforming is associated with more complex molecular changes which modify the structure and properties of the material being processed. See Shell International Petroleum Co. (1966) for a simple technical introduction to these processes.
4 That is, Badischer Anilin- und Soda-Fabrik, Cassella Farbwerke, Farbenfabrik Bayer and Hochster Farbwerke.
5 This ranking is based upon a consideration of all chemical products, not just petrochemicals.
6 Taxation arrangements ensured that the fermentation of molasses was by far the most important route to organic chemicals in the UK before World War II. However, this was an artificial situation and coal was regarded as the most appropriate raw material from a technical point of view.
7 Despite the change in their relative positions, the extent of direct competition between coal and oil should not be exaggerated. The consumption of coal for chemical synthesis in the UK, for example, increased between 1945 and 1965, but at a far slower rate than the corresponding use of oil-based feedstocks.
8 Shell began producing petrochemicals at Stanlow in 1942 by cracking a petroleum wax.

5
Technology, Markets and Growth 1950–1973

The preceding two chapters have examined the scientific and technical advances responsible for the industry's conception and the commercial and political circumstances surrounding its birth in the United States. Viewed in the context of the life-cycle framework outlined earlier (see sections 1.1 and 1.2), we have considered only the initial phase of the logistic curve of industry development, despite reviewing events over a period of approximately 70 years from the beginnings of industrial organic chemistry in Germany to the US synthetic rubber programme during World War II and the implementation of the Marshall Plan in its aftermath. In this and the next chapter, attention will be focused on the middle section of the logistic curve as represented by the spectacular growth of the petrochemical industry during what has been described by Stobaugh (1988) as its 'golden era' in the United States, Western Europe and Japan between 1950 and 1973. It is important to stress that this era is locationally specific because the industry is at a different stage in its life cycle in other parts of the world (figure 1.2). Nevertheless, the loose chronological sequence of the book is maintained by dealing with this period, whilst at the same time achieving the much more important objective of explicitly linking the various economic and technical characteristics of the high growth phase of the life cycle to the industry's changing spatial distribution. Indeed, many of these connections, such as the interrelationships between market growth, demand thresholds and process innovations associated with the search for economies of scale, which may be exemplified with reference to the United States and Western Europe during the 1950s and 1960s, are directly relevant to an understanding of the wider international dispersal of the industry in the 1970s and 1980s (see chapters 7 and 8).

This chapter is divided into five sections. The first identifies the sources of the industry's rapid growth during its golden era by disaggregating the overall pattern into a series of individual product cycles associated particularly with the development of markets for synthetic materials. The ability of individual companies to exploit these markets was dependent upon access to the relevant manufacturing technology, and the links between the factors influencing the availability of this technology, its adaptation and the proliferation of producers are explored in the second and third sections. The influence of market factors, as reflected in levels of economic development, upon the spread of petrochemical manufacture from one country to another is examined in section 5.4. Finally, these ideas are related to a brief account of the industry's development in Western Europe and Japan between 1950 and 1973.

5.1 The Nature and Sources of Growth

The growth of demand for the products of the chemical industry has consistently exceeded overall rates of economic growth in the developed world ever since 1945. This differential can be expressed as a ratio of the growth rate of the industry relative to the corresponding growth in either total industrial production or some other indicator such as gross national product (GNP). The elasticity of demand for chemicals as measured by the relationship between trends in total chemical consumption and GNP for the United States and Western Europe between 1956 and 1966 was 1.81 and 2.05 respectively (OECD 1968, 12). This differential has narrowed considerably, however, and the corresponding ratio for the United States during the 1980s was in the range 1.1 to 1.4 (Storck 1986). Despite this secular trend in the developed economies, it is important to stress that composite figures for the chemical industry conceal significant variations in the performance of its various sectors. During the 1950s and 1960s petrochemicals was the most dynamic branch of the industry, and OECD (1963b) estimates suggest that petrochemical production in Western Europe increased by a factor of 13 between 1953 and 1962, compared with only 2.5 for overall chemical production.

It has already been noted that petrochemical manufacture is part of a diverse and much larger grouping of economic activities which make up the chemical industry and that it is sufficiently important to be regarded as an industry in its own right (see sections 1.3 and 2.1). Unfortunately, this importance is not reflected in official statistics which fail to acknowledge its identity in standard industrial classification (SIC) schemes. The OECD estimate previously referred to is, therefore, unusual in its precision; the growth of the indistry is normally inferred from data relating to such categories as 'basic organic chemicals', 'plastics materials' and 'synthetic rubber', which are known to have most of their output derived from petroleum

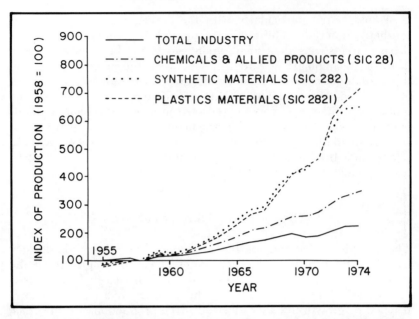

Figure 5.1 US indices of industrial production, 1955–1974 (1958 = 100) (from data in Board of Governors of the Federal Reserve System, *Industrial Production*, 1976)

sources. This approach is adopted in figures 5.1 and 5.2, which indicate the performance of the chemical industry and some of its predominantly petrochemical sectors relative to total industrial production over the same 20 year period in the United States and Western Europe respectively. The US data are more detailed and indicate differing levels of SIC disaggregation, but the general trends are similar and show that the chemical industry's position as a growth sector within the economies of the United States and Western

Table 5.1 US consumption of ethylene by derivative, 1940–1988, as percentage of total consumption

Derivative	1940	1950	1960	1970	1980	1988
Ethanol	55.6	33.3	20.4	6.7	3.0	0.9
Ethylene oxide	33.9	32.5	27.5	22.6	17.3	14.1
Ethylene dichloride	7.3	6.1	6.9	14.1	13.3	13.0
Ethyl benzene	—	12.2	10.1	8.0	7.7	7.3
LD polyethylene	—	4.1	21.4	24.6	24.4	17.7
HD polyethylene	—	—	4.5	9.6	16.7	23.9
LLD polyethylene	—	—	—	—	2.5	9.3
Others	3.2	11.8	9.2	14.4	15.1	13.8
Total	100.0	100.0	100.0	100.0	100.0	100.0

Sources: various

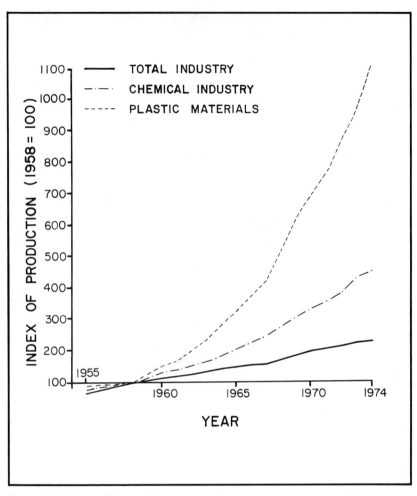

Figure 5.2 Indices of industrial production for Western Europe, 1955–1974 (1958 = 100) (from data in OECD, *The Chemical Industry*, annual reports)

Europe was paralleled at a different level of resolution by the role of petrochemicals within the chemical industry.

The inference in figures 5.1 and 5.2 that synthetic materials in general and plastics in particular were crucial to the rapid growth phase of the petrochemical industry's life cycle is confirmed by table 5.1, which indicates changing patterns of ethylene use in the United States. It has already been shown that most of the pioneering petrochemical plants in the United States before World War II were involved in the manufacture of aliphatic chemicals, especially solvents (see section 3.4). Table 5.1 indicates that nearly 90 per cent of ethylene production in 1940 was diverted to only two uses – ethanol and ethylene oxide. The former was used directly as a solvent or converted to such derivatives as ethyl ether, ethyl acetate or ethanolamine; the latter was mainly used to manufacture ethylene glycol. Although the absolute consumption of ethylene for both purposes increased steadily over the next 40 years or so, it is apparent that the demand for the various types of polyethylene in particular grew much more rapidly and that this outlet was the most important single factor driving the spectacular growth in ethylene output. Indeed, polyethylene, together with ethylene dichloride and ethyl benzene, which are themselves used to produce polyvinyl chloride (PVC) and polystyrene respectively, accounted for more than 70 per cent of US ethylene consumption in 1988. The significance of plastics is not unique to ethylene, and they consume similarly high proportions of other basic intermediates such as propylene and benzene. The importance of synthetic materials is further emphasized when fibres and elastomers are added to plastics as outlets for petrochemicals. Although table 5.1 relates to the United States, later

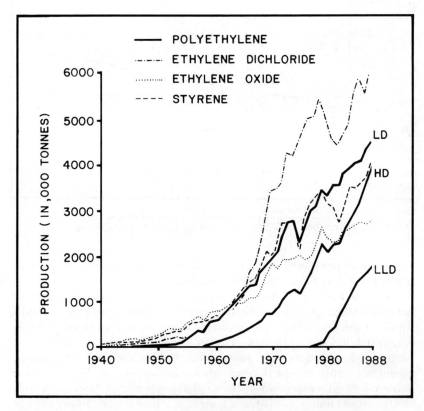

Figure 5.3 Annual US production of principal ethylene derivatives, 1940–1988

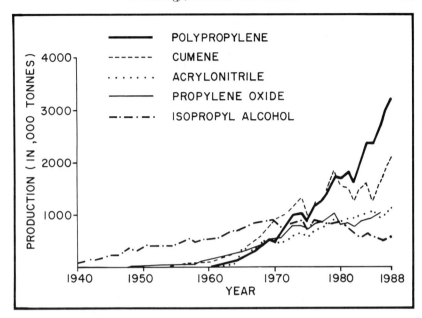

Figure 5.4 Annual US production of principal propylene derivatives, 1940–1988

producers have followed broadly similar patterns of development; if anything, synthetic materials have been more important as ethanol has never achieved elsewhere the significance associated with the industry's early development in the United States.

Implicit in the changing uses of ethylene are a series of individual product histories which themselves represent only part of the totality of products which constitute the petrochemical industry. This is reflected in figures 5.3 and 5.4, which plot the growth in US production of the principal derivatives of ethylene and propylene respectively.[1] Despite the vast number of petrochemical products, relatively few dominate its output in volume terms and most of these are associated with the manufacture of synthetic materials. It is this small group, including the various types of polyethylene, PVC (via ethylene dichloride and vinyl chloride), polystyrene (via ethyl benzene and styrene) and polypropylene, which have been mainly responsible for the post-war surge in petrochemical output (figures 5.3 and 5.4). Many of these products were neither particularly new nor petrochemical in origin (see sections 3.3 and 4.1), but their adoption was dramatically accelerated by the switch from coal to petroleum feedstocks.

The commercial introduction of synthetics in Germany and the United States before and during World War II was stimulated by actual or anticipated shortages of the equivalent natural materials (see sections 3.3 and 4.1). Their post-war growth rested upon their availability at low cost, not least because they were initially widely regarded as inferior to the natural materials they replaced. Whilst coal remained the starting material, the prospects of achieving the necessary cost reductions were poor. However, it has already been shown how process innovations motivated by the needs of the US oil refining industry for greater control over its output pattern had the incidental effect of generating a supply of by-product gases for chemical use and an interest in petroleum and natural gas as chemical raw materials (see section 3.4). The low cost of these feedstocks allowed synthetic material made from them first to obtain a foothold in the market and then to achieve the rapid rates of growth indicated in figures 5.1 to 5.4. This led to a mutually reinforcing set of influences as the high demand for ethylene and other intermediates encouraged process innovations designed to reduce their costs still further, which in turn fuelled yet more market-led growth (see sections 5.2 and 6.1). This cycle of expansion was first set in motion in the United States and then, following the post-war increase in refinery capacity and the resulting naphtha surplus, in Western Europe. Plastics, synthetic fibres and synthetic rubber were thus synonymous with petrochemicals in the United States by 1950, in Western Europe by the end of the same decade and in Japan by the 1960s.

Two components of growth, common to the marketing history of any product, were responsible for these events. First, the demand for petrochemicals was linked to the underlying trend of economic growth and, more specifically, to the performance of those sectors which represent its principal markets such as the motor vehicle, textile and construction industries. Second, and central to the industry's rapid growth, were the effects of innovation and substitution. Innovation, in marketing terms, refers to the creation of demand by meeting a previously unsatisfied (or unrecognized) need. The ability of many synthetic materials both to protect and to enhance the appearance of retail goods, for example, created a massive expansion in packaging, whilst the ease with which plastics such as polystyrene may be shaped and formed to produce finely detailed extrusions commissioned an entirely new army of model-builders. The replacement of traditional materials was, however, mainly responsible for the spectacular growth of synthetics and there is ample evidence that substitution processes tend to proceed exponentially in the early years (see Fisher and Pry 1971; Hurter and Rubinstein 1978). This was demonstrated by the success of the wartime synthetic rubber programme in the United States (see section 4.1). The pattern was repeated after World War II as synthetic fibres replaced wool and cotton in the textile industry and plastics were preferred to steel, glass, wood and paper in a host of applications (see Shell International Chemical Co. 1979). In some cases, substitution was driven

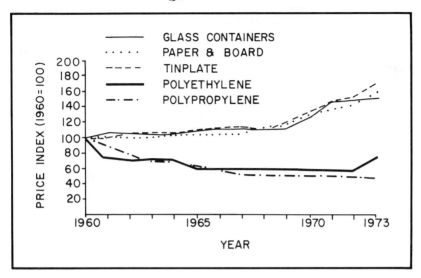

Figure 5.5 UK price indices for plastics and competing materials, 1960–1973 (1960 = 100) (Shell International Chemical Co. 1979, 7)

by the superior qualities of the new materials such as drip-dry and crease-resistant fabrics; in others, low cost was the principal attraction. Favourable trends in the price of feedstocks (see section 4.3) were reinforced by cost-reducing process innovations. These allowed the overall unit output price of SIC 282 (i.e. synthetic materials) in the United States to decline in 11 out of the 12 years between 1958 and 1971 (US Department of Commerce 1985, 98). Furthermore, these falls were taking place at the same time that price trends were moving in the opposite direction for many competing materials (figure 5.5).

The logic underlying the industry's rapid growth in the 1950s and 1960s may, of course, be employed to account for its later very different experiences in the core economies; substitution leads to the S-shaped growth curve characteristic of market saturation, and raw material costs can go up as well as down. These issues are explored in chapters 8 and 10. The rest of this chapter shifts from the analysis of output trends at the aggregate level to a consideration of the economic and technical characteristics of the industry relevant to an understanding of its spatial evolution during this phase of rapid growth in the United States, Western Europe and Japan.

5.2 The Diffusion of Technology

The geographical origin of technology frequently influences the initial location of manufacturing activities which embody the new knowledge, especially when viewed at an international scale (see section 3.1). It follows that subsequent developments which involve establishing similar activities in other locations, either within the same country or abroad, imply a connection between the diffusion of information and the dispersal of production. This connection operates on two levels. First, information spreads from an innovating firm to potential competitors. Second, it spreads from one place to another. These two dimensions of the diffusion of technology are obviously interrelated, and their relevance to an understanding of the development of the petrochemical industry during its rapid growth phase in the United States and Western Europe is explored in this section.[2] These issues are considered again in chapter 7 in the context of the progressive international dispersal of the industry in later years.

The product-cycle model postulates a link between technical change and market conditions to the extent that the innovator may initially enjoy a monopoly, especially if the product is protected by patent. Such protection can be very effective, but it may also be short-lived if the growth prospects of the product are sufficiently attractive to encourage others to try and exploit any loopholes in the patent. This erosion of technological monopoly is a precursor of other systematic changes in the nature and organization of production, including downward pressure on costs, prices and profits as more producers enter the business; accelerated output growth; and the dispersal of production to serve new geographical markets (see sections 1.1 and 1.2). The period over which these changes take place may vary widely from one product or industry to another, although the time-scale is always more compressed than the earlier research and development phase leading to the initiation of commercial production.

By the mid 1950s, most of the synthetic materials which were identified in section 5.1 as being responsible for the rapid post-war growth of the petrochemical industry were more than 20 years old in a commercial sense (see table 3.1) and very much older in a scientific sense. Indeed, several of these materials, such as polystyrene and PVC, had been discovered in the nineteenth century. Patent protection on most of these products had therefore long since expired – if it had ever existed. Generally speaking, it is the patents on the processes used to manufacture these materials and their related intermediates which have been more important in the petrochemical industry. Individual companies have, at various times, established very powerful market positions in particular products, such as ICI in methanol and Union Carbide in ethylene oxide and ethylene glycol, and earned huge sums in licensing fees as a result of technical break-throughs which have dramatically reduced production costs relative to existing processes. Despite these successes, technological monopolies based on process innovations rarely last long in petrochemicals. Following a detailed study of nine important petrochemical products,[3] Stobaugh (1988) calculated that it took only 5.7 years on average for the commercial innovator to be joined by a second producer using independently developed technology. Furthermore he estimated that, by 1974, 180 new processes had been developed for the nine products in addition to the original processes. He classifed the majority of these as 'minor' innovations because they did not threaten to displace existing processes. However minor in a technical sense, these innovations are important from a commercial perspective because they contribute to the breakdown of technological monopoly, an effect which is reinforced by Stobaugh's demonstration that 'major' process innovations are more likely to occur early in the life cycle of a product.

Considerable commercial advantages may be gained by retaining a technological monopoly for as long as possible, and great efforts are made to stop proprietary information from passing to competitors (see Stobaugh 1988, 73–4). Mansfield (1985) has suggested that the chemical industry is more successful than others in this respect, although the main thrust of his study of 100 American firms in various sectors was to emphasize the speed with which information concerning development decisions or key innovations becomes available to rivals. In the case of petrochemicals, it has already been noted how the exchange of information was actively promoted by the US government as part of its synthetic rubber programme (see section 4.1). The release of German technology in organic chemistry and synthetic materials at the end of World War II was also significant because it was available to European as well as US firms (see section 4.2). The most important factor, however, was a growing realization of the potential of petrochemicals which attracted an increasing number of chemical and oil companies into the field. This was apparent in the duplication of research effort in promising lines of enquiry (see section 3.3). Within four years of ICI's commencement of polyethylene production in 1939, for example, Union Carbide was able to introduce its own process on a commercial scale (Allen 1967).[4] This reflected the fact that polyethylene, like many other basic and intermediate petrochemicals, has a relatively simple chemical formula. Furthermore, the basic principles of polymerization established by Staudinger and others in the 1920s were widely reported in the scientific literature. This combination of uncomplicated, standard products and a tradition of publishing the results of pure scientific research has much to do with the relatively short life of process-based technological monopolies in the petrochemical industry because it helps potential imitators circumvent existing patents. Further assistance may be provided by the recruitment of key personnel from innovating firms; Spitz (1988,

317) draws attention to the increasing mobility of staff as a factor in the diffusion of information within the chemical industry, despite the obligation to secrecy frequently enshrined in legal agreements between employer and employee. This diffusion is accelerated once an innovating firm decides to license its technology. Such a decision is often motivated by the expectation that competing firms will soon be able to challenge the innovator, and there is abundant evidence from the chemical and other industries that licensing becomes more common as a technology matures (see Mansfield et al. 1979; Mansfield and Romeo 1980; Stobaugh 1988). Indeed, as different firms have developed their own processes for the manufacture of products such as polyethylene, so they have attempted to sell their technology to others; this competition amongst producer-licensers has further encouraged the dispersal of information and production, especially at the international scale (see chapter 7). The early development of BP's petrochemical interests in the United Kingdom, for example, was facilitated by the acquisition of US technology under licence from Monsanto and Oronite (a wholly owned subsidiary of Standard Oil (California)).

Licensing by manufacturing firms may be interpreted as an acknowledgement of the impossibility of retaining a technological monopoly, and the decision of when, where, how and to whom proprietary information should be released is a strategic one involving careful judgement of the balance of advantage to the innovating firm. Although the big chemical and oil companies have been the principal sources of petrochemical technology, consulting firms and the engineering contractors which specialize in the construction of chemical plant have been responsible for the development of new and the improvement of existing processes. Unlike the producers themselves, there is no ambivalence in the attitude of these organizations to the diffusion of information since their businesses depend on it. The Scientific Design Company (later Halcon-SD), for example, was formed in 1946 as a chemical engineering consultancy which has concentrated on developing petrochemical processes for sale or licensing to manufacturing firms (Landau 1981). Its activities have encouraged the post-war dispersal of the industry because 'its founders viewed Europe and later Japan as areas of great opportunity for technology acquisition and development and for technology licensing' (Spitz 1988, 319). Similarly, US chemical engineering contractors such as Kellogg, Lummus, and Stone and Webster not only built many of the oil-based industrial complexes established in Western Europe after World War II, but also acted as agents for the transfer of American technology (Freeman 1968). These contractors were not usually responsible for initial process innovations, which mainly originated with the chemical and oil companies; however, as a result of their experience in the construction, commissioning and maintenance of plant, they often made significant improvements which were incorporated in later designs.

5.3 The Proliferation of Producers

The circumstances surrounding the converging interests of oil and chemical companies in petrochemicals in the United States before, and in Western Europe immediately after, World War II were reviewed in sections 3.4 and 4.3. The relatively small number of pioneering firms were soon joined by others, initially from similar commercial backgrounds to these pioneers and later from different directions as the technology became more widely available. Many oil and chemical companies had the financial, technical and physical resources to emulate the innovators. This trend was frequently accelerated by the pooling of resources in joint ventures. British Petroleum, for example, used this strategy to establish an early presence in the European petrochemical industry through alliances with the Distillers Company in the United Kingdom, with Rhône-Poulenc in France and with Bayer in West Germany. The involvement of an increasing number of oil and chemical companies in the United States and Western Europe reflected the perceived advantages of integration: forward in the case of oil companies keen to add value to their products, backward in the case of chemical companies anxious to secure feedstock supplies. Diversification also played a part as firms in other sectors were attracted by the high growth rates of the industry. In the United States, for example, the National Distillers Products Corporation entered petrochemicals in the early 1950s in an attempt to reduce its dependence on the whiskey business (Spitz 1988, 309). Almost ten years later in the Netherlands, Dutch State Mines, which was originally established in 1902 as a coal mining company and later moved into coal-based chemistry in 1930, began using petroleum feedstocks for the first time, a policy which the National Coal Board considered following in Britain in 1968 (Ashworth 1986, 499–501). The fact that an organization such as the National Coal Board could even consider such a move emphasizes the breakdown of technology-based limits to entry. Indeed, any increase in the number of firms in a new, high technology industry is conditional upon the diffusion of the information necessary for participation.

Relatively few companies were directly involved in petrochemicals in the United States at the beginning of World War II, but the government-sponsored synthetic rubber programme encouraged others to follow the route pioneered by Shell, Standard Oil (New Jersey) and Union Carbide. Dow and Monsanto both used plants acquired from the federal government (see section 4.1) as nuclei around which to develop their embryonic interests in petrochemicals in the post-war years. B. F. Goodrich, which operated copolymer plants on behalf of the federal government, also became increasingly involved in plastics, especially polyvinyl chloride (PVC), during the war. Military demands provided a massive boost to Du Pont's new synthetic materials, Neoprene and nylon, and the success of these products had important consequences for the post-war development of the company. It was not only the future commercial direction of chemical companies that was affected by involvement in government-sponsored wartime programmes; several oil companies were drawn into petrochemicals in this way. Phillips Petroleum, for example, was one of many enlisted in the drive to increase butadiene production. From this beginning, Phillips became an important supplier of intermediates such as cyclohexane, a producer of polymers such as HD polyethylene and a developer of significant petrochemical process innovations. Standard Oil (California) was another participant in the butadiene programme. This company had begun manufacturing petrochemicals on a small scale at its Richmond, California refinery in 1935. This early experience, combined with its involvement in butadiene production, encouraged the company to establish a subsidiary (i.e. the Oronite Chemical Co.) in 1943 to promote the development and marketing of chemical products.

By the end of World War II, there was a growing realization on the part of both oil and chemical companies in the United States of the potential implicit in the alliance of synthetic materials and petroleum feedstocks. Du Pont's belated recognition of this potential has already been noted (see section 3.4), but, as the largest US chemical company, it quickly made up any lost ground. Major new manufacturing plants were established in Texas at Orange and Victoria in 1946 and 1953 respectively, as the company came to rely increasingly upon petroleum sources to supply the paraxylene required to sustain the spectacular market growth of nylon and as it diversified into ethylene and its derivatives, especially polyethylene. This shift from its traditional reliance upon coal-based chemistry was so rapid that the company was the largest (in terms of value of sales) US petrochemical producer in 1959, with an estimated 50 per cent of total sales classified as petrochemical (*Business Week* 1960, 63). The involvement of Celanese, like that of Du Pont, was primarily driven by its interest in synthetic fibres. From an initial association with cellulose acetate and later Celluloid, the company diversified into plastics during World War II, when it became committed to the idea of using natural gas as a raw material for its operations. This was reflected in the establishment of new Gulf Coast plants, first at Bishop, near Corpus Christi, in 1945 and later at Pampa, Texas in 1953. The reactions of Du Pont and Celanese were typical of US companies in organic chemicals and closely related sectors between

1945 and 1965 as most became, to a greater or lesser extent, petrochemical companies.

The ranks of petrochemical producers were also swelled by the entry of an increasing number of oil companies, which became even more influential in the industry after World War II as a result of the expanding commitments of the pre-war pioneers, Shell and Standard Oil (New Jersey), and the attempts of others to follow their lead. Beaton (1957, 676) notes that 'the role that Shell Chemical would play in the years ahead came in for a great deal of discussion in 1945'. A similar debate took place within Standard Oil (New Jersey), which pursued an essentially conservative policy in the immediate post-war years. Faced with the more aggressive approach of Shell, however, a decision was taken at the beginning of the 1950s 'to enter extensively into the manufacture of petrochemicals' (Larson et al. 1971, 770). These deliberations were paralleled in the boardrooms of many oil companies, and many reached similar conclusions. The charter of the Sun Oil Company, for example, was amended in 1952 to allow it to engage in the manufacture and sale of chemicals (Johnson 1983, 201). As early as 1944, the Texas Company (i.e. Texaco) combined with American Cyanamid to form Jefferson Chemicals which started the manufacture of ethylene oxide and ethylene glycols at Port Neches, Texas in 1946. An ethylene plant commissioned by Gulf on the site of its huge Port Arthur, Texas refinery in 1952 established this oil company as a major supplier, and it did much to promote the development of a pipeline network for the delivery of ethylene to customers throughout the emerging Gulf Coast petrochemical complex. Standard Oil (Indiana) was yet another oil company which, on the basis of research at its Whiting, Indiana refinery in the late 1940s and early 1950s, gradually extended its involvement in petrochemicals, culminating in the construction of a major complex at Chocolate Bayou, Texas in 1968 (Dedman 1984). The activities of these and other companies ensured a major role in the rapid growth of the US petrochemical industry for organizations which had traditionally restricted their manufacturing operations to the refining of oil.

Some indication of the aggregate effect of these various corporate decisions upon the commercial structure of the industry is provided by table 5.2. The highly selective choice of products is determined partly by the particular importance of ethylene and its derivatives in the growth of the petrochemical industry and partly by the availability of data. Statistics relating to the 1950s are difficult to obtain and often of dubious quality, but the general patterns in the table are probably typical of other petrochemical products, allowing for differences in the precise chronology of their life cycles. The number of producers increased into the 1970s, although trends in corporate concentration, as expressed by the percentage of total capacity

Table 5.2 Producers, capacities and concentration ratios for selected petro-chemicals in the United States, 1957, 1964, 1972 and 1990

	Ethylene	Polyethylene[a]	Ethylene oxide	Ethylene dichloride	Styrene
1957					
Number of producers	16	13	7	8	8
1964					
Number of producers	20	17	10	10	9
Capacity (thousand tonnes)	3,971	1,227	785	>894	990
Top three producers (as % of total capacity)	52.1	47.8	70.5	42.1	70.3
1972					
Numbers of producers	25	21	13	11	12
Capacity (thousand tonnes)	9,809	3,688	1,912	4,653	2,599
Top three producers (as % of total capacity)	40.5	40.8	72.0	60.8	54.1
1990					
Number of producers	22	16	12	11	8
Capacity (thousand tonnes)	18,350	10,285	3,340	8,390	4,010
Top three producers (as % of total capacity)	30.8	37.9	54.2	57.5	52.1

[a] Includes LD and HD polyethylene.
Sources: 1957, Faith et al. (1957); 1964, *European Chemical News* (Supplement), 19 June 1964; 1972, Brownstein (1972); 1990, ICI Chemicals and Polymers Ltd

controlled by the three largest producers, were more variable. The concentration ratios for ethylene, polyethylene and styrene fell during the rapid growth phase in accordance with the predictions of life-cycle models, but Union Carbide retained its historical dominance of ethylene oxide whilst Dow established a commanding position in ethylene dichloride and vinyl chloride. Two opposing patterns, which are characteristic of the petrochemical industry, are apparent in table 5.2. On the one hand, there is a tendency for more and more firms to be attracted into rapidly growing products; on the other hand, individual companies seek to establish and maintain technical advantages which allow them to become market leaders for specific products. These advantages assume an added significance when the rate of demand growth slackens, leading to a reduction in the number of producers and theoretically an increase in concentration. Tables 5.2 and 5.3 provide conflicting evidence, with no indication of increasing concentration ratios during the 1980s in the United States, despite a general fall in the number of producers, but a clear trend in this direction in Western Europe.

The link between the origins of petrochemical manufacture in Western Europe and the expansion of the oil refining industry has already been explored in section 4.3. As in the United States, the oil companies played a major role together with established European

Table 5.3 Producers, capacities and concentration ratios for selected petrochemicals in Western Europe, 1955, 1964, 1973 and 1990

	Ethylene	Polyethylene[a]	Ethylene oxide	Styrene
1955				
Number of producers	13	no data	no data	no data
Capacity (thousand tonnes)	205	no data	no data	no data
Top three producers (as % of total capacity)	52.7	no data	no data	no data
1964				
Number of producers	25	23	15	10
Capacity (thousand tonnes)	1,998	749	330	485
Top three producers (as % of total capacity)	27.6	40.3	33.6	57.7
1973				
Numbers of producers	38	40	16	15
Capacity (thousand tonnes)	11,611	5,225	1,447	>2,787
Top three producers (as % of total capacity)	24.3	18.7	41.5	40.2
1990				
Number of producers	29	26	10	12
Capacity (thousand tonnes)	16,005	9,308	1,727	4,035
Top three producers (as % of total capacity)	25.9	27.2	41.4	47.6

[a] Includes LD and HD polyethylene.
Sources: 1955 and 1990, ICI Chemicals and Polymers Ltd; 1964, *European Chemical News* (Supplement), 19 June 1964; 1973, *European Chemical News* (Supplement), 12 October 1973, 82–126

chemical companies such as ICI, Montecatini and the post-war successors to IG Farben. Although some of these companies have developed into truly global corporations, they retain distinctive national identities and their manufacturing operations were usually limited to their home countries in the early years of the industry's development in Western Europe. The effect of the commercial factors encouraging new entrants into a rapidly growing industry has been magnified by the existence of these identities. This tendency has been further reinforced by the desire of governments in some countries, such as Portugal, to create state-owned or supported enterprises to establish and operate a domestic petrochemical industry (see section 7.2). Thus the political fragmentation of Western Europe has encouraged commercial fragmentation. Paradoxically, the effort to promote economic integration through the creation of the European Economic Community (EEC) led to further proliferation of producers by attracting inward investment by US chemical companies seeking to get inside the tariff barrier, although Vernon (1971, 89) argues that much of this investment would have occurred anyway. Table 5.3, which is subject to the same limitations as table 5.2, summarizes the effect of these developments as represented by selected products. Measured in population terms, the original six members of the EEC plus the United Kingdom are very similar in size to the United States. These countries account for the major proportion of Western Europe's petrochemical capacity, and the early development of the industry in the 1950s and 1960s was almost exclusively concentrated within them. Tables 5.2 and 5.3 are, therefore, directly comparable for the purposes of relating market size to the commercial structure of the industry. As in the United States, the number of producers multiplied rapidly to the mid 1970s, but the concentration ratios are significantly lower. This contrast, which reflects the legacy of international frontiers and national markets, has limited the industry's ability to take full advantage of economies of scale (see section 6.1) and also influenced the pattern of commercial restructuring during the 1980s (see chapter 10).

5.4 Market Size and Industry Development

Strategic decisions to enter the petrochemical industry were obviously followed by investment decisions to establish manufacturing facilities, emphasizing the link between its commercial and spatial evolution. Not surprisingly, the US- and European-based companies associated with the industry's initial development concentrated their investments in their domestic markets. Proximity to raw materials in the form of a natural gas pipeline or an adjacent oil refinery was, of course, a major influence upon the choice of site. Nevertheless, viewed at a global scale, the mutually reinforcing influences of the availability of technology and market size have been the principal controls upon the timing and distribution of its development.

Figure 5.6 identifies the year to 1990 in which the petrochemical industry was first established in each country, as represented by the manufacture of ethylene from petroleum feedstocks.[5] In view of the multiplicity of petrochemical products it is difficult to provide a single unambiguous date for the industry's origin, but the overall importance of ethylene (see section 2.1) suggests that it is probably the best single yardstick for this purpose. The sequential development of the industry is related in figure 5.6 to per capita gross domestic product (GDP) in 1985[6] as a percentage of the corresponding US figure.[7] The diagram indicates a sequential hierarchy as the industry was first established in the wealthier nations before spreading to countries at lower levels of economic development, although several recent export-oriented producers such as Norway, Saudi Arabia, Qatar and Singapore seem to contradict this general trend, which is closely related to the production imitation lag described in section 3.3. This lag is consistent with the findings of

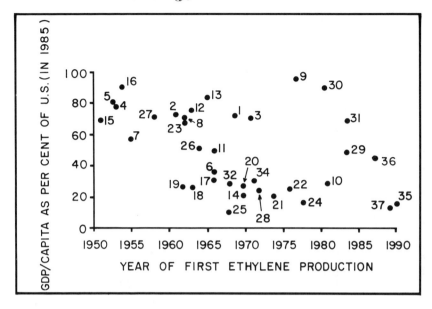

Figure 5.6 Start of ethylene production and level of economic development by country to 1990

other studies which have examined the relationship between national wealth and the establishment of domestic chemical industries (see US International Trade Commission 1985a; Gordon 1989). A similar phenomenon has been observed by Hufbauer (1966) and Stobaugh (1988) in relation to a wide range of synthetic materials and petrochemical products. These lags may be substantial, as is emphasized by the introduction of ethylene production into countries such as Saudi Arabia and Singapore more than 60 years later than the United States.

The production imitation lag as conceived by Hufbauer (1966) was explained in terms of the availability and diffusion of technology. In most cases, new products are first manufactured in their country of

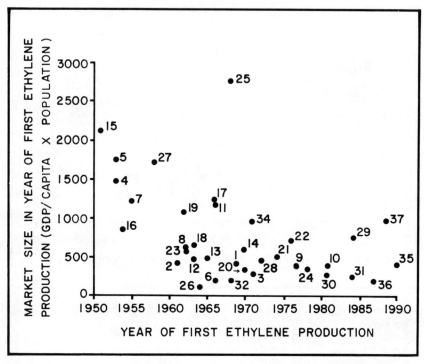

1	Austria	14	Turkey	26	Israel (figure 5.6 only)
2	Belgium	15	United Kingdom	27	Japan
3	Finland	16	Canada	28	South Korea
4	France	17	Mexico	29	Saudi Arabia
5	West Germany	18	Argentina	30	Qatar
6	Greece	19	Brazil	31	Singapore
7	Italy	20	Chile	32	Taiwan
8	Netherlands	21	Colombia	33	United States (figure 5.8 only)
9	Norway	22	Venezuela	34	Iran
10	Portugal	23	Australia	35	Iraq
11	Spain	24	Algeria	36	Libya
12	Sweden	25	India	37	Thailand
13	Switzerland				

Figure 5.7 Start of ethylene production and market size by country to 1990

origin,[8] and Stobaugh (1988, 100) found that countries which 'used locally developed technology tended to begin production about ten years before countries that had to import the technology'. However, the size of the potential market for petrochemical products seems to be an even more important influence upon the timing of the industry's establishment within a country. This potential is obviously linked to the wealth and structure of the economy as well as its absolute size. Per capita GDP provides a crude indication of the former charac-

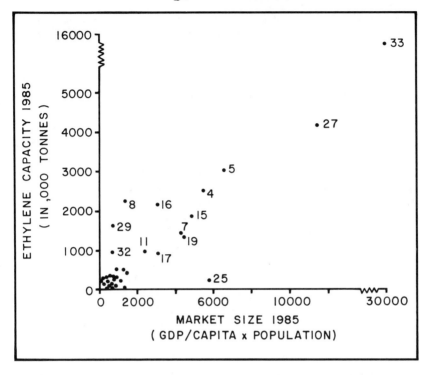

Figure 5.8 Ethylene capacity and market size by country, 1985

1 Austria	14 Turkey	26 Israel (figure 5.6 only)
2 Belgium	15 United Kingdom	27 Japan
3 Finland	16 Canada	28 South Korea
4 France	17 Mexico	29 Saudi Arabia
5 West Germany	18 Argentina	30 Qatar
6 Greece	19 Brazil	31 Singapore
7 Italy	20 Chile	32 Taiwan
8 Netherlands	21 Colombia	33 United States (figure 5.8 only)
9 Norway	22 Venezuela	34 Iran
10 Portugal	23 Australia	35 Iraq
11 Spain	24 Algeria	36 Libya
12 Sweden	25 India	37 Thailand
13 Switzerland		

teristics, but not of the latter. It is noticeable that some of the wealthier countries which seem to be late producers in figure 5.6, such as Norway, Finland, Austria and Switzerland, are relatively small in population terms; conversely, Argentina, Brazil, India and Mexico, which lie at the opposite end of the size/development spectrum, seem early. Bearing in mind the sector's role as a supplier to other industries (see section 2.2), some measure of aggregate manufacturing output seems likely to display the clearest relationship with the introduction of petrochemical manufacture. In view of the difficulty of obtaining such data, an alternative method of measuring market size is used in figure 5.7. This involves multiplying the per capita GDP in the year of the industry's establishment (standardized relative to a 1980 base) in a particular country by the country's population in the same year.[9] Despite its obvious limitations, this method produces results which make intuitive sense.[10] In particular, it has the effect of positioning some of the small, wealthy countries, which appear late in figure 5.6, closer to the general time-series trend.[11]

Market size may be expected to influence not only when the petrochemical industry becomes established within a country, but also the subsequent growth and volume of production. A clear relationship between ethylene capacity and market size (as expressed by per capita GDP × population in 1985) is evident in figure 5.8. The diagram emphasizes the skewed distribution of petrochemical capacity, with a substantial proportion of capacity concentrated in relatively few countries. Several countries have higher capacities than their national markets seem to justify, including Canada, Saudi Arabia and the Netherlands, all of which have established export-oriented industries (linked to supplying adjacent EEC countries in the case of the Netherlands). Conversely, other countries, notably India, lie well below the market size versus ethylene capacity trend line. Such 'anomalies' are, of course, partly due to the inherent weaknesses of the adopted measure of market size. They do, however, draw attention to the dangers of explaining the international distribution of the industry in terms of a deterministic response to the crossing of some kind of market threshold. Quite apart from the possibility of establishing an export-oriented industry (see chapter 8), the significance of market thresholds in triggering investment is modified by many variables. These thresholds are moving targets in the sense that the minimum efficient size of plant has tended to increase through time as a result of process innovations. The definition of minimum efficient size is itself difficult and may vary with location. The industry apparently began early in Australia, for example, where it was to some extent protected by high transport costs from imports derived from the United States and Western Europe. Even more important distortions of the relationship between market size and petrochemical development have been introduced by the entry of state-owned companies into the industry. Commercial considerations are not necessarily the principal motivation of such organizations, and the international dispersal of the industry has been strongly influenced by their activities. These issues are explored in chapter 7 and, although important, they should not obscure the validity of the general relationship between market factors and the distribution of the industry at the international scale.

5.5 Patterns of Growth in Western Europe and Japan

This relationship helps to explain the pattern of development in Western Europe as the industry was established first in the larger economies and later in a succession of countries, finishing with Portugal in 1981 (figure 5.9). As at the global scale, the market-related sequential pattern is reinforced by similar patterns in the availability and diffusion of technology. Quite apart from their elevated status in the hierarchy of European economies, West Germany and the United Kingdom would be expected to be early in the field by virtue of their traditional strengths in industrial chemistry. It is important to stress that market factors are not solely responsible for the pattern represented in figure 5.9. The availability of indigenous natural gas provided significant boosts to the Italian and French industries in the 1950s and 1960s respectively, whilst Norway's entry in 1977 was based on raw materials from the North Sea. Interpreting the pattern exclusively in market terms tends to suggest that the industry is organized on a national basis, but many firms coordinate their manufacturing and marketing activities on a European scale. Despite a clear trend towards a supranational philosophy in the largest firms, which was emphasized by the restructuring of the 1980s (see chapter 10), historical circumstances have ensured that national identities have been an important influence upon the development of the European petrochemical industry.

This development has been determined by the investment decisions of the various organizations which entered the industry after World War II. Although firms from many different commercial and geographical backgrounds ultimately became involved, three groups have played the most important role: the multinational oil companies, the principal European chemical companies and, to a lesser extent, several US chemical companies which established their own manufacturing facilities in Western Europe during the 1960s and 1970s (see section 9.4). All of these organizations are large and typically operate plants at several locations, but there are significant differences in the spatial evolution and organization of their production systems within Western Europe.

The technical and commercial factors which drew many oil companies into the industry have been reviewed earlier (see sections 3.4 and 4.3). The largest of these companies, notably BP, Esso and Shell, were already operating on a continental scale when they moved into petrochemicals, and this encouraged them to adopt a similar outlook from the beginning of their involvement in the new European industry – an outlook which is reflected in the distribution of their manufacturing facilities (figure 5.10). The major European chemical companies had generally perceived the benefits of switching from coal to petroleum as the basic raw material for organic chemical

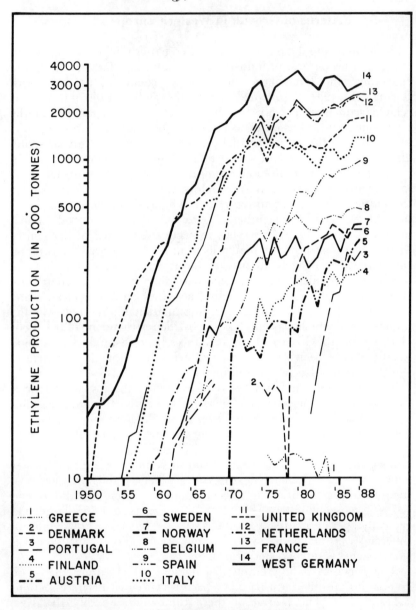

Figure 5.9 Ethylene production in Western Europe, 1950–1988

manufacture by the mid 1950s.[12] In several cases, this switch was made easier by cooperation with the oil companies which were able to supply feedstocks from refineries expanded in the immediate post-war years. BASF and Bayer in West Germany, for example,

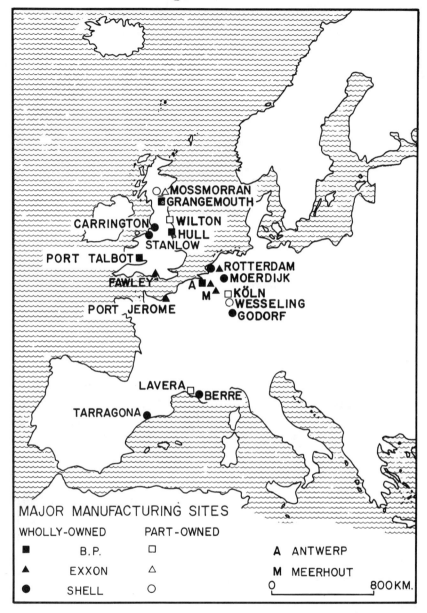

Figure 5.10 Principal petrochemical manufacturing sites of BP, Shell and Exxon in Western Europe, 1990

established enduring partnerships at an early stage with Shell and BP respectively. Others, such as ICI in the United Kingdom and Montecatini in Italy, proceeded independently into the new industry. Indeed, many European chemical companies, including Dutch State

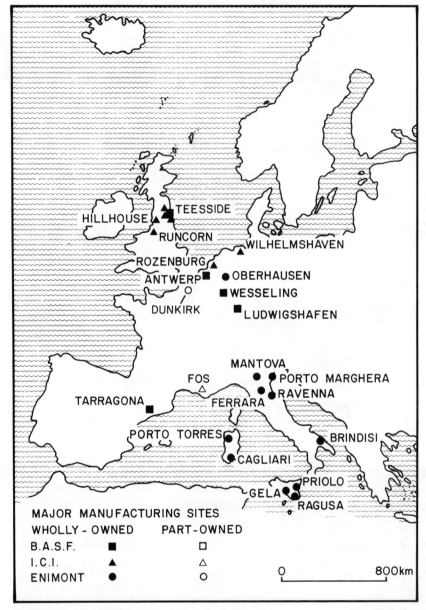

Figure 5.11 Principal petrochemical manufacturing sites of BASF, Enimont and ICI in Western Europe, 1990

Mines in the Netherlands, Rhône-Poulenc in France and Solvay in Belgium, became involved and contributed to the proliferation of producers in the 1960s (table 5.3). Despite a political commitment to economic integration and a constantly shifting pattern of corporate alliances in joint ventures organized at a continental scale, the bulk of the petrochemical capacity of the European chemical companies is concentrated in their home countries. Figure 5.11 plots the distribution of the principal production sites of the three largest – BASF, ICI and Enimont – in 1990.[13] BASF and ICI have become global corporations with worldwide production systems (see section 9.4), but their respective origins remain evident in the distribution of their manufacturing facilities within Western Europe. The national identity of Enimont[14] is even more pronounced.

Despite starting petrochemical production later than the principal countries of Western Europe, the growth of the industry in Japan was even more spectacular during the 1960s and 1970s. Ethylene production started in 1958 and Japan was second only to the United States in ethylene capacity within ten years. The circumstances surrounding the establishment of the industry in Japan were unusual (see section 7.2), but its subsequent expansion was driven by the same market dynamic operating in the United States and Western Europe. Indeed, as in other areas of their economy, the Japanese benefited from their later start because they were 'able to purchase modern processes from the West' (Spitz 1988, 382). As in Western Europe, the industry's development was closely linked to the expansion of oil refining capacity based on imported crude oil, leading to the emergence of a series of major complexes along the Pacific Coast (Adochi and Yonaga 1966).

5.6 Conclusions

Once an industry is established, its subsequent growth is driven by complex interrelationships between internal changes, affecting its technology and commercial structure, and external influences associated with the development and distribution of its markets. In the case of the petrochemical industry, these interrelationships typically produce an initially accelerating but ultimately self-regulating rate of growth as the opportunities for substitution diminish and further expansion is determined by the secular growth of the economy as a whole. Viewed in the context of markets defined in geographical terms by national boundaries, this implies a succession of partially overlapping industry growth curves. Such markets have been especially important in Western Europe where the industry's overall development has followed parallel courses in some countries such as the United Kingdom and West Germany and, at the same time, displayed a lagged sequential pattern as it has been established at later dates in smaller and/or less developed national markets. This replication of development cycles within different countries has created an industry which is more fragmented in commercial terms and more dispersed in a geographical sense than would have emerged in the absence of the political and language barriers which divide Western Europe. Similar issues have affected, and indeed restricted, the development of the industry in other parts of the world (see chapter 7), and the existence of such barriers is a reality which must be acknowledged in efforts to integrate economic and geographical perspectives within life-cycle models of industry development.

Notes

1 The United States has not only the longest production history, but also the most comprehensive output statistics for petrochemicals. The data in figures 5.3 and 5.4 were derived from the annual publication of the US International Trade Commission (i.e. *Synthetic Organic Chemicals*), although early years are based on ICI estimates.

2 The significance of the acquisition of technology in the development of the Japanese industry is more appropriately considered in chapter 7 because of the active role played by government in this process.

3 That is, phenol, methanol, vinyl chloride, styrene, acrylonitrile, cyclohexane, isoprene, orthoxylene and paraxylene.

4 ICI's discovery was in fact accidental, as described by Allen (1967) and Reader (1975).

5 Countries which had discontinued ethylene production from petroleum feedstocks by the end of 1988 (i.e. Denmark, South Africa and Egypt) are excluded from figures 5.6, 5.7 and 5.8. The United States is also excluded from figures 5.6 and 5.7.

6 These data, together with the other economic development indicators in figures 5.7 and 5.8, were derived from Summers amd Heston (1988). This is a unique data set which provides estimates of economic development using various indicators, standardized relative to a 1980 base, for most countries of the world between 1950 and 1985. It therefore provides as accurate an estimate of the comparative wealth of nations at selected points in time and of changes in their relative wealth through time as the limitations of international statistics will allow. GDP and population data for countries starting ethylene production after 1985 (i.e. Iraq, Libya and Thailand) have been estimated.

7 An alternative approach, expressing per capita GDP as a percentage of the corresponding US figure in the year of industry establishment, could also be used. However, this fails to take account of the way in which the other developed economies have caught up with the United States. In 1950, for example, per capita GDP in the principal European countries averaged 30–55 per cent of the US figure, but by 1985 the range was approximately 60–80 per cent (Summers and Heston 1988). Using the prevailing GDP for some of the early petrochemical producers such as the United Kingdom would, therefore, tend to devalue their status in the development hierarchy.

8 Hufbauer (1966, 86–7) notes some significant exceptions to this generalization.

9 Notwithstanding note 8, this approach is logical since the objective is to relate the chronology of industry establishment to absolute market size rather than to position in the development hierachy.

10 The results are not sensible in the case of India, which is excluded from figure 5.7. Despite a very low per capita GDP, the country's huge population produces an inflated indicator of market size. This example emphasizes the limitations of using per capita GDP × population as a surrogate measure of the potential demand for petrochemicals.

11 It should be noted that, although absolute size is important, other studies have suggested that national wealth as expressed by GDP or GNP is a more powerful influence upon the establishment of the chemical industry (see US International Trade Commission 1985a).

12 The switch was delayed in West Germany because the slightly later development of its oil refining industry ensured that coal-based processes remained important to the early 1960s in some of the chemical complexes of the Ruhr. Many coal-based plants were eventually converted to petroleum feedstocks.

13 Bayer and Hoechst are larger (in 1990) in terms of the value of chemical sales then both ICI and Enimont, but basic petrochemicals represent a relatively small proportion of these sales.

14 Enimont was formed in 1988 as a result of an agreement between Montedison and Enichem, the state-owned chemical company. Montedison was itself established in the early 1960s by the merger of Montecatini and the Edison Group.

6
Agglomeration in the Petrochemical Industry

The principal theme of chapter 5 was the connection between the rapid growth of the petrochemical industry and its geographical dispersal from the United States to Western Europe. The idea that the development of an industry is accompanied by the dispersal of production is not only relevant at the international scale, and similar centrifugal forces may be expected to operate within countries. On the basis of a study of several sectors in the United States, Markusen (1985, 8) notes that 'regional dispersion tendencies are a central feature of normal evolution'. Various explanations have been offered to account for this trend, including the successive establishment of plants to serve new regional markets in consumer industries, but the most important thrust of research has emphasized the connections between technical change in the manufacturing process associated with progression through the product or industry life cycle and shifts in factor requirements. Changing labour needs have been identified as the principal impetus to dispersal as process innovations allowed the progressive substitution of cheap, unskilled workers for more highly paid professional and scientific staff. It has been argued that such shifts in occupational structure have encouraged a geographical shift of production to peripheral regions to take advantage of lower labour costs (see Krumme and Hayter 1975; Norton and Rees 1979; Bluestone and Harrison 1982; Massey 1984; Markusen 1985).[1] Despite the substantial evidence in support of this hypothesis, it is probably fair to say that empirical research has been selective, focusing upon those industries most likely to fit the pattern. Thus emphasis has been placed upon sectors such as consumer electronics in which mass production techniques have been associated with the deskilling of a still significant labour input in the manufacturing process. Furthermore, technical change does not always encourage dispersal, and Schoenberger (1987) notes that the introduction of such practices as just-in-time delivery and the need for highly skilled and flexible workforces to operate and maintain sophisticated robotic equipment has created a centralizing tendency within the automobile industry.

Viewed at a national scale, the petrochemical industry has shown little evidence of dispersal, despite the efforts of some governments to encourage its establishment in peripheral regions (see chapter 11). Indeed, the most striking feature of its distribution is geographical concentration in major complexes. Table 6.1 indicates that, apart from a brief period during the 1950s when several important investments were made in the Midwest, the share of US ethylene and, by implication, petrochemical capacity in Texas and Louisiana has steadily increased to reach over 90 per cent by 1990.[2] Production in Western Europe is more dispersed for reasons discussed in chapter 5, but most of the earliest centres of production such as the Ruhr, Teesside and the Étang de Berre region in southern France remain amongst the largest concentrations of capacity.

The development of the industry in the United States provides the clearest evidence of a pattern which contradicts the dispersal hypothesis. The lack of data makes it impossible to extend table 6.1 to incorporate earlier years, but the diverse geographical and commercial origins of the industry were emphasized in section 3.4. The pre-1940 distribution of petrochemical operations indicated in figure 3.1 suggests a more dispersed pattern than the data in table 6.1. Thus, in the United States at least, centripetal tendencies seem to have been more important than centrifugal ones. This characteristic reflects the mutually reinforcing influence of raw material considerations and developments in the technology of production. The nature of this influence is explored in this chapter, which is divided into four sections. The first describes the trend towards larger plants, focusing upon the 'golden age' in the United States and Western Europe between 1950 and 1973. The implications of these trends for upstream (i.e. raw material) and downstream linkages within petrochemical complexes are reviewed in the second and third sections respectively. The role of pipeline systems in the internal and external relationships of petrochemical complexes is explored in the final section.

6.1 Economies of Scale

Models of process innovation have generally rested upon the analysis of trends in the development of individual products and the processes used to manufacture them (see section 1.1), but various attempts have been made to apply these ideas at higher levels of aggregation in studies of the oil refining (Enos 1962a; 1962b) and synthetic fibre industries (Hollander 1965). The petrochemical industry reached maturity in process terms well before the flattening of the output curve characteristic of maturity in a marketing sense. It has already

Table 6.1 Distribution of US ethylene capacity, 1950–1990

State	1950		1960		1970		1980		1990	
	thousand tonnes	as %	thousand tonnes	as %	thousand tonnes	as %	thousand tonnes	as %	thousand tonnes	as %
Texas	463	62.3	1,436	52.2	5,507	61.3	11,698	68.7	12,480	68.0
Louisiana	93	12.5	393	14.3	2,030	22.6	3,984	23.4	4,530	24.7
Others[a]	187	25.2	922	33.5	1,446	16.1	1,346	7.9	1,340	7.3
Total US	743	100.0	2,751	100.0	8,983	100.0	17,028	100.0	18,350	100.0

[a] Excludes Puerto Rico.
Sources: calculated from data in various trade journals

been noted (see section 5.2) that many basic petrochemicals are, by virtue of their precise chemical specification, standardized products from the beginning of their commercial life and that technological monopolies in the industry are usually short-lived. This in turn has tended to create severe competition which is reflected in price histories (see section 10.2). The adoption of automated, continuous-flow production systems to replace irregular batch methods is another characteristic of technology-based models of process innovation which was an early feature of the petrochemical industry. Close technical and commercial linkages ensured that, in many cases, such systems were a natural application of lessons already learned in the oil refining industry. Although the manufacture of standardized products in continuous-flow processes rapidly became the norm in the petrochemical industry, the early facilities were an order of magnitude smaller than the corresponding units in refineries. This differential has remained, since petroleum products are generally required in much larger quantities than petrochemicals, but there has been a significant increase in the size of chemical process units. This trend, which is consistent with the predictions of models of process innovation (see Abernathy and Townsend 1975; Utterback and Abernathy 1975; Thomas 1981), has been driven by efforts to exploit economies of scale. These efforts have been an important feature of the industry's development.

Economies of scale may be defined as the savings in unit costs associated with increases in the volume of production. A distinction is frequently made between static and dynamic economies of scale. The former refer to savings based on engineering principles which tend to reduce unit costs as the size of plant increases. Dynamic economies of scale are more difficult to grasp. They refer to the benefits of accumulated experience, which are usually expressed in the form of learning curves or experience curves. These usually indicate that unit costs fall through time as cumulative production increases (see Boston Consulting Group 1972; Hirschman 1964; Stobaugh and Townsend 1975). In theory, the idea may be applied at plant, firm or industry level. It is intuitively reasonable to suggest that minor modifications to an existing plant and improvements in operating procedures will allow it to be used more cost-effectively as experience of its characteristics and performance is gained. On the other hand, lessons learned from one plant may be incorporated in its successors and process innovations may be regarded as dynamic economies of scale. In fact, static and dynamic economies of scale are difficult to separate for both practical and conceptual reasons. The data required to isolate their relative contributions to falling costs at plant and firm level are rarely available to the independent re-searcher, although Hollander's (1965) study is a notable exception. Furthermore, experience curves based on cumulative output at the

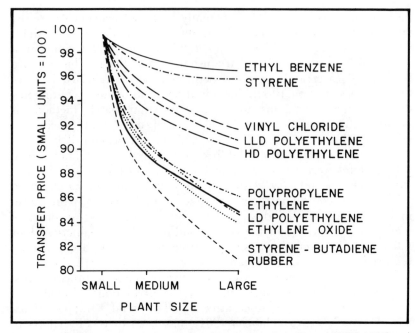

Figure 6.1 Economies of scale for selected petrochemicals (from UNIDO 1981)

industry level usually include, as part of the learning phenomenon, cost reductions resulting from static economies of scale. On the other hand, the know-how required to build bigger plants is only acquired by experience. Despite these difficulties, it is convenient to retain the distinction between the two types of scale economy. Generally speaking, the changes embodied in the dynamic version of the concept have contributed more to falling real costs in manufacturing and the chemical industry is no exception (Liebermann 1984). However, this chapter will focus on static economies of scale because of their significance in shaping the physical form of petrochemical complexes as industrial agglomerations. The role of dynamic economies of scale in the industry is explored further in chapter 10.

It is possible, using published capacity data, to demonstrate that the size of individual plants has increased through time for virtually every petrochemical product as manufacturers have attempted to exploit static economies of scale. The magnitude of these economies varies between products, with the manufacturing costs of some being more sensitive to the size factor than others. Generally speaking, the simpler processing steps involved in the production of basic intermediates such as ethylene and ammonia are better suited to large-scale operations than the more complicated downstream activities. Figure 6.1 indicates the effect of plant size upon transfer prices for a range of basic petrochemical products. These prices include production costs plus an allowance for a 25 per cent return on investment, assuming that plants operate at 85 per cent of capacity. There are significant differences between the products, although it is apparent that ethylene is one of the most sensitive to economies of scale. In view of the focal position of the cracking plants which produce ethylene within the structure of most petrochemical complexes (see section 2.2), economies of scale in this operation have implications which extend throughout the production system. Indeed, much of the downward pressure on costs in the industry during the 1960s can be traced to the introduction of progressively larger ethylene plants.

This trend was apparent in the United States, Western Europe and Japan, although there were differences in the timing and the extent of the shift towards larger units. Not surprisingly, it first became evident in the United States where the average size of new ethylene plants was more than three times that of similar plants in Western Europe in the mid 1950s (Spitz 1988, 425). This differential has subsequently narrowed, but the average ethylene capacity at European manufacturing sites in 1990 was still only 70 per cent of that in the United States, whilst the corresponding figure for Japan was approximately 60 per cent.[3] Figure 6.2 plots the capacity at commissioning of every ethylene plant in Western Europe since 1955, including units expected to come on stream before 1995. It shows a

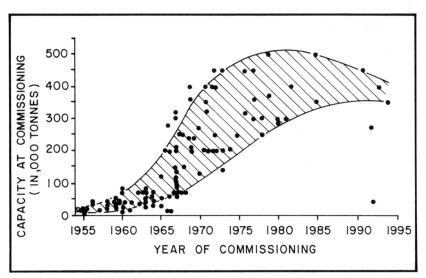

Figure 6.2 Capacity of ethylene plants at commissioning in Western Europe, 1955–1995 (from data supplied by ICI Chemicals and Polymers Ltd)

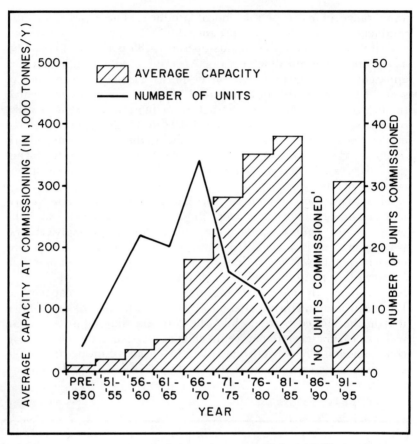

Figure 6.3 Size and number of ethylene plants commissioned in Western Europe, 1950–1995 (from data supplied by ICI Chemicals and Polymers Ltd)

gradual increase in size to the early 1960s, followed by a sharp rise and a subsequent flattening off from the mid 1970s. The initial caution was related partly to uncertainties regarding market growth in the early years of the new industry, but also to engineering factors as most European manufacturers chose to increase capacity by duplicating existing plant rather than scaling up. Futhermore, efforts to reduce the costs of ethylene production during the 1950s focused upon the problem of coproducts. It was hoped to design processes allowing better control to be achieved over the output of coproducts, minimizing the output of the less valuable ones and maximizing the yield of ethylene. These efforts achieved only limited success, and attention shifted to the development of much larger plants as a means of achieving cost reductions (see Spitz 1988, 437–56). By the early 1960s, the spectacular growth in demand was firmly established (see section 5.1) and the industry was more confident that the substantial increase in capacity implied by the introduction of larger plants could be rapidly absorbed by the market. The adoption of such plants was also promoted by US chemical engineering contractors, which were anxious to sell their experience and their designs. The aggregate annual increase in ethylene capacity in Western Europe reached a peak in 1972 when over 3 million tonnes were commissioned (figure 6.3). It is important to note that the generalized trend since 1976 is based upon relatively few units. The average capacity for 1981–5 is derived from only three installations and is strongly influenced by one very large plant. No units were commissioned in the second half of the 1980s, although several major investment projects are committed for the period between 1991 and 1995. Nevertheless, the rate of increase in total capacity and the trend towards ever larger individual units has slowed down, and possibly reversed, since the mid 1970s. This partly reflects technical factors, which ensure that the decline in unit production costs with increasing plant size in any manufacturing process typically displays diminishing returns to scale (see Moroney 1972; Pratten 1971). It is also due to changing economic conditions following the first oil price shock in 1973. This resulted in a downward revision of demand projections, which increased the risks associated with investment in very large plants, and a radical change in the structure of ethylene manufacturing costs, which reduced the significance of fixed relative to variable costs (see section 8.2). The decline in the average size of units scheduled for completion in the 1990s (figure 6.3) probably reflects caution about the anticipated growth in demand, since modern units are generally designed to allow subsequent expansion.

The typical fall in capital costs per unit of installed ethylene capacity reflects static economies of scale and is based upon the mutually reinforcing effects of economies of increased dimensions and plant indivisibilities. Examples of these effects include respectively the fact that the capacity of a pressure vessel may be doubled by using less than twice the surface area of steel, and the need for a certain minimum number of measuring instruments to monitor reaction conditions in both large and small process units. Such situations are familiar to chemical engineers and are described by the relationships of the following form:

$$I^A = I^B \, (C^A/C^B)^n$$

where I represents investment cost, C represents capacity, and A and B are two plants which are identical but for their capacities. The critical variable in the relationship is the exponent n, which has been empirically demonstrated to lie within the range 0.4 to 0.8 for various chemical products and to average 0.58 for ethylene plants (Axtell and Robertson 1986, 21).

Static economies of scale influence operating as well as construction costs. Table 6.2 is derived from a paper originally published in 1966 which incorporated the experience and reflected the expectations of Shell, which was in the vanguard of new developments in ethylene manufacture (Braber 1966). It is representative of the commercial logic underlying the push towards larger units during the 1960s. The anticipated decline in unit manufacturing costs between 1955 and 1975 was linked to the combined effect of external economic influences, notably a fall in the price of naphtha feedstock over the 20 year period, and internal technical factors related to the introduction of larger plants. The data in table 6.2 assume that the plants each operate at capacity and that their coproducts achieve directly comparable premium uses (see section 2.2).[4] The table distinguishes between fixed costs, which remain essentially the same regardless of production, and variable costs, which are related to the level of output. It is clear that the most significant savings associated with the use of larger plants derive from the fixed portion of total costs. This can itself be divided into two elements related to labour and capital charges. Labour costs are fixed because the numbers and type of personnel required to operate a plant remain the same regardless of the volume of production. Capital-related costs include maintenance, overheads and an allowance for depreciation. These tend to reflect the downward trend of construction costs per tonne of output based on the static economies of scale already described. Thus it is these capital-related fixed charges which contribute most to the fall in ethylene manufacturing cost in a 200,000 tons per year plant as compared with one of 20,000 tons per year (table 6.2).

Table 6.2 Hypothetical ethylene manufacturing costs, 1955–1975 (£/tonne)

| | Plant size (tonnes/year) and date | | |
	20,000 (1955)	100,000 (1965)	200,000 (1975)[a]
Variable			
Net feed cost	15	5	5
Chemicals	1	1	1
Utilities	19	10	8
Total variable	35	16	14
Fixed			
Labour/overheads	11	4	2
Maintenance	4	2	1
Depreciation	31	10	8
Total fixed	46	16	11
Total	81	32	25

[a] Prediction based on assumption of no inflation since 1965.
Source: Braber (1966)

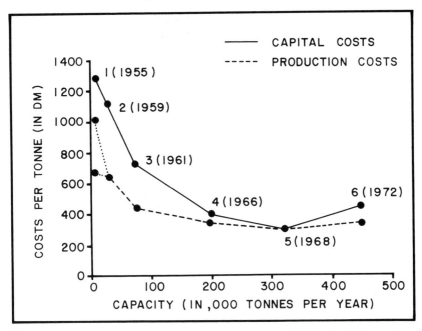

Figure 6.4 Size and costs of ethylene plants operated by Rheinische Olefinwerke Wesseling, 1955–1972 (from Hansen 1975)

The data in table 6.2 are hypothetical, but the size/cost relationship is confirmed by figure 6.4. This is based on the operating experience of Rheinische Olefinwerke Wesseling (ROW), which is one of the largest ethylene producers in Western Europe (Hansen 1975). The data points correspond to six ethylene plants commissioned at ROW's Wesseling (West Germany) complex between 1955 and 1972. Costs for each plant are expressed in Deutschmarks (DM) and defined in a consistent and comparable fashion, whilst assumptions regarding operating rate, feedstock price, coproduct values and return on investment are held constant throughout the period. The figure emphasizes that the exponent n in the cost/size relationship does not remain constant. The greatest fall in unit costs (both capital and production) occurs between the third unit (75,000 tonnes per year) and the fourth unit (200,000 tonnes per year); here $n = 0.56$. The value of n rises successively to 0.75 and 1.5 with the next two investments. The increase in unit capital costs between 320,000 and 540,000 tonnes per year was mainly due to a sharp rise in construction costs. Although based on the experience of a specific company, the relationship indicated in figure 6.4 is supported by many other examples which suggest that not only is there a limit to economies of scale in ethylene manufacture, but also the cost curve begins to turn upwards beyond a certain point. This point of inflexion cannot be defined precisely because it varies with prevailing economic and corporate circumstances, but the potential diseconomies of scale associated with the construction and operation of very large plants are well documented (see Holroyd 1967; Walley and Robinson 1972; Gilbourne et al. 1978). Nevertheless, the average size of new ethylene plants by the early 1970s was an order of magnitude higher than only 10–15 years earlier, and this had important consequences for the structure and development of the industrial complexes based upon them.

6.2 Raw Materials, Economies of Scale and Intranational Location

Raw material factors have strongly influenced both the initial choice of site for petrochemical facilities within the United States, Western Europe and Japan and also the subsequent growth of the industrial complexes which developed around them. It has already been shown that petrochemicals may be manufactured from oil- or gas-based raw materials (see section 2.2). Gas-based feedstocks such as ethane and propane have sustained the industry in the United States, although oil-based materials such as naphtha and gas oil have increased in importance since the early 1970s, to account for 25–35 per cent of ethylene production by the late 1980s. The position is reversed in Western Europe and Japan where the industry has relied almost exclusively upon oil-based feedstocks. This contrast has had important consequences for comparative advantage in petrochemicals at the international scale (see chapter 8) and has also affected the nature of the industry's functional and geographical relationship with oil refining activities.

The early links between oil refining and petrochemical operations in the United States were described in chapter 4. Despite the operation of petrochemical facilities based on by-product gases at refineries such as Baton Rouge (Exxon), Whiting (Amoco) and Torrance (Mobil) for over 40 years, such arrangements could not have sustained the post-war growth of the industry. Indeed, less than 1 per cent of US ethylene production in 1987 was derived from refinery gases (SRI International). Natural gas supplies were an important influence upon the location of Union Carbide's pioneering petrochemical operations in West Virginia (see section 3.4) and similar considerations motivated the company's decision in 1939 to establish a complex at Texas City. Other companies, including Dow and Monsanto, were also drawn to the Gulf Coast region by the prospect of cheap natural gas (see section 4.1). Gas-based feedstocks fuelled the impressive post-war growth of the industry; this coincided with a massive expansion of natural gas, which increased its share of US primary energy consumption from 14.1 per cent in 1945 to 33.7 per cent 20 years later (De Golyer and MacNaughton 1985). This was achieved by the rapid development of pipeline systems which delivered gas from Texas, Louisiana and Oklahoma to the markets of the Northeast and Midwest. The rapid penetration of natural gas in the US energy market reflected the substantial size of the resource base as the volume of proven reserves increased steadily to 1967, as well as its qualities as a premium fuel. The petrochemical industry was a beneficiary of this trend, which guaranteed the availability of increasing quantities of natural gas liquids (NGLs) for ethylene manufacture. This was emphasized by a survey of 60 companies with petrochemical operations in Texas, in which 47 of the respondents identified 'nearness to raw material' as the principal location factor (Whitehorn 1973, 9).

NGL mixes are generally separated from natural gas at the producing fields. Various strategies are adopted in the subsequent fractionation of these mixes to isolate the individual components used in petrochemical manufacture (i.e. ethane, propane and butane). Integrated companies such as Exxon and Shell, with interests in natural gas production, oil refining and petrochemical manufacture, may divert NGL streams from one or many of their fields through fractionation plants which are dedicated to meeting the feedstock requirements of their own petrochemical facilities. Pipelines bind these integrated corporate systems together and permit considerable flexibility in the relative location of gas production, fractionation and petrochemical activities. Similar principles apply in the case of non-integrated systems, where the ownership of the various inputs to, outputs from and elements of the system may be divided between many companies. The largest fractionation units typically operate as intermediaries between the gas producers and the petrochemical industry, handling NGL mixes from numerous sources, providing storage facilities and supplying feedstock to many different petrochemical users. These units are the focal points of complex pipeline networks linking raw material suppliers and petrochemical producers throughout the Gulf Coast region. Mont Belvieu, to the east of Houston, is by far the most important centre, accounting for more than 50 per cent of total capacity in centralized fractionation facilities. Its significance extends beyond its role within the Gulf Coast production system, and feedstock prices at Mont Belvieu serve as a basic reference point for the international petrochemical industry. Nevertheless, there is no downstream manufacturing at Mont Belvieu itself. This emphasizes that although raw material availability is responsible for the concentration of US petrochemical capacity in Texas and Louisiana (table 6.1), extensive pipeline networks ensure that feedstocks can be delivered to virtually any location within the

Gulf Coast region (see Shanafelt 1977). A complex intraregional pattern has developed, including several major multicompany agglomerations and various relatively isolated centres of production built around the activities of a single dominant firm.

Ownership seems to have influenced the location of petrochemical plants relative to oil refineries. Almost without exception, oil companies which became involved in petrochemicals made their new investments within or adjacent to existing refineries. The location of some of the earliest and largest agglomerations of petrochemical manufacture such as the Houston Ship Channel and the Golden Triangle formed by Port Arthur, Orange and Beaumont was thus determined by the established pattern of the oil refining industry.[5] The availability of land and infrastructure was probably more important than feedstocks in encouraging the oil companies to adopt this policy, since the site requirements of oil refineries and petrochemical plants are similar. These include flat land, water for cooling and process use and, ideally, access to port facilities. On the other hand, many of the major chemical companies have had no difficulty in meeting these requirements and obtaining their feedstocks without locating adjacent to an oil refinery.

The much greater importance of oil- relative to gas-based feedstocks in Western Europe and Japan is reflected in the closer geographical association between the two types of activities as compared with the United States. Molle and Wever (1984, 87) suggest that 43 out of a total of 48 sites manufacturing ethylene in Western Europe in 1980 'were located in the vicinity of one or more oil refineries'. The subjectivity implicit in this statement makes direct comparison impossible, but there is no doubt that the spatial juxtaposition of oil refining and petrochemical operations is less overwhelming in the United States.[6] The origins of the relationships between the two industries in Western Europe were described in section 4.3, especially the implications of the naphtha surplus. This surplus, together with the fact that naphtha cracking yields not only ethylene but also various components suitable for blending into gasoline, fuel oil and other petroleum products, made location adjacent to a refinery a natural choice for most of the early petrochemical plants, especially those established by or with the participation of oil companies. Initially petrochemical operations were often regarded as subsidiary to oil refining activities, but the nature of this relationship within individual complexes changed as petrochemical feedstock requirements increased.

Figure 6.5 represents these changes in the form of a simple descriptive model. It is based upon a study of input–output links within several complexes in the United Kingdom (Chapman 1973). Despite this fairly narrow empirical base, the model may be applied to other oil-based industrial complexes in Western Europe and Japan.

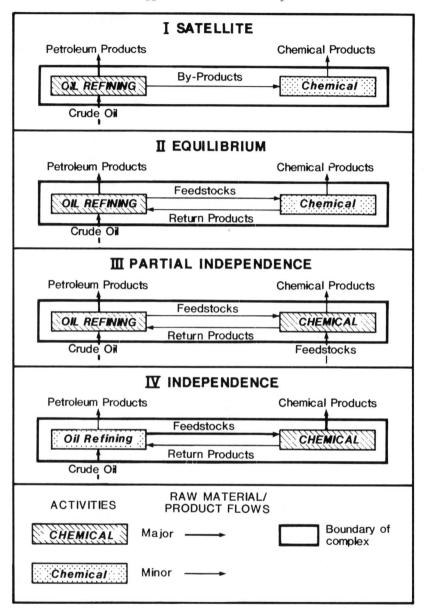

Figure 6.5 Model of changing linkages within oil refinery and Petrochemical complexes

It is suggestive of an evolutionary sequence, but there is no uni-directional development path through which all oil-based complexes must proceed. Generally speaking, the use of by-product refinery gases for petrochemical manufacture has never had the same role in

Western Europe and Japan that it did in promoting some of the earliest developments in the United States (see section 3.4). Nevertheless, where by-product gases are used, petrochemical manufacture is little more than a 'satellite' activity (figure 6.5) which is fully integrated with refining operations. 'Equilibrium' in figure 6.5 refers to a situation in which an adjacent refinery is able both to meet the needs of a linked petrochemical complex for liquid feedstocks such as naphtha and also to absorb the various return products within its processing scheme. Such equilibrium is difficult to maintain if, as occurred during the 1960s, demand for petrochemicals is rising faster than that for petroleum products; feedstocks may have to be imported from elsewhere, making the petrochemical operation partially independent of the adjacent refinery. Such imports are frequently obtained from other refineries within the same organization in the case of integrated oil companies (Chapman 1974b). Viewed from a geographical perspective, they may be derived from local sources, where the petrochemical operation is part of a larger multi-company complex such as Rotterdam, or if necessary from distant ones. Petrochemical capacity soon exceeded the capability of the domestic refining industry in Japan, for example, and substantial imports of foreign (mainly Middle East) naphtha were required to sustain its rapid growth from the mid 1960s.

It is important to appreciate that the distinction between equilibrium and 'partial independence' in figure 6.5 does not imply a deterministic one-way progression, as the policies of BP at its Grangemouth complex in Scotland during the 1950s and 1960s demonstrate (Chapman 1974a). In the early years, chemical feedstock requirements were met by direct transfers from the refinery. As newer and larger ethylene plants were introduced, adequate supplies of feedstock could only be produced at Grangemouth by modifying the refinery processing scheme and thus affecting its output of other petroleum products. The supply of chemical feedstocks was only one relatively minor aspect of the refinery's function, and any advantage gained by adjusting its processing scheme to meet the increasing raw material needs of the chemical plants would be more than offset by imbalances created between the supply and demand for other products within its market area. Nevertheless, a point was reached in 1968 when BP considered that such adjustments became worthwhile, and measures were taken to restore the internal equilibrum of the complex.

Whilst an individual complex may accord with the satellite, equilibrium and partial independence models at various periods of its development, 'independence' (figure 6.5) is not part of the same evolutionary sequence. It represents a situation in which oil refining activities are geared to the production of petrochemical feedstocks rather than conventional petroleum products. Such petrochemical refineries may be regarded as a form of backward integration by chemical companies to secure their raw material supplies, in contrast to the forward integration which propelled many oil companies into petrochemicals (see section 9.5). In some cases, such as the Petrosar operation at Corunna in Ontario which came on stream in 1978, the refinery and associated petrochemical facilities are conceived as a coordinated project on a greenfield site. In others the petrochemical facilities precede the refinery, which is established only when feed-stock requirements reach such a level that a tied local supply is perceived to be advantageous. ICI, for example, started oil refining at North Tees in 1963, more than ten years after its first ethylene plant was commissioned just across the River Tees at Wilton. Prior to this development, which was a joint venture with Phillips Petroleum, ICI had purchased naphtha under contract from Shell-Mex and BP. No Shell or BP refineries were located on Teesside at that time, and the feedstock was delivered from various sources within the corporate systems of the sypplying companies. A much more recent example of a petrochemical refinery is provided by Dow's plant at Freeport, Texas.[7] This came on stream in 1980, 40 years later than the original petrochemical units on the site it was designed to serve (see section 9.5). Most oil-based petrochemical operations are not linked to such purpose-built refineries, but these examples indicate the extent of the transformation in the relationship between the two types of activity resulting from the increasing scale of petrochemical operations as measured by trends in overall output and the size of individual process units.

6.3 Economies of Scale, Coproducts and Agglomeration

The increasing scale of petrochemical activities has implications not only for their relationship with oil refining on the input side, but also for the pattern of downstream development. This is most evident in the manufacture of ethylene, since the full realization of potential economies of scale is dependent upon finding premium uses for the various coproducts of the cracking process. The significance of these coproducts and their relationship to the choice of feedstock was emphasized in chapter 2.[8] Estimates of the effects of plant size upon the unit costs of ethylene production typically make optimistic as-sumptions about the use of coproducts. These involve crediting them with a nominal value reflecting their downstream use as chemical intermediates and refinery products. If coproduct propylene, for example, is converted into polypropylene for sale rather than burnt as works fuel, the overall economics of the cracking operation are much more favourable and the unit cost of ethylene is correspond-ingly reduced. Indeed, the benefits of increasing scale are largely eliminated if appropriate uses cannot be found for the full range of products. There is a substantial literature which explores these issues from an economic perspective (see Frank and Lambrix 1966; Walley and Robinson 1972; Gilbourne et al. 1978; Axtell and Robertson 1986). However, they also have geographical significance to the extent that the technical and commercial logic of operating large oil-based ethylene plants generates a momentum of development which tends to promote further agglomeration in massive industrial complexes.

The concept of a model industrial complex in which successive stages of production are linked together to form a fully integrated production-consumption system has been used as planning objective in both the public and the private sector. Various attempts have been made to identify such complexes for development purposes (see Roepke et al. 1974; Czamanski and Ablas 1979; Norcliffe and Kotseff 1980). More spcifically, the petrochemical industry has been perceived as the focus of development strategies based on the creation of a self-sustaining industrial complex (Isard et al. 1959). The role of the industry in regional development and its external relationships with other sectors are considered in chapter 10. Attention is now focused upon the internal structure of individual complexes and, in particular, upon the difficulties involved in achieving in reality the kind of equilibrium between interdependent activities which is so easy to portray in theoretical programming models.

Detailed statistics on linkages within industrial complexes are hard to obtain. There have been few published studies which make the connection between such linkages and the spatial form of oil-based industrial complexes. Most of these rest upon circumstantial evidence rather than direct measurement of input–output relationships (see Chardonnet 1958; Wever 1966; Mittmann 1974). Chapman's (1973) study is an exception which, by tracing the development of several complexes in the United Kingdom, emphasizes that internal equilibrium is rarely achieved. Where the responsibility for apparently interdependent activities is divided between different companies, the obvious over-the-fence transfers from the upstream to the downstream operation are often supplemented by purchases from elsewhere. Such behaviour is motivated by the desire to avoid dependence upon a single supplier and it emphasizes that, although transfer economies may be responsible for the proximity of interdependent activities within a complex, the relationship is not always straightforward.

Commercial fragmentation is not the only factor complicating input–output relationships. Even where related activities are controlled by a single company, it is often impossible to maintain internal equilibrium because the system is ultimately driven by business considerations. Designing a complex upon technical and engineering principles to maximize the input–output balance between its various elements will not necessarily produce the optimal economic solution if it results in a production pattern which takes no account of the market-place. Nevertheless there is no doubt that maintaining such a balance, within the constraints imposed by economic realities, is an important influence upon the design, operation and development of the complexes controlled by the major companies.

A distinction may be drawn between technical responses, which aim to achieve better coordination of existing activities within a complex, and commercial ones, which involve changing the pattern of activities. Greater control over the output of coproducts from the cracking process offers the prospect of achieving a closer match to the requirements of downstream processes. Different feedstocks produce different yield patterns (figure 2.4), and there has been a trend since the 1970s towards the design of more flexible cracking plants capable of operating on a wider range of feedstocks (Richter et al. 1978). This trend has been motivated mainly by the desire to take advantage of variations in the relative price of feedstocks in a more unstable oil price environment (see chapter 8), but it has had the incidental effect of allowing desired yield patterns to play a greater part in optimizing the choice of feedstock. Variations in reaction conditions provide another source of operational flexibility, and adjustments in temperature, pressure and residence time allow the balance of coproducts from a given feedstock to be modified (see section 2.2). Although such possibilities are important influences upon operational decisions, other responses to the problem of coproducts involve more strategic decisions.

The historical significance of by-products as a source of technical slack promoting growth and diversification in the chemical industry was emphasized in chapter 3. The exploitation of the coproducts of ethylene from the cracking process is consistent with this theme. The issue was of particular concern in Western Europe during the 1950s because of the reliance upon naphtha feedstock, which produced a wider range of coproducts then the equivalent NGL-based operations in the United States. Attention was focused especially upon propylene, which was typically produced in a ratio to ethylene of 0.75:1 to 0.85:1.[9] The most significant development at the industry level was the discovery and commercial exploitation of polypropylene. A number of US companies and Montecatini in Italy were independently working on this polymer in the early 1950s. This research reflected the science-push effect of the search for an analogous polymer to polyethylene, but there is no doubt that the commercial development of polypropylene was accelerated in Western Europe and Japan by the widespread availability of coproduct propylene. These events at the industry scale were paralleled at a corporate level by efforts to develop propylene outlets within individual complexes.

This was a major preoccupation of BP,[10] for example, at Grangemouth during the 1950s and 1960s when the company used joint ventures to acquire US technology for propylene-based products.

The connection between coproduct utilization and the realization of economies of scale in ethylene production creates a technical and economic momentum which promotes the characteristic agglomeration of the petrochemical industry, since the installation of a new ethylene plant is accompanied by the construction of related downstream units. Thus economies of scale and functional linkages combine to encourage further expansion at existing centres of production. Geographical inertia based upon economies of scale at plant level is often reinforced by more general agglomeration economies. These may be internal to the firm, and include such factors as the availability of site infrastructure and land which tend to favour the location of incremental capacity at established rather than greenfield sites. Other benefits of agglomeration may be external to the firm. Major multicompany complexes provide opportunities for individual firms to obtain economic and strategic advantages from diversifying their sources of supply. This applies both to producers of basic intermediates in their relations with suppliers of raw materials such as naphtha, and also to their customers. Most ethylene transfers within Western Europe are internal to integrated companies, but a significant merchant market exists in the United States where buyers certainly benefit from the competition fostered by the existence of alternative suppliers within the Gulf Coast petrochemical complex. Opportunities for product swaps, which minimize the adverse effects of both scheduled and unexpected plant shutdowns, are enhanced by geographical concentration. Other external economies within major complexes include the availability of specialized services associated with maintenance and repair as well as storage and transport facilities capable of handling a wide range of chemical products. Services associated with the disposal of waste products may be provided more cost-effectively on a cooperative basis. An important factor encouraging petrochemical development at Bayport, near Houston during the 1970s, for example, was the construction of a central waste treatment facility serving several firms.

6.4 Economies of Scale and Pipelines

The concentrated spatial form of oil-based industrial complexes is essentially based upon transfer economies gained by the adjacent location of interdependent processes. The significance of these economies is reinforced by the nature of many of the intermediates transferred between the different stages of production. Gases, freezing mixtures and corrosive liquids, which are difficult and expensive to transport over long distances, are often used in petrochemical manufacture. These characteristics are responsible for the role of linkages in promoting agglomeration. The centripetal influence tends to weaken, however, as the proceessing chain moves further downstream. The materials involved in the later stages (with the exception of crude oil) are generally easier to handle so that adjacent location becomes less important. The manufacture of such polymers as polyethylene and polypropylene involves the transformation, under varying conditions of temperature and pressure, of gases into solid pellets and powders. Scale factors are also important in determining the stage in the processing chain at which centripetal tendencies are replaced by centrifugal ones encouraging the dispersal of downstream activities. The significance of economies of scale in the manufacture of basic intermediates and first- and second-stage derivatives has already been emphasized (figure 6.1). These have been mutually reinforcing as the construction of large cracking plants has been accompanied by increases in the size of downstream units utilizing their products. The rate of increase in the size of these downstream units has been slower, however, creating a widening gap between the capacity of individual ethylene producing and ethylene consuming plants. Furthermore, a discontinuity can be identified in most processing chains where large-scale, continuous-flow methods of production are replaced by entirely different technologies which generally involve smaller scales of operation. This discontinuity defines not only the boundary between the petrochemical and the plastics industry, for example, but also the fulcrum in the balance of centripetal and centrifugal forces influencing location.[11]

Accepting this distinction, the logic of the arguments developed in this chapter suggests that economies of scale at plant level may be expected to reinforce the centripetal tendencies affecting primary processing. It has been shown that the realization of economies of scale in ethylene manufacture, for example, depends upon the rapid buildup of downstream capacity to match the increased volume of potential production from the cracking process (see Peters 1966; Gilbourne et al. 1978). This has become more difficult for two reasons. The growing divergence between the optimal size of cracking plants and the downstream units which utilize their products has already been noted. This may be regarded as an essentially technical matter which may be resolved by careful planning at the design stage of a new complex. Figure 6.6 illustrates a more fundamental economic problem. It indicates the typical S-shaped long term growth in demand and superimposes upon it the step-like increases in capacity associated with the introduction of progressively larger individual production units. There is a clear dilemma facing the producer in meeting projected demand and, at the same time, operating at the limits of prevailing technology. Reconciling these

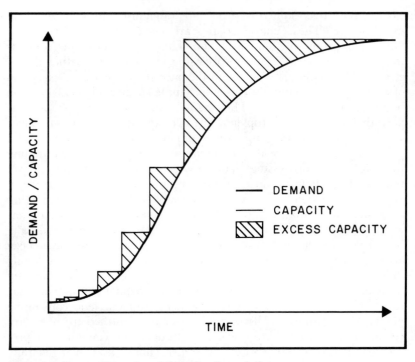

Figure 6.6 Demand/capacity relationships through time

two objectives implies inevitable periods of excess capacity which tend to increase in magnitude and duration as larger plants are built and the pace of demand growth slackens. Increased market share is the only way these periods can be minimized. However, the consequences of all producers pursuing this strategy are obvious. These are explored in chapter 10, which examines the links between economies of scale, competitive behaviour and overcapacity at the industry scale. One response to the problem at the level of the individual firm or production complex has been to develop pipeline networks capable of distributing basic intermediates to more extensive and dispersed production systems. By allowing bulk movements over long distances, such networks have weakened the centripetal influence of economies of scale at plant level upon related downstream investments since adjacent location is no longer essential.

The most significant developments in the pipeline transportation of chemicals have been associated with ethylene because of its crucial role within the petrochemical industry and also because of the supply/demand difficulties created by the trend towards larger units. The low boiling point of ethylene ($-103.7°C$ at 760 mmHg) presents serious transportation problems. Although increased pressure raises this threshold, ethylene is usually handled at atmospheric pressure (i.e. refrigerated) in road, rail and marine shipments. Such methods of transport are, however, expensive and potentially hazardous. Road and rail are generally used for short term movements and are totally unsuited to the kind of bulk, continuous transfers required to sustain a downstream plant. Larger quantities may be moved by sea and several companies, including Esso, ICI and Shell, have found it expedient on occasion to make regular shipments between their European manufacturing sites to balance ethylene supply and demand within their corporate systems. Nevertheless, the quantities involved are small by comparison with pipeline movements.

The economics of pipeline transportation are well documented with reference to oil and oil products (see Hubbard 1967; Manners 1971, 114–27). The same general principles apply to ethylene. Transport costs are influenced by volume and distance, and are usually met by the supplier when ethylene capacity exceeds demand and by the purchaser when the market situation is reversed. Capital costs are substantial and construction is only justified when a high load factor can be guaranteed.[12] These costs are themselves subject to considerable economies of scale. The potential benefits of pipeline networks have, therefore, increased with the volume of ethylene production and their development has paralleled that of the industry itself. The concept was first applied in the United States. The 'Texas spaghetti bowl' linking oil refineries, fractionation plants, underground storage and petrochmical sites in the Gulf Coast region developed rapidly from the late 1940s. This system emerged in piecemeal fashion rather than as a result of any grand design, although Gulf's activities in establishing pipelines to distribute ethylene from its Port Arthur complex from 1950 were important in promoting the idea. The system is used both for arm's-length transactions and for transfers between the sites of multiplant companies. Many materials are moved in this way, but ethylene is by far the most important chemical product.

Pipeline transfer of ethylene within Western Europe began in 1938 as part of a pioneering network of chemical pipelines in the Ruhr (Isting 1970). The development of the international system indicated in figure 6.7 is, however, much more recent. As in the United States, this system emerged as a result of the coordination of previously independent links which were conceived to meet the requirements of specific companies rather than as part of an integrated network. Most of these links were established during the 1960s, and two separate systems – one linking complexes in the Dutch and Belgian parts of the Schelde estuary, the other focused on the Rhine-Ruhr complexes in West Germany – were operational by 1968. These systems were joined in 1971 with the construction of a link between Beek (South Limburg) and Antwerp (figure 6.7). Subsequent

Figure 6.7 Ethylene pipelines in Benelux and West Germany, 1990

developments have added to the network, which extends from Ludwigshafen in the south to Rozenburg in the north. This system is the most important but not the only one for ethylene movement in Western Europe; others, involving intra- rather than international transfer, have been established in the United Kingdom, France, the Netherlands and Bavaria in West Germany. These systems offer important operational advantages to connected firms. The impact of plant failures which starve downstream units of ethylene at a particular complex are less serious if alternative sources can be arranged at short notice. The prospects of securing emergency supplies are obviously much better if there is access to a wider system. Similarly, transport costs may be reduced by swap deals in which one producing company supplies the customer of another from its own, nearer facility in return for a corresponding arrangement elsewhere. Long term swaps tend to undermine the viability of pipeline systems, however, since they reduce the overall throughput, thereby diminishing the revenues accruing to the operator of the system which in turn leads to higher tariffs to users.

The potential benefits of pipeline systems extend beyond operational matters to include strategic considerations. For example, they remove the necessity for the adjacent location of ethylene producing and consuming facilities. This possibility has partially offset the tendency for economies of scale in ethylene manufacture to promote further agglomeration since ethylene consumers, previously restricted in their choice of location to a major complex, may draw their feedstock from any point along a pipeline. Esso's polyethylene plant at Meerhout in Belgium (figure 6.7) is an example, and at least one million tonnes of ethylene consuming capacity on the Aethylen Rohrleitungs Gesellschaft (ARG) system are built at distances of 65–200 km from their sources of supply. ARG was formed in 1968 as an equal partnership of six companies to operate a T-shaped system extending from Marl in the Ruhr to Wesseling near Köln and across to Antwerp. A similar system was established during the 1960s in the United Kingdon, where each of the four national ethylene producers have access to a network extending from Fife in Scotland to Merseyside.

The existence of such networks raises issues which extend beyond the logistics of ethylene supply and the location of individual plants. Bearing in mind the problems of matching ethylene supply and demand associated with the introduction of larger units (figure 6.6), a system involving several companies presents the opportunity to coordinate much more than their day-to-day operations. Investment programmes may also be coordinated to minimize the problems of surplus capacity associated with the independent construction of large cracking plants. Thus new investment may be organized on a cyclical basis with each company taking its turn so that any excess capacity generated by a new plant is small in relation to total demand and more easily assimilated throughout the system. In theory this kind of arrangement must, at times, have seemed very attractive to the industry; in practice such a level of cooperation has never been achieved, as the massive ethylene and derivative overcapacity in the late 1970s and early 1980s testifies. On the other hand, there is no doubt that some collaboration relevant to investment planning has taken place. In the United Kingdom, for example, special provisions within the 1968 Restrictive Trade Practices Act permitted the exchange of information between companies in circumstances deemed important to the national economic interest. With government approval, the three principal UK petrochemical producers, BP, ICI and Shell, took advantage of this provision for a number of years prior to the country's entry into the European Economic Community (see Rees 1974, 207; Grant et al. 1988, 30–1).

6.5 Conclusions

The significance of economies of scale during the rapid growth phase of the petrochemical industry's development is consistent with the emphasis upon cost-reducing process innovations predicted by technology-based life-cycle models. The search for such economies has emphasized the capital-intensive nature of petrochemical production which has been a characteristic of the industry from its inception. This characteristic has ensured that labour costs, which have been identified as a key factor encouraging the dispersal of production with increasing maturity in other industries, have played no significant role in the evolution of the petrochemical industry.[13] Indeed, the massive capital sums involved in the construction of bigger and bigger units tend to emphasize the commitment of individual companies to existing sites, not least because of the knock-on effects generated by functional linkages between interdependent processes. Thus developments in the technology of production have subsequently reinforced a predisposition towards agglomeration associated with the influence of raw materials upon location. In the United States, this influence has created the concentration of capacity in Texas and Louisiana; in Western Europe it has been responsible for the close geographical association between the oil refining and petrochemical industries. Pipeline systems, especially for the movement of ethylene, have to some extent offset the combined effects of raw material availability, economies of scale and linkages in promoting the development of large complexes at the regional level. Intracorporate systems certainly permit individual companies to retain a more dispersed distribution of downstream activities at several sites than would otherwise be possible if ethylene from large cracking plants had to be used at the point of production. In the case of cooperative systems involving many companies, the effects upon plant location are limited because it is the existing nodes which determine the shape of the network rather than vice versa.

Notes

1 These same arguments have also been used to account for dispersal at the international scale (see chapter 7).
2 The dominance of Texas and Louisiana is greatest in the production of base chemicals and intermediates and is less overwhelming when downstream products are included (see Adib 1983).
3 This comparison is based not on the size of individual production units, but on a calculation which involves dividing total capacity by the number of separate sites (defined in terms of corporate ownership) at which ethylene is manufactured. In several cases, the ethylene capacity at a site may include more than one unit. Thus the comparison is really between the size of sites rather than of units. Such data are, however, easier to obtain from published sources and the comparison probably gives a reasonable indication of differences at plant level.
4 Failure to operate a plant at or near to its capacity significantly increases the unit costs of production. This issue is examined more fully in sections 8.2 and 10.2.
5 The evolution of the Gulf Coast petrochemical region is described more fully in section 11.2.
6 The significance of functional linkages has probably increased as oil-based feedstocks have accounted for a growing share of US ethylene production since the early 1970s.
7 This investment, which was based on the expectation that oil-based feedstocks would replace NGLs as the preferred raw material in the Gulf Coast region, proved to be a costly strategic error and the plant was mothballed after only six months.
8 The significance of coproducts is much greater in the case of oil- rather than gas-based operations because of differences in the yield patterns (see figure 2.4).
9 The corresponding ratio in modern plants is closer to 0.5:1.
10 BP had only a 50 per cent stake in the Grangemouth petrochemical complex before 1967.
11 This fulcrum has implications, which are considered in chapter 10, for the role of the petrochemical industry in regional development.
12 Ethylene pipelines may, in certain circumstances, provide operational flexibility in coping with unscheduled plant failures. Thus investment may be partially justified as an insurance measure. Hoechst has, for example, gained such benefits from its Köln–Frankfurt pipeline.
13 Although siting decisions, such as for Dutch State Mine's Geleen, have been influenced by the availability of labour in declining coal mining areas.

7
Government Policies and Internationalization

Insights into the spatial evolution of industries at the global scale may be derived from a massive literature concerned with various aspects of the process of economic development. The most explicit theoretical analysis of this topic is provided by Vernon's (1966; 1979) link between the product cycle and the location of manufacturing activities (see section 1.2). This work is based upon the assumption that the international distribution of industry is determined by the actions of multinational companies. By definition, the various theories of foreign direct investment, which obviously aid our understanding of the world distribution of manufacturing, are restricted to these companies (see Agarwal 1980; Dunning 1988). Despite their considerable and growing influence in shaping the world map of industrial activity, this map also reflects the actions of private sector and state-owned enterprises which operate at the national scale. Although there is no place for the small firm in petrochemical manufacture, the industry incorporates a diversity of organizational forms and its spatial evolution must acknowledge the differing goals and strategies of its various participants (see section 2.3).

The prominent role in the industry of global corporations from the top rank of the world's largest businesses has meant that foreign direct investment has been an important mechanism contributing to its dispersal from the core economies. However, there is no doubt that national governments have promoted the industry in an ever-widening range of countries either by indirect means such as trade policies or by direct intervention through the creation of state-owned companies. Regarding ethylene as an indicator of petrochemical development (for the reasons discussed in previous chapters), table 7.1 emphasizes the substantial involvement of the state in promoting the industry outside the core economies since the mid 1960s.[1] This represents a major change from the earlier history of the industry in the United States and Western Europe where the private sector, sometimes supported by government for strategic purposes, was the principal, driving force. In these circumstances, the industry's spatial evolution at the international scale may be characterized as the result of a complex interaction between essentially centrifugal tendencies originating in the core economies and reflected in the operations of the multinationals, and a kind of spontaneous development in the periphery initiated by national governments. This dichotomy is, of course, an oversimplification in the sense that the actions of these agents of change are not only mutually interdependent but also often directly linked through the medium of joint ventures (table 7.1). Nevertheless, it is possible to make a distinction between them on the basis of their respective roles as the *initiators* of development. In this chapter and, to a lesser extent, the next, the emphasis is placed upon the role of government, whilst chapter 9 approaches the question of the location of international investment from the perspective of the multinationals.

An important prerequisite for the internationalization of the industry, especially where development is initiated by governments rather than multinationals, is the availability of the necessary technology which, as demonstrated in earlier chapters, originated in the United States and Western Europe. This is discussed below, before

Table 7.1 State involvement in initiation of ethylene production in countries since 1966

Country	Startup year	State participation			Private sector
		Majority	Joint venture	Minority	
Greece	1966				X
Spain	1966	X			
Mexico	1966	X			
India	1968				X
Taiwan	1968		X		
Austria	1969				X
Chile	1970	X			
Turkey	1970	X			
Finland	1971	X			
Iran	1971	X			
South Korea	1972		X		
Colombia	1974	X			
Venezuela	1976	X			
Norway	1977			X	
Algeria	1978	X			
Portugal	1981	X			
Qatar	1981	X			
Saudi Arabia	1984		X		
Singapore	1984		X		
Libya	1987	X			
Thailand	1989	X			
Iraq	1990	X			

an attempt is made in the second section to explain why the industry
has attracted the interest of governments and development agencies.
Subsequent sections describe the various patterns of petrochemical
development associated with import substitution strategies of
industrialization.

7.1 North–South Technology Transfer in Petrochemicals

The source and subsequent diffusion of proprietary technical information is an important element of the industry life cycle. 'New'
industries embody 'new' technology, even if such technology represents something less than a fundamental advance in existing
knowledge. The significance of technology for the evolution of the
petrochemical industry has already been reviewed in the context
of its corporate and geographical origins (chapter 3) and the link
between the erosion of technological monopolies and the proliferation
of producers in the United States and Western Europe (chapter 5).
This proliferation emphasized the short duration of production
imitation lags within the core economies (section 3.3), but much
longer delays, of 50 years or more, have been associated with
the industry's introduction into the peripheral economies of the
developing world. This characteristic of petrochemicals is typical of
other industries, and the significance of and reasons for such lags are
the principal concerns of a massive literature concerned with the role
of technology transfer in shaping the economic and political relationship between the developed and the developing world. Such transfers
may occur as commercial transactions between companies, but,
where they also involve exchanges between countries, they frequently
assume a wider significance which encourages the intervention
of governments. Such intervention is generally associated with the
desire of the recipient country not only to acquire technology,
but also to ensure that it is effectively absorbed to maximize the
long term benefits accruing to the society and economy. Although
important from an economic development perspective, these issues
are peripheral to this study, which is more concerned with the availability of technology as an influence upon the spatial evolution of
the petrochemical industry. The increasing number of countries
with petrochemical industries (figure 1.4), many of which have been
established without relying upon investment by foreign multinationals (table 7.1), is predicated upon the diffusion of the required
technology.

The general factors contributing to the erosion of technological
monopolies in petrochemicals have already been reviewed (section
5.2). Stobaugh's (1984; 1988) analysis of the histories of nine petrochemical products 'chronicle a strong decline in the economic power

of the manufacturing firms that own technology – principally multinational enterprises' (Stobaugh 1984, 170). This decline reflects the activities of successful imitators, and competitive pressures encourage process owners to license their technology because any advantage is likely to be transient. This pattern of process improvement is linked to the age of the product. Eventually, the law of diminishing returns ensures that the potential rewards from further improvements become less attractive. The widespread availability of competing processes under licence further weakens the case for independent process development since the negotiating position of licensees relative to licensers becomes progressively stronger. Stobaugh (1984; 1988) noted a sharp increase in the rate of international licensing when a product was more than 30 years old (in terms of commercial manufacture). This increased availability of technology, together with the prospect of more favourable terms in a buyers' market, is clearly relevant to the petrochemical aspirations of developing countries. A study of the introduction of manufacturing facilities for 26 selected petrochemical products into Latin America to 1975 suggested that an average of 16 possible suppliers of technology existed for each product,[2] an average which will certainly have increased in subsequent years since 'the diffusion of existing technologies and the development of close substitutes for existing products seems to be accelerating' (Cortes and Bocock 1984, 24). These suppliers are of two broad types – producers and non-producers. The former include the major multinationals, which have been the principal innovators within the industry, and a large group of smaller companies; the latter are composed of specialized chemical engineering firms and contractors.

Multinational enterprises generally prefer to retain control of their technology as long as possible, although some, such as Union Carbide, have traditionally been more willing to license at an earlier stage. Stobaugh (1984, 164) established that the initial sale of technology by firms manufacturing a product with proprietary technology did not occur until 22 years (median) after its original commercialization. This figure implies that a multinational enterprise will initially choose to meet demand for its product in a developing country by exports from its domestic facilities. If import barriers make this difficult, the second option is to establish a wholly owned subsidiary to build and operate a plant within the market. The plant is likely to be of suboptimal size, partly because of the limitations of the market and partly because of the risks of foreign investment. Such strategies become more difficult to sustain, however, in the face of increasing competition from alternative technologies developed independently by smaller manufacturing firms and chemical engineering specialists.

Stobaugh's population of firms included both the major multinationals and the many smaller firms that were attracted into the industry during its rapid growth in the 1950s and 1960s (section 5.3). Most of these new entrants were and remain primarily concerned with serving their respective national markets, but many have successfully developed their own process technology which they have been keen to license overseas. The greater enthusiasm of smaller companies for international licensing as compared with multinational enterprises is well documented and reflects the fact that this is a less expensive and risky approach than direct investment in unfamiliar territory (see Wilson 1977). Furthermore, firms supplying domestic markets are less likely than multinationals to lose sales as a result of encouraging new producers overseas. These considerations certainly influence licensing behaviour in the petrochemical industry (Stobaugh 1984; 1988). Governments either own or have a significant stake in many of the smaller European petrochemical producers such as Statoil (Norway) and Neste Oy (Finland). The influence of the state is less direct, but probably no less significant, in the case of Japanese companies such as Mitsubishi and Sumitomo. These formal and informal relationships have allowed the transfer of petrochemical technology to developing countries to be officially encouraged for diplomatic reasons by the exporting nation. French and Japanese national interests in the Middle East have, for example, been linked to the activities of their companies in providing technical assistance to petrochemical projects in Qatar and Iran respectively (Office of Technology Assessment 1984).

As already noted (section 5.3), the various non-producing organizations involved in petrochemical process development are in the business of selling information and, unlike their competitors with manufacturing interests, are not faced with the problem of balancing licence income against possible losses from reduced product sales. The clearest evidence of the growing importance of non-producers is provided by Cortes and Bocock (1984, 41), who calculate that only 18 per cent of plants involved in the manufacture of their chosen petrochemicals in Latin America built before 1960 were based on technology supplied by non-producers. The corresponding percentages for 1960–9 and 1970–5 were 44 and 53 respectively. This trend reflects the fact that the developing world represents a major new market for their expertise. Indeed the attractions of this market have been emphasized during the 1980s by lack of opportunities in the traditional centres of petrochemical production (see chapter 10). The fact that the non-producing companies tend to be relatively stronger in the basic processes associated with olefins and aromatics rather than in downstream operations has further increased their significance in dealing with governments, because it is the upstream end of the industry which has attracted the highest levels of state intervention. Furthermore, certain countries, notably Mexico, seem to have positively discriminated in favour of non-producing companies as sources of foreign technology as a consequence of a politically motivated desire to avoid dealing with the multinationals (Cortes and Bocock 1984, 31). Yet another political dimension of the technology transfer process is highlighted by Sercovich (1980), who emphasizes that the Brazilian choice of Technip, the French state-owned engineering firm, as the principal agent supervising the design and construction of the country's third petrochemical complex in Rio Grande do Sul was made not because it was the cheapest or most experienced contractor, but because it was prepared to offer most in terms of the communication of expertise to native Brazilians. The importance attached to such considerations and the submission of four competing bids for this project in the late 1970s emphasize that access to technology (at a price) has not, for some time, been a problem limiting the internationalization of the petrochemical industry.[3]

7.2 Petrochemicals and National Economic Development Strategies

The widespread availability of the necessary technology, together with the recirculation via the international financial system of surplus revenues accumulated by oil producing countries during the 1970s, encouraged many governments to promote national petrochemical industries as part of ambitious development projects. The extent of state intervention and commitment has varied from one country to another, but several have made the creation of a domestic petrochemical capability an explicit element of their wider industrialization objectives. Japan was the model for many of these countries. The Ministry of International Trade and Industry (MITI), the state agency with responsibility for industrial strategy, published a document outlining 'measures promoting the petrochemical industry' in 1955 (Adochi and Yonaga 1966). These measures, which were designed to encourage private sector investment in the industry, included steps to increase the availability of low cost feedstocks (i.e. naphtha) and to provide protection from imports. MITI also intervened in the creation of new companies, based on alliances of existing chemical enterprises, to build and operate the four petrochemical complexes which were established during the first phase of the industry's development to 1960. These complexes were almost entirely dependent upon foreign (mainly US) technology acquired under licence. The apparent success of Japanese policy encouraged others to follow a similar route. Government intervention has, for example, played a key role in the establishment of the industry in Taiwan and South Korea, both of which started industrialization by encouraging light, labour-intensive industries such as textiles and then moved into heavy, capital goods industries such as petro-chemicals. In the case of South Korea, the Second Five Year Plan (begun in 1967) made the formation of a heavy chemical industry a priority, and this culminated in the commissioning of the country's first petrochemical complex at Ulsan in 1972. Many other countries which have not achieved significant levels of petrochemical pro-duction are nevertheless committed to this objective, including Pakistan, Indonesia and the Philippines (UNIDO 1985a).

The attractions of the petrochemical industry as an instrument of development policy rest upon its position as a strategic industry within the modern economy. During the 1960s, its rapid rates of growth within the core economies made it an obvious target for developing countries keen to promote industrialization (Mercier 1966). Its extensive linkages with other buoyant sectors such as plastics and synthetic fibres seemed to offer the prospect of replicat-ing the growth dynamic associated with the industry in the United States, Western Europe and Japan (see section 5.1). Furthermore, the industry acquired a certain symbolic or prestige value in the aspirations of many developing countries because of its perceived position at the leading edge of contemporary industrial technology. These images have been strongly reinforced by international agencies, especially the United Nations Industrial Development Organization (UNIDO) which was established in 1965 to promote industrialization in developing countries. UNIDO has actively encouraged the dis-semination of information about the industry via numerous con-ferences and publications (see UNIDO 1969a; 1969b; 1970a; 1970b; 1973; 1982; 1983a; 1983b; 1985a; 1985b; 1985c; 1985d; United Nations 1966). The agency identified petrochemicals as a priority sector in the 1975 Lima Declaration, which maintained that the developing countries should account for at least 25 per cent of world industrial output by 2000 and supported this commitment by a prediction of a major shift in the global distribution of petrochemical capacity (UNIDO 1978).

Identifying the factors influencing the prospects for petrochemical development has been a consistent theme in the various publications of UNIDO, which have emphasized the primary constraint of market size. The general relationship between petrochemical manufacture and levels of economic development has already been discussed in chapter 2, and the significance of this relationship for the timing of the industry's establishment within different countries was explored in section 5.4. The critical role of market size rests upon the fact that import substitution has been by far the most important single motivation for government sponsorship of the industry. Indeed, the industry is representative of what has been termed second-stage import substitution (Balassa 1981). This is designed to replace imports of intermediate goods and producer and consumer durables. It follows a first stage which focuses upon non-durables, usually including clothing and shoes. Even in countries such as Japan and South Korea, which later became significant exporters of petrochemicals, the initial objective was to replace imports. Unfortunately, the attempts of many developing countries to establish their own petrochemical industries coincided with the big increase in optimal plant size during the 1960s and early 1970s in the relatively mature industries of the core economies (see chapter 6). Furthermore, the benefits of scale were generally greater in basic operations such as ethylene production, which governments perceived to be crucial to their ambitions, then in downstream activities which attracted less active state intervention. In these circumstances, most developing countries (other than those with very large markets, such as Brazil) were faced with a number of options: abandoning the idea of establishing a petrochemical industry; basing their industry upon suboptimal manufacturing plants; building world-scale facilities with the intention of exporting product surplus to domestic requirements; and coordinating investment with other countries within the framework of organized trading blocs.

No petrochemical development is the only realistic option facing the majority of Third World countries in the foreseeable future (UNIDO 1985c; US International Trade Commission 1985a). This conclusion has been reinforced by the rise of export-oriented industries based upon low cost raw materials in the Middle East and Canada during the 1980s (see chapter 8). These have effectively pre-empted developments elsewhere and have also made it more difficult for other countries to consider temporary exports to bridge the gap between the capacity of a world-scale plant and the growth of domestic demand. This strategy has never been easy anyway because of the problem of competing in international markets with experienced multinationals with effective sales and distribution networks.

In practice, most petrochemical facilities constructed for import substitution purposes in developing countries have been small by comparison with prevailing standards in the United States, Western Europe and Japan. This has been true of plants established by foreign direct investment and by state-owned corporations. Protected by tariff walls, such plants typically produce high cost products with adverse consequences for the downstream industries which depend upon them (see section 9.3). In these circumstances, the pursuit of self-sufficiency in petrochemicals is not necessarily a rational strategy (Adelman and Zimmerman 1974). Indeed, this conclusion seems to have been reached by many developing countries on a more general policy level as outward-looking, export-oriented strategies have replaced import substitution as the preferred approach to industrialization since the mid 1960s (see Donges 1976; Balassa 1981; Chenery et al. 1986).

Cooperation in supranational groupings theoretically permits countries to take advantage of economies of scale despite the limitations of their individual markets. This collective approach to petrochemical development has been advocated by UNIDO (1970b; 1973; 1983a; 1985a; 1985c). Various groupings exist. The Gulf Cooperation Council was formed in 1981, ostensibly to coordinate industrial planning between Saudi Arabia, Bahrain, Kuwait, Qatar, the United Arab Emirates and Oman, although security considerations have been the main focus of common interest. Nevertheless, at least one joint petrochemical project (i.e. Gulf Petrochemical Industries' ammonia/methanol plant) has been undertaken by Kuwait, Qatar and Saudi Arabia, and further cooperation is a declared objective. The Association of South East Asian Nations (ASEAN) has a similar commitment to industrial cooperation within its charter. How effective such arrangements are in subordinating national interests to the collective welfare is debatable. The most ambitious example affecting the petrochemical industry proved to be a conspicuous failure. Various schemes to create a Latin American common market were proposed during the 1960s. These prompted studies which demonstrated the potential benefits of such a grouping in promoting industrialization (see Behrman 1972; Carnoy 1972). In fact, a smaller bloc was created in 1969 when Bolivia, Colombia, Ecuador, Peru and Venezuela formed the Andean Common Market (ANCOM). A petrochemical programme for ANCOM was announced in 1975. This allocated production of specific chemicals to each member state to avoid the proliferation of small, inefficient plants. However, this scheme has never been implemented, and Venezuela has pressed ahead independently with major investments whilst the other states have assigned a very low priority to petrochemicals. The failure of this scheme, which is not really surprising in view of the political realities, only serves to emphasize the significance of the market size constraint facing most developing countries with petrochemical ambitions, and underlines the fact that most poorer countries have little prospect of achieving these ambitions.

Market factors are by definition the principal influence upon petrochemical developments associated with import substitution policies. However, the industry is also associated with a different kind of economic development strategy aimed at adding value to indigenous hydrocarbon resources by producing petrochemicals for export. The oil price increases of 1973–4 and 1979 fundamentally changed the pattern of international comparative advantage in basic petrochemicals in favour of the major oil and gas producers. The nature and significance of this change is considered in the next chapter, but figure 7.1 indicates the relative significance of raw

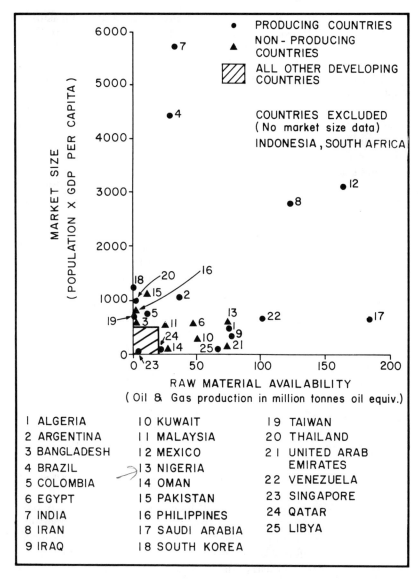

Figure 7.1 Market size, raw material availability and petrochemical production in developing countries, 1990 (market and raw material data 1985)

material and market factors as influences upon petrochemical developments within the Third World. The two axes measure market size, expressed as population × GDP per capita, and raw material endowment, indicated by oil and gas production in million tonnes of oil equivalent. Both axes utilize 1985 data, although the distinction between petrochemical producers and non-producers relates to the situation in 1990.[4] The difficulties of providing a true measure of market size have already been discussed (see section 5.4) and it is clear that other indicators of raw material availability could be used, including oil and gas reserves. Possibly the most direct measure is the quantity of natural gas that is flared (i.e. burnt) for want of a market. Such gas could be and has been used as a petrochemical feedstock. It has been estimated that the volume of gas wastefully flared in Saudi Arabia in 1982 incorporated the ethane feedstock equivalent to the requirements of 13 ethylene plants each producing 500,000 tonnes per year (US Department of Commerce 1986, 59).[5] To the extent that such gas is produced in association with oil, however, oil and gas (excluding flared material) production is a reasonable and more readily available measure of raw material availability. Despite these difficulties in calibrating the axes, figure 7.1 provides a crude typology of countries with respect to the principal determinants of petrochemical development at the macro-level. The distributions are highly skewed in the sense that not only are there few giant-market countries, but also the hydrocarbon-rich nations are a small minority of the population of developing countries. The vast majority have small markets, little or no hydrocarbon resources and, therefore, poor prospects of becoming petrochemical producers. These countries are positioned in the bottom left-hand corner of figure 7.1 and, with the exception of Singapore which has overcome these handicaps, are not identified on the diagram. Of the remaining countries which are identified, a distinction is made between producers and non-producers (in 1990). All of the identified non-producers may be regarded as potential candidates for the establishment of basic petrochemical industries; most, including Malaysia, Nigeria and the Philippines, have prepared plans with varying degrees of confidence that they will actually be implemented.[6]

Import substitution has stimulated petrochemical development in all of the countries adjacent to the vertical (market size) axis in figure 7.1, and the rest of the chapter will focus upon these cases. A basic issue facing any country wishing to encourage the development of a particular sector for import substitution purposes is the appropriate balance between foreign and domestic investment. In the case of a capital-intensive industry such as petrochemicals there is little chance within developing countries that indigenous private capital will be able to mobilize the necessary resources, and the problem therefore centres upon the respective roles of the state and foreign multinationals. These roles are explored in the remainder of this chapter.

7.3 Foreign Direct Investment and Import Substitution

Spatial patterns of petrochemical investment by the multinationals may be analysed in the context of corporate strategies (chapter 9) or from the perspective of the host countries. Several developing countries have deliberately encouraged foreign direct investment as a means of promoting industrialization, especially during the early stages of this process. A combination of stick and carrot measures have been used. On the negative side, high tariffs and restrictions on imports make it difficult for multinationals to supply markets from facilities in their home countries, whilst favourable tax treatment and limited controls on the repatriation of earnings are typical positive inducements. Such policies have certainly influenced the growth of the industry in Latin America which, as figure 5.6 and table 7.1 indicate, was associated with some of the earliest developments outside the core economies. By the early 1970s, 18 to 20 foreign, predominantly US, companies had producing affiliates serving protected national markets in Latin America (Behrman 1972, 156).

Despite the very early involvement of its government is setting up the first petrochemical plant in Latin America, in 1943, Argentina most clearly demonstrates the impact of foreign investment. Legislation in the late 1950s to encourage such investment resulted in several petrochemical developments during the 1960s by companies such as Dow, Du Pont, ICI, Koppers and Monsanto, operating independently or in joint ventures either with one another or with Argentinian private capital (Gatti et al. 1966). By the end of the decade, the industry was 'dominated by the international companies' (Behrman 1972, 157). Despite its early start, the Argentinian petrochemical industry has subsequently developed very slowly as these companies have been reluctant to increase their exposure in a politically unstable situation. Other Latin American countries, including Chile, Colombia and Peru, followed a similar pattern of early but very limited multinational investment in small petrochemical plants, mainly linked to the production of fertilizers rather than ethylene and its derivatives. Even in Mexico, which has consistently limited the scope for multinational involvement within its economy, foreign capital represented 35 per cent of total investment in the petrochemical industry at the end of the 1960s (Behrman 1972, 156).

The large size of the Brazilian market provided the country with greater leverage in its dealings with the multinationals than the other Latin American countries seeking to promote industrialization through import substitution in the 1950s and 1960s.[7] Faced with prevailing Brazilian policies, these companies were obliged to produce behind the tariff wall, or surrender the market to others willing to do so. Despite the creation in 1953 of Petrobràs, the state-owned oil company, the government formally acknowledged in the following year that the petrochemical industry 'should as far as possible be set up by private enterprise' (Brandaõ et al. 1966, 723). Significant investments were made by foreign companies, especially in downstream operations such as the production of bulk polymers for the plastics and synthetic fibre industries (UNIDO 1969c). The chemical industry was second only to motor vehicles by 1960 in terms of the cumulative total of foreign investment (Bergsman 1970, 78). However, the multinationals were reluctant to invest in basic petrochemicals because of uncertainties regarding the limits of the monopoly of Petrobràs, since official policy, whilst encouraging private enterprise, did not preclude the direct involvement of the state (Evans 1977). Nevertheless, a further expression of a predisposition towards the private sector in 1965 persuaded Union Carbide and Phillips to submit plans for the manufacture of olefins and aromatics respectively. In the event, Phillips subsequently withdrew its plans and Union Carbide chose to use the ill-fated Wulff technology. Its plant, like others elsewhere in the world, never achieved its design performance. Union Carbide therefore failed to translate its early involvement in the Brazilian petrochemical industry into a long term advantage and the initiative passed into the hands of state agencies (see section 7.4).

With the exception of India, where Union Carbide, Hoechst and Shell were involved in projects which established the first naphtha-based ethylene plants during the late 1960s, the industry has been created in the developing world outside Latin America by partnerships between state agencies and foreign capital. The involvement of US multinationals in Latin America was viewed as an extension of American diplomacy by both the donors and the recipients and was actively encouraged by the federal government in Washington. This geopolitical dimension was less important in South East Asia where the slightly later development of the industry also contributed to the reduced significance of foreign direct investment. The belief that reliance upon such investment was inconsistent with national economic independence gained strength during the 1970s, when the wider availability of petrochemical technology (see section 7.1) ensured that governments could establish the industry upon their own terms rather than those of the multinationals.

7.4 Public Sector Investment and Import Substitution

The shift in the political climate was reflected in Latin America in certain changes to the existing organizational structure of the industry in several countries. Mexico has been committed to extensive state involvement in the oil and petrochemical industries since the expulsion of all foreign oil companies in 1938 (Petróleos Mexicanos 1966). The state-owned oil company Pemex embodies this commitment, and it has a legislative monopoly of the production of basic petrochemicals and many intermediates. The limits of this monopoly have varied from time to time as the list of so-called 'secondary' petrochemicals which the private sector may produce has been modified. The monopoly was extended and strengthened during the late 1960s and the early 1970s to include several existing foreign-owned plants. Their owners were obliged to surrender control of these plants if they attempted to expand their capacity. Furthermore, foreign participation in the manufacture of secondary petrochemicals was limited to a maximum holding of 40 per cent in any single company. Thus the Mexican industry has remained firmly under state control from its inception and Pemex, as the sole owner of the principal manufacturing complexes, has the responsibility of trying to meet the import substitution objective which prompted the entry into petrochemicals.[8]

As already noted, Brazil has always adopted a less hostile view of foreign participation in petrochemicals than Mexico and has never made a formal declaration reserving particular branches of the industry to the state. Nevertheless, Petroquisa, which was created in 1967 as a wholly owned subsidiary of Petrobràs, has played a major role in the subsequent development of the industry. There is evidence that the decision to create Petroquisa was influenced by the desire of the local entrepreneurs associated with the establishment of the country's first major petrochemical complex in São Paulo to encourage the involvement of Petrobràs, as a means of guaranteeing feedstock supplies, in a three-way partnership which would also include a foreign company, Phillips Petroleum (Evans 1977, 49). This formula incorporating the state and both local and foreign private capital has been used in several later petrochemical schemes in Brazil, although the extent of Petroquisa's involvement tends to increase with the scale of the project. Generally speaking Petroquisa takes a majority position in very large core facilities.

Despite the encouragement and early significance of foreign direct investment in Argentina, the production of basic petrochemicals was reserved to the state in 1973. Chile had adopted a similar position from the beginning, although the relatively limited down-stream operations remain in the hands of foreign companies. Venezuela became the most significant new Latin American producer when a major olefin-based complex came on stream at El Tablazo, near Maracaibo in 1976.[9] The comparatively late development of the industry in Venezuela is surprising in view of its resource base. The foreign companies had no real commitment to the development of Venezuelan petrochemical capacity, and the state enterprise Instituto Venezolano de Petroquímica (IVP), which has been formed as early as 1956, was never able to achieve its petrochemical ambitions through a combination of inefficiency and under funding. Its functions were taken over by Pequiven in 1977. This is analogous to Petroquisa in Brazil, since it is a subsidiary of the state oil company which was formed following nationalization in 1976. Pequiven has pursued a similar strategy to Petroquisa of encouraging joint ventures with private capital including foreign companies such as Dow, Dutch State Mines, Phillips and Shell.

The history of the petrochemical industry in Latin America since the mid 1960s emphasizes that, despite variations from one country to another, the state has played a major role in its development. Cortes and Bocock (1984, 84) indicate that the proportion of wholly nationally owned (including both state and private sector) plants included within their study of the Latin American industry increased from 30 per cent for facilities built before 1960 to 56 per cent for those built between 1970 and 1975. Corresponding time-series data are not available for state participation alone, but it is known that the state was involved in 82 per cent of the plants identified within the study as being under local (i.e. national) ownership, regardless of the date of their construction (Cortes and Bocock 1984, 85). Several factors contributed to the shift towards greater state involvement. It partly reflected the changing political climate towards foreign investment in the developing world, which has already been noted. This shift in attitude was indirectly reinforced by the activities of international agencies such as UNIDO. By emphasizing the importance of petrochemicals in second-stage import substitution, UNIDO made governments more aware of the industry's strategic importance and, therefore, more sensitive to the question of ownership. Closely linked to this was the wish not only to promote the industry, but also to gain access to and control over its technology. The transfer and, more important, the absorption of technology was regarded as essential to the process of industrialization, and continued foreign ownership seemed incompatible with this goal. The fact that the multinationals which had traditionally dominated the world industry were no longer the only suppliers of technology was clearly a welcome development from the perspective of Latin American governments.

Similar factors have shaped the development of the industry in Taiwan and South Korea. The emergence of these countries as major petrochemical producers was contemporaneous with the state-sponsored expansion of the industry in Latin America. In both countries, foreign investment was encouraged in establishing the industry, but only in joint ventures with state-owned enterprises and/or local capital. Foreign participation was regarded as a means of securing not only technology but also much needed capital. Thus, in considering possible foreign partners in establishing the first petrochemical complex in South Korea, the government's 'choice of who was to undertake manufacture and what technology they were to employ was inseparable from who was to provide at least some of the capital' (Enos and Park 1988, 62). Government influence upon the pattern of petrochemical development in South Korea has been considerable, and certainly greater than its typical 50 per cent stake in the equity of participating firms would suggest (see Enos and Park 1988). This influence has extended from the initial identification of petrochemicals as a priority sector through to various supportive measures during operation. As well as setting production targets for the industry, government intervention in the early stages included the promotion of indigenous private sector companies capable of contributing to its development, the initiation of contacts with potential foreign partners, the conduct of subsequent negotiations and the provision of suitable sites and infrastructure. Once established, the industry has been further sustained by appropriate education and training policies and by the manipulation of input prices to ensure low cost feedstocks. Similar arrangements have maintained the international competitiveness of the industry in Taiwan, where the state-owned Chinese Petroleum Corporation has used its monopoly of the country's refining capacity to protect the petrochemical industry from increases in the price of naphtha resulting from events in the international oil market (see Industrial Bank of Japan 1978). The basic policy has been to link input prices to those prevailing on the United States Gulf Coast through the operation of a petrochemical stabilization fund.

7.5 Patterns of Development

There have been wide variations in the extent to which individual countries have succeeded in replacing imported petrochemicals with domestic production. Generalizations are difficult because of the multiplicity of products and rapidly shifting patterns of international trade. Japanese policy, for example, ensured that the country became self-sufficient in petrochemicals before the end of the 1960s and then a major exporter. Similar successes in Taiwan and South Korea have, however, contributed to a loss of export markets in South East Asia, and Japan turned full circle in 1985 by becoming a net importer of ethylene derivatives, 30 years after the original policy decision to promote the industry as an import substitution strategy. Brazil is another country which had achieved an export capability by the end of the 1980s, whereas India and Mexico, for example, continued to rely heavily upon imports. Although the trade balance is the ultimate yardstick against which import substitution policies are judged, our concern is with their impact upon the development of the industry rather than with evaluating the success or failure of these policies in achieving their objective. In reviewing events over a period of 25–30 years, it is possible to identify patterns associated with the evolution of the industry in the many countries which initially promoted it for import substitution purposes.

There is some evidence of sequential changes in the respective

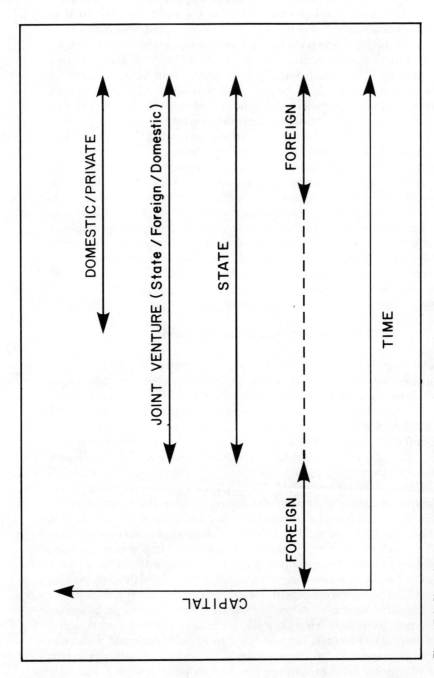

Figure 7.2 Changing patterns of ownership in national petrochemical industries

roles of multinational, state and local private capital in the development of national petrochemical industries (figure 7.2). Foreign direct investment was largely responsible for introducing the industry to Latin America.[10] The plants were generally small and it required the later intervention of the state to promote investment in the facilities, which provided the basis for establishing fully integrated petrochemical industries. The extent of this intervention varied from one country to another, as did the nature of the relationship between the state, foreign capital and local capital. In Mexico, opportunities for private, especially foreign, capital have been strictly limited by the comprehensive scope of public ownership in the industry. Most other countries have encouraged foreign investment in joint ventures with the state and local interests. Nevertheless, there is no doubt that government agencies have been decisive in initiating and accelerating the development of the petrochemical industry in most Third World countries.

State intervention is not necessarily viewed as a permanent commitment. The absorption of technical know-how has always been an important aspect of the official promotion of the petrochemical industry in developing countries. Successful absorption implies an expanding role for local private capital as the industry develops. In the case of Japan, the country already had a substantial chemical industry with large private enterprises created by a process of government-sponsored consolidation during the 1930s. Although these companies had little knowledge of petrochemical technology, they were quickly able to absorb and adapt expertise from abroad (see Spitz 1988, 375–84). The state therefore was the catalyst in encouraging Japanese companies to enter petrochemicals and in facilitating their acquisition of foreign technology, but did not need to create state-owned corporations to actually utilize the technology. Japanese success in establishing a petrochemical industry encouraged others to do the same.

The difficulties facing these imitators were much greater. By comparison with the countries of Latin America and the rest of South East Asia, Japan was at a more advanced level of development when it started petrochemical production. Studies of technology transfer have emphasized that the problems increase as the development gap between the donor and recipient countries widens (see OECD 1981). As far as the petrochemical industry is concerned, this has meant that Japan has been unique outside Western Europe in having an indigenous private sector with the management skills and financial resources necessary to assume responsibility (sometimes in partnership with foreign interests) for the industry's development from the beginning. State intervention in other countries has, in many cases, been a pragmatic response to the lack of such skills and resources, rather than an ideological commitment. This is emphasized by efforts to encourage greater involvement of indigenous private capital. Local participation in construction activities is one measure of involvement, and studies by Sercovich (1980) and Enos and Park (1988) have demonstrated the expanding domestic content of supplies and services in the later petrochemical complexes built in Brazil and South Korea respectively. By contrast Algeria, which was one of the first OPEC nations to establish an export-oriented petrochemical industry, has been much less successful because it purchased the technology before creating a socio-economic infrastructure capable of absorbing it (Papageorgiou 1985). Although local involvement in the construction of state- or foreign-owned plants is welcome from a development perspective, the direct entry of local capital into the production and marketing of petrochemicals is even more important. Apart from the special case of Japan, South Korea and Taiwan have been most successful in this respect. Despite the key role of the state in establishing their industries, the proportion of total petrochemical capacity owned by the state relative to private sector firms has declined in both countries. Formosa Plastic Corporation based in Taiwan is undoubtedly *the* success story as it has become a multi-national in its own right.

Formosa Plastic is, for example, directly involved in the Brazilian industry. This involvement reflects something of a change in attitude towards foreign investment in many developing countries during the 1980s. Having previously either discouraged such investment or limited it to joint ventures with local partners, several countries started encouraging foreign participation. Mexico eased some of its restrictions in 1986 by reducing the list of basic petrochemicals reserved for Pemex (Comisión Petroquímica Mexicana 1986). This list was further reduced in 1989 to 20 products, including the olefins and aromatics, but excluding such important commodities as styrene, polyethylene (HD and LD) and vinyl chloride (US International Trade Commission 1989). The 40 per cent restriction upon foreign participation in secondary petrochemicals was also removed, allowing 100 per cent ownership of plants manufacturing a wide range of products including polypropylene. These moves were an acknowledgement of the Mexican failure to achieve the goal of self-sufficiency in petrochemicals and of the impossibility of achieving it in the future on the basis of indigenous investment, bearing in mind the acute capital shortage resulting from the country's international debt problem. The Mexican situation is to some extent unique because of the substantial gap between domestic capacity and demand, but steps to attract foreign investment by countries such as Brazil, South Korea and Taiwan are part of a more general shift of direction by many developing countries toward export-oriented industrial policies and away from import substitution. This shift has implications for the petrochemical industry to the extent that the multinationals may

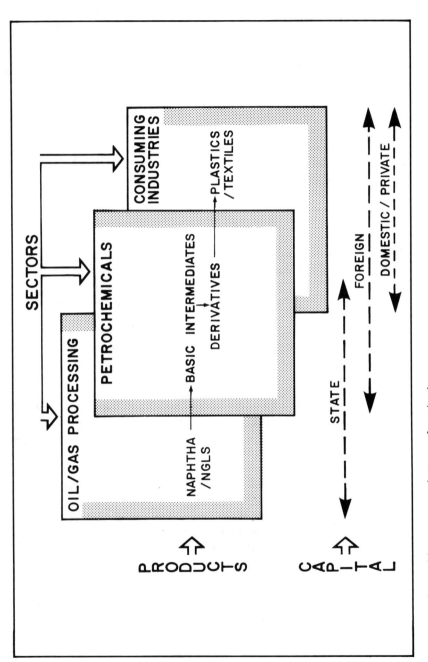

Figure 7.3 Ownership patterns and stages of production

be persuaded to establish plants which contribute to export earnings (see chapter 9). The wheel has turned full circle from the very early multinational investments prompted by import substitution policies in Latin America (figure 7.2).

Temporal changes in the organizational structure of national petrochemical industries established as part of import substitution strategies have been linked to the technology of the industry. Figure 7.3 suggests that state agencies are typically associated with the primary operations such as oil refining and the production of basic intermediates and that the involvement of private capital, both foreign and domestic, increases progressively downstream. The diagram is a very generalized representation which incorporates a broad spectrum of commercial possibilities. The distinction between the stages is not always precise, and the diagram extends beyond the boundaries of the petrochemical industry to include oil refining at the input end and consuming sectors at the output end. Nevertheless, the overall pattern is well established. In their study of the Latin American industry Cortes and Bocock (1984, 85) made a distinction between basic, intermediate and final petrochemical products, and noted that public sector participation declined from 73 to 56 and 42 per cent respectively of the plants in each of these categories. There are several reasons for this pattern. Investment in upstream activities is viewed by governments as a major influence upon the rate and direction of the industry's development, and foreign control of these strategic activities is widely regarded as undesirable. Conversely, the multinationals are reluctant to make the kind of massive investments required by these basic facilities without the close collaboration of the state because of the political risks associated with operations in developing countries. These substantial capital requirements also tend to exclude local private interests from the upstream stages. Generally speaking, the capital threshold falls with each downstream step in the processing chain as scale factors become less important and, therefore, the opportunities for local involvement improve. On the other hand, product differentiation increases in the downstream stages and technology may be less readily available than at the other end of the chain. In these circumstances, proprietary technology may provide leverage to foreign companies wishing to secure a niche within the industry.

A logical consequence of figure 7.3 is that the way in which the industry develops, in terms of either forward integration from a raw material base or backward integration from a downstream demand, will be an important influence upon the evolution of its commercial structure. The strategy adopted may be expected to vary depending upon a country's position with respect to the key determinants of market size and raw material availability (figure 7.1). Thus forward integration is the only route for resource-rich, small-market countries,

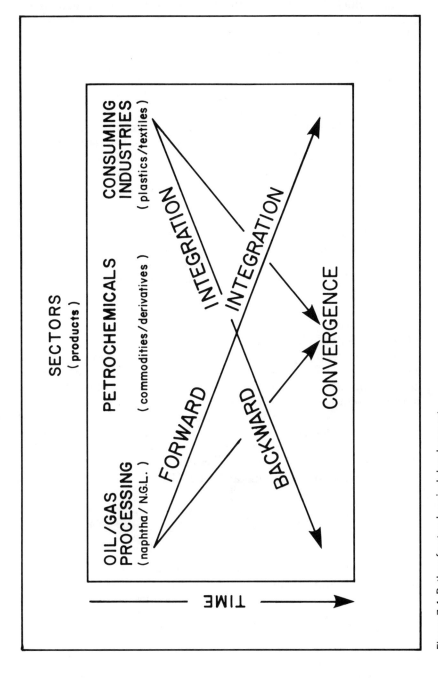

Figure 7.4 Paths of petrochemical development

whilst the import substitution policies pursued by most developing nations which have entered the industry are, by definition, based upon backward integration. In practice, however, it is more appropriate to characterize their approach as convergent – involving a combination of both (figure 7.4). Even where the replacement of imports was the primary motivation for promoting the industry, an existing refinery has, in most cases, served as the focus for the initial investments. The refinery invariably supplied at least some of the feedstock, and the petrochemical industry in Latin America and South East Asia has generally followed the West European rather than the US pattern of dependence upon oil- rather than gas-based raw materials. The South Korean experience illustrates the import substitution approach in the context of an export-oriented industrialization strategy. The establishment of a textile industry was a key element of the country's First Five Year Plan (1961–6). This was geared not only to meeting domestic demand, but also to developing an export capability. Most of the materials used by this industry were petrochemical products such as nylon, acrylic and polyester fibres. At the beginning of the 1960s these were all imported, but they were all derived from domestic sources by 1980 (Enos and Park 1988, 51). Nevertheless, the establishment of South Korea's first oil refinery at Ulsan during the First Five Year Plan was a prerequisite to the subsequent commitment to petrochemicals in the following planning period. A similar pattern of development occurred in Brazil, Mexico and Taiwan, where the oil refining and downstream industries were in place before the petrochemical sector was introduced to fill the gap between them. The actual sequence in which specific operations are introduced to fill this gap will vary from one country to another; it can be shown that a completely integrated national industry is not necessarily the optimal solution from an economic development perspective, as continued imports of selected commodities and derivatives may be cheaper than the initiation of domestic production (Trevino and Rudd 1980).

7.6 Conclusions

It is clear that the policies of governments have played a major role in the establishment of the petrochemical industry within more and more countries outside the core economies of North America, Western Europe and Japan since the mid 1960s. The connection between innovation and the initial location of industries was explored in chapter 3, and the diffusion of innovations may be expected to shape the pattern of their subsequent application. Such diffusion is implicit in life-cycle analogies to the extent that the loss of patent protection and successful imitation inevitably erode the technological monopolies of pioneering firms. Diffusion of technical information between firms has a geographical dimension which is most significant when it involves transfers from one country to another. The experience of the petrochemical industry demonstrates that as the information necessary for manufacture becomes more widely available, the major producing companies responsible for the key innovations within the industry progressively lose control over the rate and direction of its diffusion. In these circumstances, the negotiating position of the recipients relative to the suppliers of technology is strengthened and, with it, the ability of governments in developing countries to influence the behaviour of multinational corporations. The essential outcome of this influence in the case of the petrochemical industry has been its more rapid introduction in a wider range of countries than would have occurred if its development had been determined exclusively by the investment strategies of the multinational corporations in accordance with their own objectives rather than those of national governments.

This conclusion has implications for prevailing ideas concerning the spatial evolution of industries at the global scale. First of all, it emphasizes the limitations of the technology-based concept of the new international division of labour which has dominated much of the 1980s literature on industrialization in the Third World. The technology of the petrochemical industry is such that labour costs have never been a significant factor, and its manufacturing operations have, in an important sense, been standardized from the beginning because of their dependence upon continuous-flow techniques rather than batch processing. Despite the fact that some of the world's largest industrial corporations are active in the industry, its internationalization cannot be attributed to a kind of corporate imperialism. Certainly the diffusion paradigm is appropriate to the increasing availability of the know-how which was a precondition for the industry's development outside the core economies, but the initiative in seeking out and applying these technologies largely came from the periphery. This initiative was predominantly government inspired, although local private capital was important in Brazil. The stimulus to government intervention was generally linked to a wider policy commitment to import substitution, emphasizing that the industry's spatial evolution at the global scale cannot be regarded as the inevitable outcome of an internal dynamic, but has also been strongly influenced by external forces associated with the political economy of the development process. This conclusion is reinforced by the evidence of the next chapter, which turns from the place of the petrochemical industry in import substitution strategies to consider the impact of the export-oriented policies of resource-rich governments in the Middle East.

Notes

1 It is important to note that ethylene was not necessarily the first petro-chemical product to be manufactured in these countries.

2 This average overstates the choice available to the recipient because different processes may use different inputs and yield different by-products – that is, they are not necessarily *direct* competitors.

3 Despite their historic significance, Spitz (1988, 545) notes that the in-dependent petrochemical research organizations such as Scientific Design had largely disappeared by the late 1980s.

4 Iran is identified as a producer, although its small refinery-based ethylene unit at Abadan and its much larger partially completed complex at Bandar Khomeini are thought to have been destroyed in the war with Iraq.

5 Ironically, by the time the new Saudi ethylene plants were commissioned, the sharp fall in oil production meant that supplies of associated gas (and ethane) were less abundant than assumed at the planning stage (see section 8.3).

6 Some of the countries indicated as non-producers in figure 7.1 have established non-ethylene-based activities which may be defined as petro-chemical operations, notably related to the production of fertilizers.

7 Mexico also had a large market, but never attempted to base its industrialization upon the attraction of foreign direct investment.

8 Significant policy changes in 1986 and 1989 enhanced the opportunities for foreign participation (see section 7.5).

9 Venezuela began petrochemical production with a fertilizer complex at Morón in 1963.

10 Stobaugh (1971, 40) suggests that for many products there were enough alternative sources of technology even during the 1950s for governments in countries such as Argentina to have insisted upon local control of manufacturing facilities. The acceptance of foreign control was therefore a conscious policy choice rather than a necessary price for petrochemical development.

8
Oil Politics, Energy Policies and Location

Its dependence upon oil and natural gas as both feedstock and energy source makes petrochemical manufacture one of the most energy intensive of industries (see US Department of Commerce 1982, 25–6; OECD 1985, 23–6), and trends in the availability and cost of these raw materials may therefore be expected to have influenced its evolution. It has already been noted that the falling real cost of oil and gas contributed to the rapid growth of the industry by initially encouraging a switch from coal-based chemistry and later enhancing the substitution effect (see chapters 3 and 5). Furthermore, the geographical concentrations of petrochemical capacity in Texas and Louisiana and in the oil refining centres of Western Europe and Japan are clearly related to raw material factors. Nevertheless, these influences upon plant siting were set within a growth momentum at the industry level that reflected the mutually reinforcing dynamic of technical change and market development. Despite some concern in the United States during the 1960s regarding the adequacy and cost of raw materials for petrochemical manufacture relative to Western Europe and Japan, such considerations played little part in influencing the rate and pattern of the industry's growth at the international scale. The price rises engineered by the Organization of Petroleum Exporting Countries (OPEC) in 1973 and 1979, together with the subsequent instability of the international oil market during the 1980s, created a very different situation. Quite apart from their indirect effects upon the industry related to their impacts upon overall rates of economic growth, these price increases radically altered cost structures within the industry, especially in basic processing operations. In these circumstances, the cost of raw materials acquired much greater significance as an influence upon investment decisions. Widening geographical differentials in the cost of raw materials were created by the actions of OPEC and the policy reactions of oil consuming countries. These differentials were large enough to ensure that comparative advantage based upon raw material costs suddenly become a major influence upon patterns of trade and investment at the international scale. A questionnaire survey of major US petrochemical producers carried out in 1986–7, for example, emphasized that feedstock and fuel costs were not only regarded as by far the most important influence upon their prevailing competitive situation, but were also unanimously viewed as the greatest area of future concern (US International Trade Commission 1987).

This chapter attempts to explain the nature of these changes. It examines the role of raw material costs in shaping the development of the industry at the macro-level rather than short term operational responses to spatial and temporal variations in these costs. Emphasis is placed upon the implications for the industry of government responses to the circumstances created by the oil price shocks. The effects of these circumstances upon corporate location strategies and upon the restructuring of the industry are considered further in chapters 9 and 10 respectively. This chapter is divided into five sections. The first draws attention to some general problems involved in determining the role of changing raw material costs within the industry; the second examines the place of raw material costs in the economics of ethylene manufacture; the third assesses the link between these costs and the emergence of new petrochemical producers in the Middle East; the fourth considers the impact of events in the international oil market, as mediated by domestic energy policies, upon the competitive position of the US industry relative to Western Europe and Japan; and the final section further illustrates some of the complex interactions between raw material costs, public policies and the evolution of the industry since the oil price shocks with reference to the case of Canada.

8.1 Determining Raw Material Costs

It has already been emphasized that the petrochemical industry is defined in terms of its dependence upon oil and natural gas rather than the distinctiveness of its products, many of which may be derived from other organic materials such as coal. This dependence has ensured very close technical and commercial links with the oil industry. Despite the great importance of petrochemicals within the modern economy, the sector is, in many respects, the junior partner in this relationship. The share of total world oil demand (excluding the centrally planned economies) consumed, as fuel and feedstock, in petrochemical manufacture increased from 2.5 per cent in 1960 to 7.5 per cent by 1988 (Shell International Petroleum Co. 1990, 2). Although the increase is significant, the proportion remains small. With the exception of ethane, virtually all of the oil- and gas-based raw materials used by the industry have alternative, and quantitatively much more important, uses in energy markets. Naphtha, for example, is primarily used within oil refineries as a component of gasoline; liquefied petroleum gases such as propane and butane are more familiar as bottled gases than as petrochemical feedstocks. This situation has important consequences for the industry because the alternative fuel value of any hydrocarbon defines the lower limit of its value as a petrochemical feedstock. What happens in the much bigger fuel markets, therefore, largely determines the cost of raw materials to the petrochemical industry.

Understanding the pricing of petrochemical feedstocks is often made even more difficult because transactions do not take place in an open market. Many oil companies supply feedstocks to their petrochemical plants from sources, such as gas processing installations and oil refineries, that are internal to the organization. Transfer pricing arrangements are, therefore, an important influence upon the cost to the petrochemical operation. Indeed, many basic petrochemical plants manufacturing olefins and aromatics are regarded by their owners, especially in the United States, as integral parts of the oil refineries with which they are associated; they are designed to operate in a scavenging role, using whatever suitable feedstock happens to be surplus to refinery requirements. The fact that this can be done draws attention to another complication – the interchangeability of feedstocks.

The possibility of using different raw materials to manufacture the same basic intermediates was emphasized in chapter 2. In the past, individual units were usually designed to operate on feedstocks within narrowly defined boiling ranges,[1] but there has been a clear trend, from the 1970s onwards, towards greater flexibility. This has primarily been driven by the instability of feedstock prices after the oil price shocks as the industry has sought ways of responding to short term changes in the relative costs of, for example, naphtha and propane. Such flexibility makes evaluation of comparative advantage very difficult, not only because it blurs the distinction between oil- and gas-based operations on the input (i.e. cost) side, but also because different feedstocks yield different combinations of coproducts on the output (i.e. revenue) side (see chapter 2).

All of the various technical problems in assessing the role of raw material costs in the economics of the industry are compounded by political factors. These costs are frequently influenced by decisions which reflect international and domestic energy politics. Potential impacts upon the petrochemical industry are rarely a consideration in these decisions. Thus, unlike other raw-material-based industries, such as iron and steel, the availability and costs of its basic inputs are determined not by the operation of factor markets which are internal to, or an extension of, the industry, but by circumstances in another

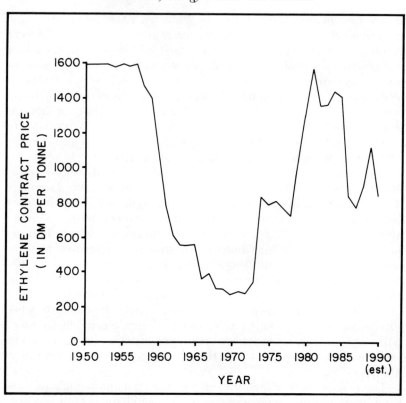

Figure 8.1 Ethylene price trends in Western Europe, 1950–1990 (from data supplied by ICI Chemicals and Polymers Ltd)

sector over which many producers have little or no control. These issues may be illustrated with reference to ethylene manufacture which, as previously noted, is a key operation, providing the most important basic intermediate upon which many downstream activities are based. Depending upon the type of feedstock used, the process may also yield several other coproducts, such as propylene and butadiene (figure 2.4), which are significant intermediates in their own right.

8.2 Raw Materials and the Economics of Ethylene Production

Many petrochemical products, including ethylene, are standard commodities in which cost rather than product differentiation is the basis for competition; trends in their manufacture may be related to the product life-cycle concept, which predicts increasing cost competition with the onset of maturity. The role of economies of scale in this progression has already been examined in chapter 6, and figure 8.1 plots long term trends in ethylene contract prices in Western Europe.[2] The data are expressed in current values rather than standardized relative to a particular base year, and the fall in ethylene prices during the 1960s was clearly substantial. A similar pattern occurred in the United States, where the price remained in the range 4.7–5.0 cents per pound (i.e. $104–110 per tonne) throughout the 1950s and into the early 1960s and then fell to approximately 3 cents per pound ($66 per tonne) by 1972. These trends coincided with the big increase in the size of individual cracking plants (figure 6.2) and reflected the impact of economies of scale during a period of stable or gradually declining raw material costs (figures 8.2 and 8.3). The shift to larger plants, however, had the effect of changing the relative importance of the fixed and variable components of ethylene production costs. This is evident in table 6.2, in which variable costs (mainly feedstock and fuel) increase their share of total costs from 43 to 56 per cent as plant capacity rises from 20,000 to 200,000 tonnes per year.[3] This shift is an indirect consequence of the various technical factors, already discussed in chapter 6, which reduce the significance of fixed costs per unit of production as plant size increases. Economies of scale are an important element of the life-cycle model and, in capital-intensive industries such as petrochemicals which are based upon the processing of raw materials, they imply that the costs of these basic inputs become more important influences upon the economics of production as products and industry mature. This conclusion remains valid even if the unit cost of raw materials remains constant, and it rests upon the interaction of various technical and economic changes which are internal to the industry. In the case of petrochemicals, however, the external oil price shocks sharply reinforced this trend.

The prices of specific petrochemical feedstocks broadly reflect trends in oil prices, although the relationship is not always straightforward because of the problems of price determination referred to earlier. This correlation is evident in figure 8.2, which plots naphtha and crude prices in Western Europe. The diagram also indicates a general fall in the premium for naphtha over crude since the mid 1960s, although annual figures conceal significant short term fluctuations in the ratio as real and imagined shortages of naphtha have caused the market for this feedstock to magnify swings in crude prices. Just as the Rotterdam spot market for naphtha is the key indicator of feedstock price in Western Europe, so the ethane price at Mont Belvieu, Texas is the reference point in the United States. This reflects Mont Belvieu's position as the largest single concentration of fractionation and storage capacity (see section 6.2). Figure 8.3 is a generalized representation of ethane price trends and their relationship to those of crude oil. The oil price is the average refinery

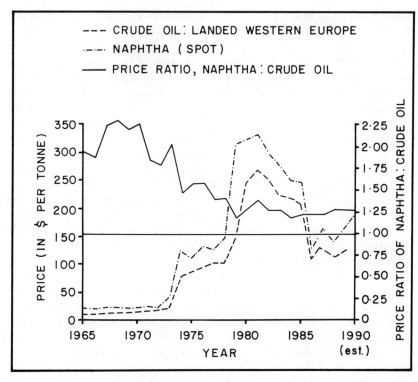

Figure 8.2 Crude oil and naphtha prices in Western Europe, 1965–1990 (from data supplied by ICI Chemicals and Polymers Ltd)

acquisition cost estimated by the US Department of Energy and is a composite figure incorporating the appropriate balance of domestic and imported crude as processed each year. The ethane price is the unit sales value published by the US International Trade Commission. These data have several limitations. Actual prices paid often diverge from posted prices because of the contractual terms between supplier and customer, a situation which is made even more complex when the two parties are part of the same integrated company.[4] Geographical variations reflecting local supply and demand conditions are not apparent in national figures. Furthermore, the broad temporal trends suggested by figure 8.3 conceal the short term fluctuations which are so important for operational purposes. Finally, it is worth emphasizing that the strategic investment decisions which shape the development of the industry are made on the basis of *expectations* of feedstock price and availability rather than with the perfect knowledge of hindsight.[5] Despite those various difficulties of measurement and interpretation, figure 8.3 provides a synoptic view of price trends for the most important single petrochemical feedstock

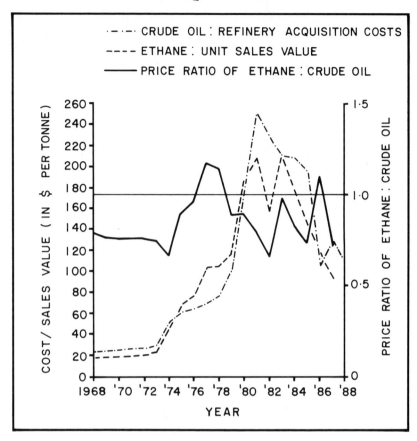

Figure 8.3 Crude oil and ethane prices in the United States, 1968–1988 (from data published by Energy Information Administration and US International Trade Commission)

in the United States. It is evident that the ratio of ethane price to oil price has fluctuated considerably; this has prompted shifts, within the limits imposed by the specifications of existing plant, in the proportion of ethylene derived by the US petrochemical industry from ethane as compared with other feedstocks such as naphtha and gas oil. Although the price of ethane in the United States is most directly linked to that of natural gas, figure 8.3 emphasizes that, viewed at a very general level, it is set within the overall framework established by events in the international oil market. The effect of the oil shocks upon the US ethane price is clear, despite the rigidities imposed by the complexities of domestic energy policy (see section 8.4). Thus although such national policy influences, together with differences in the technical characteristics of their respective petrochemical industries, ensured that the impact of these shocks was not necessarily the same in the United States, Western Europe and Japan, the structure of ethylene production costs was radically altered in all three areas.

There have been many published estimates of ethylene production costs along similar lines to those presented in table 6.2 (see Peters 1966; Braber 1966; Frank and Lambrix 1966; Mercier 1966; Gilbourne et al. 1978; OECD 1985; Axtell and Robertson 1986; Fayad and Motamen 1986; SRI International). They incorporate different assumptions regarding the many variables which influence such calculations. These include the values ascribed to coproducts; the operating rate as a percentage of total capacity; methods of estimating depreciation on fixed capital and of allocating overheads; technical specifications such as plant size and type of feedstock used; and the presumed location of the hypothetical plant, which may influence capital charges because of geographical variations in construction costs. Contemporaneous estimates are affected by all of these factors, but further problems are introduced when attention is focused upon changes through time and, in particular, upon the contribution of a specific factor such as raw material costs. Although relatively mature, the technology of ethylene production is not static and advances in furnace design have, for example, resulted in improvements in energy efficiency. More obviously, the trend towards larger units makes it difficult to separate the effects of scale factors from changing feedstock prices as influences upon total costs. Estimates made at different times incorporate financial assumptions about interest rates and depreciation, for example, which reflect prevailing economic circumstances. The generally lower levels of inflation in the 1960s as compared with the 1980s ensure that the bases of cost estimates made during these periods are totally different. Direct comparison of such estimates in an attempt to assess the changing role of raw material costs is, therefore, meaningless.

Despite these difficulties, there is no doubt that the petrochemical industry's production function, as exemplified by the manufacture of ethylene, was changed dramatically by the oil price shocks. This is apparent in figure 8.4, which describes the cost structures of a typical naphtha-based ethylene plant in Western Europe at various dates. This begs obvious questions regarding the definitions and assumptions upon which the comparisons are based, but there is no doubt that the general pattern is valid. The impact of changes in raw material costs tends to decline with each downstream step in the processing chain. The focal position of the cracking operation, however, ensures that changes at this stage have knock-on effects further down the line. Overall, the events of 1973 and 1979 transformed the industry from a capital-intensive activity of high fixed costs to a variable cost business dominated by feedstock and energy

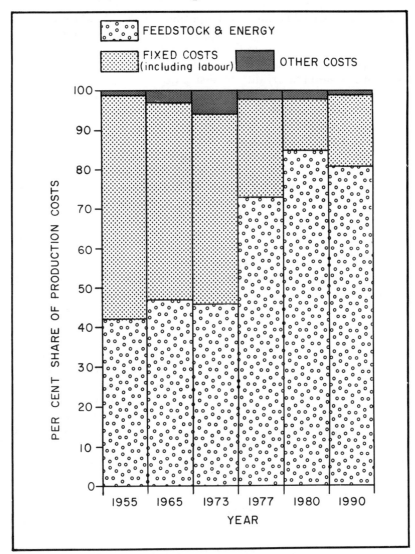

Figure 8.4 Changing structure of ethylene production costs in Western Europe, 1955–1990 (estimates from various sources)

considerations. Significant falls in the price of oil and therefore feedstock in 1986 to levels comparable with those prevailing before the second oil shock (figures 8.2 and 8.3) reversed this trend, but the 1990 cost structure in figure 8.4 confirms the continuing validity of the generalization. Indeed, the changes induced by the oil price shocks were sufficiently dramatic to precipitate decisions which have had lasting effects upon the industry's development.

One way of evaluating the significance of the variables affecting major capital investment decisions is the technique of sensitivity analysis. This represents profitability as a function of one variable (or of the percentage change in that variable), holding other variables constant. It simplifies reality by disregarding the interdependence of the variables and it seeks only to illustrate their relative importance. The analysis relates to a hypothetical plant and incorporates assumptions regarding its technical specifications, capital cost and operating costs. Figure 8.5 plots the results of such an analysis for a newly built 450,000 tonnes per year naphtha cracker operating at full capacity in Western Europe in the economic conditions prevailing in 1980, immediately after the second oil price shock.[6] The vertical axis measures the computed pre-tax net return, expressed as a percentage of the fixed capital, on a replacement cost basis. The horizontal axis indicates the percentage change from the base case assumptions. The point of intersection shows a return of approximately 5 per cent under these assumptions. The steepness of the slope of the lines for each variable away from this point is an indication of their influence upon rate of return: the steeper the line, the more important the variable. It is clear that the cost of naphtha is the most influential determinant of profitability. A corresponding analysis for a gas-based cracking plant located on the US Gulf Coast in 1981 produced slightly different results, with declines in ethylene price and capacity utilization, closely followed by increases in feedstock costs, imposing the most severe penalties (US Department of Commerce 1982).[7] The conclusions of these studies are, of course, specific to the period when they were carried out, but they help to explain why raw material costs dominated the operational and strategic thinking of the industry in the late 1970s and the early 1980s. They also demonstrate how major temporal changes in these costs created the opportunity for relatively minor spatial variations in them to influence the geography of the industry. The nature and significance of these variations are explored in the rest of this chapter.

8.3 Resource-Based Petrochemical Developments

The oil shocks added a new dimension to the internationalization of the petrochemical industry. The interaction of the diffusion of technology and the essentially market-led dispersal implicit in import substitution strategies was reviewed in chapter 7. The emergence of new producers in North Africa and the Middle East since the late 1970s has been driven by raw material factors and geared towards export rather than domestic markets. There have been several detailed studies of the political economy of resource-based industrialization in hydrocarbon-rich countries (see Turner and Bedore 1979; Al Wattari

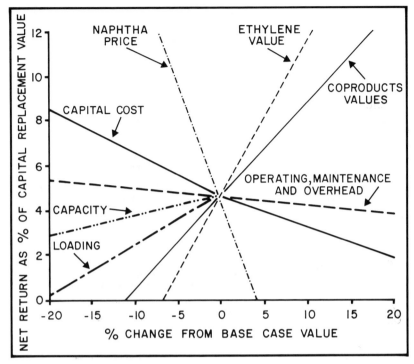

Figure 8.5 Sensitivity analysis for ethylene production costs in Western Europe, 1980 (OECD 1985, 64)

1980; El Mallakh and El Mallakh 1982; Fesharaki and Isaak 1983; Auty 1988a; 1990; Stauffer 1988) as well as specific studies of the place of petrochemicals within such development strategies (see OECD 1985; Tandy 1986). Our concern here is limited to an under-standing of the nature and extent of petrochemical investment in these countries, its relationship to developments elsewhere and its implications for the evolution of the industry at the global scale.

Petrochemical developments in the Middle East and North Africa fall into two categories related to their use of different components of natural gas. Those which utilize methane are primarily concerned with the production of nitrogenous fertilizers (i.e. ammonia, urea and ammonium sulphate) and methanol. Fertilizer production was the first to be established, and the earliest development took place in Kuwait in 1966. Most other gas-rich countries have followed this lead, and exports from the Middle East have become an estab-lished feature of the international trade in fertilizers. Investment in methanol generally came later and was less substantial, reflect-ing its more limited market (although technical advances suggest that this intermediate will become more important in the future).

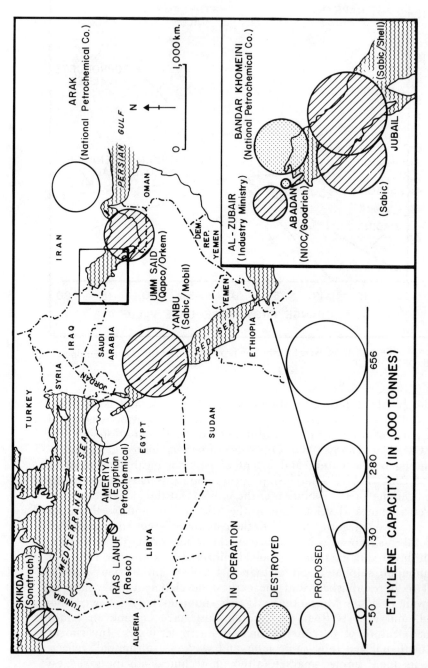

Figure 8.6 Ethylene capacity in North Africa and Middle East, 1990

The methane derivatives fall outside the definition of petrochemical manufacture adopted in chapter 2 for the purposes of this book, and it is the various operations based on ethane which constitute the second, more relevant aspect of petrochemical production. Figure 8.6 indicates the distribution of ethylene and, by implication, derivative capacity in the Middle East and North Africa. It emphasizes the particular importance of developments in Saudi Arabia. Algeria was the first OPEC member outside Latin America to establish an ethane-based petrochemical complex in 1978.[8] It was followed by Qatar in 1981 and Saudi Arabia in 1985. Both Iran and Iraq started the construction of similar complexes in the late 1970s. These were principal targets during the war of 1980–8 between the two countries, and Iran's Bandar Khomeini complex was largely destroyed. Despite the suspension or abandonment of plans for further capacity in Egypt, Kuwait and Libya, total investment by OPEC members in the region has been substantial. By 1990, these countries accounted for approximately 5 per cent of world (excluding the centrally planned economies) ethylene capacity, compared with virtually nothing ten years earlier. Indeed these developments have been more important that these figures suggest, in terms of both their direct and their indirect impacts upon the international distribution of the industry. They have obviously added a new element to the overall pattern; less obviously, by virtue of their export orientation they have contributed to capacity reductions and discouraged new investment in Western Europe and Japan (see chapter 10).

The cost of feedstock to specific petrochemical plants is difficult to judge at the best of times, but is especially problematic in the Middle East. Attention during the early 1980s focused on Saudi Arabia, and most estimates anticipated that its new ethylene plants would be based on ethane priced in the range \$0–25 per tonne (see UNIDO 1983b; US International Trade Commission 1985c; 1987; 1989; OECD 1985; Stauffer 1988). This compared with prevailing prices of \$150–210 per tonne on the US Gulf Coast and \$275–320 per tonne for naphtha in Western Europe (figures 8.2 and 8.3).[9] An even more important consideration was the expectation not only of further increases in the costs of raw materials outside the oil-rich countries, but also of widespread anxiety about security of supply following the second oil shock. It was this combination of economic and political factors which generated real apprehension about the possible effects of developments in oil-rich countries upon traditional centres of petrochemical production (see US International Trade Commission 1983; Glass 1985).

The very low cost of feedstock in these countries ultimately reflects the lack of alternative uses for their gas resources. The huge quantities that have previously been wastefully flared in Saudi Arabia have already been mentioned in chapter 7. To the extent that much of this gas has been associated with oil production, there has been limited control over its output which has, in the past, far exceeded domestic requirements. Furthermore, opportunities for export have been limited. The pattern of energy supply and demand at the international scale ensures that gas pipelines from the Middle East are rarely feasible for both economic and political reasons. Although a maritime trade in liquefied petroleum gases (i.e. propane and butane) has developed since the 1970s, the quantities involved are a fraction of the volume potentially available, whilst shipments of methane and ethane are a very expensive way of transporting energy. Indeed, ethane is unique as a petrochemical feedstock in having a high cost of transportation and no alternative use except as a fuel near the point of production. All of these factors mean that natural gas in the Middle East has a very low intrinsic value. Indeed, the price charged to petrochemical users of ethane in Saudi Arabia is probably based upon a formula which assumes zero value at the wellhead plus an element intended to cover the costs of building and operating the infrastructure required to collect natural gas from the many different fields, to extract the ethane component and to deliver it to the petrochemical plants.[10]

The low feedstock costs of the oil-rich countries do not necessarily guarantee a comparative advantage in basic petrochemicals. The ambitious scale of the Saudi projects exceeded any previous petrochemical developments in the Middle East, and construction costs were expected to be significantly higher than in the industrialized countries. Lack of experience and the need to import manufactured materials and equipment suggested that investment costs would be 1.3 to 1.5 times higher per unit of installed capacity relative to the US Gulf Coast (see OECD 1985; Fayad and Motamen 1986). In fact, the engineering contractors confounded some of the more pessimistic estimates and, boosted by the use of innovative modular construction techniques, most of the Saudi projects were completed on or ahead of schedule. Despite this achievement, these projects had to compete not only with new facilities in the traditional centres of production, but also with existing plants which had already been fully depreciated for accounting purposes. In addition to these capital-related factors, there are good reasons for expecting operating costs, other than feedstock charges, to be higher in the Middle East. The lack of trained personnel and the need to acquire the necessary skills inflate labour costs. A further penalty of poor labour quality is its effect upon plant performance. The importance of high levels of capacity utilization in the economics of basic petrochemical production was emphasized in the preceding section. Sonatrach's petrochemical facilities have, for example, consistently failed to achieve design performance, mainly because of the limitations of Algerian labour and management (Papageorgiou 1985).[11] Another reason for the underutilization of capacity has been shortage of feedstock. Levels of OPEC oil and, therefore, associated gas production during the 1980s have fallen far below the levels anticipated when petrochemical projects were originally planned. The ethylene plant in Qatar, for example, operated at less than 50 per cent of capacity between 1981 and 1984 as a result of limited ethane supplies (Tandy 1986, 110–11), and Stauffer (1988) emphasizes the very real constraint imposed by a shortage of natural gas upon the immediate industrial ambitions of several Middle Eastern states.

The possibility of new petrochemical capacity in the Middle East inspired many attempts in the early 1980s to estimate the relative costs of ethylene production in different parts of the world (see US International Trade Commission 1983; OECD 1985). Figure 8.7 summarizes the results of such an analysis. It indicates the projected

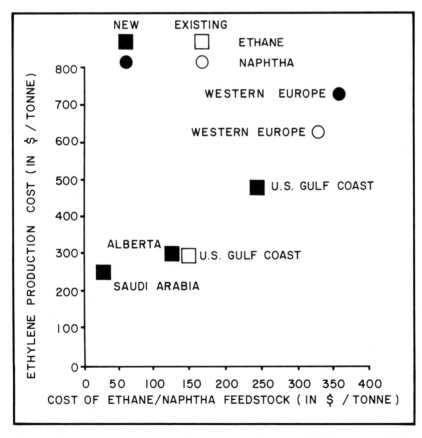

Figure 8.7 Predicted variations in ethylene production cost, 1980 (based on OECD 1985, 66)

range in production costs under 1980 economic conditions for both
naphtha- and ethane-based units with assumed capacities of 450,000
tonnes per year. The diagram incorporates many assumptions[12] and
can only be regarded as indicative. Furthermore, the estimates are of
historic rather than contemporary interest, but they reflect the circumstances in which the decisions to proceed with the Saudi projects
were taken. Nevertheless, it is apparent that production costs vary
considerably depending upon the type of feedstock and location,
with a new plant in Saudi Arabia predicted to have a significant
advantage relative to similar facilities in the United States and,
especially, Western Europe. The advantage over completely amortized
established units is much lower, with the typical ethane unit of
equivalent size on the US Gulf Coast having only marginally higher
costs.

Bearing in mind the export orientation of the Saudi projects, their
success ultimately depends upon delivered costs in target markets
rather than upon production costs. This complicates the usual
forecasting problems arising from the long lead times of major
petrochemical projects. Oil price fluctuations are a major source of
uncertainty. The ability of Saudi plants to compete with local facilities in overseas markets is enhanced as oil prices rise. In the case of
Western Europe, an oil price of approximately $125 per tonne was
the critical threshold for ethylene derivatives in 1990. At this level,
delivered costs (including duty) were broadly similar to those of a
fully depreciated naphtha-based European plant. The balance of
advantage swung progressively in favour of Saudi facilities as the
price rose above this level. Saudi planning in the immediate aftermath of the second oil shock was based upon the presumption that
OPEC would retain control of the international oil market and,
therefore, guarantee the competitive advantage of basic petrochemical
facilities in the Middle East. Ironically, the international oil price
remained well above the threshold of $125 per tonne during the
construction of the Saudi facilities, only to fall below this level soon
after their commissioning (figure 8.2). By late 1990, however, the
Iraqi invasion of Kuwait prompted a return to the levels prevailing
ten years earlier when the Saudi commitment to large-scale petrochemical investments was made. These events emphasize the difficulties facing those responsible for any major investment decision in
petrochemicals. Further uncertainties are related to the estimation of
demand and price levels four to five years ahead and, in the case of
export-oriented projects, the additional problems of forecasting future
transport costs and tariff levels.[13] It is very difficult to know exactly
what estimates were made, at the planning stage, of the anticipated
returns on these projects. However, in evaluating the results of a
wide range of large-scale energy-intensive industrial developments
conceived in the euphoria (from an OPEC perspective) of the

second oil shock, Auty (1990, 88) notes that feasibility studies were 'universally overoptimistic'. Many foreign companies became involved in several ethane-based petrochemical projects established in the Middle East since 1980, but their participation has been based upon more than purely commercial judgements.

Apart from a French involvement in the establishment of the Qatar Petrochemical Company's complex at Umm Sa'id, foreign interest has focused upon Saudi Arabia, where both US and Japanese companies operate as 50/50 partners with the state-owned Saudi Basic Industries Corporation (SABIC) in several different projects (figure 8.6). Similar arrangements were made before the 1979 revolution in Iran between the National Petrochemical Company and a Japanese group led by Mitsui to establish an ethylene and derivatives complex at Bandar Khomeini. The importance attached to foreign partners, especially in Saudi Arabia, contrasts with the emphasis upon state control typical of most developing countries which have entered petrochemicals for the purposes of import substitution (see chapter 7). Where investment is export driven, as in the Middle East, the expertise of foreign companies may be crucial in penetrating overseas markets. Such considerations were certainly important in the case of Saudi Arabia, and the agreements with the various partners in its petrochemical projects all required these partners to assume a heavy initial responsibility for marketing. This responsibility emphasises the apparent paradox that these companies have in many cases been drawn into competing, if not directly with themselves, then certainly with others which are part of the same global organization (such as the chemical subsidiaries of Exxon and Shell in Western Europe). Furthermore, these companies chose to embark upon this strategy at a time when the depressing effect of the second oil shock upon the world economy was creating serious overcapacity problems in their traditional centres of production (see chapter 10).

This paradox, together with the undoubted risks of involvement in the Middle East, subsequently emphasized by the Iran–Iraq War and the invasion of Kuwait, suggests that it was the politics of the oil industry rather than the economics of the petrochemical industry that were decisive in getting the Saudi projects off the ground. Concerns regarding the security of oil supply strongly influenced the actions of both the oil companies and the governments of importing countries in the uncertain economic environment following the second oil shock. It has already been noted in chapter 7 that French and Japanese involvement in promoting the petrochemical ambitions of the oil producing countries received official encouragement as part of a wider objective of securing national political interests in a sensitive area of the world. Corporate, rather than state, diplomacy seems to have guided the actions of the US oil companies. Guaranteed access through negotiated entitlements to Saudi crude oil in amounts linked to the extent of their participation was a major attraction to these companies. The absence of the multinational chemical companies, which could certainly have provided similar expertise, provides circumstantial evidence in support of this conclusion. Of this group only Dow displayed any serious interest, withdrawing in 1982 from negotiations with SABIC to establish an ethylene plant. This suggests that the leverage provided by Saudi domination of world crude oil production and reserves was, for obvious reasons, more effective in dealing with oil companies than with chemical companies.

Overall, the establishment of the petrochemical industry during the late 1970s and the early 1980s in the oil-rich countries in general and in Saudi Arabia in particular rested upon political decisions which changed the economic environment. These petrochemical ambitions were not new. Early declarations of interest (see United Nations 1966; UNIDO 1970b; 1973) were translated into fertilizer projects which were commissioned in several countries before the first oil shock. These and later ethane-based operations have been promoted by Arab governments because they add value to their raw materials and also represent a limited move away from dependence upon oil exports. Chapter 7 emphasized that such projects and the technology they embody have also been viewed as contributing to wider development strategies in which industrialization is regarded as the key to ambitious programmes of economic and social transformation. In some cases, notably the deposed Shah's belief in Iran's destiny as an economic superpower, considerations of prestige have reinforced the political commitment to the industry. It has been demonstrated that the success of the OPEC countries in achieving the major oil price jumps of 1973 and 1979 significantly improved their prospects of fulfilling this commitment because of its impact upon the behaviour of certain multinational companies. Furthermore, it is clear that the assessments of risks and returns applied to the kind of investment made in Saudi Arabia during the 1980s have not followed normal commercial practice. The provision of infrastructure and finance on very favourable terms has meant that these investments have been heavily underwritten by the state, which has also been willing to accept relatively low rates of return.

8.4 US Energy Policy and International Comparative Advantage

The freedom of oil-rich countries to price feedstocks at whatever level is necessary to allow their petrochemical exports to remain competitive in international markets is not shared by other producers. It has been shown that the cost of raw materials to the industry outside these countries broadly reflects trends in the international oil price (see section 8.2). Nevertheless governments have, at various times, influenced the raw material costs of the industry operating within their jurisdiction. In some cases, actions have been designed to promote its initial development. By removing or relaxing taxes upon naphtha feedstocks, both the United Kingdom and Japan, for example, effectively reduced the costs of raw materials to their embryonic petrochemical industries in the late 1940s and 1960s respectively. In other cases, such as South Korea and Taiwan, the main objective has been to protect established industries from some of the adverse effects of the oil price shocks. Despite these examples, political intervention targeted upon the raw material costs of the petrochemical industry has been the exception rather than the rule. The indirect effects of energy policies, framed to achieve wider goals and objectives, have been far more important, even though these effects have not always been intended or anticipated by those responsible for their formulation. The importance of these policies has increased as a result of the oil price shocks as governments in several major countries have attempted to modify the impact of these events upon their economies by intervening in energy markets. In this and the subsequent section an attempt is made to evaluate the effect of policies influencing raw material costs upon the development of the petrochemical industry, and especially upon the economics of operating in different locations. Such policy-based differentials have arisen both within and, more significantly, between countries, contributing to shifts in the regional distribution of the industry at the national level, and affecting comparative advantage, trade and therefore patterns of investment and disinvestment at the global scale. These issues are considered first with reference to the US petrochemical industry and, in the next section, with reference to Canada. The US industry is important not only in a national context, but also because of its major share of the international trade in petrochemicals.[14] In these circumstances, policy effects upon its competitive position have important consequences for the industry in other countries. Canada is an interesting case because it has taken advantage of its hydrocarbon resources to develop an export capability since the first oil shock.

Government regulation has long been a feature of the US oil industry. This characteristic is surprising in view of the aggressive promotion of free enterprise by many of its participants and lobby groups. This apparent contradiction has its origins in the history of the industry. The United States was self-sufficient in oil to the late 1940s and it was therefore able to develop national oil policies regardless of events elsewhere in the world. This traditional self-sufficiency increased sensitivities towards the strategic implications of growing dependence upon imported oil. These sensitivities were exploited by the powerful oil lobby which had its own reasons for wishing to discourage imports of foreign oil. The evolution of US oil policy in response to these various influences is a massive topic (see Nash 1968; Bohi and Russell 1978). Overall this policy has been forced, by the realities of rising energy consumption and a dwindling resource base, to come to terms with increasing dependence upon imported oil and to acknowledge the impossibility of insulating the United States from the international oil system. Acceptance of this situation has, however, been reluctant and various regulations were responsible for periodic shifts in the relationship between domestic and foreign oil prices.

Conservation regulations introduced during the 1930s, especially in Texas, effectively organized oil producers into a state-run cartel which fixed prices by regulating production. After World War II, these institutional controls on output became difficult to sustain as world oil prices dropped below US prices and imports began to encroach upon domestic markets. This competition was unwelcome to US oil producers, who persuaded the federal government first to urge voluntary restraint upon importing companies in 1954 and then to impose a mandatory ceiling in 1959. Subsequent battles over the implementation of this programme resulted in a progressively more complex array of regulations and exceptions which operated until 1972. These measures had several effects, including the promotion of exploration and production, which in turn accelerated the depletion of the country's resource base, and higher oil prices to consumers than would have been the case if cheap imports had been allowed unrestricted entry. The situation changed dramatically with the first oil price shock in 1973, which reversed the price relationship between domestic and imported oil. The US industry no longer needed protection from imports, and controls were lifted in 1973.[15] Despite the increasing significance of imports, which reached a peak of 46.5 per cent of total oil consumption in 1977 (Energy Information Administration 1989), the introduction of price controls on petroleum and petroleum products in 1974 cushioned the impact of the 1973 shock upon consumers. In this new environment it was the consumers rather than the producers who were the principal beneficiaries of government intervention, and price levels were generally lower than in other industrialized countries. This had the predictable consequence of discouraging investment in the domestic industry, and the cycle of policy swings and roundabouts was finally broken in 1981 with a commitment to dismantle the complex structure of government regulations affecting supply, demand and price in the US oil and gas industry. This effectively ended a 30 year effort to insulate the United States from the international oil system and resulted in the convergence of domestic and world oil prices.

Figure 8.8 indicates the net result of these policies since 1968.

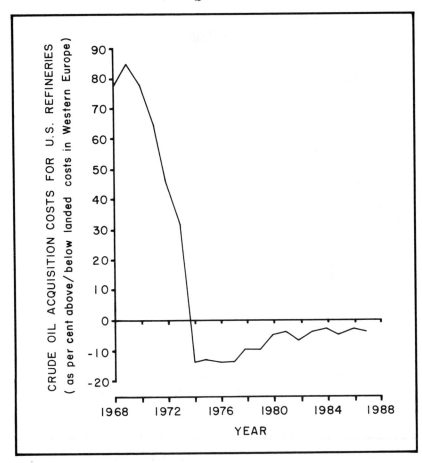

Figure 8.8 Crude oil acquisition costs for US refineries relative to landed cost of oil in Western Europe, 1968–1987

The average landed costs of crude oil in Western Europe provide a yardstick against which US prices, as expressed by average refinery acquisition costs, are measured. The discrepancy would be even more marked if average wellhead price rather than refinery acquisition cost were represented in figure 8.8, since the differential is suppressed by the inclusion of a proportion of imported oil in the feedstock slate to US refineries. Nevertheless, figure 8.8 confirms that the production of refined products in the US was derived from significantly more expensive raw material before 1973. The diagram only begins at 1968 because of the limitations of federal statistics, but the premium paid by US refineries certainly persisted throughout the 1950s and 1960s when the petrochemical industry was developing. The relationship was sharply reversed following the first oil shock, but deregulation

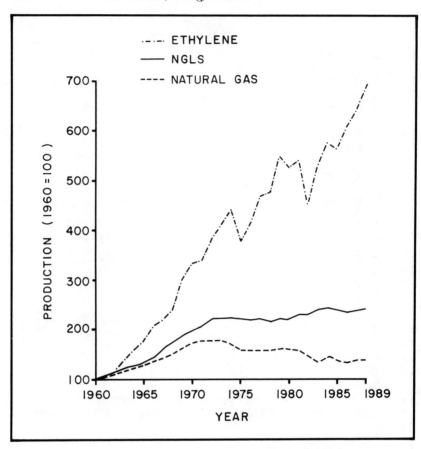

Figure 8.9 US natural gas, NGLs and ethylene production, 1960–1989 (1960 = 100)

has resulted in a convergence towards European (and world) levels since 1981. The differentials indicated in figure 8.8 have influenced the competitive position of the US petrochemical industry in overseas markets. The various regulations have also affected individual US producers in different ways, depending upon the nature and sources of their feedstock and, in some cases, upon their location.

Raw material availability, initially from oil refineries and then from natural gas processing plants, was decisive in the concentration of petrochemical capacity in the Gulf Coast region during the 1940s and 1950s (see chapters 4 and 6). Figure 8.9 plots trends in natural gas, NGLs and ethylene production. The rapid growth of natural gas guaranteed abundant NGLs which could be extracted as required, but by-product refinery gases continued to meet a significant proportion of the industry's feedstock needs during the 1950s and ethane recovery increased slowly. This abundance was reflected in very low prices (figure 8.3). Indeed, feedstock price was not really an issue because the market could absorb as much as the industry could produce. This market extended beyond the United States. The industry was not yet established in Japan, and Western Europe was a major importer (see chapter 5). With no foreign competition, plentiful feedstocks and an apparently insatiable market, raw material costs were of little concern to the US industry at this stage of its development.

The spectacular growth of the industry during the 1960s prompted concern about the inadequacy of its raw material supplies towards the end of the decade (see Kirby 1970; Petrochemical Energy Group 1974). Dow, for example, 'thought that by the eighties natural gas would either not be available – at any price – or would be rationed away from the chemical companies' (Morner 1977, 315). Such assessments reflected the fact that ethylene output was increasing at more than twice the rate of natural gas production (figure 8.9) and it encouraged several companies to consider naphtha as an alternative feedstock and to invest in oil-based cracking plants. Non-integrated chemical companies such as Dow and Union Carbide, which were not involved in oil production and refining, were more concerned about NGLs supplies, especially ethane, than the chemical subsidiaries of oil companies such as Exxon and Shell, which had access to captive naphtha from their own refineries. The problem was aggravated by the Mandatory Oil Import Program (MOIP) introduced in 1959. By limiting access to cheaper foreign oil, this raised the input prices of US refineries (figure 8.8) which in turn made their output of naphtha and gas oil more expensive than the corresponding fractions in Western Europe and Japan. Higher gasoline demand increased the pressure on naphtha supplies and further inflated its price as a chemical feedstock. This situation led to a protracted campaign, which revealed significant differences in the positions and interests of individual companies within the industry, to secure free access to foreign naphtha and a relaxation of the restrictions imposed by the MOIP. The so-called Heavy Liquids Program was introduced in 1972 to allow imports of foreign crude and refined fractions designated for petrochemical use.

It is difficult to separate objective analysis from vested interest in evaluating the arguments regarding the overall effect of the MOIP upon the development of the US petrochemical industry. The extent of the shift from gas- to oil-based feedstocks, arising from doubts about ethane supplies, was probably inhibited by uncertainty over access to foreign naphtha (Brown 1970). However, claims that protection of the US oil industry by the MOIP undermined the international competitiveness of the petrochemical industry and diverted investment overseas were exaggerated (see Kirby 1970). Raw materials were a less important element in the total costs of basic petrochemical production during the 1960s, and the differences between feedstock prices in the United States and elsewhere were probably not sufficient to induce any major redistribution of investment by the multinationals. It is true that the 1960s witnessed a substantial increase in the involvement of US companies in Western Europe, but this was a defensive response to indigenous developments in countries such as the United Kingdom and a recognition of the need to establish a manufacturing presence to maintain a market share previously served by exports (see chapter 9). There is no evidence that this investment was motivated by lower raw material costs in Western Europe.

One development that certainly was influenced by such considerations was the emergence of Puerto Rico as a new oil refining and petrochemical centre. The island was exempt from the restrictions of the MOIP and was conveniently placed to receive low cost oil and naphtha from Venezuela and Curaçao. By virtue of its constitutional relationship with the United States, the Commonwealth of Puerto Rico has unrestricted access to the mainland market. This freedom from US customs duties has been used to promote the industrialization of the island ever since Operation Bootstrap in the 1950s. Several companies, including Union Carbide and Phillips, established petrochemical facilities on Puerto Rico in the late 1960s. These developments were inspired by the differential between the higher feedstock prices on the Gulf Coast and the lower ones on the island. This differential, reinforced by various investment incentives, provided sufficient margin to cover the shipping charges incurred in delivering petrochemical products to the mainland. Ironically, this advantage disappeared after the oil price shocks when Puerto Rico's geographical position isolated its refineries and petrochemical plants from the mainland raw materials that were now cheaper than the Venezuelan feedstocks which had provided the original justification for their establishment (figure 8.8). This reversal precipitated a collapse of these activities that was almost as rapid as their rise (see chapter 11).

What was bad for Puerto Rico was good for the rest of the US petrochemical industry. Furthermore, the various arguments which had been used to favour investment in oil- rather than gas-based cracking plants in the late 1960s and early 1970s were invalidated by the new situation in which US feedstocks became cheaper than those available to producers in Western Europe and Japan. Price controls applied to both NGLs and naphtha, but their immediate influence was to make the former more attractive as petrochemical feedstocks. On the other hand, by discouraging exploration and production, artificially low natural gas prices resurrected fears of a future ethane shortage. These conflicting short- and long-term signals encouraged many producers to hedge their bets by modifying existing and designing new cracking plants to operate on both oil- and gas-based feedstocks.

The most important consequence of the interaction of the oil price shocks and the continued regulation of oil and gas prices in the United States was upon competitive relations at the international scale. By the mid 1970s, US domination of the industry had been challenged by Western Europe and Japan which, taken together, broadly matched US petrochemical capacity. As the volume and complexity of international trade increased, so its participants became more sensitive to political distortions of comparative advantage. US energy policy was widely regarded in Western Europe and Japan as such a distortion, especially in view of the sharply increased importance of feedstock and energy in the costs of petrochemical production after the oil price shocks. Not all of the observed differences in feedstock costs (figures 8.2 and 8.3) could be attributed to policy factors. Refinery economics in the United States are very different from those in Western Europe and Japan, mainly as a result of the emphasis upon gasolines. This has complex influences upon the price and availability of feedstocks to the petrochemical industry. The bulk of the naphtha used for petrochemical purposes in the United States is sold within vertically integrated organizations. Purchases on the spot market are less important than in Western Europe. This contrast was a significant influence upon feedstock prices at the time of the oil shocks because the operations of the spot market tended to magnify fluctuations attributable to changes in the price of crude oil. The flexibility of the US petrochemical industry and its extensive choice of indigenous feedstocks, especially within the vast complex of oil refineries, gas plants and pipelines of the Gulf Coast, is a further source of competitive advantage relative to the much more fragmented industries of Western Europe and Japan. Nevertheless, even US observers acknowledge that these natural advantages were strongly reinforced by energy policy (see Langston 1983; Campbell 1983). It is virtually impossible to isolate the individual sources of comparative advantage, but there is no doubt that feedstock costs were significantly lower than their European counterparts in the late 1970s (figures 8.2 and 8.3) and that this was largely responsible for a sharp increase in the volume of US exports, especially in the immediate aftermath of the second oil price shock (Campbell 1983, 28). This increased competition in their domestic markets was particularly unwelcome in Western Europe and Japan as a result of the effect of the recession of the early 1980s upon their petrochemical industries (see chapter 10).

The phased deregulation of the US oil and gas industry which started in 1981 was more or less completed by the end of the decade. This process progressively reduced the differential between US and world energy prices which was, in turn, reflected in the price of petrochemical feedstocks. The complexities of petrochemical economics are such that this has not resulted in the emergence of global pricing for key commodities such as ethylene, and significant geographical differences remain. Nevertheless, the role of US energy policies, which first increased and then reduced the raw material costs of the US petrochemical industry relative to its counterparts in Western Europe and Japan over more than 20 years in the 1960s and 1970s, in contributing to variations in international comparative advantage was progressively diminished during the 1980s. There is, however, no guarantee that this will be a permanent situation. Perhaps the principal lesson of the recent past is the speed with which the balance of economic advantage may change between one location and another in this raw-material-based industry. Generally speaking, these shifts have occurred at the international scale, but the development of the Canadian industry since the mid 1970s illustrates the way in which domestic policy responses to international events may affect competitive relations at the national level.

8.5 Canada: the Politics of Intranational Comparative Advantage

Although the Canadian petrochemical industry is concentrated in three separate centres of production (figure 8.10),[16] it is the dichotomy between its eastern (i.e. Sarnia/Montreal) and western (i.e. Alberta) branches which is crucial to an understanding of its development (see Seifried 1989). The origins of the industry in Canada may be traced to styrene and butadiene plants built at Sarnia as part of the wartime synthetic rubber programme (figure 4.2). These units subsequently became the focus of post-war petrochemical expansion, together with a second, smaller complex established at Montreal in the 1950s (Shell Oil Co. of Canada 1956). Both of these complexes were based on naphtha feedstocks derived from local refineries and their output mainly served domestic markets. The commissioning of two large ethylene plants in Alberta in 1979 and 1984 represented a radical change in the character and distribution of the industry within Canada. These, together with associated downstream facilities, were primarily conceived as export plants and were based upon ethane feedstock extracted from the province's natural gas. Thus the industry in Alberta developed not only for different reasons, but also from a different raw material base, than its counterpart in eastern Canada.

The idea of establishing a substantial petrochemical industry in Alberta has a long history and is linked to the economic development aspirations of successive provincial governments, which have been

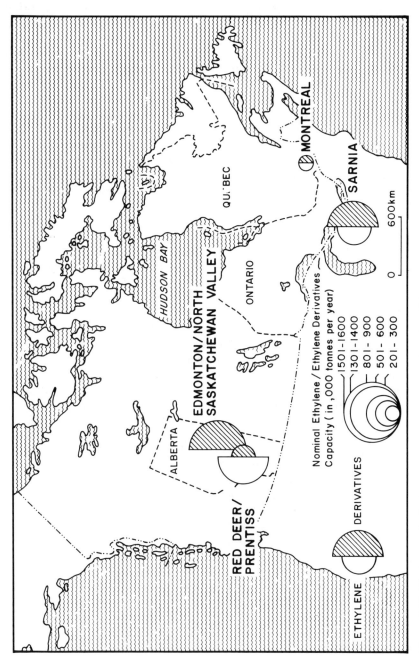

Figure 8.10 Ethylene and ethylene derivatives capacity in Canada, 1990

anxious to promote oil- and gas-based industrialization (see section 11.3). Various companies, including Dow, were actively exploring these possibilities immediately before the first oil shock, which encouraged them to proceed rapidly from the feasibility stage to the submission of specific proposals. These were analogous to developments in the Middle East to the extent that they were driven by perceptions of a raw material cost advantage (Chapman 1985a). This advantage appeared to be even more substantial immediately after the second oil price jump, when Alberta became the focus of a corporate scramble for access to its ethane and the ethylene manufactured from this resource (see section 9.5 and Chapman 1985b). This scramble was motivated by both political and economic considerations. For many companies, investment in Alberta was a more attractive approach to obtaining low cost raw materials than involvement in Saudi Arabia. The risks of direct investment in the Middle East were considerable, and the obligation to enter into a partnership with a state-owned enterprise was a further deterrent to many. By contrast, Alberta was widely regarded, in the uncertain atmosphere created by the oil price shocks, as one of the few politically secure sources of uncommitted ethane in the world. Its attractions were reinforced by the response of the Canadian federal government to these shocks.

Government regulation of oil and gas prices in Canada coincided with the introduction of similar measures in the United States, and domestic prices were set by agreement with the Alberta government in 1973.[17] The original intention was simply to ameliorate the impact of the external shock upon the Canadian economy by allowing domestic prices to reach international levels within four years (Energy, Mines and Resources Canada 1976), but the gap actually widened as a result of the second oil price shock. This prompted the introduction of the National Energy Program (NEP) in 1980, which had the principal objective of insulating Canada from the international energy market (Energy, Mines and Resources Canada 1980). The NEP created a new pricing regime for domestic oil and gas involving incremental rises every six months (figure 8.11). The schedule of price increases anticipated a substantial rise in the price of oil to Canadian consumers, but the architects of the NEP were confident that the international price would also continue to rise, ensuring that Canadian prices would remain lower. This assumption proved false and this error of judgement was decisive in the ultimate abandonment of the NEP. It was also important in determining the impact of the NEP upon the Canadian petrochemical industry.

Government intervention in Canadian energy markets initially benefited the national petrochemical industry by suppressing both oil- and gas-based feedstock prices below world levels (Steinbaum and Rothman 1984). The NEP, however, had a differential effect

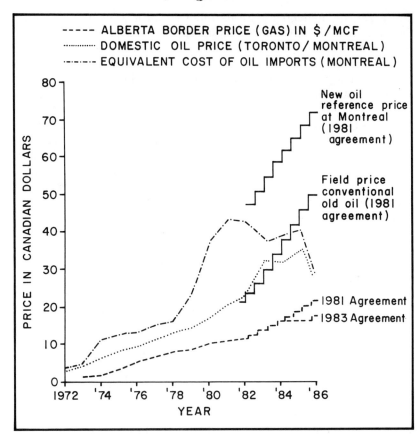

Figure 8.11 Canadian oil and gas prices, 1972–1986

upon its eastern and western branches because the schedule of six monthly increases in gas prices stipulated in the NEP involved a more gradual rise than the corresponding programme for oil. This difference was related to the strategic objective of encouraging a shift away from oil to natural gas in patterns of energy consumption to take account of the relative domestic reserve positions of the two hydrocarbons. An incidental effect of this policy was to further improve the economics of the gas-based petrochemical industry in Alberta, since the regulated domestic price for natural gas was the principal variable determining the cost of its ethane feedstock. These controlled price increases seemed to guarantee a substantial and growing cost advantage in view of the more rapid projected upward trend in international oil prices, and this expectation was reflected in the enthusiasm of potential petrochemical investors in Alberta at the beginning of the 1980s.

In fact, the delivered price of imported oil to Canadian refineries began to fall in 1980 whilst domestic crude continued to rise in price under the terms of the NEP (figure 8.11). As the gap progressively narrowed, oil-based petrochemical producers in eastern Canada found themselves committed by contractual obligations to purchase domestic raw materials at a time when imported feedstocks could be obtained more cheaply on the spot market. This squeeze made them increasingly uncompetitive both in international terms and relative to operations in Alberta, which used cheaper gas-based feedstock. The cost of feedstocks used by the largest ethylene producer in eastern Canada in 1982, for example, was Canadian $150 million more than the cost of a weighted average mix of feedstocks used by an equivalent plant on the US Gulf Coast (Wood 1986).

In these circumstances, it is not surprising that companies heavily involved in the Montreal and Sarnia complexes were first to express dissatisfaction with the continued operation of the NEP in the face of declining international oil prices, and a formal approach was made to the federal government in October 1982 calling for a more flexible policy which would distinguish between the petrochemical and conventional energy uses of oil and gas. This appeal was resented by most of the participants in the Alberta complex because it was felt that any assistance to the eastern producers may have provoked retaliatory action by other countries, thereby threatening the markets of the export-oriented western industry. This view was taken despite the fact that the same trends in international oil prices which were affecting the eastern producers were also undermining the viability of the Alberta complex. Indeed, the direct link between the cost of ethane and the regulated six monthly increases in natural gas prices (i.e. the Alberta border price in figure 8.11) meant that the raw material costs of the Alberta complex were moving in the opposite direction to corresponding costs elsewhere in the world. This situation threatened the viability of the entire complex, and the continued weakness of the international oil price convinced its participants that the NEP was damaging to their interests as well as those of the eastern producers.[18] Accordingly, the two branches of the industry attempted to reconcile their differences in a unified submission to the federal government which stressed 'the need to obtain market related prices for feedstock' (Petrochemical Industry Task Force 1984, iii).

Changing political circumstances within Canada, rather than the representations of the petrochemical industry, resulted in the abandonment of the NEP and a commitment to the deregulation of oil and gas prices in 1985. This change of direction was consistent with similar, earlier moves in the United States. Indeed, the most important general effect of deregulation has been to ensure that feedstock costs to the Canadian industry will be linked to, and effectively determined by, trends in the United States – a connection reinforced by the commercial ties of common ownership linking several of the principal corporate actors on both sides of the border (see Chapman 1988; 1989). Overall, questions of feedstock supply and cost have been the principal strategic concerns of the Canadian petrochemical industry since the first oil price shock – a characteristic it shares with the industry in other countries. The recent history of the industry, especially between 1975 and 1985, demonstrates the way in which government intervention in energy markets has been a major influence upon these concerns, not least because it has, at various times, affected producers in different locations in different ways.

8.6 Conclusions

Spatial variations in the availability and cost of raw materials have traditionally been viewed as a major influence upon the location of certain types of manufacturing industry. In the case of petrochemicals, this influence operates at two different scales. At the national level, location decisions have been strongly influenced by proximity to feedstock, whether derived from natural gas processing plants or from oil refineries, for reasons discussed in chapter 6. The role of raw materials is, however, less evident at the international scale where interactions of technology on the supply side and markets on the demand side have resulted in a general correlation between the distribution of the industry and levels of economic development (see chapter 5). Nevertheless, it is clear that the sharp increases in the international oil price in 1973 and 1979 had a bigger impact upon petrochemical manufacture than upon most other sectors. These events represented a parametric shock which changed the course of the industry's long term evolution, including, to a limited extent, its distribution. The emergence of new centres of petrochemical production, notably in Saudi Arabia and Canada, was the most obvious of these changes. These investments were conceived to serve export markets and, as such, the motivating factors were quite different from those driving the development of the industry in other countries prior to the oil price shocks. Nevertheless, the competitive relations of the industry within and between established centres of production were also affected by this parametric shock. These effects partly reflected technical factors, especially the distinction between the predominantly gas-based industry of the United States and the oil-based industries of Western Europe and Japan. They were also shaped by the reactions of governments in oil consuming countries to the oil price increases. These reactions were determined not by any particular concern for the petrochemical industry, but by wider considerations of energy policy. The facts that the development of the industry has been influenced by the oil price shocks and that the nature of this influence has been modified, often in an almost incidental way, by the actions of governments, emphasize that industry evolution cannot be explained exclusively in terms of the operation of some kind of internal technological and economic imperative. External events, determined by political rather than economic considerations, may have essentially unpredictable effects on patterns of industry development. They are, therefore, impossible to accommodate within deterministic evolutionary models. Furthermore, in attempting to generalize about such patterns, there is a danger of relegating firms within the industry, which are responsible for creating these patterns, to the status of economic pawns in a game over which they have no control. This is obviously inappropriate for an industry in which several of the world's largest business organizations are major participants. The next chapter takes a more disaggregated view by examining corporate strategies within the context of the broader influences considered to this point.

Notes

1 The boiling range refers to the upper and lower temperature limits within which a specified group of hydrocarbon compounds passes from the liquid to the vapour state at normal atmospheric pressure. Light distillates such as naphtha have an approximate range of 30°C to 205°C. A fully flexible modern cracking plant may accept feedstocks from ethane, with a boiling point of −88.6°C, to gas oil, with a boiling range of 180°C to 370°C.
2 The data in figure 8.1 should be regarded as indicative of general trends, bearing in mind the difficulties of establishing any single ethylene price at the scale of the United States and Western Europe.
3 See chapter 6 for a discussion of the assumptions upon which table 6.2 is based.
4 Nevertheless, the US International Trade Commission data for ethane do provide a reasonable indication of average transaction prices.
5 The construction of several new naphtha/gas-oil-based ethylene plants in the United States at the beginning of the 1970s was, for example, stimulated by an anticipated ethane shortage which failed to materialize.
6 The detailed assumptions upon which this analysis is based are described in OECD (1985, 58–65).
7 Some of the implications of low rates of capacity utilization are discussed in chapter 10.
8 Small-scale petrochemical operations using refinery gases started at Abadan in Iran as early as 1971.
9 It is important to stress that, because of the very different economics of gas- and oil-based cracking plants, naphtha and ethane are not directly comparable as feedstocks for ethylene.
10 Stauffer (1988, 7) notes that Saudi pricing policy requires industrial gas

price contracts to be renegotiated when a venture reaches a threshold rate of return of approximately 15 per cent. However, it is the starting price which influences the initial investment decision.

11 It is worth noting that the Saudi plants have performed much better in this respect than facilities elsewhere in North Africa and the Middle East.

12 See note 6.

13 These uncertainties are emphasized by the continuing efforts of the Gulf Cooperation Council to establish a free trade area with the EEC, mainly to improve market access for petrochemical products. This diplomacy has created tensions within the EEC between DGI (External relations), which favours such an arrangement, and DGIII (Industry), which opposes it.

14 For example, the US accounted for 22 per cent (by value) of total world exports of ethylene and benzene derivatives in 1985 (US International Trade Commission 1987, 2–6).

15 In fact, import controls were lifted *before* the first oil price shock in October 1973. This decision was a consequence of an energy shortage which was itself created by institutional factors influencing the supply of and demand for natural gas.

16 There are two separate centres in Alberta, one near Red Deer and the other in the valley of the North Saskatchewan River near Edmonton. These centres are linked by pipelines.

17 The National Oil Policy from 1961 to 1973, which divided the Canadian market into two halves served by domestic and imported oil, did not involve substantial government interference in pricing.

18 The dichotomy between eastern and western interests was not always clear-cut, since many firms were and are represented in both branches of the industry. Nevertheless, these differences are real, even if their relative significance varies with corporate circumstances.

9
Corporate Strategies and Internationalization

Previous chapters have emphasized the role of government as an influence upon the international distribution of the petrochemical industry as reflected in the direct involvement of the public sector in many developing countries and in such indirect effects upon comparative advantage as trade and energy policies. Despite the undoubted significance of government in modifying the business environment of the private sector, large multinational corporations are the principal agents of change in many global industries. Several of the largest such corporations are involved in petrochemicals, and it follows that their strategies have played an important role in shaping the development of the industry at the international scale. Certainly, the chemical industry accounts for a significant proportion of total foreign direct investment and it figures prominently in overseas investment by both US and British companies (Dicken 1986, 66 and 72). It is very difficult to estimate what part of this is accounted for by petrochemicals, but it is reasonable to infer that the share is substantial.

9.1 Industry Evolution, Corporate Strategies and International Location

Table 9.1 provides an indication of the importance of foreign direct investment in the petrochemical industry by focusing upon a single product. It shows the proportion of world ethylene capacity at selected dates accounted for by foreign direct investment (i.e. capacity located in one country that is ultimately owned by a company based in another). This illustration probably tends to underestimate the overall significance of foreign direct investment in the industry because of the tendency for such basic processing operations to be regarded in many countries as strategic functions which should be carried out by national companies whether in the public or the private sector

Table 9.1 Foreign direct investment in ethylene, 1950–1990

Year	Ethylene capacity (thousand tonnes)			Foreign direct investment as %	
	World[a]	World excluding US	Foreign direct investment[b]	of world	of world excluding US
1950	757	14	0	0	0
1960	3,696	896	290	7.8	32.4
1970	19,459	10,160	2,830	14.5	27.8
1980	42,372	24,894	5,540	13.1	22.2
1990	53,259	34,909	5,554	10.4	15.9

[a] Excluding centrally planned economies.
[b] Shell's operations in the US are assumed to be 100 per cent US owned. Elsewhere they are assumed to be Dutch/UK-owned on a 60/40 basis.
Sources: Various

(chapter 7). It is, however, impracticable to obtain corresponding time-series data for downstream products. Various assumptions are incorporated in table 9.1. For example, ownership of capacity is split on a pro rata basis in the case of joint ventures so that only half of the capacity of a specific plant is regarded as foreign direct investment where one of the partners in a 50/50 venture is headquartered in another country. This is obviously somewhat artificial, but table 9.1 does give a reasonable general impression of the importance of foreign direct investment. In fact, there is no foreign direct investment in ethylene in the United States, and the level of involvement in Japan is limited to minority participation in joint ventures with domestic interests. The bulk of this activity is concentrated in Western Europe. Indeed, more than one-third of world ethylene capacity outside the United States and Japan was foreign owned in 1960 and 1970, much of it by US companies. These proportions have subsequently declined, partly as a result of a strategic withdrawal from basic petrochemicals by some of these companies and partly as a result of the rise of new national producers in several developing countries. Nevertheless, the table emphasizes that foreign direct investment has played a significant role in the spatial evolution of petrochemical manufacture at the international scale. This chapter attempts to describe and explain this process, which may be conceived as a kind of corporate dispersal from the core economies in which the industry first developed, and especially from the United States.

There is a massive literature on the reasons for foreign direct investment which is reflected in Dunning's (1988) formulation of an 'eclectic paradigm' to account for the phenomenon. There are two basic types of overseas investment – market oriented, and supply or cost oriented. The former is intended to influence the revenue side of the firm's operations and the latter is focused upon the input side.

These two principal motivations for foreign direct investment may be linked to the product and industry life-cycle concepts. One of the most obvious ways of increasing sales in the face of the slower growth rates associated with maturity is to seek out new geographical markets, and there is no doubt that the bulk of foreign direct investment in manufacturing has been associated with this kind of horizontal expansion across national boundaries. More recently, the life-cycle concept has been applied in a very different way to account for cost-oriented investments in which mature, standardized manufacturing operations have been established in places such as South East Asia to take advantage of cheap labour. Supply-oriented investments may be regarded as a special case of cost orientation in resource-based industries. They are normally motivated by a desire to secure access to a localized resource. The locational pull of this resource may, however, be radically altered by some kind of discontinuity in the industry's development such as the oil price shock described in the preceding chapter.

The connections between foreign direct investment and life-cycle concepts are important. On the one hand, the evolution of industries is ultimately determined by decisions of individual economic actors that are perceived to be rational within the context of prevailing economic circumstances. On the other hand, these circumstances are themselves determined by certain basic forces, implicit in the life-cycle concept, which drive the development of industries. Thus the behaviour, and specifically the locational behaviour, of firms rests upon foundations which are, in a sense, part of this external dynamic. This is not to deny that large firms, especially in oligopolistic situations, cannot shape the development of the industries in which they are involved, but simply to emphasize that their strategic choices are frequently constrained and directed by a kind of evolutionary momentum at industry level.

9.2 Serving Foreign Markets

The general relationship between market size and the spatial evolution of the petrochemical industry at the international scale has already been discussed (see section 5.4). It was noted that the industry tends first to be established in countries with the largest domestic markets and then to trickle down a hierarchy of market size (figures 5.6 and 5.7). No attempt was made to distinguish between the respective roles of private sector companies and state enterprises in contributing to the observed pattern or to isolate the role of foreign, as opposed to national, investment. Although state intervention, motivated by a combination of economic and political considerations, has certainly accelerated the international development of the industry by effectively disregarding technology-based market size thresholds for petrochemical production (see section 7.4), foreign investments by multinational enterprises based in the United States and Western Europe have contributed to the process. Most of this investment has been market led, but it is important to recognize that direct investment in foreign production facilities is only one of three basic strategies for serving overseas markets. Before focusing upon the contribution of such investment to the international dispersal of the industry, it is desirable to place it in the context of the alternative approaches of licensing proprietary technology to foreign producers and exporting from domestic facilities.

The inevitable erosion of technological monopolies is associated with the adoption of a progressively more relaxed attitude to licensing on the part of innovating companies. Nevertheless, it has already been shown that in petrochemicals most producing companies (as opposed to non-producers such as chemical engineering consultancies and contractors) are reluctant to make their technology available to others until threatened by competing technologies (see sections 5.2 and 7.1). This implies that the preferred initial strategy in meeting a perceived foreign demand will be either exports or investment in overseas facilities rather than licensing.[1] Dow, for example, has always been cautious in its licensing policies, and this caution drew the company into overseas production during the 1950s as a consequence of the efforts of foreign manufacturers and entrepreneurs to obtain permission to use its technology (Whitehead 1968, 219).

Notwithstanding such pressures encouraging foreign direct investment, there is no doubt that Dow, like the rest of the companies involved in the post-war expansion of the US petrochemical industry, enjoyed substantial and increasing exports during the 1950s and the early 1960s. Imports were negligible. This is not surprising in view of the industry's flying start in the United States (see chapter 4). Figure 9.1 indicates US trade in petrochemicals since 1972. The data are based on aggregate statistics for the four-digit SIC codes which most closely correspond to accepted definitions of the petrochemical industry.[2] Much more detailed data are published by the Department of Commerce, but these tend to confuse rather than clarify because they are influenced by circumstances specific to individual products. Much of the period covered by figure 9.1 was especially favourable for the US industry, which benefited from the effect of domestic energy policy in suppressing the impact of the oil price shocks upon its feedstock costs (see section 8.4). Thus petrochemical imports were approximately one-third the value of exports after the first oil shock, and the ratio fell to almost one-quarter in 1980 when the raw material cost advantage was further enhanced after the second oil shock. However, figure 9.1 shows a reversal of this trend in the 1980s as the ratio of imports to exports rose above 0.5. This still

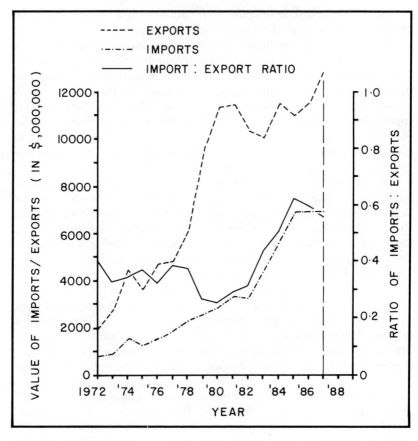

Figure 9.1 US trade in petrochemicals, 1972–1987 (from data in US Department of Commerce 1988, 12–3)

means, of course, that the United States exports twice as much as it imports, but its traditional dominance of world petrochemical markets is expected to progressively weaken, and the reduction of its positive trade balance became a matter of policy concern during the 1980s (see US International Trade Commission 1985b; 1987; MIT Commission on Industrial Productivity 1989). This trend is expected to continue as a consequence of diminished opportunities for export as the industry develops in other countries and of the growth of imports from new raw-material-based producers. A substantial proportion of the increased imports during the 1980s were, for example, derived from Alberta and took the form of intracorporate transfers by US companies such as Dow and Union Carbide which have played a major part in the expansion of the Canadian industry.

Stobaugh (1970; 1988) has used the experience of the US industry to postulate 'a neotechnology account of international trade' which explores the relationships between the geographical origins of technology, patterns of trade and foreign direct investment. He argues that foreign direct investment typically follows an initial phase during which foreign markets are served by exports. Such investment is frequently a defensive reaction to the entry of local competition within these markets.[3] Thus the initial trade surplus is based upon a technological advantage and the erosion of this advantage leads to the decline of the early phase of 'technology-gap' shipments. This analysis suggests that although market growth is obviously important in stimulating foreign direct investment, the decision to replace exports by overseas production is directly linked to the diffusion of technology (see sections 5.2 and 7.1). In the case of the US chemical industry this was reflected in a fundamental shift in the relationship between the values of exports and foreign production during the 1960s. In 1957, sales of chemicals and allied products from US plants abroad were 1.75 times the value of exports from facilities in the United States itself; ten years later the ratio had increased to 3.2 in the context of a tripling in the combined value of total foreign sales from both sources during the same period (Spitz 1988, 370). This implies a substantial rise in the level of foreign direct investment. It is important to stress that it is not only the major US-based oil and chemical companies which have established manufacturing facilities in foreign markets. Similar pressures, which became apparent somewhat later because of the chronology of the industry's evolution, have prompted a corresponding strategic response by their European counterparts, a response which has included direct investment in North America.

9.3 Government Policies and Foreign Direct Investment

Whatever factors may encourage a shift from exports to foreign production as a means of serving overseas markets in a world free from political and institutional influences upon trade and investment are reinforced by the presence of such influences in reality. The most important policy influences favouring foreign direct investment are normally associated with the actions of the recipients of such investment, but the willingness of major companies to start manufacturing oveseas may be affected by government initiatives taken in their home country. High levels of foreign direct investment were indicative of the US dominance of the international petrochemical industry in the 1950s and especially the 1960s, but the implementation of the Marshall Plan indirectly fostered the growth of the industry in Western Europe (see section 4.3) and the Eisenhower administration subsequently used tax concessions to encourage foreign investment by US companies. Private capital was effectively recruited in the pursuit of US foreign policy objectives 'on the assumption that the establishment of financial stability and industrial development, particularly in Europe and Latin America, would ultimately reduce the need for American economic and military aid and thus reduce government spending' (Taylor and Sudnik 1984, 190). Company histories emphasize that these tax concessions were taken into account in boardroom discussions of foreign expansion (see Whitehead 1968, 219) and there is no doubt that Latin America and Western Europe were the principal destinations for US petrochemical investment in the 1950s and 1960s. On the other hand, Sorey (1980) notes, with reference to Dow, that increasing foreign direct investment almost inevitably leads to a divergence between perceptions of national and corporate interests. Thus, by the early 1970s, increasing concern was being expressed in the United States about the diversion of investment and, by implication, employment to foreign countries, a concern which became central to the debate over the 'deindustrialization of America' in the 1980s (see Bluestone and Harrison 1982).

The factors influencing the attitudes of host governments towards inward investment in petrochemicals have already been discussed in chapter 7. It was shown that these attitudes tend to change through time. Some of the earliest petrochemical producing countries outside North America and Western Europe, such as Argentina, initially welcomed such investment as a means of establishing a vital new industry and, more optimistically, of securing access to its technology. As this technology became more widely available in the 1960s and 1970s, however, state enterprises assumed the primary role in the international dispersal of the industry. Nevertheless, opportunities remained for the major multinationals to participate in the expansion of national petrochemical industries in such countries as Brazil and Taiwan. The opportunities were, on the one hand, constrained by policies which reserved certain activities and products to indigenous enterprises and, on the other hand, promoted by tariff barriers offering protection from competing imports. Although it has already been observed that the diffusion of technology relaxed an important constraint upon the international dispersal of the industry (see sections 5.2 and 7.1), the concurrent trend to progressively larger units (see chapter 6) had the opposite effect by raising the market size threshold required to sustain optimal levels of production. Tariffs have been used to overcome this difficulty, allowing small plants, or large units operating below capacity, to supply a protected market with relatively high cost products. In many cases, this strategy has been used to nurture an indigenous state-owned industry (see section 7.4), but it has also been employed to attract foreign direct investment.

The part played by foreign direct investment in the origins of the petrochemical industry in Latin America has already been described (see section 7.3). Almost without exception, the principal role in its subsequent development in these countries passed to public or private national enterprises. In Australia, however, foreign companies, initially attracted by import substitution policies, have remained the dominant force. Figure 5.6 emphasizes the apparently early establishment of the Australian industry relative to the hierarchy of national market size. Belgium, which is well placed with respect to the economic core of Western Europe, is the only smaller market in which ethylene manufacture started before Australia. Furthermore, the bulk of the Australian market is itself divided between the two major metropolitan areas of Sydney and Melbourne and this is reflected in the distribution of petrochemical capacity. In these circumstances, it is not surprising that the Australian industry has, from the very beginning, been characterized by small plants and high costs. This problem was aggravated by the fact that its establishment during the 1960s more or less coincided with the rush to exploit economies of scale in North America, Western Europe and Japan (see chapter 6). The consequences of this from the point of view of the industry were offset by government policies which provided tariff protection, and the petrochemical industry was an important strand of a wider objective of promoting industrialization by import substitution. These policies persuaded many of the major players in the industry, such as Dow, Esso, Monsanto, Union Carbide and Shell, to construct wholly owned or majority-owned facilities in Australia. This flurry of foreign direct investment in the 1960s was probably accelerated by the kind of competitive reactions described in the next section, but there is little doubt that the initial interest of the multinationals was stimulated by the actions of government, which shifted the balance of advantage towards local production and made it difficult for these same organizations to continue supplying the Australian market by exports from their existing facilities (Rimmer 1968). Once it was established, however, the constraints of the relatively small domestic market, together with the emergence in the 1980s of major export producers, meant that the Australian petrochemical industry has required almost permanent tariff protection to survive.

9.4 Markets and International Location Strategies

Government policies may accelerate foreign direct investment by large companies in response to perceived market opportunities, but, viewed from a corporate perspective, such investment is often a natural route to growth. The logic of product and industry life cycles suggests that companies are both pushed overseas as domestic markets mature and rates of growth slacken and also pulled by the attractions of repeating the cycle in an undeveloped market. Indeed, it has been argued that the deceleration of consumption in developed market economies has been the driving force behind the internationalization of production in many sectors (Clairmonte and Cavanagh 1985). The empirical evidence in support of this generalization is considerable. It includes studies in the business history tradition of the behaviour of individual companies (see Chandler 1986) as well as statistical analyses relating aggregate patterns of foreign direct investment to various measures of market size (see Agarwal 1980). Overall, it is apparent that 'the more developed a country, the more attractive it is to investors' (Moran 1979, 161).[4] Adjacent countries seem to be more attractive than distant ones; it has been shown that Canada and Mexico, for example, are the preferred first destinations for US companies venturing into foreign production (Kravis and Lipsey 1982). Indeed, the inter-related influences of market size and geographical proximity have been incorporated in various models which represent the spatial growth of large corporations from national to international scales of operation (see Chapman and Walker 1991, 101–5).

International location strategies are influenced not only by market trends, but also by the actions of competitors. It has already been noted that foreign direct investment is often a defensive reaction to the emergence of domestic competition in markets previously served by exports (see section 9.2). The imperative to respond is frequently reinforced by government policies in these markets (see section 9.3). Competition may also come from other multinationals, and the phenomena of follow-the-leader behaviour and oligopolistic reaction are well documented. These ideas are usually attributed to Knickerbocker (1973), and rest upon the proposition that a decision to establish production in a given market by a leading enterprise in an oligopolistic industry is likely to precipitate similar moves by its principal competitors. It can be shown that such imitative behaviour is a risk-reducing strategy for each individual company which may also work to the mutual benefit of all members of the oligopoly (see Vernon and Wells 1986, 13–14). Such behaviour tends to produce a temporal bunching and a geographical clustering of investment. This is evident not only at the national scale as investment is focused upon a particular country, but also at the regional level as it is concentrated in specific areas of the same country. Although the phenomenon was first described with reference to the behaviour of US companies (see Vernon 1971; Knickerbocker 1973; Rees 1978), it is also evident in the later internationalization of Japanese companies (Dunning 1986).

In applying these ideas regarding the influence of market factors upon patterns of foreign direct investment in the petrochemical industry, it is helpful to distinguish between the respective roles of the oil and chemical companies. Shell and Exxon in particular played a pioneering role in the development of the industry (see section 3.4) and this is reflected in their position in the league table of companies ranked according to the value of their chemical sales (table 2.2). Most of the organizations which integrated forward from oil into petrochemicals were already familiar with multinational operations when they took this step. In Western Europe, for example, the oil companies adopted a continental perspective from the beginning whilst the traditional European chemical companies retained much clearer national identities in production and marketing. By 1955, Shell had refineries at eleven separate sites in six European countries, Exxon five in five countries and BP seven in three countries. These have been the most important of several oil companies to participate in the European petrochemical industry. Functional linkages, together with practical considerations of land availability, encouraged them to coordinate their petrochemical investments with their existing refineries (Chapman 1973; 1974a; 1974b), resulting in the early establishment of production on a European scale (figure 5.10). Thus the combination of in-house raw materials and an existing structure of multinational operation enabled those oil companies which recognized the market opportunities in petrochemicals to build up rapidly a formidable international presence. This is illustrated in figure 9.2, which emphasizes the extent of Shell's foreign direct investment in petrochemicals in 1965 – a dispersal which was not matched by even the most internationalized of the traditional chemical companies.

Despite their position amongst the ranks of the largest industrial organizations and their early technological contributions, the principal traditional chemical companies generally lagged behind Shell and Exxon in the creation of international networks of petrochemical production. The reasons for this were partly historical. Certainly Du Pont, ICI and IG Farben operated beyond their respective national boundaries before World War II, but to a limited extent. A complex system of agreements and alliances, which maintained a highly effective cartel in the inter-war years, contributed to this situation (see Reader 1975; Taylor and Sudnik 1984). The geographical allocation of markets was one aspect of the cartel which limited its members to involvement in specific territories and, therefore, restrained their spatial expansion. The breakdown of the cartel, which was hastened by the way in which the new technology drew the oil companies into the chemical industry, removed this restriction and most of the major chemical companies reconsidered their attitudes towards foreign direct investment from 1960 onwards. In the United States, Dow and Monsanto were quickly followed by Du Pont and Union Carbide in actively seeking out opportunities for overseas production, whilst in

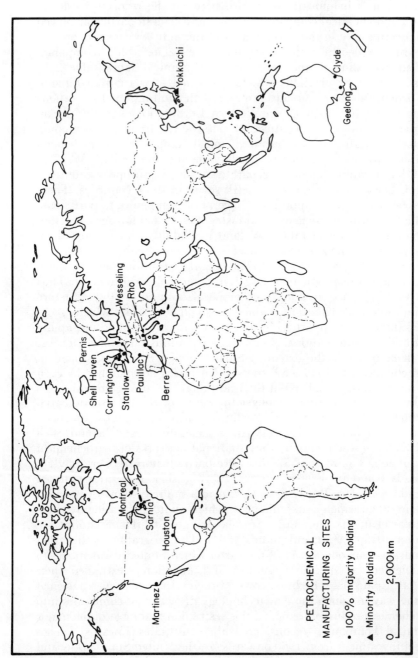

Figure 9.2 Principal petrochemical manufacturing sites of Shell, 1965 (from data supplied by Shell International Chemical Co.)

Western Europe, ICI and to a lesser extent BASF responded in a similar fashion. The outcome of these events was the emergence of 'a new international order' in the chemical industry which impelled the companies into foreign direct investment 'within each other's formerly sacrosanct territories as well as into hitherto undeveloped regions in Asia and Latin America' (Taylor and Sudnik 1984, 195). The factors contributing to this change may be illustrated by looking in more detail at the strategies of two companies – Dow and ICI.

Of the principal US chemical companies, Dow has been the most aggressive investor in overseas petrochemical production. By 1989, its domestic facilities accounted for only 53 per cent of the total value of its assets or 'gross plant properties' (Dow Chemical Co. 1989). The existence of surplus domestic capacity, boosted to meet war-time demand, initially encouraged the company to seek out export markets, but its entry into foreign production was rather haphazard as it became involved in more and more joint ventures in response to overtures by foreign companies wishing to acquire its technology (Whitehead 1968, 246). Dow Chemical International was created in 1959 to coordinate these operations. More significant, however, was a conscious decision made in the early 1960s, following an internal battle at board level, to 'globalize' the company (Sorey 1980, 208). Since taking this decision, Dow has consistently pursued a policy of market-led expansion with emphasis upon the dispersal of production facilities within many countries rather than the establishment of relatively few export-oriented plants in strategic locations. This preference is based upon a recognition of the advantages of local production, not least the political ones in dealing with governments, a desire to spread the risks of foreign investment and a belief in the pre-emptive value of such a presence as a deterrent to potential competitors.

Unlike Dow, ICI was already involved in foreign production before World War II. However, its initial interest in establishing overseas petrochemical (as opposed to non-petrochemical) operations more or less coincided with that of Dow when it created a European Council in 1960 to study the desirability of large-scale manufacture within the EEC. Although the pull of anticipated market growth in continental Europe stimulated this debate, the company was subsequently pushed in the same direction by the limitations of the UK market.[5] Indeed, Pettigrew (1985, 53) maintains that the company was weakened in the 1970s by its dependence on the United Kingdom and that the relatively poor performance of the domestic economy was influential in reinforcing the diversion of investment overseas. Whatever early doubts may have accompanied the internationalization of this traditionally British-based company, it clearly recognized the advantages of 'geographical balance' by the late 1970s (Harvey-Jones 1988, 44). This balance has been provided by focusing

Table 9.2 ICI group employment by geographic area, 1970, 1980 and 1989

Area	1970 Number	%	1980 Number	%	1989 Number	%
United Kingdom	137,000	72.1	84,300	58.9	54,700	40.9
Continental Western Europe	—	—	10,800	7.5	16,700	12.5
Americas	—	—	19,900	13.9	33,900	25.3
Australasia, Japan and Far East	53,000	27.9	15,700	11.0	16,700	12.5
Indian Subcontinent	—	—	10,600	7.4		
Other countries	—	—	1,900	1.3	11,800	9.8
Total	190,000	100.0	143,200	100.0	133,800	100.0

Source: 1970 and 1980, Clarke (1985, 125); 1989, ICI PLC Annual Report

attention upon Europe on the one hand and the United States on the other. A polyethylene plant commissioned in 1966 at Rozenburg in the Netherlands was ICI's first continental foothold in petrochemical production. This was later followed by investment in France and, most significantly, in what was originally planned as a major manufacturing complex at Wilhelmshaven in West Germany. ICI's determination to make an impact in the United States was announced by the acquisition of Atlas Chemical in 1971. However, it subsequently made substantial direct investments in grass-roots petrochemical facilities in the Gulf Coast complex at Corpus Christi[6] and Bayport[7] in Texas. With the benefit of hindsight, the timing of ICI's investments at Wilhelmshaven and Corpus Christi proved disastrous. Both came on stream in 1980, coinciding with a collapse in the industry in the wake of the second oil shock (see chapter 10). Although the company subsequently pulled out of the Corpus Christi venture, the long term shift in the geographical balance of the company is apparent in table 9.2 and figure 9.3[8].

In reviewing the changing geography of companies such as Dow and ICI, it is important to remember that these geographies are not necessarily independent of one another. The chemical industry in general and the petrochemical industry in particular provide many examples of interactive behaviour at the world scale which has influenced corporate investment and location decisions. Such behaviour contributes to the international dispersal of the industry in two quite different ways. The entry of a newcomer into a company's traditional territory, especially its home market, frequently provokes a counter-attack in the market of the intruder. Rather different is the situation in which one company decides to establish production facilities within a relatively new and growing market and is rapidly followed by others in accordance with Knickerbocker's (1973) oligopolistic reaction.

The breakdown of the cartel which characterized the international chemical industry before World War II is apparent in several tit-

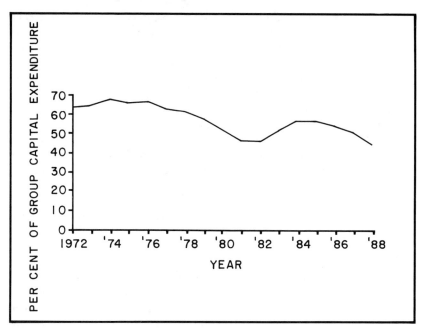

Figure 9.3 UK share of ICI group capital expenditure, 1972–1988, three year running mean (from data in ICI PLC annual reports)

for-tat reactions associated with the frequently strained relations between US and European producers. Du Pont's first manufacturing plant in Western Europe was, for example, conceived as a retaliation to what, from the American company's viewpoint, was an unwelcome move by ICI when it acquired a dye plant in the United States in 1956 (Taylor and Sudnik 1984, 190). On the other hand, the major European chemical companies certainly viewed investment in the United States as a natural reaction to American activities in Western Europe during the 1960s. This reaction has gathered momentum to the extent that an estimated one-quarter of the US chemical industry was foreign owned by the end of the 1980s (MIT Commission on Industrial Productivity 1989, 38).

Chemical companies were a part of what Servan-Schreiber (1968) characterized as 'the American challenge' to European industry during the 1960s, and their arrival clearly demonstrates the nature and significance of follow-the-leader behaviour. The influx of US investment was concentrated in the prevailing high technology sectors such as computers and petrochemicals (Dunning 1970). Although US companies retained a lead in certain areas of petro-chemistry, that lead was threatened by the diffusion of technology and the independent research efforts of their European competitors. The arrival of the US chemical companies was, like American investment in other sectors of European industry (Blackbourn 1974), essentially a defensive reaction designed to protect their positions in a valuable market. Some indication of its importance is provided by trade statistics. In 1959, for example, when most of the major US chemical companies were either considering or committed to investment in Western Europe, the value of organic chemicals exported from the United States to the member countries of the Organization for European Economic Cooperation was almost four times as great as the reverse flow. The corresponding ratio for synthetic plastic materials was more than 18 to 1 (OECD 1962). The most important contributions to this situation were the products, such as polyethylene, styrene and ethylene glycol, which were driving the growth of the petrochemical industry.

The buoyant market, the rise of indigenous producers and the threat to continued imports posed by the formation of the EEC in 1957 led many US chemical companies to review and reach similar conclusions about the desirability of direct investment in Europe (see Whitehead 1968; Forrestal 1977; Taylor and Sudnik 1984). Not all of this investment was in petrochemicals. Firms such as Air Products, Lubrizol, and Rohm and Haas were in other areas of the chemical industry, whilst Du Pont and Monsanto concentrated upon downstream operations such as plastics and synthetic fibres rather than the production of basic intermediates. The most important petrochemical investments were made by Union Carbide and Dow. The former company established a manufacturing presence in 1958 with polyethylene and ethylene oxide plants in the United Kingdom at Grangemouth and Fawley respectively, but its commitment increased sharply with the startup of much larger facilities for the same products at Antwerp in 1967. Dow made an even more significant move at about the same time when it established its Dutch complex at Terneuzen which was conceived as the European equivalent of its massive Freeport operation in Texas (Whitehead 1968, 249). Dow later reinforced its commitment to Europe with major investments at Stade in West Germany and Tarragona in Spain. These companies were followed by others, such as Hercules, Oxirane and USI, during the 1970s. These developments boosted the growth of the industry in Western Europe and reduced the trade deficit in chemicals with the United States as the companies replaced exports from their domestic plants with production from their new European facilities. By 1980, an estimated 95 per cent of Dow's sales in Europe were locally produced (Kidder, Peabody and Co. 1980). Unlike most of their European counterparts, the US chemical companies regarded the European market from the outset on a continental scale and planned their operations accordingly. One consequence of this has been a concentration of investments in the Benelux area. This is apparent in figure 9.4, which plots the distribution of the European manu-

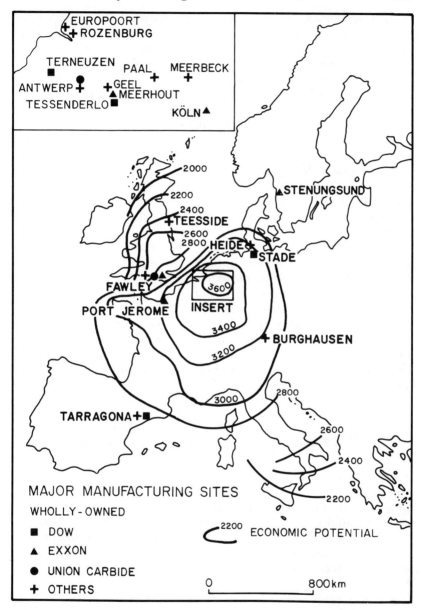

Figure 9.4 Principal petrochemical manufacturing sites of US chemical companies in Western Europe, 1979

facturing facilities of the US chemical companies at the zenith of their involvement in 1979, relative to a crude measure of economic potential originally calculated at approximately the same time that many of these companies were making their location decisions (Clark et al. 1969).[9] Based upon a gravity model formulation incorporating variables relating market size (as measured by population and income levels) to transport costs and the effect of tariffs, this calculation confirms the intuitively obvious impression that Benelux and the Ruhr constitute the economic centre of gravity in Western Europe – an impression which seems to have strongly influenced not only the location decisions of US chemical companies during the 1960s and 1970s, but also inward investment in other sectors (Hamilton 1976).

The entry of US chemical companies into Western Europe is perhaps the best example of the way in which competitive reactions have, by exaggerating the impact of market-led growth, shaped the evolution of the international petrochemical industry. It is not the only one, however, and it has already been noted that the simultaneous involvement of several multinationals in establishing the Australian industry suggests a similar effect. A flurry of foreign investment in petrochemical capacity in Argentina in the late 1960s was also consistent with this pattern. It has been argued that Dow, for example, carried through a huge investment at Bahia Blanca, despite a hostile political environment in Argentina, 'to prevent any potential sales from going to competitors' (Sorey 1980, 339). Looking ahead, it seems likely that South East Asia will become the focus of multinational interest in the 1990s in view of the encouraging prospects for market growth (see UNIDO 1985a; Vergara and Brown 1988). The probable involvement of Japanese companies, which are already established in Singapore, for example, will further complicate the pattern of competitive action and reaction.

9.5 Raw Materials and Location Strategies

Markets are not the only stimulus to foreign direct investments. Analyses of the apparent redistribution of many manufacturing industries towards the newly industrializing countries have emphasized the ability of the global corporation to fragment its operations to take advantage of the new international division of labour. This advantage is essentially cost based and is related to variations in the price and productivity of labour between countries. Such considerations are not decisive in the capital-intensive petrochemical industry, but corresponding variations in raw material costs have affected investment and location decisions at the international scale. It has not only been the cost of raw materials that has entered the business calculus; equally important have been concerns about security of supply. The bases of these interrelated issues have already been reviewed in chapter 8. The impact upon the petrochemical industry was also discussed with reference to its role in the economic development aspirations of governments and to the almost incidental effect

of various policy responses to the oil price shocks upon the competitive relations of established producers. By concentrating upon policy
issues from the perspective of governments, relatively little attention
was paid to the way in which individual companies responded to the
new situation created by the actions of OPEC. In many cases, these
responses have had only indirect effects upon the geography of the
industry. Backward integration to secure raw materials supply by
appropriate investment at existing locations or by acquisitions may
change the geography of the company concerned, but produce no
major shift at industry level. On the other hand, investment attracted
to new locations by the availability of raw materials is an explicitly
geographical response which, if undertaken by many companies,
may bring about such a shift. In making this distinction between
what may be termed spatial and non-spatial corporate responses to
matters of raw material cost and supply, it is important to recognize
that the two are often closely related.

These matters have always been of greater concern to the chemical
companies than to the oil companies, which usually moved into
petrochemicals from a secure raw material position. As early as 1927
Union Carbide considered backward integration into oil refining, and
it has already been shown how this and the other principal US
chemical companies contributed to the emergence of the Gulf Coast
petrochemical complex when they were drawn to the oil and gas
fields of Texas in the immediate post-war years (see section 4.1). The
realization that the future of the organic chemical industry lay with
oil rather than coal was not the only reason why the chemical
companies were interested in securing their sources of feedstock.
Their apprehension was reinforced by the activities of the oil companies which were both suppliers of raw material and competitors,
prompting fears of 'a fatal squeeze' (Harvey-Jones 1988, 30). These
fears were greatest in Europe because of the dependence upon refinery
naphtha rather than natural gas as in the United States. Petrochemical producers in France and Italy were, perhaps, less appre-
hensive because of the extensive involvement of the state in both
upstream and downstream sectors. This meant that they were less
directly threatened by the squeeze from the oil companies. ICI
and the German big three had no such protection. ICI undertook
'a constant re-examination of [its] oil strategy' during the 1960s
(Harvey-Jones 1988, 30), which resulted in very early participation
in North Sea exploration and in the establishment of an oil refinery
on Teesside to meet the feedstock needs of its existing petrochemical
complex at Wilton. Similar moves were made by several other
companies attracted by the concept of the chemical refinery (see
section 6.2), whilst BASF acquired Wintershall, a small German oil
company, in 1969.

Strategies of backward integration towards raw material supplies which seemed prudent in the 1960s became axiomatic following the oil price shocks. These reflected not only the new economics of petrochemical manufacture (see section 8.2), but also the new politics of oil supply. European naphtha prices were, for example, rising faster than oil prices in 1979–80 (figure 8.2). Fears of further price escalation and, more important, supply disruptions reinforced the attractions of backward integration. Du Pont's acquisition of Conoco in 1981 was, at the time, the largest takeover in American history and it encumbered Du Pont, traditionally very conservative in its financial affairs, with an unaccustomed debt. The move was largely driven by the uncertainties surrounding the future supply and cost of the raw materials essential to the company's petrochemical operations (Taylor and Sudnik 1984, xviii).

Similar thinking lay behind Dow's decision to construct an oil refinery adjacent to its huge Freeport complex in Texas (Morner 1977). In addition to its concerns about the international situation, Dow also believed that prevailing levels of US NGL production could not be sustained and that it was prudent to shift towards liquid feedstocks such as naphtha and gas oil derived from oil. The Freeport refinery was, to some extent, a continuation of Dow's traditional 'pursuit of corporate self-sufficiency' (Sorey 1980, 338) which had previously led, for example, to the acquisition of interests in oil and gas fields in Texas and Louisiana. It was designed to handle high sulphur and heavy (i.e. low cost) crudes. It came on stream in 1980 and shut down after only six months' operation, proving to be one of the more spectacular business disasters arising when the assumptions of rising international oil prices and constrained supplies which underpinned the investment decision were contradicted by the events of the early 1980s.[10] Dow's venture into oil refining implied no major shift in the geographical pattern of its activities because it was focused upon an existing complex. However, the company was also involved in another type of strategic response to the oil shocks which did have geographical implications – the search for new locations with secure access to low cost raw materials. This strategy was pursued at the international scale and represented a very different kind of foreign direct investment from the market-led moves prevailing in the 1960s.

It was noted in chapter 8 that the initiative for petrochemical developments in the Middle East came from governments rather than the private sector. However, it was also noted that the most significant of these developments, in Saudi Arabia, have nearly all involved direct equity participation by US, Japanese and other multinationals. From the Saudi perspective, these participants contributed technology, expertise and established marketing systems as well as capital. As far as the foreign participants were concerned, these ventures could be viewed as a reluctant acknowlegement of the

Saudi determination to proceed with its plans and of its ability to carry them through with or without such participation. Bearing in mind the projected feedstock cost advantage, it could be regarded as a case of 'If you can't beat them, join them.' On the other hand there was real scepticism in the early 1980s about the feasibility of Saudi ambitions, and it has already been suggested that the oil companies in particular were probably drawn into these projects more by their desire to secure their oil supplies than by their interest in petro-chemicals (see section 8.3).

However ambiguous the views of the major multinationals regarding direct investment in the Middle East, there is no doubt that the impact of the oil price shocks upon the economics of petrochemical manufacture stimulated commercial interest in general locations and in specific sites with access to low cost raw materials, especially sources of NGLs. Some improbably schemes were conceived in the panic engendered by the 1979 jump in oil prices. For example, a proposal to establish a petrochemical complex in Alaska using gas from the North Slope would probably have required an oil price in excess of $50 per barrel to be viable (Spitz 1988, 489). More realistically, the preferred locations were those which combined these raw material advantages with reasonable proximity to the principal markets and a socio-economic environment that minimized the risks of political interference in corporate activities. These requirements were fulfilled by Alberta in Canada and also by various locations oriented towards the activities of the oil industry in the North Sea.

The origins of the commercial interest in Alberta and the impact of Canadian energy policies upon the development of the industry in the province were considered in section 8.3, but the extent of the scramble for access to its ethane resources was not described (see Chapman 1985b). In the five years between 1977 and 1982, the Alberta Energy Resources Conservation Board (ERCB), which is the regulatory authority responsible for the issue of industrial develop-ment permits for projects utilizing the oil and gas resources of the province, was swamped with applications for proposed petrochemical facilities. These included methane-based operations, and aromatics as well as ethylene and its derivatives. Although many of these applications were made by Canadian interests, most incorporated varying levels of foreign participation. US oil and chemical com-panies were particularly active in the struggle for access to resources, including Celanese,[11] Dow, Du Pont, Exxon and Union Carbide. European and Japanese interests were also represented in several proposals. The total raw material requirements of these various schemes almost certainly outstripped the potential available supply and their combined output would also have flooded the market. Thus the intrigues focused on the ERCB in Calgary and the Ministry of Economic Development in Edmonton were part of a high-level battle between several of the major players in the international petro-chemical industry not only to secure access to raw materials, but also to deny access to others and thereby obtain a pre-emptive advantage in furture rounds of investment. In this sense, events in Alberta from the mid 1970s to the early 1980s may be regarded as a variation on the follow-the-leader behaviour associated with market-led foreign investment in the 1960s (see section 9.4).

Interest in Alberta waned after 1982 as a combination of declining international oil prices and the rigidities of prevailing Canadian energy policy eroded its raw material cost advantage (see section 8.5). Furthermore, many projects never got off the drawing board, either because their advocates were unable to secure control of sufficient feedstock or because they had second thoughts about the viability of their proposals. Nevertheless, there were significant winners in this battle for resources, in particular the Alberta-based Nova group and Dow Chemical. The investments made by these and other companies such as Union Carbide and Shell have been substantial enough not only to radically change the geography of petrochemical manufacture in Canada (figure 8.10), but also to intro-duce a significant new element in the international pattern of the industry. In view of its export orientation, the Alberta complex, which accounted for approximately 6 per cent of North American ethylene capacity in 1990, has implications for future developments in its principal markets in the Pacific Rim and the United States. It has, for example, had a dramatic effect on the balance of trade between Canada and the United States in LD/LLD polyethylene, styrene, vinyl chloride and ethylene glycol (Chapman 1989).

The possibility of using raw materials from the North Sea as feedstocks for petrochemical manufacture was recognized at an early stage in its development as an offshore hydrocarbon province, and such activities were included in predictions of energy-based industrial complexes focused upon the gas pipeline landfalls in eastern England (Odell 1968). These never materialized, but various observers have drawn attention to the opportunities (see Chemicals EDC 1976; Chapman 1977). The establishment of the Norwegian petrochemical industry was, for example, directly linked to the availability of North Sea feedstocks. The decision to deliver oil and associated gas from the Norwegian Ekofisk field by pipeline to a terminal located close to ICI's existing petrochemical operations on Teesside prompted the British company to enter negotiations with the Norwegian chemical company Norsk Hydro in 1973 to explore the possibility of estab-lishing a jointly owned ethylene plant based on ethane extracted at the terminal. The plan was abandoned when Norsk Hydro decided to proceed with its own scheme in Norway. This decision was con-sistent with the desire of the Norwegian government to maximize the national economic benefits of its North Sea resources, and it required the return by tanker from Teesside of the raw material for ethylene manufacture. Following an extensive review of alternative sites, the new petrochemical complex was built in the district of Bamble, south-west of Oslo, and commissioned in 1977. Norsk Hydro had been considering entry into petrochemicals for some time, but the availability of raw materials from the North Sea certainly accelerated its decision.

Although private sector interests were the principal participants in the Norwegian petrochemical project, it seems likely that hidden government inducements or pressures were influential in its implementation. Corresponding initiatives in the United Kingdom came from the private sector. Specific proposals to establish a gas gathering system to collect ethane from many fields and to deliver it to coastal terminals for onward transmission to chemical sites were published in 1976 (Williams-Merz 1976). ICI actively promoted various derivatives of this scheme in conjunction with the three other major UK petrochemical producers (i.e. BP, Esso and Shell). Other companies, notably Dow, gave serious consideration to the possibility of establishing entirely new complexes and, in the interlude between the first oil shock and the growing realization of a looming overcapacity problem in Western Europe (see chapter 10), many believed that access to North Sea ethane was an important source of competitive advantage that raised the prospect of a much larger UK petrochemical industry exporting to the rest of Western Europe (Chemicals EDC 1976; Chapman 1977). In the event, only one greenfield site was developed when Shell and Esso established a jointly owned ethylene plant at Mossmorran in Scotland in 1986. This is supplied with ethane ultimately derived from fields in the northern North Sea. These fields are owned by the same companies, and this level of integration almost certainly allows Shell and Esso to adopt transfer pricing arrangements which ensure that the Mossmorran plant is a cost leader in Western Europe. Expansion plans that will make this one of the largest ethylene plants in the world by 1992 provide circumstantial evidence in support of this conclusion. Shell and Esso are, of course, long established petrochemical producers in the United Kindom and Western Europe, and it cannot be argued that North Sea feedstock has brought about a fundamental change in the geography of the international petrochemical industry comparable with events in Saudi Arabia and Alberta. On the other hand, the Mossmorran project has resulted in a reorientation of the continental petrochemical systems of the two companies, dirverting investment from sites elsewhere in the United Kingdom and mainland Europe. Another indirect consequence has been to reinforce the efforts of competitors in Western Europe, such as BASF, BP and ICI, to minimize their raw material costs, usually by enhancing the flexibility of their operations to take advantage of fluctuations in the price of the various alternative feedstocks and by making arrangements to secure access to them (see section 8.2).

9.6 Conclusions

It was certain oil companies, notably Shell and Exxon, rather than the traditional chemical companies which were the first to move into production on an international scale, building upon existing organizational structures associated with their oil refining operations. Some chemical companies, such as Du Pont and ICI, had experience of international production before World War II, but on nothing like the same scale as the oil majors which could be regarded as the earliest global corporations. When the chemical companies made the switch to oil- and gas-based feedstocks as raw materials for the manufacture of organic chemicals, their first moves were, not surprisingly, made in their home countries. However, viewed over the half century since the end of World War II, it is evident that foreign direct investment by both oil and chemical companies has played a significant role in the evolution of the international petrochemical industry and that the geographical pattern of this investment has changed through time.

US companies were the earliest significant foreign investors in petrochemicals, as would be expected given their lead in the industry (see chapters 3 and 4). By 1970, the foreign direct investments of US chemical companies (mainly in petrochemicals) amounted to $13 billion, which was one-third of their domestic plant investment.[12] No other US industry approached this total and ratio (US International Trade Commission 1987, 5–9). Despite a substantial presence in Latin America and Australia, the most distinctive feature of this early US investment abroad was its concentration in Western Europe. The influx of US companies more or less coincided with, and was partly responsible for, an increased interest in foreign investment on the part of the principal European chemical companies such as ICI. Initially, this focused upon a shift from national to continental systems of production at the European scale, but this was rapidly followed by moves into the United States itself. However, the timing of these latter moves was such that the emphasis was more upon high value chemicals such as pharmaceuticals than upon petrochemicals, which were showing clear signs of maturity in US and European markets by the mid 1970s.

This maturity, combined with the impact of the oil price shocks, produced a very different kind of foreign investment in the late 1970s, in terms of both its motivation and its geographical distribution. At the same time that many of the US chemical companies were pulling out of Western Europe as part of their restructuring efforts (see chapter 10), raw materials replaced markets as the dominant influence upon strategic planning within the industry, and this was reflected in developments in Alberta and Saudi Arabia. By the time the later of these investments were coming on stream, the diminished ability of OPEC to control the international oil price was already apparent; most planning within the industry by the end of the 1980s was based upon assumptions which regarded major discontinuities of the kind that occurred in the 1970s as much less likely than a gradual increase towards $35–45 per barrel by the end of the century.[13] This does not mean that raw material costs will become irrelevant in evaluating comparative advantage. Indeed, it seems likely that, having already made a huge investment in the necessary infrastructure, Saudi Arabia in particular will retain a substantial advantage which will ultimately be reflected in an increasing share of world capacity. On the other hand, a smoother trend in oil prices suggests that, viewed in the perspective of its long term evolution, the preoccupation with raw material costs and availability at the international scale that characterized the industry between 1975 and 1985 will prove to be an aberration. If this is correct, market factors will once again become the principal controls upon the geographical pattern of growth.

South East Asia is expected to offer the greatest new market opportunities in the 1990s because of the position of countries such as Thailand and Indonesia on the logistic curve of demand growth. The extent to which foreign multinationals will participate in this expansion of perochemical production will obviously depend upon the attitudes of host governments towards inward investment. These attitudes mellowed somewhat during the 1980s as developing countries found themselves desperately short of the capital needed to embark upon major projects such as petrochemical complexes, and this has created joint venture opportunities for the multinationals. Such opportunities will probably arise in South East Asia, which may also become an increasingly important source of, as well as a destination for, foreign direct investment. The petrochemical industries of South Korea and Taiwan are sufficiently well developed for national firms to consider direct investments in North America and Western Europe, possibly following the globalization strategies of major customers such as Hyundai.

Notes

1 Company size is a significant variable influencing this judgement. Small companies which make an important breakthrough may be more willing to license because they do not have the financial resources to embark upon expensive (and risky) foreign investment.

2 That is, SICs 2821, 2822, 2824, 2843, 2865, 2869, 2873 and 2895.
3 This pattern is not unique to petrochemicals. Numerous studies of the behaviour of US companies in many industries have suggested that exporters have invested in foreign production to protect an established market position (see Moran 1979).
4 Although cost-reducing strategies linked to the new international division of labour have drawn multinational companies into many less developed countries, this generalization remains valid.
5 Another push factor relevant to many of ICI's basic chemical operations was the high cost of energy in the United Kingdom compared with other European countries. This has long been a matter of concern to the British chemical industry, and it has been suggested that lower electricity costs in West Germany had a strong bearing on the opening of ICI's Wilhelmshaven complex (Clarke 1985, 134).
6 Corpus Christi Petrochemical was a joint venture of ICI, Solvay and Champlain Petroleum.
7 Sold to Cain Chemical Inc. in 1987.
8 These trends relate to the total activities of ICI rather than just its petrochemicals and plastics operations, which accounted for 19 and 29 per cent of group turnover and trading profit respectively in 1988 (ICI 1989, 111).
9 A significant withdrawal occurred during the 1980s for reasons discussed in chapter 10.
10 Dow's experience emphasizes that vertical integration (both backwards and forwards) is not necessarily the best strategy in petrochemicals (see Burgess 1983).
11 Acquired by Hoechst in 1986.
12 The substantial petrochemical investments by US oil companies are excluded from this figure.
13 The invasion of Kuwait by Iraq at the time of writing and the confusion created in the international oil market by this action emphasizes the fragile nature of such assumptions.

10
Restructuring in the Petrochemical Industry

Previous chapters have portrayed the development of the petro-chemical industry as a story of rapid and continuous growth associated with its establishment in an increasing number of countries. An abrupt reversal of these trends occurred in the early 1980s, at least within the developed economies of the United States, Western Europe and Japan. Similar reversals occurred in several other basic industries, prompting references to a restructuring crisis distinguished by such features as intense competition, declining profitability, slower increases or even falls in productivity and output, and under-utilization of capacity. No analysis of the evolution of the industry would be complete without reference to this period. Before focusing upon the particular circumstances of the petrochemical industry, however, it is desirable to place them within a wider perspective.

10.1 Restructuring, Life Cycles and Location

The concept of restructuring may, to some extent, be accommodated within the life-cycle framework which has been used throughout this book. Markusen's (1985) profit-cycle model was described in chapter 1. This is an extension of the product-cycle idea which seeks to identify and account for various systematic changes common to the long term evolution of many industries, focusing especially upon profitability (figure 1.1). The model suggests that a combination of severe competition, which is a legacy of the attraction of new entrants during its rapid growth phase, and market saturation typically result in a profit squeeze as an industry matures. It also indicates that this situation frequently leads to a restructuring process involving an organizational concentration of production as relatively few firms acquire the assets of others.[1] These acquisitions are then followed by rationalization schemes which reduce both total capacity and the number of production sites in an attempt to secure control of output and prices to restore profitability. Viewed in this way, restructuring is a natural aspect of industry evolution involving a gradual readjustment to changing circumstances. This conceptualization does not accord with the traumatic events in the developed economies during the later 1970s and early 1980s. Studies of many industries, including steel (Hogan 1983; Bradbury 1987), oil refining (Bachetta 1978; Wijetilleke and Ody 1984) and motor vehicles (Holmes 1987) have emphasized that the extent of their restructuring experiences could not be explained adequately in such incremental terms.

Certain characteristic corporate responses to uncertainty, which encourage over investment and therefore magnify the negative effects of increasing competition and diminishing rates of market growth, often ensure that restructuring is a painful process associated with discontinuous rather than gradual change. Capital investment necessarily involves speculation on an uncertain future, and it seems that firms tend to be optimistic rather than pessimistic (or realistic) in assessing their prospects. In theory, the rate of profit regulates the level of investment, attracting capital to areas of growth and discouraging it in less promising areas. In practice, firms often exaggerate growth potential and, on the other hand, are frequently slow to grasp the full significance of declining performance.[2] Bandwagon effects, in which capital is drawn into an industry by a set of mutually reinforcing expectations (or delusions?), are well documented and almost inevitably result in over investment (Strange 1986). By contrast, the very real difficulties of distinguishing short term fluctuations from secular trends virtually guarantee a delayed response to the onset of market maturity. This is reinforced in many cases by a reluctance on the part of senior management to acknowledge unwelcome trends and to hang on in the hope of better times (Clair 1984). The effect of such behavioural tendencies towards optimism and inertia in contributing to overcapacity by delaying any moves towards rationalization is reinforced by other factors. It is a paradox of product and industry life cycles that the pressures of cost competition encourage a search for and the greatest exploitation of economies of scale just before rates of market growth begin to slacken off. In these circumstances, it is often difficult to match the big jump in capacity resulting from the commissioning of a new plant to the more gradual rate of increase in demand (figure 6.6). This technical problem may be aggravated by competitive strategies in which individual companies attempt to pre-empt others by getting their investment in first in the hope of securing greater market share. It is easy to appreciate that the collective result of such behaviour is an endemic tendency to overcapacity.

Behavioural responses to uncertainty may aggravate, but do not usually precipitate, restructuring crises within industries. The development of individual industries takes place within the wider context of national and international economies. Whilst propulsive sectors may act as engines of economic growth in the long perspective of history, the immediate fortunes of industries are shaped by prevailing economic circumstances. The nature of change in these circumstances is beyond the scope of this book, but there is no doubt that many industries, including petrochemicals, were adversely affected in the 1970s by a downward shift in overall rates of growth within the developed economies relative to previous experience during the postwar boom and, more specifically, by the global recession of 1981–2. The role of the 1973–4 and the 1978–9 oil price rises as causal mechanisms in these macro-economic changes is a matter of debate, but the impact of these price shocks upon the petrochemical industry was considerable (see chapter 8). This impact more or less coincided with the maturation of markets for many petrochemical products, resulting in a combination of negative influences upon the industry: those implicit in the internal dynamic of the life cycle, and those linked with external economic circumstances.

Restructuring has important geographical dimensions. At community and regional level, it may be associated with devastating effects upon economic well-being as contractions and plant closures precipitate major job losses. In some cases, capacity reductions in one place may be matched by corresponding increases elsewhere as production is transferred to more attractive (usually lower cost) locations. This kind of switch is apparent in the influence of 'the new international division of labour' upon corporate location strategies in industries such as textiles and consumer electronics (see Dicken 1986). The experience of deindustrialization, especially in the United Kingdom, has prompted a new awareness in the geographical literature that the distribution of industry is a consequence of both investment *and* disinvestment decisions. More specifically, attempts have been made to identify the variables influencing rationalization strategies within multi plant companies, especially those influencing the allocation of capacity between different production sites, and to place these strategies at enterprise level within the broader context of restructuring at industry level (see Massey and Meegan 1979; Watts and Stafford 1986). This approach is adopted in the rest of this chapter, which traces the background to and the various consequences of the restructuring crisis in the petrochemical industry.[3]

10.2 Origins of the Restructuring Crisis

Viewed in marketing terms, the life-cycle concept implies an ultimate deceleration of growth as a consequence of diminishing substitution opportunities and market saturation. The dynamics of the growth process in the case of petrochemicals were described in section 5.1, where it was noted that trends at the industry level were the sum of many individual product life cycles (figures 5.3 and 5.4). As the rate of product innovation has slowed down, so too has the impetus provided by the initiation of new life cycles to the aggregate growth of the petrochemical industry, leading to a situation in which its performance has more closely matched overall rates of economic growth rather than exceeded it by the kind of margins displayed in the 1950s and 1960s (see figures 5.1 and 5.2). With the benefit of hindsight, these trends seem entirely predictable, but there is abundant evidence of an apparent failure by the participants in the industry to perceive the implications of approaching maturity. Forecasts made in the 1970s consistently overestimated the growth of demand for petrochemicals.[4] Figure 10.1 indicates the discrepancies between the projected and actual consumption of ethylene in the European Economic Community during the 1970s, for example, and similar errors have been made in forecasts relating to the United States and, more ambitiously, to the entire world (see Robertson 1986; Vergara and Brown 1988, 7–9). To the extent that they guided investment decisions, such errors contributed to the overcapacity problems of the later 1970s and early 1980s and, bearing in mind the expectation of slower growth built into the life-cycle concept, it is necessary to appreciate the circumstances in which the forecasts were made in order to understand why they were so consistently wrong.

The extent of, and factors contributing to, the surge of new entrants to the petrochemical industry in the United States and Western Europe during the 1950s and 1960s was described in chapter 5. In several countries, notably France and Italy, the commercial attractions of the industry were reinforced by political considerations as state-supported or -owned companies joined the rush. Less direct but equally influential encouragement was offered in Japan, leading to a similar proliferation of producers and manufacturing sites in the 1960s (see section 7.2). The principal effect of this influx, which was made possible by the diffusion of technology, was to create a commercial environment characterized by competitive pricing and low profits. Thus the 1960s have been described as a period of 'profitless growth' in petrochemicals (Spitz 1988, 390). The basis of this growth has already been discussed (see chapter 5) and the sources of the associated profit squeeze are represented in figure 10.2, which is based upon the work of Stobaugh and Townsend (1975). The nature of this squeeze is worth examining in some detail because, although the possibility of such a squeeze was either not recognized by new entrants or not enough of a deterrent to their ambitions, its reality ultimately affected their survival prospects when the crisis came.

There is ample evidence of long term falls in the real price of petrochemical products prior to the oil price shocks. Although these

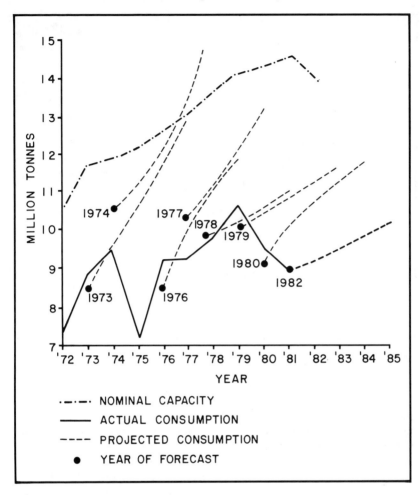

Figure 10.1 Projected and actual ethylene consumption in EEC, 1972–1985 (OECD 1985, 79)

external shocks had a profound effect upon the industry (see chapter 8), this effect was magnified by the incipient internal pressures represented in figure 10.2. Stobaugh and Townsend (1975) demonstrated a downward trend in the constant dollar price of eight different products in the United States from the year they each first became commercially available to 1972. In the case of phenol, this represented a continuous time series of almost 60 years, whilst more recent introductions such as vinyl chloride and acrylonitrile span a period of approximately 20 years (figure 10.3). More recent studies by Stobaugh (1988) have confirmed the validity of the model represented in figure 10.2 on the basis of data for 82 petrochemical

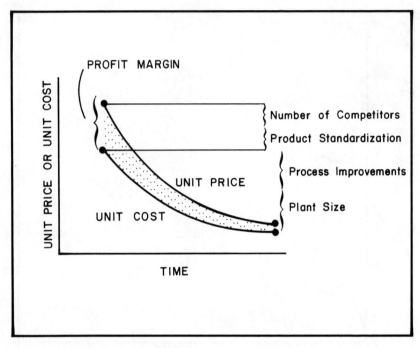

Figure 10.2 Sources of profit squeeze in petrochemicals, reprinted from the *Journal of Marketing Research*, published by the American Marketing Association (Stobaugh and Townsend 1975, 20)

products in the US market. Similar price trends have been described in other, less comprehensive, studies (see Shell International Chemical Co. 1979; US Department of Commerce 1985). In the case of the United States, Stobaugh and Townsend (1975) demonstrated that this downward pressure on prices was directly linked to the entry of new competitors, a conclusion reinforced by the more recent work of Liebermann (1984). These findings reflected not only the erosion of oligopoly power, but also the willingness of new entrants, especially those diversifying into petrochemicals from other sectors, to accept lower returns on investment. Such moves were made easier as a result of the fact that virtually all liquid and gaseous petro-chemicals are standard products in which monopolies cannot be maintained once the appropriate technology becomes available. Solid petrochemicals such as polymers, fibres and elastomers may be differentiated, offering a better chance of defending market share on the basis of specification rather than price. Nevertheless it is clear that, for many petrochemical products, lower prices are the only way a new entrant can break into the market, especially when faced with the problem of rapidly achieving the high utilization rates necessary for the efficient operation of a new, world-scale plant. The aggregate

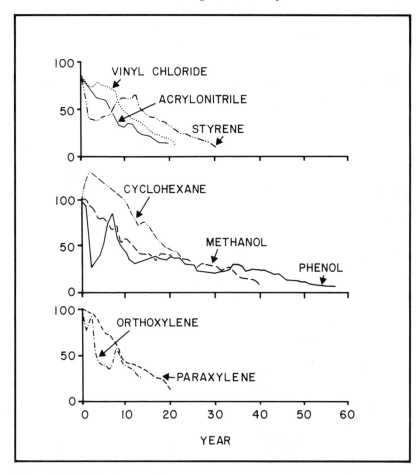

Figure 10.3 Price index trends in constant dollars for eight petrochemical products from year of first availability of price data to 1972 (reprinted from the *Journal of Marketing Research*, published by The American Marketing Association, reproduced in Stobaugh, 1988, 70)

effect of many such decisions by different entrants is the downward trending price curve represented in figure 10.2.

Pressure on prices is closely related to pressure on costs, since the competitive markets of maturity require firms to search constantly for cheaper and more efficient methods of production. These methods tend to become more routine and standardized with the passage of time. A distinction was made in section 6.1 between the contributions of static and dynamic economies of scale to falling unit costs. The significance of static economies of scale linked to the introduction of larger production units was emphasized in chapter 6, but dynamic economies of scale reflected in the learning curve effect have been even more important influences upon costs and therefore upon prices (see Nelson and Winter 1977; Liebermann 1987).

Process innovations in petrochemicals vary widely in their impact upon existing practices. Most are minor improvements associated with, for example, better yields, energy savings or fewer steps in a sequence of reactions. Such advances are not enough to provide an overwhelming competitive advantage relative to the majority of existing producers, but they tend to place pressure on the smallest and/or least efficient which is evident in the aggregate industry cost curve. More dramatic effects are produced by the relatively few process innovations, such as ICI's low pressure methanol process, which involve more radical changes.[5] However, Stobaugh (1988, 20–7) has shown that such breakthroughs tend to be made early in the life of a new product when they contribute to the initially steep decline of the cost curve (figure 10.2). Subsequent downward pressure is mainly due to the cumulative effect of minor process innovations, an effect which is reinforced by the speed with which such innovations become generally available throughout the industry (see section 5.2). Thus the experience or learning curve has certainly operated in the case of petrochemicals, but more at the industry level rather than to the benefit of individual producers (Spitz 1988, 391).

There is considerable evidence of the squeeze on profits implied by the convergence of the declining cost and price curves in figure 10.2. The financial performance of the US chemical industry has, for example, deteriorated steadily over a long period (figure 10.4). Throughout the 1950s and 1960s the percentage rate of return on capital constantly exceeded the figure for manufacturing as a whole, but the relationship has been reversed in several years since 1978. Figure 10.4 relates to the chemical and allied products industry as a whole (SIC 28) and therefore obscures the performance of the petrochemical sector. This has in fact been significantly worse, and the profitability of basic chemicals manufacture, which is largely synonymous with petrochemicals, fell below the average for all manufacturing industries in the United States as early as the late 1950s and has largely remained in that position ever since (Spitz 1988, 524). These unfavourable trends in the United States were paralleled by similar ones in Western Europe and Japan. Figure 10.5 indicates a general fall in the profitability of petrochemicals in Western Europe between 1967 and 1987, expressed in terms of the pre-tax net income (in constant US dollars) of the major companies. Indeed, most of these companies were losing huge sums of money on their petrochemical operations by the early 1980s (Bower 1986).

These losses were not only the outcome of the cost-price squeeze. Figure 10.2 suggests a trend towards lower profits, but does not predict losses. It assumes that the pressures of competition will result in a gradual shift to an equilibrium position in which profits are just

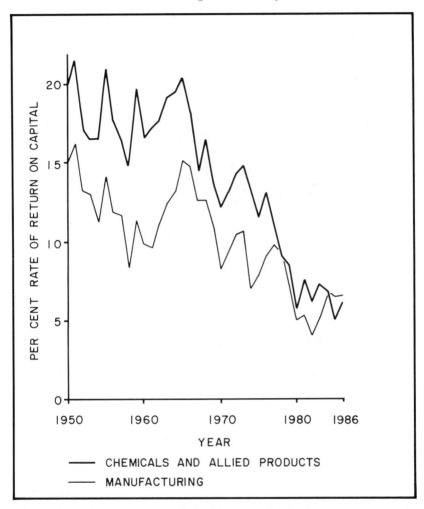

Figure 10.4 Rates of return on capital in manufacturing and chemicals and allied products in US, 1950–1986 (from data in US Department of Commerce 1988)

sufficient to attract the incremental investment necessary to meet demand. Such adjustments are often difficult to achieve in reality. The petrochemical industry in the 1960s and early 1970s was characterized by a dangerous combination of optimism about future growth and severe cost competition. Both of these circumstances encouraged individual producers to build larger plants – on the one hand to serve what was expected to remain a repidly growing market, and on the other hand to take full advantage of economies of scale. This kind of logic influenced the behaviour of existing producers as established

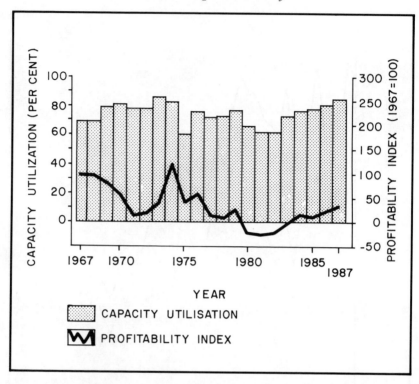

Figure 10.5 Utilization and profitability per petrochemical tonne in Western
Europe, 1967–1987 (Shell International Petroleum Co. 1990)

plants became commercially obsolescent long before the end of their
technical and engineering design lives and were replaced by newer,
bigger units. It also influenced the behaviour of new entrants, for
whom an all-or-nothing approach was the only realistic option in an
industry so strongly influenced by economies of scale. These pressures
towards larger plants increased the importance of accurate forecasting and the difficulty of matching supply and demand (figure
6.6). Indeed, the attempts to resolve this latter difficulty at corporate
level tended to aggravate it at industry level. New entrants, for
example, often believed that they could rapidly secure the high
utilization rates upon which the economies of large plants depend by
exploiting state-of-the-art technology to outcompete and take market
share from older facilities. Even where investment was not originally
based upon this strategic premise, but was planned to match an
assumed increase in demand, newcomers frequently overestimated
such increases and were, therefore, pushed into direct competition
with existing producers. The latter were, in turn, impelled to defend
their market share to maintain plant loadings. This sequence of

events associated with strategic initiatives and tactical responses was repeated many times over as more and more oil, chemical and other companies were attracted into the industry in the United States, Western Europe and Japan (see section 5.3). By definition these new entrants were inexperienced and were, therefore, more likely to make forecasting errors or, in the case of some state-owned enterprises, to disregard unwelcome predictions. Certainly the bandwagon effect was a feature of the petrochemical industry in the 1960s and early 1970s, when it was believed that marked growth would rapidly absorb any surplus capacity. Pettigrew (1985, 263) characterizes the attitude in the ICI Plastics Division during the 1960s, for example, as 'growth forever, profits forever', a climate of confidence that was shared by others in the industry. As plants became progressively larger, however, the risks associated with this mentality became greater, not only because of the higher capital costs but also because the magnitude of any overinvestment, as measured by the time lag between the jump in capacity resulting from the commissioning of a new plant and the catching up of demand, increased (figure 6.6).

The general factors, associated with the complex interaction between costs, prices, profits, technical change and competitive behaviour, leading to the restructuring crisis in petrochemicals may be regarded as internal to the industry. However, a number of more specific external factors also contributed to the industry's problems. In the cases of Western Europe and Japan these were reflected in deteriorating trade performances during the 1970s. As already noted in section 8.4, the US industry enjoyed a significant comparative advantage following the oil price shocks, and European producers faced increased competition in their domestic markets from US imports. This assault from the west was matched by a new threat from the east as Comecon countries, which had established their own petrochemical industries on the basis of Western technology, began exporting in significant quantities to Western Europe. These pressures upon domestic markets were made worse by reduced export opportunities as countries which had previously relied upon imports from Western Europe became self-sufficient (see chapter 7). In the case of the Middle East, the scale of development raised the prospect not only of lost export markets, but also of yet another unwelcome source of low cost imports into Western Europe. Similar factors affected the competitive position of the Japanese industry which had rapidly built up a substantial export capability in the 1960s and early 1970s, mainly aimed at South East Asian markets. The establishment and subsequent rapid growth of the petrochemical industry in Taiwan and South Korea first limited, and then posed a direct challenge to, potential Japanese exports. These developments, together with the new resource-based operations in the Middle East and especially in Alberta, fundamentally changed the situation of the

Japanese industry, which was forced to reassess its objectives and to
drastically reduce its capacity. Indeed, Japan became a net importer
of ethylene derivatives in 1985 for the first time since the early 1960s.

The oil shocks clearly had a negative effect upon the competitive
positions of the European and Japanese industries. More specifically,
they contributed to the overcapacity problem as a result of short
term responses to the uncertainties created in petrochemical markets
in the wake of the shocks and also as a result of long term impacts
upon patterns of demand. Paradoxically, the 1973–4 oil shock was
followed by a surge in petrochemical demand as fears of future
shortages and further raw-material-driven price increases led to
panic buying and the accumulation of inventory stocks. The immediate effect of this was good news for the industry, and 1974 was a
highly profitable year in all the developed economies (figure 10.5).
Unfortunately this experience conveyed the wrong signals to the
industry, encouraging companies to embark upon major capacity
expansions, such as ICI's Corpus Christi and Wilhelmshaven projects (see section 9.4), which subsequently came on stream just in
time to face the recession of 1981–2. Most observers believe that this
recession was itself partly triggered by the second oil shock. As a
basic industry at an early stage in the chain of production, petrochemical manufacture was, like steel, especially vulnerable and
amongst the first to be affected by the downturn in demand. The
threat posed by the recession loomed even larger in the minds of
executives within the industry as a result of fears that the reversal in
the long term decline in the price of petrochemical products (figure
10.3) would undermine their position relative to competing materials,
thereby weakening the substitution effect and further depressing
demand.[6]

Overall, it is evident that a combination of factors contributed to
the emergence of chronic overcapacity in the petrochemical industry
by 1980. Some of these factors were internal to the industry and had
their origins in patterns of competitive behaviour established during
the era of profitless growth. Others were external to the industry,
especially the numerous direct and indirect effects of the oil price
shocks. Figure 10.6 illustrates the magnitude of the problem by
expressing actual output as a percentage of nameplate capacity[7] for
selected products in Western Europe between 1978 and 1989. The
diagram emphasizes that aggregate measures of capacity utilization
at the industry level (figure 10.5) may conceal wide differences
between individual products. Polypropylene, which is a relatively
young product, maintained generally high utilization rates in the
context of a steady increase in production, whilst the performance
of the more mature LD polyethylene was worse despite significant
reductions in capacity between 1980 and 1985.[8] Nevertheless the products identified in figure 10.6, especially ethylene, may be regarded

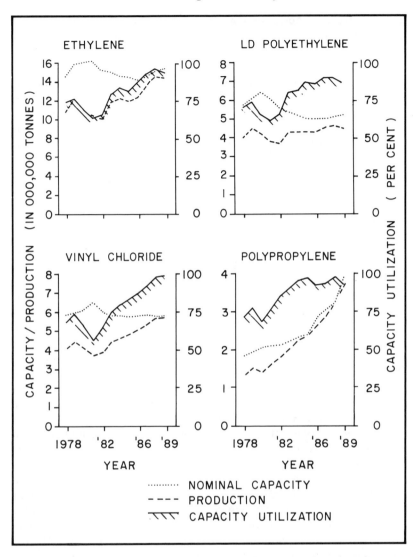

Figure 10.6 Nominal capacity, production and utilization rates for selected petrochemical products in Western Europe, 1978–1989 (from data supplied by ICI Chemicals and Polymers Ltd)

as representative of the industry as a whole, in which operating rates reached a nadir of 60–65 per cent in 1981 and 1982. This experience was replicated in Japan, and these were also the worst years in the United States where operating rates never fell as low. Bearing in mind the importance of capacity utilization as a variable in the economics of petrochemical production (as exemplified by ethylene in section 8.2), the close correlation between operating rate and profitability in figure 10.5 is not surprising. The problems of the industry were made worse by the need to finance much of this surplus capacity embodied in new plants at much higher interest rates than were expected when investment decisions were originally taken. Even the largest private sector and state-owned corporations which dominate the industry could not sustain the kinds of losses that were experienced in 1981 and 1982 when the urgency of the overcapacity problem was clear to all.

10.3 Criteria for Closure

The market solution to overcapacity may, in theory, be expected to achieve a closer correspondence between potential supply and demand as a result of a natural selection process driven by commercial imperatives. This idea is implicit in the concept of the *survival matrix* which was developed by Chem Systems, an international consulting firm specializing in economic forecasting for the chemical industry. This company prepared a comprehensive multiclient study of the European petrochemical industry incorporating detailed analyses of the economics of more than 150 separate petrochemical plants owned by approximately 30 companies (Chem Systems International Ltd 1983). Information was derived from published sources and from interviews with senior management. The study was undertaken in the context of the serious overcapacity problem prevailing in the European petrochemical industry, and a major objective was to measure the extent of this problem under different economic scenarios projected to 1990. More specifically, it attempted to assess, for a range of products, the vulnerability of individual plants to closure under each of these scenarios. Central to the analysis was the distinction between *leader* and *laggard* plants which were used as yardsticks against which the performance of actual plants was compared. These model plants were defined in terms of operating costs, with leader and laggard plants at opposite ends of the spectrum.[9] Costs were assumed to be influenced by such factors as plant vintage, capacity and technology. Such costs were not the only dimension of the survival matrix, since the viability of a plant is also determined by its market prospects or business position. In many cases the position is strongly influenced by corporate structure, and a firm with a captive market for a particular product within a vertically integrated complex has an important advantage over a rival selling in merchant markets. Other variables shaping the assessment of business position included the flexibility of the plant as affected by, for example, its ability to use alternative feedstocks or to modify its pattern of output, and its accessibility to potential markets which

may be influenced by, amongst other things, its location on pipeline
networks.

Figure 10.7 is a representation of a hypothetical survival matrix.
The scores for cost rating and business position are expressed over a
range from −20 to +20 about a median of zero on each axis. There is
an element of subjective judgement in deriving these scores. Nevertheless, the basic principle is that the lowest cost plant has a cost
rating of +20 and the operation with the most favourable business
position scores +20 on the vertical axis. Conversely, scores of −20
are given to the plants with the highest costs and poorest strategic
position. The division of the matrix into two halves implies an
equal weighting to the variables incorporated within the two axes
in determining overall survival prospects. The distinction between
competitive and non-competitive plants is not always clear; hence
the grey area along the diagonal. The knock-on effects for linked
operations within an integrated complex may, for example, tip the
balance in favour of retaining an otherwise marginal unit. Further-

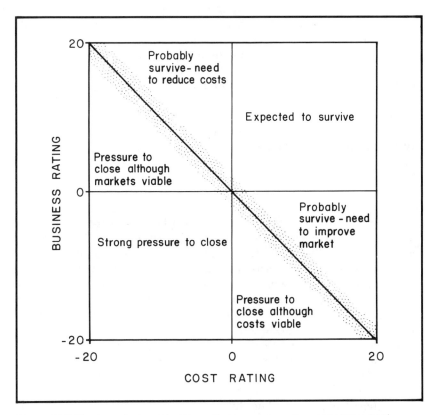

Figure 10.7 Plant survival matrix (Chem Systems International Ltd 1983, I-23)

more, the calibration of the scales is not immutable, and withdrawals may significantly improve the business position of remaining plants that were previously at risk.

The survival matrix concept is applied in figure 10.8 to 66 cracking plants in Western Europe that were either operational or recently closed when the Chem Systems study was published in 1983. Account is also taken of subsequent closures to 1990. Similar matrices were assembled for other products; however, as the core units supplying ethylene, propylene and other basic intermediates to downstream operations, cracking plants exemplify both the nature of the general overcapacity problem in the industry in the early 1980s and also the difficulties involved in solving it. The total nameplate capacity of the operational units identified in figure 10.8 amounts to approximately 16 million tonnes of ethylene, compared with Chem Systems' median demand forecast of 12 million tonnes by 1990.[10] Assuming a 90 per cent utilization rate, this suggested a required nameplate capacity of 13.3 million tonnes. The lines parallel to the main diagonal in figure 10.8 identify increments of 1 million tonnes obtained by adding the capacity of the individual units lying to the left of each line. The diagram suggests that between 4 and 5 million tonnes could be removed without involving any units to the right of the main diagonal. Despite its value in identifying vulnerable capacity, the objective appraisal implicit in the survival matrix is easier for independent observers than for those faced with closure decisions. This was clearly acknowledged by Chem Systems in the original study, which noted a number of plants with strong exit barriers (figure 10.7). The existence of such plants emphasized the many obstacles to restructuring within the industry.

10.4 Obstacles to Restructuring

The survival matrix is an interesting idea because it seeks to provide a rationale for restructuring at the industry level (Baden-Fuller and Longley 1988). It finds parallels in attempts to understand the factors determining patterns of plant closure at corporate level. Watts and Stafford (1986) have drawn together empirical material from studies of multiplant firms in a wide range of industries with a view to identifying a similar rationale shaping the selective closure of factories within corporate systems. In reviewing the evidence, they draw attention to the difficulty of identifying any clear set of decision rules, an observation that certainly applies to petrochemicals. The procedures for evaluating new investments are well known (see Axtell and Robertson 1986), but the financial criteria for plant closure are often ambiguous. The huge capital investments involved in the petrochemical industry make the distinction between cash and

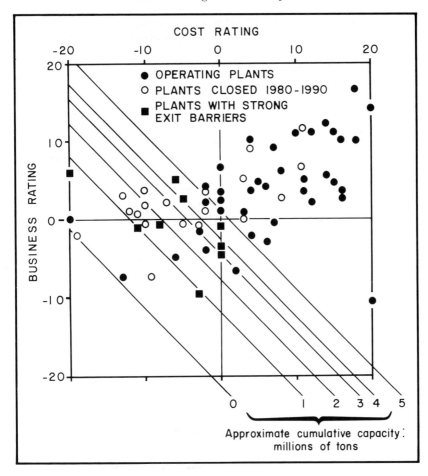

Figure 10.8 Survival matrix for ethylene plants in Western Europe, 1990 (from data supplied by Chem Systems International Ltd)

replacement costs particularly important. The former include only the direct costs of keeping a plant in production, including site overheads; the latter also take account of depreciation, which is typically a major item in the balance sheet of petrochemical operations, as well as interest charges, capital costs and corporate overheads. Where overcapacity prevails and reinvestment is a distant prospect, return on capital is less important than maintaining a positive return on a cash cost basis. Actually shutting down a plant may be very expensive, involving writing off its residual value, dismantling and site clearance in addition to possible redundancy payments. Furthermore, the saving on site overheads may be minimal if the plant is only one of many within a larger complex. In these circumstances, the continued operation of a plant which is making a considerable loss in conventional accounting terms may be a sensible strategy, provided the cash costs are less than the value of the product. However, the cumulative effect of many such 'rational' decisions made at corporate level will be to delay the restructuring of the industry.

The huge capital costs characteristic of the industry create a psychological as well as a financial barrier to restructuring. Studies based upon interviews with senior management have emphasized that decisions to shut down capacity become more and more difficult as the magnitude of the commitment, as reflected in the size of the plant, increases (see Bower 1986; Grant et al. 1988, 207–42). This was especially true of some later entrants to the industry as companies attempted to convince themselves that they held a competitive edge based upon superior technology or management skills. Thus 'pessimism at the sector level was seen as compatible with optimism at the industry level' (Grant et al. 1988, 223). Although this suggests wishful thinking on a grand scale, there is no doubt that the consequences of capacity reduction were much more serious for some companies than for others, notably those that were single plant producers of a particular product. In these circumstances, rationalization implies total withdrawal from a product line rather than the less extreme step of selective closure available to a multiplant company. This difficulty is often made worse by the domino effect which may result from the shutdown of individual units within an integrated complex. The importance of linkages within such complexes was emphasized in chapter 6, which also drew attention to the significance of coproducts. Multiple products are a feature of many petrochemical processes, making it impossible to reduce the output of one without affecting the output of others.

These various psychological, financial and technical barriers to capacity reduction are exemplified by ethylene. They were acknowledged in the Chem Systems (1983) study of the European petrochemical industry. Thus several plants in the most unfavourable quadrant of figure 10.8 have 'strong exit barriers'. One of the most compelling of these barriers is the fact that many European ethylene producers are single plant operations. Indeed, figure 10.8 emphasizes that, although the majority of ethylene plants closed during the 1980s lay in the weaker half of the matrix, there were several notable exceptions in the most favourable quadrant. These were a consequence of the actions of multiplant companies closing their poorest units which were, nevertheless, ranked ahead of many other single plant operations. The commercial constraint to closure facing such operations may be reinforced by political factors where national petrochemical industries are effectively dependent upon a single unit as in, amongst others, Austria and Sweden. Such dependence at the national level is closely related to the problem of geographical isolation. Proximity to alternative suppliers, a highly developed pipeline network, a substantial merchant market and an absence of international frontiers limiting the movement of commodities such as ethylene and propylene made it easier for participants in the US Gulf Coast complex to shut down capacity than for many of their counterparts in the more fragmented European market. This was especially true for plants in Italy and France that were not linked to the principal pipeline systems (figure 6.7). Generally speaking, the availability of coproducts was a constraint upon the rationalization of ethylene capacity more in Western Europe and Japan than in the United States. This reflected the greater importance of liquid rather than gaseous feedstocks for ethylene production which, as noted in section 6.3, ensures that coproducts are more influential in the economics of the cracking operation. The downstream consequences of plant closure are, therefore, more extensive because they affect not only ethylene consuming plants but also activities based upon the other products of cracking such as propylene and butadiene. This domino effect is even more difficult to control when responsibility for downstream units is divided between many companies. Several of the Japanese complexes, for example, were originally conceived as multicompany *combinatos*. This commercial fragmentation was helpful in financing their expansion, but it subsequently hindered their rationalization.

Viewed from the strictly commercial perspective incorporated within the two axes of the survival matrix, it is evident that the petrochemical industry, as exemplified by the case of ethylene, is characterized by a degree of structural inertia which inhibited the reduction of capacity in the early 1980s. This inertia was reinforced in many cases by the intrusion of political considerations, especially in Western Europe where state ownership is a significant factor in many countries. The reasons for the involvement of the public sector in the industry were discussed in chapter 7, and it has been suggested that this involvement delayed the restructuring of the European petrochemical industry because it introduced non-commercial criteria into the decision making process (see Bower 1986; MIT Commission on Industrial Productivity 1989). These include the desire to maintain a national petrochemical industry, and concern for the negative social and economic impacts of plant closures in peripheral regions (see chapter 11). There is no doubt, for example, that the state-owned Portuguese complex at Sines, which came on stream during the trough of the recession in 1981, operated on a totally uneconomic basis for many years. This is an extreme case, but there is considerable evidence that political influence inhibited the introduction of commercial criteria into the bureaucracies of the Italian and especially the French petrochemical industries, delaying their responses to the overcapacity problem of the early 1980s (see Bower 1986; Baden-Fuller and Longley 1988).

To the extent that it involves a reduction in the number of producers as well as a contraction of capacity, industry restructuring raises issues of antitrust (in the United States) and competition (in Western Europe) policy. By discouraging both mergers and the exchange of information between companies, such policy may inhibit industry rationalization. A study of the restructuring of the US chemical industry concluded that antitrust regulations, specifically those relating to mergers and acquisitions, require modification to permit 'firms to adjust quickly to fundamental changes in the market place' (MIT Commission on Industrial Productivity 1989, 58). Similarly, Bower (1986, 61) suggests that the Directorate of the European Commission responsible for enforcing competition policy 'has virtually defeated the efforts of companies to construct cross-national deals that reduce capacity [in petrochemicals]'. The evidence outlined in the next two sections tends to contradict this assessment, but Bower's study does draw attention to a real constraint upon corporate freedom of action.

10.5 Approaches to Restructuring

The mismatch between the potential supply of and demand for many petrochemical products that was reflected in the underutilization of capacity in the early 1980s (figure 10.6) affected all branches of the industry in the developed economies. The international scope of the problem was most apparent in Western Europe, where the origins of the industry ensured that it retained a separate national identity in countries that were more appropriately regarded as part of the same continental market. In these circumstances, attempts to deal with the problem in one country inevitably influenced the situation in neighbouring countries, whether as an incidental side-effect or as a matter of deliberate policy. Various approaches to restructuring may be identified involving differing levels of cooperation between companies and governments. Companies may take unilateral action to reduce capacity, or they may become involved in bi- or multi-lateral deals with others to achieve the same objective (Beynon 1982). Such *autonomous restructuring* depends upon market forces to restore equilibrium between supply and demand. *Organized restructuring* implies an overall policy conceived and directed at industry level on the basis of cooperative arrangements allocating capacity reductions between individual producers. Such arrangements may also involve the participation of national or supranational government agencies, which may simply sanction plans formulated by the industry or may take a more active role in policy making. These various approaches to restructuring are examined in this section as they relate to the petrochemical industry, proceeding from unilateral corporate actions to cooperative schemes. This is followed by a review of events in each of the main areas of production. Such a geographical breakdown is appropriate because the relative import- ance of the different approaches as applied to the problems of the industry in the early 1980s varied between the different areas, with the United States associated with market-driven autonomous changes, Japan adopting a more interventionist stance and Western Europe lying somewhere in between.

Unilateral corporate action may take various forms and have dif- fering impacts both upon the position of the company concerned and upon the overall situation at industry level. Reductions in capacity may be achieved by either temporary or permanent closure of indi- vidual process units.[11] In some cases plant closure is synonymous with site closure, although the latter is usually a more drastic step in the petrochemical industry involving the simultaneous shutdown of several units. All of these actions may be regarded as *tactical* responses to an overcapacity problem. In the case of multiplant enterprises, such responses are designed to concentrate production in the best locations; the intention is to trim capacity rather than cease production altogether. However, total withdrawal from a particular line of business is another *strategic* option. This may take several forms. The most extreme step, which may be taken by large, diver- sified organizations, is to leave a sector completely and direct their resources elsewhere. A less radical alternative is selective withdrawal from particular markets, whether defined in terms of products or geographical areas. Despite the logic of economic theory it is import- ant to recognize that such unilateral corporate actions will not necesarily produce an optimal outcome at the industry level. Fur- thermore, many strategic responses are not truly unilateral because they usually involve selling facilites to other companies so that the effect of such moves upon the overcapacity problem actually depends upon what the purchasers do with their inherited facilities.

Bi- and multilateral corporate initiatives are often intended to secure more specific outcomes in the sense that the participants have established mutually acceptable objectives which may include capacity reduction. Implicit in such arrangements is an acknowl- edgement that changes in industry structure may be necessary to overcome at least some of the obstacles to capacity contraction described in section 10.4. Typically, these changes involve the concentration of production in fewer hands, and they are consistent with life-cycle models which predict such a trend in the later stages of industry evolution (figure 1.1) This transformation may be achieved by a variety of mechanisms. Mergers and joint ventures, frequently related to technology sharing and acquisition in times of growth, are associated with different motivations during maturity when they may be a prelude to selective closures within an enlarged grouping. Similar rationalization may occur following the aggressive takeover of one company by another, as numerous case studies have demonstrated (see Massey and Meegan 1979; Todd 1985). Portfolio swaps are a more unusual step towards concentration and rationalization which have been tried in the petrochemical industry. These involve agreements between companies to exchange their respective interests in specific products so that each withdraws from one (or more) line(s) of business but acquires an increased market share in the retained product(s), which in turn permits a greater influence upon future capacity and output.

Mergers, takeovers and portfolio swaps normally involve only two parties. There are, however, various circumstances in which multilateral arrangements may facilitate capacity reduction. These may range from informal discussions between companies to cartels intended to influence far more than the rationalization of capacity. A uniquely Japanese approach was a tour of European facilities arranged by MITI for the chief executives of 12 of the country's leading petrochemical companies in 1983. This was designed to emphasize the magnitude of the overcapacity problem and, according to an MITI official quoted by Bower (1986, 189), to 'help build co-operative relationships' amongst the travellers. The creation of the Association of Petrochemical Producers in Europe (APPE) in 1985 as a sector group within Conseil Européen des Fédérations de l'Industrie Chimique (CEFIC), which represents the interests of the chemical industry at the European level, was principally motivated by the overcapacity problem and the need to facilitate the assembly and dissemination of information relevant to its solution. Thus it serves as a channel through which aggregate data on such matters as new investment and levels of capacity utilization may be directed to its member companies (Grant et al. 1988, 193–5). The activities of commercial consultancies such as Chem Systems and Parpinelli Tecnon also facilitate the circulation of information, since their various studies are heavily based upon intelligence gained from discussions with the companies that are themselves their principal customers.

In their desire to provide better information services to their members, industry associations such as APPE must be sensitive to potential breaches of antitrust and competition policy. Cartels have played an important role in the history of the chemical industry (see Reader 1975; Mirow and Maurer 1982; Taylor and Sudnik 1984), and there is evidence that these practices have not entirely disappeared from the modern industry (UN Conference on Trade and Development 1979). Indeed, a substantial number of chemical companies were fined by the European Commission in 1986 and 1988 for operating illegal price fixing and production sharing arrangements for polypropylene, LD polyethylene and PVC during the early 1980s. The existence of these arrangements indicates that a very high degree of cooperation was widely perceived in the industry to be a sensible response to its overcapacity problem.[12] The fact that the European Commission did not share this view underlines the wider policy implications of industry restructuring. These implications suggest that government may either inhibit or promote the restructuring process depending upon its attitude towards attempts to increase industry concentration.

The restructuring of the US petrochemical industry has been extensively described elsewhere (see US International Trade Commission 1983; 1985b; Bower 1986; MIT Commission on Industrial Productivity 1989). This restructuring was achieved exclusively by autonomous corporate actions involving selective closures within multiplant enterprises and conscious attempts to reduce dependence upon petrochemicals relative to other activities. In some cases, such as Monsanto, corporate reorientation involved almost complete withdrawal from the petrochemical industry. Retrospective assessments of these events have suggested that, by comparison with Western Europe and Japan, the restructuring of the US industry was a relatively smooth transition to the slower growth rates of maturity which vindicated the free market approach (see Bower 1986; MIT Commission on Industrial Productivity 1989). However, such assessments tend to disregard the additional obstacles to change imposed, in particular, by the commercial and geographical fragmentation of the European industry.

Petrochemicals was not the first European industry to be faced with a chronic overcapacity problem. Iron and steel and synthetic fibres had previously attracted considerable political attention, including the direct intervention of the European Commission (see Commission of the European Communities 1981; Shaw and Shaw 1983). Similar intervention was considered for petrochemicals in 1982 at a meeting between members of the Commission and representatives of several major companies. Views within the industry were divided, with its weaker members, mainly French and Belgian companies, favouring some kind of EC programme, whilst the British, German and Dutch were opposed (Grant et al. 1988, 226–31). Accordingly, no agreement for a crisis cartel was reached. Nevertheless, the meeting was important in securing formal recognition at the highest political level of the industry's overcapacity problem. In particular, it became clear that the Commission was prepared to adopt a sympathetic attitude towards agreements and information sharing arrangements aimed at a coordinated reduction of capacity (rather than the price fixing scheme which many companies actually tried). Bearing in mind its traditional vigour in the implementation of competition and trade policies, these signals by the Commission were important in paving the way for a variety of different approaches to the overcapacity problem ranging from unilateral corporate actions to direct government intervention.

Many companies shut down capacity. At least 12 plants were closed in the United Kingdom in 1981–2 (Fayad and Motamen 1986, 96) and similar moves were made by BASF and Hoechst in West Germany. New investment was still undertaken, however, and severe cost competition encouraged some companies to replace older units with new facilities. The commissioning of the Shell/Exxon joint venture ethylene plant at Mossmorran in Scotland in 1985 was, for example, directly responsible for the shutdown of facilities at Carrington, near Manchester (Shell) and at Köln (Exxon). The impact of US investment upon the development of the European petrochemical industry during its rapid growth phase in the 1960s has already been described (section 9.4). This influx became an exodus 25 years later when, faced with a very different prospect in a mature industry, most of the same companies ceased production in Western Europe. In some cases, such as Gulf's Europoort complex, this withdrawal immediately resulted in plant shutdown. More often, the facilities were acquired by European firms. For example, BP purchased all of Union Carbide's commodity chemical business in Europe, whilst BASF took over several of Monsanto's facilities. Such responses to the US withdrawal contributed to the consolidation of the European petrochemical industry by reducing the number of producers and facilitating the rationalization of capacity by the enlarged survivors.

Consolidation was not limited to the opportunitites presented by the US withdrawal, and a spate of mergers and takeovers occurred during the 1980s. The number of PVC producers, for example, fell from 29 to 17 between 1980 and 1983 (Bower 1986, 28) and similar trends have been apparent in other branches of the industry (table 5.2). A deal involving the exchange of facilities by BP and ICI was one of the more imaginative approaches to restructuring. Under this scheme, which was conceived in 1981 and finally implemented in 1984 after securing the approval of both the British government and the European Commission, BP withdrew from vinyl chloride and PVC in Europe whilst ICI pulled out of LD polyethylene. By transferring ownership of certain facilities and shutting down others, the positions of BP and ICI in each of these markets was considerably strengthened. Similar considerations have underpinned attempts to rationalize the French and Italian petrochemical industries, where the situation has been complicated by the involvement of both state-owned and private sector companies.

Various historical and political factors have ensured that the state has always played an active role in the French and Italian chemical industries. This role has had many consequences, including effects upon location (see chapter 11). It has also influenced the approach to the overcapacity problem as a result of the politicization of the decision making process. Indeed, the economic problems of the French-owned (i.e. private sector) petrochemical industry resulted in its nationalization in 1983, a step which certainly delayed plant closures (Bower 1986, 137–46). In the Italian case, the picture was distorted by the complex relationship between the private sector company Montedison and its state-owned counterpart ENI. Various attempts were made during the 1980s to clarify the division of responsibilities between them. Once again the overcapacity problem provided the stimulus to this continuous reappraisal, which has involved portfolio swaps between the public and private sector along the lines of the BP/ICI deal as well as the merging of common petrochemical interests in Enimont, which became one of the world's largest chemical companies when formed in 1989.[13]

The role of government was very different in Japan, where influence was exerted indirectly through the actions of MITI rather than by state ownership. The significance of MITI in the establishment of the Japanese petrochemical industry was emphasized in section 7.2. In just the same way that the agency promoted petrochemicals as part of an overall industrial strategy in the 1950s, so it facilitated the restructuring of the industry in the same spirit of comprehensive economic planning in the 1980s. It was recognized that, 25 years on, the prospects of the industry were very different. This was due not simply to the inevitable slowdown of maturity, but also to a belief that the Japanese dependence on imported oil and gas seriously weakened its competitive position in petrochemicals relative to the Middle East, Canada, the United States and even Western Europe. Declining exports and increasing import penetration at the beginning of the 1980s reinforced this assessment and prompted a fundamental review both of the overcapacity problem and of the industry's place in the national economy. This was undertaken by a committee of the Industrial Structure Council which 'is the central forum used by MITI to establish broad political consensus behind major policy objectives' (Bower 1986, 202). Broadly speaking, this review suggested a reorientation of the Japanese chemical industry away from commodity petrochemicals and towards high value, high technology products such as advanced materials (Suzuki 1982). More immediately, it was recognized that a major restructuring of the petrochemical industry was necessary to improve operating rates and profitability. The changes required to achieve these objectives were made easier by legislation in 1983. This was directed towards a number of depressed industries including petrochemicals. It established precise targets for capacity reduction by 1985, advocated fewer producers to eliminate 'abnormal competition' and encouraged geographical concentration in the most favoured locations. The real significance of these various measures was the deliberate attempt to create a political and institutional environment conducive to the restructuring of depressed industries. Thus, despite the absence of direct state ownership, the influence of government upon the restructuring of petrochemicals in Japan was, by virtue of MITI's mediating role between the political and business communities, much greater than in Western Europe.

10.6 Consequences of Restructuring

The basic objective of the restructuring process was to achieve, at both corporate and industry levels, a closer match between production and available capacity, bearing in mind the importance of maintaining high utilization rates for the economics of petrochemical plants. It has already been noted (see section 10.2) that the over-capacity problem was greater for some products than others, but figures 10.5 and 10.6 are indicative of the transformation achieved in Western Europe between the beginning and end of the 1980s. This improvement was based upon initial cutbacks in capacity followed, after 1985, by a general recovery of production. Taking ethylene as the most appropriate indicator for the performance of the industry as a whole, the 90–95 per cent operating rates[14] achieved between 1987 and 1989 (figure 10.6) were not only a dramatic turnaround compared with a few years earlier, but also a significant improvement on the 70–80 per cent levels characteristic of the 1970s.

The real commercial significance of these trends lies in their direct link to profit margins. These margins obviously depend upon the relationship between feedstock costs and product prices, but they are also strongly influenced by operating rates, as figure 10.5 implies. Indeed, company accounts suggest that 1988 and 1989 were highly profitable years in the petrochemical business. Thus the restructuring process was successful as measured by the bottom line of corporate balance sheets. The beneficiaries of this process were fewer in number than the losers at the beginning of the period as a result of the concentration of production in the various subsectors of the industry (see section 10.5). Generally speaking, the position of the oil companies in basic petrochemicals was strengthened relative to the traditional chemical companies, which diverted resources into other areas such as pharmaceuticals. Another consequence of the restructuring process is evident in employment. Virtually all petrochemicals producers regarded job losses as an integral part of their restructuring programmes, and the effects of these decisions were apparent in employment statistics (figure 10.9).

It has been suggested that relocation may be an important dimen-

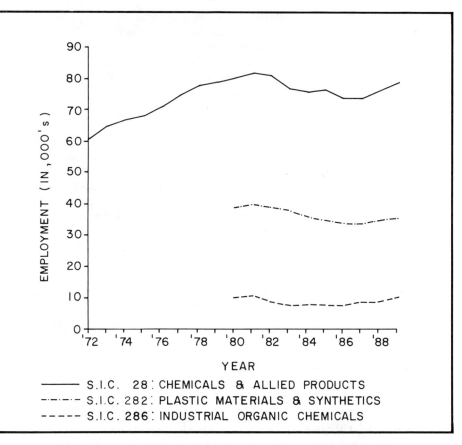

Figure 10.9 Employment in SIC 28 (chemicals and allied products), SIC 282 (plastics and synthetic materials) and SIC 286 (industrial organic chemicals) in Texas, 1972–1989 (data supplied by Texas Employment Commission)

sion of the restructuring of industries (see Storper and Walker 1989, 90). This view has been encouraged by the apparent collapse of the economic base of communities associated with industries such as steel or textiles. It is, therefore, relevant to consider whether the restructuring of the petrochemical industry has resulted in any shift in its distribution within the developed economies. More specifically, it may be hypothesized that the kind of logic implicit in the *survival matrix* as applied to plants in section 10.3 might have a geographical component operating at the aggregate industry level, with selective closures resulting in the elimination of capacity in the least favoured locations and a tendency towards a more optimal distribution. This proposition assumes greater significance in Western Europe as compared with the United States and Japan because of the

politicization of the industry associated with its fragmentation
between different countries. There was, for example, initial resent-
ment in the United Kingdom that, by responding quickly to the need
for capacity reduction, its industry was assuming a disproportionate
share of the burden of rationalization (Chemicals EDC 1984). Reference to the distribution of ethylene capacity within Western Europe
at the beginning and end of the 1980s, however, suggests that these
concerns were misplaced. Thus, of the top five countries, which
accounted for more than 75 per cent of total capacity and production
in 1990, the United Kingdom and the Netherlands showed a relative
gain over the period, whilst the shares of France, Italy and especially
West Germany declined. Whatever shifts took place, notably in the
fortunes of the United Kingdom and West Germany, reflected the
commissioning and closure of relatively few large plants rather than
any fundamental change in the geography of the industry.

In analysing the spatial consequences of restructuring within the
petrochemical industry it is important to make a distinction between
factory (or site) closures and plant closures. The two are synonymous
in many industries and the terms are often used interchangeably.[15]
In the case of petrochemicals, however, 'factories' often take the
form of integrated complexes manufacturing multiple products in
numerous interconnected 'plants'. Although functional linkages
ensure that the closure of one plant may adversely affect the operation of others within the complex (i.e. the domino effect), it is nevertheless possible to achieve major capacity reduction without the total
closure of a particular site. Indeed, shutdown plants are frequently
mothballed for long periods before a decision is taken to dismantle
them so that there may be no obvious changes in the appearance of
the site. Despite substantial disinvestment involving numerous plant
closures during the early 1980s, very few manufacturing sites were
abandoned to the extent that might have been expected in other
industries experiencing similar contractions in capacity. Thus derelict
engineering works, shipyards and steel mills have often provided
mute testimony to the impact of deindustrialization within developed
economies, but abandoned petrochemical complexes are unusual;
Gulf's Europoort operation, which shut down at the beginning of the
1980s, is perhaps the most spectacular example. Thus the basic
geography of the petrochemical industry in Western Europe, as
reflected in the location of the principal centres of production, was
little changed by the commercial upheavals of the 1980s.

Even if these upheavals did not have a major impact upon spatial
patterns at the industry scale, they did require significant adjustments at corporate level as the larger companies reviewed their
options for reducing capacity. Generally speaking, this involved
concentrating the output of specific products on the most efficient
units subject to the logistical constraints imposed by the availability

of feedstock and patterns of downstream use. In many cases, the commercial changes associated with the restructuring process meant that these adjustments occurred within the context of a corporate system modified by the effects of mergers, takeovers, portfolio swaps and other shifts of ownership. ICI has, for example, had a significant impact upon patterns of vinyl chloride and PVC production in Western Europe as a result of first an agreement with BP in 1984, and second a joint venture with Enichem in 1986. The former deal led to the closure of BP's vinyl chloride and PVC plants at Baglan Bay and Barry in South Wales, whilst the arrangement with Enichem led to the creation of European Vinyls Corporation (EVC) which effectively merged the vinyl chloride and PVC interests of the parent companies in Western Europe (figure 10.10). This merger was immediately followed by substantial reductions in PVC capacity at the various sites inherited by the new company, which has sub-sequently created a sales and distribution organization to optimize marketing arrangements on a continental scale. The creation of EVC, which supplies approximately 20 per cent of the European PVC market, has involved little change in the geography of vinyl chloride and PVC production since its output is derived from the same sites operated by its parent companies before the merger.[16] This continuity does, however, conceal significant changes in the organization of production. These changes, especially the shutdown of older units on these sites, were facilitated by the consolidation of the previously separate operations of the parent companies.

10.7 Conclusions

The experience of petrochemical manufacture within the developed economies during the early 1980s emphasizes that trends in output and capacity do not necessarily follow the smooth curve predicted by life-cycle models. In this case, the temporal coincidence of an internal tendency towards overinvestment, based upon the interaction of both behavioural and technical factors, and the external shock associated with the second jump in oil prices, resulted in a significant blip in the industry's long term evolution. However, it is also clear that there is no question that the industry has reached a point at which output may be expected to begin a steady, terminal decline within the developed economies. Indeed, the improvement in operating rates towards the end of the 1980s has resulted in a series of additions to capacity that will come on stream during the 1990s. These additions will not alter the progressive global shift in the distribution of the petrochemical industry away from the core economies, but they emphasize that this shift is a consequence of differential rates of growth rather than absolute decline or transfers of production of the

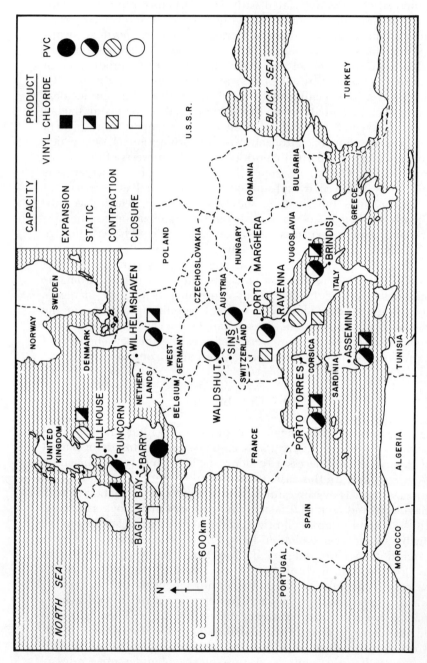

Figure 10.10 Rationalization of ICI/Enichem vinyl chloride and PVC production, 1982–1990

type associated with industries such as consumer electronics. It is therefore not surprising that the impact of the restructuring crisis upon the geography of the industry *within* the developed economies was negligible, with the principal centres of production remaining the same at the beginning and end of the 1980s. Employment within these centres has, however, often fallen drastically as a result of the further substitution of capital for labour in an already capital-intensive industry, and of the slowdown in investment and hence construction activity. These employment effects have drawn attention to the connection between the evolution of the industry and the development of the regions and communities with which it is associated – a connection that is explored in the next chapter.

Notes

1 Such a response, associated with normal-plus profits in Markusen's terminology, does not always occur. She also acknowledges the possibility of continuing destructive competition leading to normal-minus profits and the accelerated demise of the industry (see section 1.1).

2 It must be acknowledged that some firms tend to be overoptimistic in good times and excessively pessimistic in bad times. This tends to exaggerate the cyclical nature of the petrochemical business rather than encourage persistent overcapacity.

3 The regional development impacts are examined in chapter 11.

4 Paradoxically, forecasts made during the industry's rapid growth in the 1950s and 1960s generally erred on the side of caution, and the experience possibly fostered an atmosphere of overoptimism which contributed to the mistakes of the 1970s.

5 This process is unusual in the sense that it was introduced 43 years after synthetic methanol first entered commercial production (Stobaugh 1988, 115).

6 These fears were not in fact realized, and whatever decline in petrochemical demand actually occurred seems to have been unrelated to any price induced weakening of the substitution effect.

7 This is the theoretical design capacity and is rarely achieved in practice as a result of normal operational limitations such as breakdowns and routine maintenance. Thus figure 10.6 tends to exaggerate overcapacity, since effective (i.e. realistic) capacity is generally assumed to be 90–95 per cent of nominal or nameplate capacity.

8 Competition from younger linear low density (LLD) polyethylene aggravated the problems of maturity for low density (LD) polyethylene. Technical advances in the early 1980s, for example, allowed the manufacture of much thinner LD polyethylene films by blending with LLD polyethylene. By replacing heavier gauge films in many applications, these new films led to sharp falls in LD polyethylene demand.

9 The leader corresponded to the lowest cost type of plant generally available to participate in the industry. It excluded plants which derived their advantages from special situations, such as artificially low transfer

prices on feedstocks. The cost of production for the leader was, therefore, not necessarily the absolute minimum in the industry. Similarly, the laggard plant was the highest cost surviving facility remaining operational for economic rather than social or political reasons. It too was not necessarily the most extreme case.

10 By 1990 ethylene demand was in fact running at approximately 15 million tonnes, emphasizing the difficulty of making such predictions.

11 The distinction between temporary and permanent closure is not always clear in the petrochemical industry, as many units that are initially mothballed are never recommissioned.

12 In fact, the huge losses sustained by most participants suggest that these arrangements were remarkably unsuccessful, although they probably delayed the shutdown of surplus capacity.

13 The future of Enimont and the relationship between public and private sector in the Italian petrochemical industry continue to be uncertain at the time of writing (in 1990).

14 See note 6.

15 Watts and Stafford (1986, 206), for example, refer to the plant as 'the basic unit by which a closure decision is expressed in regional space'.

16 The manufacturing plants continue (in 1990) to be operated by the parent companies which supply products to EVC.

11
Petrochemicals, Regions and Public Policy

The evolution of industries and the development of regions are inextricably linked (see section 1.2). The traditional association of particular regions with particular industries has, to some extent, been replaced by differentiation upon the basis of position within systems of production related to spatial divisions of labour operated by large corporations. Thus certain core regions account for a disproportionate share of high order functions such as head offices and R and D facilities, whilst routine manufacturing is carried out in peripheral regions. Although such relationships now play an important role in the spatial organization of production within countries, Markusen (1987, 23) notes, with reference to the United States, that 'sectoral differentiation remains a potent factor in contemporary regionalism.' The potency of this factor depends upon the geography of individual industries; those that are highly clustered are obviously more influential than those that are widely dispersed (see Lubove 1969; Doxiadis 1966). One of the most distinctive features of the petrochemical industry is its agglomeration in large complexes (see chapter 6). This characteristic has ensured that it has had a major impact upon the fortunes of regional economies. These fortunes have reflected those of the industry, so that places such as south-east Texas have passed through the full range of economic experiences from spectacular growth to catastrophic decline in less than a generation. The nature of these experiences and their implications for regional development policy are explored in this chapter, which is divided into four sections. The first reviews the nature of petrochemicals as a propulsive industry; the second illustrates this characteristic with reference to the economy of the US Gulf Coast; the third reviews attempts to harness this role in the context of growth centre policies; and the fourth considers some of the regional consequences of the industry's maturity.

11.1 Petrochemicals as a Propulsive Industry

The concept of lead or propulsive industries was introduced in section 1.2, where it was noted that industries in the early phase of their life cycle may serve as engines of growth at national and regional levels. This idea, which is implicit in the work of many economists such as Rostow, Schumpeter and Freeman, was developed by Perroux (1950) who adopted the term *pôles de croissance* (i.e. growth poles) to describe the focuses of growth within an economic system. These are conceptualized not as geographic locations but as functional nodes, consisting of clusters of industries around which fields of economic forces are organized. These forces are both centrifugal and centripetal and are transmitted through the economic system by transactions between plants, firms and sectors. Propulsive industries play an important role in this process. They are characterized not only by rapid growth on such indices as output, employment and investment but, more important, by the ability to transmit this growth to other sectors. The operation of normal multiplier mechanisms ensures a kind of ripple effect from any rapidly growing sector, but this effect seems to be enhanced in the case of propulsive industries as a result of their extensive connections throughout the economic system. These connections are maintained by information flows and physical linkages.

As far as information flows are concerned, the real significance of propulsive industries derives from their role in the diffusion of innovations. It has already been observed that innovations are ultimately responsible for the creation of industries (see sections 1.1 and 3.1), but the impact of innovations such as the silicon chip clearly extends far beyond any single sector. Indeed, 'a small number of industries may be responsible for generating a vastly disproportionate amount of total technological change in the economy' (Rosenberg 1979, 46). Scherer (1982) attempted to indentify these industries by constructing a 'technology flows matrix' based upon an analysis of R and D expenditures and invention patents in the United States. In reviewing these patents, a distinction was made between industries of origin and industries of use in order to identify sectors that were exporting technology to others. Major differences between industries were revealed, with some, including petro-chemicals,[1] especially active in providing new technology to a broad array of using industries, a conclusion which is consistent with the chemical industry's traditional role as an agent of change in other sectors including textiles and metals. There is, in fact, a strong positive correlation between technology flows and physical flows which is both statistical and causal. Numerous studies, employing historical and contemporary evidence, have emphasized the import-ance of producer goods industries, which typically have extensive input (i.e. backward) and output (i.e. forward) linkages, as sources of technology (see Rosenberg 1976; 1979; 1986; Scherer 1982; Kline and Rosenberg 1986). Thus a propulsive sector often exerts a kind of demand-pull effect upon its suppliers, stimulating more rapid rates of technical change in response to the pressures of demand, and a science-push effect upon its customers, encouraging a search for new applications for new materials.

These innovation effects are arguably the essential characteristic of a propulsive industry, but the possession of extensive physical linkages magnifies the impact of purchases and sales upon levels of production in other sectors. The extent of this impact is revealed by conventional input–output analyses which show how a unit increase in output or sales in one sector generates, through the operation of the multiplier, increases in other sectors. The central role of the petrochemical industry in the modern economy, as demonstrated by such analyses, was emphasized in chapter 2. Thus petrochemicals has, in its pervasive influence upon both innovation and output, the key qualities of a propulsive industry, and it is not surprising that it figures prominently in various attempts to identify sectors suitable for promoting economic development.[2] Most have been content to equate these sectors with Perroux's concept of growth poles in abstract economic space (see Hirschman 1958; Kuznets 1966; Roepke et al. 1974; Lever 1980), but others have made the significant jump to growth centres in geographic space by making the explicit connection between linkages and agglomeration (see Czamanski 1976; Norcliffe 1979). This connection is important since many studies were, despite their common dependence upon apparently abstract input–output models, intended to provide practical guidance to policy makers wishing to steer economic development to specific regions. Indeed, they were often motivated by a desire to replicate the economic experiences of established industrial complexes. In the case of petrochemicals, it was the spectacular growth of places such as Rotterdam, Teesside and, above all, the communities of the US Gulf Coast which provided the inspiration for attempts to use the industry as an instrument of regional development policy. It is, therefore, desirable to consider the characteristics of such spontaneous regional complexes before evaluating the success or failure of planned growth centres.

11.2 Sectoral Growth and Regional Growth: Petrochemicals on the US Gulf Coast

Although not always clear, it is possible to make a distinction between a specific industrial complex and the wider regional complex of which it forms a part. The characteristic agglomeration of oil-based industrial complexes was explained in chapter 6 in terms of the combined effects of functional linkages, transfer economies and scale factors. Several studies have explored the internal structure of individual complexes (see Wever 1966; Chapman 1973; 1974a; Shanafelt 1977; Molle and Wever 1984), but few have placed these complexes within the overall socio-economic structure of the regions in which they are located. Pratt's (1980) study of the upper Texas Gulf Coast is an important exception. The existence of this work, together with the relatively long history and massive concentration of petrochemical activity, makes the Gulf Coast the most appropriate illustration of the regional impact of the growth of the industry.

Pratt (1980, 4) eloquently observes that 'The imprint of petroleum on the pattern of regional development [in the upper Texas Gulf Coast] stands out vividly, like a brightly lighted refinery against the early morning sky on the coastal plain.' He identifies oil refining as 'the engine of growth that helped power more than seventy-five years of regional development at a pace that was unusual even by the standards of a nation accustomed to rapid economic growth' (Pratt 1980, 4–5). Certainly, the Gulf Coast was clearly established by 1947 as the greatest regional concentration of oil refining capacity in the United States (and in the world), a situation which contributed to its emergence as the dominant centre of petrochemical production. Having decided to move into petrochemicals, it made technical and economic sense for oil companies such as Shell and Gulf to locate their new facilities within or adjacent to their principal refineries (see section 4.1). The attractions of the region were further enhanced by the availability of natural gas which drew chemical companies such as Dow and Union Carbide to the Gulf Coast. Indeed, the propulsive role of the refining industry was, to a considerable extent, inherited by petrochemicals which became 'the catalyst for the second spurt of regional growth in the modern era' (Pratt 1980, 105).

The progressive concentration of US petrochemical capacity in Texas and Louisiana (table 6.1) conceals a significant dispersal of facilities within a series of separate but interconnected complexes extending from Corpus Christi in the west to the Mississippi corridor linking Baton Rouge and New Orleans in the east (figure 11.1). This pattern broadly corresponds to the distribution of refinery capacity, a correspondence based upon the technical and commercial relationships between the two industries. The Golden Triangle defined by Beaumont, Orange and Port Arthur was the initial focus of the Gulf Coast oil refining industry, reflecting the magnetic attraction of the huge Spindletop discovery in 1901. By the end of World War II, however, the more dispersed contemporary pattern of refinery capacity was established and Houston had replaced the Golden Triangle as the principal centre. This pattern provided the geographical framework for the new petrochemical industry since, with

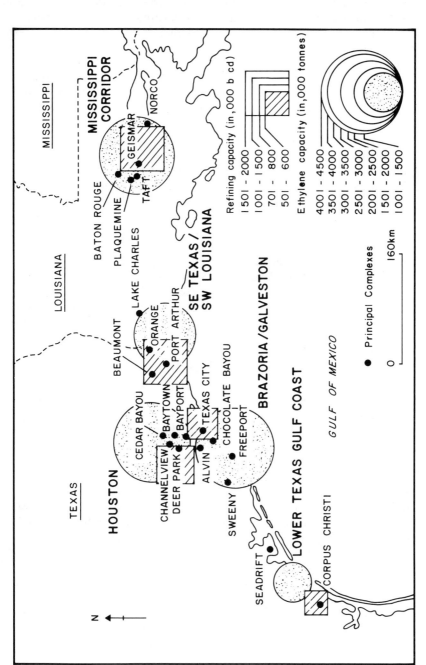

Figure 11.1 Oil refining and petrochemical regions on US Gulf Coast, 1990

the significant exception of Dow's Freeport operation, virtually all of the early petrochemical plants were located in close proximity to oil refineries. The Houston Ship Channel soon became the largest concentration of petrochemical facilities and experienced very rapid growth in the late 1940s and early 1950s. By 1960, few large sites with Channel frontages remained available and new companies wishing to build plants in the Houston area were obliged to seek alternatives such as Channelview and Cedar Bayou to the north and east respectively, both of which were developed in the 1960s. The existing refining complexes of the Golden Triangle and Texas City also attracted considerable petrochemical development during and immediately after World War II. It has already been noted that the functional relationship between oil refining and petrochemical operations that was so important to some of the earliest developments rapidly became less significant as NGLs rather than refinery feedstocks supported the industry's expansion, and accessibility to a natural gas processing facility or pipeline system was, therefore, the basic locational requirement (see section 6.2). In these circumstances, several petrochemical plants have been built on large greenfield sites in relatively remote locations on the coastal plain between Galveston and Corpus Christi. Some of these, such as Freeport (Dow), Victoria (Du Pont) and Seadrift (Union Carbide) were operational before the mid 1950s; others, such as Bay City (Celanese),[3] Alvin (Monsanto)[4] and Chocolate Bayou (Amoco), came on stream in the 1960s. These site choices may have been influenced by the problems of acquiring land in such congested areas as the Houston Ship Channel. Although Exxon's Baton Rouge refinery played an important part in the early development of petrochemical technology (see section 3.4), the major expansion of the industry in Louisiana occurred later than in Texas. Up to the mid 1950s, this facility and the refining complex established during and immediately after World War II at Lake Charles were the only significant centres of petrochemical production in Louisiana. However, a whole series of new plants were built along the banks of the Mississippi between Baton Rouge and New Orleans during the 1960s and 1970s, and these ensured a significant jump in Louisiana's share of US petrochemical capacity (table 6.1).

Various indicators may be used to measure the growth of the Gulf Coast petrochemical complex. The dominating presence of tanks and towers makes a massive physical impac upon the landscape. The Houston Ship Channel is, for example, flanked by an almost uninterrupted procession of oil refineries and petrochemical plants over a distance of approximately 25 km, whilst the three sites operated by Dow at Freeport are, taken together, probably the largest single company petrochemical complex in the world. A growing number of firms contributed to the creation of such distinctive industrial landscapes. Whitehorn (1973, 7) notes that four firms started petrochemical operations in Texas[5] during the 1930s and that these were joined by a further 15, 21 and 17 respectively in each of the following decades to 1970. Employment, which is perhaps the most obvious indicator of the regional economic significance of petrochemical manufacturing, is difficult to measure accurately because the industry is not differentiated in most official statistics, although Adib (1983) has estimated that 68 per cent of total employment in SIC 28 (i.e. chemicals and allied products) in Texas and Louisiana in 1977 could be classified as 'petrochemical'. It is also difficult to obtain a clear picture of long term employment trends as a result of periodic changes in the definition of the geographical units to which the data relate. Figure 11.2 uses the example of the Beaumont–Port Arthur metropolitan statistical area (MSA) (i.e. the Golden Triangle). It is clear that oil refining and petrochemicals have consistently accounted for a major proportion of manufacturing employment since 1950, although their relative contributions have changed during the period. As previously noted, this area was the initial focus of oil refining activity on the Gulf Coast and the industry had been established for almost half a century by 1950. Viewed at the regional scale it was therefore already a mature industry, and this is reflected in generally stable or even slightly falling employment

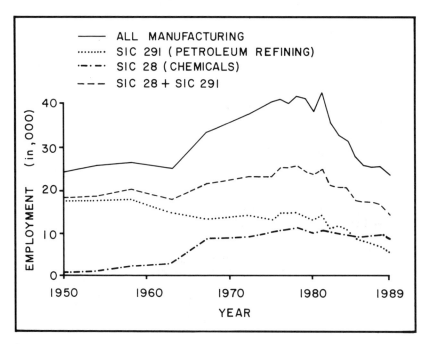

Figure 11.2 Employment in manufacturing, petroleum refining (SIC 291) and chemicals (SIC 28) in Beaumont–Port Arthur MSA, 1950–1989

levels to the end of the 1970s. Employment in the new petrochemical industry showed a very different trend, starting from a very low level, increasing sharply in the 1960s and then growing more steadily in the 1970s. Although the very early development of oil refining in the Golden Triangle ensured that employment in this sector stabilized and began to fall earlier than in later refining centres such as Lake Charles and Corpus Christi, the general trend of employment in petrochemicals indicated in figure 11.2 is typical of other parts of the Gulf Coast industrial complex.

An important characteristic of both oil refining and petrochemical manufacture is not only that they are capital intensive, but also that their capital intensity has increased through time. Pratt (1980, 97) notes that increasing automation 'gradually weakened the strongest direct linkage between the refineries and the regional economy'. This effect is easy to express for oil refining since crude throughput capacity provides a reliable single measure of potential output. It is much more difficult to derive an equivalent indicator for the multi product petrochemical industry, and the problem is compounded by the failure of official statistics to identify petrochemicals as an employment category. Table 11.1 uses ethylene capacity as a surrogate measure of petrochemical output and employment in SIC 28, which certainly includes non-petrochemical activities. It combines data for the Houston primary metropolitan statistical area (PMSA) and the Beaumont–Port Arthur MSA which together account for a significant proportion of petrochemical capacity on the Gulf Coast. Even allowing for the severe limitations of the method and the data, the steady increase in capacity per employee is both striking and significant.

Paradoxically, the high levels of construction activity required to achieve the increase in capacity and the technological advances responsible for the trend towards more capital-intensive methods of production apparent in table 11.1 themselves created many new jobs. Indeed, the absolute numbers employed in contract construction

Table 11.1 Ethylene capacity and employment in chemicals (SIC 28) in Houston PMSA and Beaumont–Port Arthur MSA, 1950–1989

Year	Employment in SIC 28 (approx.)	Ethylene capacity (thousand tonnes)	Capacity per employee (thousand tonnes)
1950	7,200	169	0.023
1960	14,700	488	0.033
1970	28,500	2,304	0.081
1980	35,400	6,082	0.172
1989	34,600	6,365	0.184

Source: employment from US Census of Manufactures (1950, 1960, 1970) and Texas Employment Commission (1980, 1989); ethylene capacity from various sources

in Beaumont–Port Arthur MSA have generally been greater than in either SIC 28 or SIC 291 (petroleum refining), although these numbers have closely followed the ups and downs of the leading sectors. Much the same pattern may be observed not only in the various subregional economies of the Gulf Coast, but also in other places dominated by the oil refining and petrochemical industries. Petrochemical complexes throughout the developed world had the appearance of permanent construction sites during the boom years. The employment generated by this activity was further enhanced by construction in other sectors related to and sustained by the propulsive effect of oil refinery and petrochemical expansion, as well as by construction in the residential sector. Pratt (1980) notes, with reference to the Gulf Coast, that this propulsive effect was not confined to the construction industry. Thus he identifies iron and steel, shipbuilding, metals fabrication, packaging and miscellaneous transportation activities as part of the 'oil-related complex of industries', based initially upon the expansion of production and refining and latterly upon these operations plus petrochemical manufacture, which has given the Gulf Coast economy its distinctive regional identity over a period of more than half a century.

Various attempts have been made to represent the character of this economy in more formal terms using input–output analysis. This technique is usually employed to reveal the structure of national economies, but several input–output studies of the Texas and Louisiana economies have suggested that the petrochemical industry generates substantial income and employment effects (see Grubb 1973; Whitehorn 1973; Rice and Scott 1974; Texas Department of Water Resources 1983). There are many problems involved in measuring these effects with any precision, not least the fact that input–output studies usually depend upon SIC definitions which do not identify petrochemicals as a distinctive sector. Various methodological problems compound this practical difficulty and it is not surprising that estimates of the multiplier effects of the petrochemical industry cover a fairly wide range. Most estimates agree, however, that petrochemicals has a greater multiplier effect than most other industries. These estimates usually relate to national economies and it is difficult to translate such projections into local and regional impacts. Nevertheless, common sense suggests that these impacts must be directly related to the significance of oil refining and petrochemicals within individual communities. Certainly, the income effects of growth within these industries are enhanced by their tradition of high wages and salaries relative to many other manufacturing sectors. This tradition is firmly established on the Gulf Coast and it seems to have become a feature of these industries in other countries as well. Thus, whether viewed in terms of functional linkages or income generation, the propulsive effect of the petrochemical industry upon regional economies during its rapid growth phase was considerable. Observing this effect in established centres of production, policy makers tried to reproduce it elsewhere and the petrochemical industry became inextricably linked with growth centre strategies of regional economic development during the 1960s.

11.3 Petrochemicals and Growth Centres

These strategies were sometimes focused upon existing complexes which, because of their rapid growth, were regarded as potential agents of regional economic change. They were even more attractive when they happened to be located in peripheral or declining regions. All but one of the major centres of petrochemical production in the United Kingdom, for example, lay within the boundaries of prevailing development areas in 1966. This was a coincidental association since all of these complexes had their origins in location decisions taken before these areas were defined. Nevertheless, a government publication in 1963 specifically identified the Grangemouth petrochemical complex as an appropriate nucleus for the development of a more diversified industrial complex (Cmnd 2188, 1963). ICI's Teesside complex was similarly identified in another policy document relating to north-east England (Cmnd 2206, 1963). In fact, no serious attempt was made to evaluate the assumptions upon which these proposals were based, especially the proposition that the downstream linkages of the petrochemical industry could be translated into new industrial development in activities such as plastics fabrication. Indeed, it could be argued that the principal beneficiaries from the official approval of these growth centres were the companies that were already there rather than any more broadly defined community of regional interest.

Investment grants were a widely used form of regional subsidy in Western Europe during the 1960s and 1970s when capital expenditure in petrochemicals was, generally, running at high levels. The capital-intensive nature of the industry and, at least in the United Kingdom, its concentration in areas qualifying for such grants, ensured that companies such as ICI, BP and Shell received substantial sums of money under these schemes. Figure 11.3 indicates the share of all regional development grant payments in Cleveland (i.e. mainly Teesside) received by ICI. During the 1970s, these payments met 40–50 per cent of total capital investment in the oil and chemical industries on Teesside. The wisdom of such grants from a regional development perspective has always been a matter of debate (see Chisholm 1970; Chapman 1971; Warren 1971). Quite apart from the problem of subsidizing investment rather than employment creation,

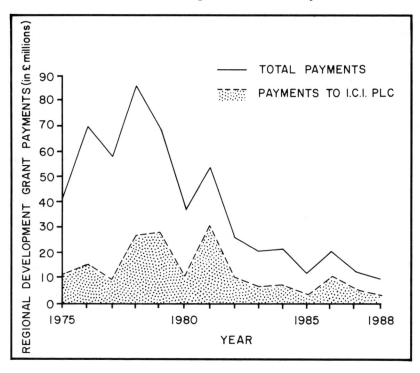

Figure 11.3 Regional development grant payments in Cleveland, 1975–1988 (from data provided by Cleveland County Council)

which is usually the principal objective in regional policy, it has never been clear that these grants actually influenced the location of new investment. Indeed, in the case of the UK petrochemical industry there is no doubt that, given the technical and economic advantages of adding capacity at existing rather than greenfield sites, many companies gratefully accepted the bonus of investment grants for projects they would have undertaken anyway. This is not to deny the possibility that such grants may influence corporate decisions;[6] but the balance of evidence suggests that it is the industry rather than the regions which got the better side of the bargain. This conclusion is reinforced when account is taken of other aspects of public sector support for private investment in petrochemicals. Hudson (1983) emphasizes the magnitude of infrastructure investment in transport, public utilities and land reclamation that has been undertaken by governments in many Western European countries in efforts to accommodate the needs of the oil refining and petrochemical industries for extensive coastal sites. Both Pratt (1980) and Feagin (1988) have drawn attention to the fact that, even in Texas, where government intervention is anathema and 'free enterprise is the gospel', public agencies have an enabling role in providing the infrastructural framework for the development of these industries.

Many of the uncertainties surrounding attempts to persuade private enterprise to act in a manner consistent with regional development objectives may be removed by direct state intervention in leading sectors such as petrochemicals. France and especially Italy provide the clearest examples of this in Western Europe. Regional development considerations were not a major reason for the involvement of the state in the petrochemical industries of these countries, but it is clear that such considerations have influenced the investment and location decisions of the relevant companies. In France, the discovery of natural gas at Lacq in the south-west at the beginning of the 1950s was seen from the outset as an opportunity to establish a new petrochemical industry in a relatively undeveloped region (Darwent 1969). Deliberate geographic dispersion of the industry also contributed to the construction of ethylene plants at Carling in the south-east and at Dunkirk in the north (Bower 1986, 138). In Italy, the industry has been closely associated with the efforts of successive Italian governments to promote the development of the *mezzogiorno*. More public funds have been devoted to the support of the petrochemical industry in southern Italy than any other manufacturing sector: 40.4 per cent of total loans and 23.6 per cent of the grants to all industries in the *mezzogiorno* between 1951 and 1974 were accounted for by 'chemicals' (Rodgers 1979, 30). The results of this commitment are apparent in several large petrochemical complexes, notably at Brindisi and in a coastal zone between Siracusa and Augusta in Sicily. Sardinia has also qualified for assistance under the *mezzogiorno* programme, and substantial investments in petrochemicals have occurred at the northern and southern ends of the island at Porto Torres and Cagliari respectively.

Regional development has been a primary concern in Italy, where state-owned corporations in petrochemicals and other industries have been required to direct specific proportions of their capital investment to the *mezzogiorno*. It has been secondary to other policy objectives in most countries which have, nevertheless, taken account of the potential regional development role of the petrochemical industry. Its growth in Brazil and Mexico, for example, was motivated by import substitution, but both countries recognized that this national economic strategy could have undesirable regional effects by concentrating economic growth in the principal cities. Public sector control of core petrochemical operations (see section 7.4) has allowed regional development considerations to influence the location of such operations in both countries. Brazil's first petrochemical pole was established in São Paulo, but the second and third were deliberately sited in relatively undeveloped regions at Camaçari and Triunfo.[7] Explicit commitments to utilize these complexes as catalysts of regional growth were made by the agencies responsible for coordinating their development (CONPETRO 1978; COPENE 1982). Similar thinking is evident in Mexico, and it has been suggested that differential pricing of petrochemical feedstocks and intermediates by Pemex is used to encourage downstream investment in approved locations (US International Trade Commission 1985c; 1989).

As with petrochemical developments motivated by import substitution, those linked to the exploitation of indigenous raw materials have been promoted by governments for reasons of national rather than regional economic development (see sections 7.2 and 8.3). Nevertheless, governments in this situation have been aware of the possibilities of using the industry 'to hasten the spatial decentralization of economic activity' (Auty 1990, 226). Viewed at a Canadian scale, developments in Alberta have, by bringing about a fundamental shift in the distribution of the country's petrochemical industry, contributed to expansion in the periphery relative to the economic heartland of Ontario and Quebec (figure 8.10). The distinction between national and regional interests has sometimes been confused in the context of Canadian federal politics and the strained diplomatic relations between Edmonton and Ottawa arising from disputes over the appropriate level of domestic energy prices following the oil price shocks (see section 8.5). The idea of establishing petrochemical facilities in Alberta as part of a provincial strategy of encouraging oil- and gas-based industrialization can be traced back to the 1950s (Alberta Research Council 1957; 1962). This idea came to fruition in the 1970s when the new developments contributed to some measure of economic decentralization within the province as a result of political persuasion, leading to the location of several facilities in the Red Deer area rather than in either of the two dominant metropolitan centres of Calgary and Edomonton (Seifried 1984). Similar considerations seem to have influenced the Saudi choice of Al Jubail and Yanbu as locations for major industrial complexes in the northern part of the country, well away from Jedda and the south-west (Auty 1988b).

Puerto Rico is another place where the petrochemical industry has been viewed as an agent of economic change at both national and regional level. The circumstances attracting the industry to the island were described in section 8.4. These circumstances were regarded as an opportunity both by the firms within the industry and by the island's economic development administration (FOMENTO). As far as the latter was concerned, there seemed to be a real prospect of translating an abstract development model into reality. The most comprehensive theoretical consideration of the potential value of the petrochemical industry as an instrument of regional development policy is provided by the work of Isard et al. (1959). This study used comparative cost techniques to present a case for the establishment of a fully integrated oil-based industrial complex in Puerto Rico. Particular emphasis was placed upon the role of functional linkages between interdependent processes in creating opportunities for the development of a wide range of operations, from oil refining and basic petrochemical processing to the production of synthetic fibres. Encouraged by the persuasive technical and economic logic of this study, FOMENTO placed great faith in oil refining and petro-chemicals as key elements of its industrialization strategy, a strategy which included a deliberate attempt to divert economic growth away from metropolitan San Juan on the north coast by concentrating petrochemical investment on the opposite side of the island. This policy was widely regarded during the 1960s as a model for other developing countries (UNIDO 1970b, 29).

Although substantial investments were made by companies such as Union Carbide, Phillips and Sun, employment fell far short of the expectations of FOMENTO (Chapman 1982). These expectations were based upon the belief that the capital-intensive oil refining and petrochemical operations would stimulate more labour-intensive downstream developments, leading to the creation of as many as 50,000 direct jobs by 1980 (Hulten 1973, 12). In fact, employment in these sectors plus plastics and synthetic fibres peaked at approxi-mately 9000 in 1976. This was followed, for reasons discussed in section 8.4, by a succession of plant closures, including the key operations of Commonwealth Oil Refining and Union Carbide, resulting in the virtual disappearance by the early 1980s of the growth pole which had been the source of so much optimism less than ten years earlier. By 1990 employment in oil refining (SIC 291) was just over 1000, and stood at just 78 in plastics and synthetic materials (SIC 282)![8] The extent of this collapse has been especially dramatic in Puerto Rico, but petrochemical complexes conceived as growth centres in remote locations generally seem to have fallen short of the expectations of planners. In the case of the Saudi complexes at Al Jubail and Yanbu, for example, 'the expected proliferation of linked industries was notably muted' (Auty 1990, 241). In reviewing the Italian policy of concentrating public investment in the *mezzogiorno* in capital-intensive basic sectors such as steel and petrochemicals, Rodgers (1979, 125–6) observes that 'their contribution to the increase of employment was not nearly as great as the proponents of southern development had envisaged. There was virtually no spin-off or multiplier effect such as the growth of small- and medium-sized establishments that were linked to the basic industries.' This has been especially true of the petrochemical industry, and Rodgers (1979, 155) describes the influence of the major complex at Gela in southern Sicily upon its surrounding area as 'extraordinarily small'. With reference to Sardinia, King (1977, 100) notes the existence of 'glaring discrepancies between plan forecasts and outcomes'. Some of the most spectacular discrepancies in employment projections once again stem from the failure of the petrochemical industry to generate jobs in downstream activities, which seems to have been a common thread in the experiences of many different places (Chapman 1984).

This failure partly reflects unreasonable expectations, and the sense of disappointment has often been all the more acute because of initial overoptimism. This has frequently rested upon wishful thinking rather than considered and informed analysis (Chapman 1984). Bearing in mind the kind of areas in which these policies have been pursued, the agencies responsible for their execution have sometimes lacked the necessary expertise and possessed only a rudimentary knowledge of the technology and economics of the petrochemical industry. In these circumstances, unreasonable expectations may actually be fostered by companies which recognize the importance attached to employment creation by planning agencies. Referring to the involvement of the Sun Oil Company in a refinery and lube oil complex in Puerto Rico, Johnson (1983, 171) notes that ' "petrochemical" had a special magic for Puerto Ricans.' The company was sensitive to this 'magic' and, in its negotiations with FOMENTO, 'touched upon the possibility of future investment in petrochemical manufacture ... leading to the creation of more than 1000 jobs' (Johnson 1983, 174). Indeed, the line between good intentions and deliberate misrepresentation has often been blurred, with corporate submissions to development agencies frequently accompanied by flow charts indicating a dazzling array of linkages between various stages and sectors of production and implying the possibility of extensive downstream developments with substantial job creation potential. Willingness to manipulate the misconceptions of planners is hardly surprising. It has already been noted that the industry has, over the years, received substantial state support for its capital investments in the form of grants, loans and infrastructure subsidies. Much of this support has been based upon the premise that the industry serves as a catalyst to regional development; it therefore has good reason to discourage any serious questioning of this premise.

Several factors prevent the undoubtedly extensive technical linkages between basic petrochemical manufacture and other industries from being realized in diversified complexes of interdependent activities. The nature of petrochemical products changes fundamentally as they pass through the different stages of production. The technical factors which encourage the agglomeration of basic manufacturing processes are less relevant in the later stages. Products generally become more elaborate and less uniform with each stage of the manufacturing process. Cooperation with individual consumers is an important factor affecting the volume and specification of plant production; location relative to major customers becomes more significant than proximity to sources of raw material. This locational shift

274   *Petrochemicals, Regions and Public Policy*

is reinforced by the fact that solid process materials, which are
relatively easy to transport, tend to replace the less stable liquids and
gases which draw the earlier stages of production together. The
different techniques employed in the manufacture and manipulation
of plastic materials ensure that this stage in the conversion process
is generally regarded as the responsibility of the plastics industry,
whereas the initial operations are considered to fall within the scope
of the petrochemical industry. Similar distinctions apply to the production of petroleum-derived synthetic fibres. The manufacture of
basic intermediates is performed within petrochemical complexes,
but their conversion into fibres is carried out by the textile industry,
whose spinning facilities are affected by an entirely different set of
locational factors.

Although petrochemical investment may stimulate economic
growth in a national context, there is no guarantee that this growth
will be focused around the site of the basic operation. In Italy, for
example, increasing evidence has been assembled to suggest that
state support for industrial investment in the *mezzogiorno* has actually
contributed more to economic growth elsewhere in Italy (Rodgers
1979, 146). Podbielski (1978) contrasts the experiences of large-
scale industrial projects in the centre-north of Italy with the results
achieved by similar developments in the south. Whereas linkages
frequently produced the desired local and regional multiplier effects
in the case of northern plants, Podbielski (1978, 158) observes
that, with respect to the *mezzogiorno*, 'industrial underdevelopment
produced a vicious circle whereby the isolation in which the large
industrial complexes operated hampered the creation of a network of
complementary minor industries of a modern and competitive type
while the lack of such industries in turn compelled the large plants to
maintain their close interdependence with outside enterprises and
to continue their isolation.' Auty (1990, 239) reaches essentially
the same conclusion in a study of the impact of resource-based
industrialization in several oil producing countries, noting that 'increasing remoteness is positively associated with stunted and delayed
linkages.'

The relationship between regional and national economic systems
is closely linked to the issue of external control and the compatibility
of corporate and government objectives. The petrochemical industry
is dominated by large companies which operate on an international
scale. Although these companies may acknowledge the desirability of
promoting local employment when negotiating with governments
to establish within an area, evidence suggests that considerations
important to the goal of regional development are very low on the
corporate list of priorities. Indeed there is no reason, in a capitalist
system, why they should be on the list at all. There are many
examples of situations in which the interests of private sector

companies involved in petrochemical manufacture and those of regional development agencies have diverged. The removal of NGLs and ethylene by pipeline from Alberta is central to the commercial strategies of companies such as Dow and Nova, but these transfers support developments in eastern Canada, thereby limiting the opportunities for further petrochemical expansion within the province (Chapman 1985b). This is a continuing cause of concern to the Alberta government. In some cases, public investment may itself have contradictory effects. Kinsey (1979) suggests that the provision of a high quality port infrastructure at Fos associated with the Aire Métropolitaine Marseillaise growth centre in southern France facilitated the export of basic petrochemical products from complexes at Berre and Lavera and, therefore, indirectly reduced the chances for local processing. Similarly in Puerto Rico, the freedom of access to the United States mainland, which helped to make basic petrochemical operations attractive to the private corporations, at the same time reduced the prospects of downstream development since export of bulk intermediates such as benzene to mainland markets for further processing was more economic than shipment of downstream products. The problem is often aggravated by the tendency of large companies to internalize their linkages, whether in the form of physical or information flows (Ettlinger 1984). This tends to reinforce the enclave mentality associated with many major capital-intensive projects in remote locations as potential multiplier effects are channelled elsewhere in the corporate system.

11.4 Restructuring and Regional Development

The leakage of multiplier effects is not only a problem for isolated complexes in peripheral regions, and several observers have noted that many elements of the oil-related complex of the Gulf Coast are ultimately controlled from headquarters elsewhere in the United States (see Pratt 1980; Rees 1984; Feagin 1988). This pattern of absentee ownership may be partly responsible for the much greater importance of backward rather than forward linkages in stimulating economic development within the region. In analysing the nature of the Gulf Coast oil-related complex, Pratt (1980, 130) emphasizes the significance of such activities as metal manufacture and fabrication, specialized chemical engineering design and construction, as well as miscellaneous supply industries associated with transportation and distribution functions. Much of the complex has, therefore, been geared to supplying the capital goods and infrastructure required to sustain the expanding output of petroleum and petrochemical products. The move into petrochemicals from an existing refining base was by far the most significant downstream development, but this exploitation of forward linkages did not go much beyond basic and intermediate stages in the processing chain. There was always an expectation of such a progression, and it was noted in 1955 that 'The production of end products from chemicals may well be the next stage in the industrialization of the Texas Gulf Coast Country' (Clark 1955, 242). The same author was also perceptive enough to observe that 'The manufacturing of end products would employ far more numerous workers, and small, locally-owned plants for this purpose would keep the profits within the region' (Clark 1955, 241).

The limited extent of downstream development within the Gulf Coast complex based on forward linkages from basic petrochemical production has several implications. On a general level, it draws attention to the shaky empirical foundation for one of the key assumptions underpinning the growth centre policies described in the preceding section. Furthermore, the fact that backward linkages from oil refining and, later, petrochemical operations clearly stimulated the growth of various supply industries on the Gulf Coast did not guarantee a similar effect elsewhere. Investment in oil refining and petrochemicals in this region was sustained, over a long period, at a level several orders of magnitude higher than in any other corresponding area. Individual complexes, however impressive on the ground, will not generate sufficient demand for supporting supplies and services to justify the sort of investments in, for example, metals manufacture and fabrication that were attracted to the Gulf Coast by the simultaneous development of numerous such complexes. Indeed, some of the economic benefits arising from the backward linkages of petrochemical expansion in other parts of the world have probably leaked to the Houston area as a result of the international business of specialist chemical engineering contractors based in the city.[9]

Quite apart from its implications for growth centre policies based upon new petrochemical complexes, the relative lack of downstream development has clear implications for regional economies associated with existing complexes. These implications, which were either ignored or pushed into the background when the industry was growing rapidly, became a matter of major policy concern in the wake of its restructuring crisis. It has already been noted that this crisis resulted in major job losses in national petrochemical industries (see section 10.6). The economic impact of these job losses was concentrated in particular regions because of the characteristically agglomerated spatial distribution of the industry. In the case of the Gulf Coast, these impacts were only part of a major recession which affected all branches of its oil-based economy in the early 1980s (see Weinstein et al. 1985; Weinstein and Gross 1987). This recession became an economic tailspin as plant closures and job losses in oil refining and petrochemicals depressed levels of activity and employment in related sectors, especially construction. The magnitude of these negative multiplier effects was made worse by the predominance of backward linkages in the oil-related industrial complex. This ensured that events were largely driven by the supply-side problems of the oil industry and that there was little opportunity for demand-led stimuli from outside the region to cushion the impact of these problems by supporting forward-linked downstream activities located within it. Although every metropolitan area along the Gulf Coast experienced large declines in manufacturing employment in the early 1980s, there was considerable variation in their magnitude, ranging from a fall of only 4.8 per cent in Lafayette between 1980 and 1984 to 33.3 per cent in Lake Charles (Weinstein et al. 1985, 26). Broadly speaking, these variations reflected differences in the relative import-ance of oil refining and petrochemicals within overall employment structures. Although Houston has attracted most attention in analyses of oil-related cycles of boom and bust (see Feagin 1985; Center for Public Policy 1989), places such as Lake Charles and Beaumont–Port Arthur are much more dependent upon the manufacturing, as distinct from the exploration and production, aspects of this business. The fall in oil refining and petrochemical employment over approxi-mately ten years to its nadir in 1987 was, therefore, more sharply felt in some communities than in others.

The contrast between rapid growth during the 1960s and 1970s and spectacular decline during the 1980s was, for example, clearly evident in the experience of the Golden Triangle (figure 11.2). Annual unemployment rates for the Beaumont–Port Arthur MSA, which were significantly below the US average before 1980, exceeded more than 14 per cent of the labour force at the depths of the recession. Indeed, the total employment base of the region, which had increased steadily over a long period mainly as a result of the propulsive effect of growth in oil refining, petrochemicals and related construction activity, began to fall in 1981 and by 1988 had returned to the level of 1975, representing a loss of almost 30,000 jobs in just eight years. This loss has resulted not only in higher unemployment, but also in significant outmigration. Indeed, the unemployment figures would have been even higher, but for this contraction in the labour force from its 1983 peak. Trends in personal income are yet another measure of decline. Real per capita income levels within the Golden Triangle grew steadily during the 1970s and they exceeded the national average as late as 1982; by 1988, however, they were over 20 per cent below it (John Gray Institute 1989, 4).

Although the transformation from growth to problem area has probably been more spectacular in the Golden Triangle, other com-munities dominated by oil refining and petrochemicals have had similar experiences. This is true not only of the US Gulf Coast, but also of oil-based industrial complexes in Western Europe and Japan. In the United Kingdom, for example, Teesside was one of the most buoyant regional economies during the 1960s, mainly as a result of the rapid growth of petrochemical manufacture. Contemporary optimism about the future of this industry and the region found expression in one of the earliest strategic land use and transportation plans produced in the United Kingdom (Teesplan 1969). This envisaged substantial expansion in population and employment to 1991, a projection largely based upon the assumption that the rates of growth associated with such modern industries as petrochemicals during the 1960s could be sustained. In the event, the Teesside of the 1980s bore little resemblance to the images fostered by Teesplan, with unemployment consistently above the national average and reaching a peak of over 22 per cent in 1984 (Cleveland County Council n.d.).

Such problems have prompted policy responses at local and regional level aimed at providing alternative sources of employment. Bearing in mind the fact that the planning failures of the industry partly contributed to the restructuring crisis (see section 10.2), it is difficult to criticize government agencies for not anticipating the scale of the problem. The track record of growth made decline seem all the more improbable. Lip-service was paid to the desirability of economic diversification in places such as Houston during the boom years, but the pace of expansion diverted attention from the possibility of slump. When the collapse came, therefore, the policy response was crisis driven. In the case of the Gulf Coast economy in general and the city of Houston in particular, the problems of the petrochemical industry were only part of a more general recession affecting all branches of the oil- and gas-based regional economy. Nevertheless, these problems were serious enough to have a major impact within specific communities, an impact which resurrected the essentially dormant commitment to economic diversification and prompted what was, for Texas, an almost apocalyptic acknowledgement of 'the need to plan' at state and local level (see City of Beaumont 1986; Strategic Economic Policy Commission 1989). The same commitment to diversification, to be achieved by the attraction of inward investment and by the promotion of internal economic regeneration, is evident in the planning strategies of communities facing similar problems elsewhere (see Cleveland County Council n.d.).

Regional policy within developed economies has traditionally concentrated upon encouraging multiplant enterprises to establish branch factories in problem areas. This approach placed considerable emphasis upon the presumed attractions of cheap, preferably unorganized labour (Massey 1984). The pool of such potentially mobile industrial investment generally dried up in the 1980s as the macro-economic circumstances which contributed to the problems of the petrochemical industry also affected other sectors. Even if such investment were available, oil refining and petrochemical centres would not be very attractive destinations. Research in the United Kingdom has suggested that areas with an established heavy industrial tradition were generally not the preferred locations for branch plant operations attracted by regional policy incentives during the 1960s, even if unemployment was high (Massey and Meegan 1978). Most inward investors, especially in light, assembly-type industries, were drawn towards unskilled, inexperienced, often female labour and avoided blue-collar male labour familiar with the working practices of a particular sector. Viewed from a corporate perspective, it seems that these practices were often perceived as bad habits that may be difficult to break, especially when supported by the power of well established trade unions. Furthermore, such unions frequently encouraged wage expectations that proved remarkably durable in the face of high unemployment and, therefore, raised baseline labour costs for inward investors. All of these arguments, which were used to explain why some places found it difficult to attract incoming firms during the 1960s, may be applied to the situation of oil refining and petrochemical centres in the 1980s. In south-east Texas, for example, the combination of traditionally high wages and a reputation for antagonistic labour–management relations, based upon the confrontation between the irresistible force of the Oil, Chemical and Atomic Workers (OCAW) and the immovable objects represented by some of the major oil and chemical companies, is acknowledged to have 'hampered industrial recruitment efforts' (John Gray Institute 1989, 5).

Another obstacle to such efforts which south-east Texas shares with other oil refining and petrochemical centres is the negative environmental image associated with these activities, which both rank high on any list of polluting industries. The fact that they are typically concentrated in major complexes only serves to reinforce the problem of dealing with such externalities as air and water pollution and the disposal of toxic wastes (Chapman 1983). Although these and other polluting industries have generally improved their operating standards in the face of mounting legislative pressures, there is no doubt that an environmental price has been paid for earlier growth; this is evident in the appearance of the landscape and, in some cases, in the health of the population (see Chapman 1980; Pratt 1980; Feagin 1988). Cobb (1982) notes that such matters were long subordinated to economic development objectives in the drive to industrialize the southern United States since the 1930s, but that there was a belated recognition that this approach would ultimately prove counter-productive. This is confirmed by the severe problems facing those responsible for selling places such as Beaumont–Port Arthur to potential inward investors and by the importance attached to policies of environmental improvement in overcoming these problems.

The difficulties of attracting inward investment place greater pressure on attempts to promote economic regeneration at the local or regional level. This grass-roots approach is also consistent with the encouragement of entrepreneurial initiatives as a means of reducing dependence upon externally owned manufacturing plants. The kind of job losses sustained in oil refining, petrochemicals and other industries during the 1980s often induced a feeling of helplessness in the face of economic disaster which in turn stimulated interest in community-based initiatives. Where job losses were a consequence of decisions taken by a single major employer, external control seemed even more undesirable. This situation is not unusual in the petrochemical industry, as the position of ICI on Teesside, BASF in Ludwigshafen and Dow at Freeport–Lake Jackson testifies. Attempts to assist existing small and medium businesses and to promote new firms have been a common thread in the policy response to the contraction of petrochemical employment in such communities. This support typically includes business advice as well as financial assistance funded from local and regional sources. It is often targeted upon specific geographical areas. Enterprise zones attracting special assistance for industrial development are, for example, identified within both the Teesside conurbation and the Beaumont–Port Arthur MSA.

Establishing enterprise zones and small business development programmes is, of course, no guarantee of success, and the prospects for replacing job losses in oil refining and petrochemicals on the basis of such essentially local economic development initiatives are not good. The scale of the job losses in the 1980s far exceeded what could be regarded as realistic targets for compensating growth in the small business sector. It is well known that spin-offs from larger organizations are one important mechanism of new firm formation, especially in younger industries. Many of the major participants in petrochemicals are also involved in other branches of the chemical industry which offer greater scope for small, science-based firms. Where the establishments of such organizations incorporate R and D as well as manufacturing functions, opportunities for spin-off ventures may arise and may indeed be encouraged by the parent firm. A technology park next to ICI's Billingham manufacturing site on Teesside, for example, was established and promoted by both the company and local development agencies in the late 1980s. It attempts to build on the region's chemical tradition by providing facilities for small firms in such areas as biotechnology, process control, instrumentation and plastics. Although such developments seem logical extensions of this tradition, the industrial inheritance is often an obstacle rather than an incentive to the growth of small business. Numerous studies have demonstrated significant spatial variations in rates of new firm formation and, in particular, a tendency for these rates to be suppressed in communities dominated by individual industries and employers (see Mason 1987; Mason and Harrison 1985). This negative effect upon the entrepreneurial spirit seems to be most apparent where the dominant industry is at the mature stage of its development, and has been explained in terms of the stultifying influence of established technologies and working practices which discourage innovation and initiative (Markusen 1985). Whatever the reasons, it seems that oil refining and petrochemical centres are not conducive to a dynamic small firm sector. This is, for example, identified as a problem on Teesside (Cleveland County Council n.d.). Similarly, a study of past and possible future employment change in the United States, whilst optimistic about Texas, placed petrochemical-dominated centres such as Beaumont–Port Arthur and Longview well down a list of 239 areas ranked according to growth prospects to 1997 (Birch 1987).

11.5 Conclusions

The role of manufacturing as an agent of economic change at various spatial scales is one of the most important reasons for understanding the dynamics of industry evolution. The place of the petrochemical industry as such an agent at the national level was reviewed earlier (see section 7.2) and attention in this chapter has focused upon its link to economic development at the regional scale. This is a massive topic and, although an attempt has been made to incorporate evidence from many sources, it must be acknowledged that this evidence is heavily biased towards US and British examples. Despite this limitation, it is possible to derive a number of general conclusions about the regional development and policy implications of the life-cycle concept as applied to the petrochemical industry.

There is no doubt that the industry has fulfilled all the requirements of a growth pole as defined by Perroux. The timing of this propulsive function within national economies has obviously varied according to the chronology of the industry's development in different countries. Thus some of the newer producers, especially those with potentially large domestic markets such as Brazil, Mexico and Indonesia, can hope to replicate the rapid growth phase experienced 30 or 40 years earlier in the United States, Western Europe and Japan. There is less certainty that this propulsive effect at the national scale (i.e. growth pole) may be reproduced at the regional level (i.e. growth centre). In particular, it should not be assumed that the economic experience of the US Gulf Coast since World War II, which was partly based upon the petrochemical industry, can be transferred elsewhere. Close examination of this experience reveals that forward linkages from petrochemicals have been limited, and that the growth of the regional economy has been driven primarily by upstream oil and gas production and by various sectors supporting oil refining and petrochemical manufacture. These supporting activities represent backward linkages relative to oil refining and petrochemical operations. The translation of such linkages into a substantial regional complex of oil-related industries has been made possible by the huge scale of both production and manufacturing based on oil and natural gas. No other region in the world approaches the level of oil refining and petrochemical capacity concentrated along the Gulf Coast of Texas and Louisiana. The demands upon supplying industries generated within this zone are therefore unique, and there is no reason to suppose that backward linkages from the much more limited levels of oil refining and petrochemical invest-ment found in other regions will induce corresponding developments. Indeed, for most petrochemical complexes, construction activity is the only supply-side linkage guaranteed to produce a significant economic impact at the local or regional scale. This is an important consideration whilst the industry is growing rapidly when investment in new plant is more or less continuous. With the onset of maturity, however, this activity slows down, leading to a drastic fall in con-struction employment in addition to job losses associated with the intensification of production on existing plant. There is, therefore, a mutually reinforcing downward spiral in employment. In many cases, this spiral only serves to emphasize the limited extent of downstream employment based on forward linkages from petro-chemicals into plastics fabrication, textiles and so on. A series of target industry studies were, for example, undertaken in the early 1980s to identify suitable sectors to promote economic diversification in several Gulf Coast communities such as the Golden Triangle and Lake Charles (see Weinstein and Gross 1983; Gross and Vulkovic 1984). The fact that these and similar, more recent, studies (see John Gray Institute 1989) favoured the encouragement of plastics fabrication was itself an admission that one of the most natural routes to economic diversification had failed to materialize on any major scale after more than a generation of basic petrochemical production. This in turn suggests that the advocates of growth centre policies based on petrochemical investment in other places had failed to carry out the most obvious empirical check of the models which shaped their thinking. If downstream development was limited in Texas and Louisiana, why should it appear in Puerto Rico and Sicily?

The question acquired a new urgency when restructuring and rationalization revealed all too clearly the implications of over-dependence upon petrochemicals and prompted renewed efforts at diversification by regional development agencies and pressure groups. Paradoxically, the industry that was, in times of growth, regarded as presenting opportunities for diversification became, in some respects, a liability which frustrated these efforts. It has been observed that, contrary to the reasoning of neoclassical theory which views industrial location as a response to existing spatial variations in factor costs and market opportunities, industries may create their own conditions for growth within a region (see Hudson 1988; Storper and Walker 1989). In so doing, they may also diminish the prospects for the development of other industries within the same region. Thus the overwhelming presence of the oil refining and petrochemical industries in places such as Lake Charles and Ludwigshafen largely determined the character of the labour market, creating a predominantly blue-collar tradition of employment in large companies unfavourable to entrepreneurship and new-firm formation. More controversially, this presence often makes itself felt in the institutions of local and regional politics because the economic interests of these industries and the communities they dominate are seen to coincide. The success of the oil industry in shaping various dimensions of public policy to its own advantage in Texas, for example, is well documented (see Pratt 1980; Feagin 1988). Attempts to deal with the problem of pollution from oil refineries and petrochemical plants highlight the nature of the dilemma facing public agencies. The argument that stricter standards of pollution control will damage the prosperity of the industries and, therefore, of the communities which depend upon them has frequently been deployed to resist political pressures to clean up their operations (see Chapman 1980; Pratt 1980, 225–52). The implied threat to wage packets in such communities is clear for all to see. Even if this argument is accepted, it is essentially short term in its outlook since there is little doubt that external perceptions of a polluted, unattractive and unhealthy environment make it very difficult to sell such communities to inward investors and especially to the kinds of industries which represent real diversification of the economic base away from oil and chemicals and also offer genuine prospect for sustained growth.

Viewed over the perspective of 30 or 40 years of development, the experience of petrochemicals is consistent with the proposition that employment growth is ultimately replaced by job losses in all industries. The regional development consequences of this cycle are that much greater when, as with petrochemicals, the industry is characterized by geographical clustering in huge concentrations of capacity. There is no reason to suppose that the restructuring crisis of the early 1980s heralds the imminent demise of the petrochemical industry and, therefore, the economic collapse of the places in which it is located. Nevertheless, the logic of the life-cycle model suggests that the boom periods of the 1960s and 1970s are unlikely to return within the developed economies and that the future expansion of capacity will be more gradual. The lesson of this and other, older industries for those concerned with regional development is the need to recognize at an early stage the dangers of overdependence upon a particular sector. This prompt recognition is required not only because of the inevitability of, at best, diminished growth and, at worst, total shutdown, but also because the task of diversification becomes progressively more difficult as the cycle proceeds as a result of regional characteristics inherited from the dominant industry.

Notes

1 Scherer does not actually identify petrochemicals as a sector, but he does draw attention to 'industrial organic chemicals' and 'synthetic resins, fibers and rubbers'.
2 The limitations of official statistics ensure that petrochemicals are always hidden within other sectors of the type described in note 1.
3 Now Hoechst.
4 Now Amoco.
5 The number locating on the Gulf Coast is not identified, but the vast majority were certainly drawn to this region.
6 An internal ICI report (February 1984) concerned with the relative cost of operating chemical plant in various Western European countries noted that investment incentives and taxation were the dominant factors.
7 The development of a fourth pole in Rio de Janeiro, using NGLs from the offshore Campos field, began in 1987.
8 Employment data provided by Economic Development Administration.
9 The fact that many firms which were established to serve the oil and petrochemical industries on the Gulf Coast have developed an international capability may itself inhibit the emergence of locally based suppliers.

12
Geographical Perspectives on the Evolution of an Industry

The objective of this book has been to explain the evolution and, in particular, the *spatial* evolution of an industry which has been at the heart of some of the most important developments within the world economy during the second half of the twentieth century. The geographical coverage of the book has extended from the regional to the international scale, and its historical scope has embraced a period of approximately 100 years from the laboratory origins of polymer science and petrochemistry to the massive operations of the modern petrochemical industry. The approach adopted has been eclectic in the sense that it has drawn upon ideas from a variety of disciplines in seeking to provide an understanding of the variables shaping the industry's development. By focusing upon long run evolution and especially upon the influence of innovation, innovation diffusion and patterns of technical change, the book has acknowledged the contributions of economic historians and economists in these areas. In attempting to explore the spatial dimensions of the industry's development, it also draws upon the work of geographers with their traditional interest in location.

Life-cycle concepts are a recurrent theme, applied at different levels of economic resolution from product to sector and to industry. Although the book has consistently referred to the petrochemical 'industry', it is worth remembering that the manufacture of petrochemicals is only part of the chemical industry. Indeed, in defining the scope of this study it was noted (in section 2.1) that, despite the vast number of petrochemical products, total output is dominated by relatively few. The book has focused upon the principal olefin derivatives which, together with the aromatics, may be regarded as a reasonably coherent sector bound together by internal linkages based upon the principles of hydrocarbon chemistry and sharing a variety of common economic characteristics reflected in the organization and location of production. One of the most fundamental of these characteristics has been a secular change in the rate of growth in output which has resulted in the logistic curve of cumulative capacity (or production) observed in a succession of countries and major world regions starting with the United States (figures 1.2 and 1.3). Figure 12.1 represents this change for Western Europe in terms of the growth (or decline) of petrochemicals and plastics relative to the prevailing average for industrial production as a whole.[1] The growth premium displays considerable variation from one year to the next, mainly as a result of the effect of stock changes (Burgess et al. 1988). Nevertheless, a general trendline has been superimposed upon these fluctuations which suggests a convergence, over a period of 40 years, from rates of growth more than 20 per cent higher towards the norm for overall industrial production. This is consistent with a gradual weakening of market penetration at a macro-scale. The trend does not, of course, indicate absolute decline (unless a major recession

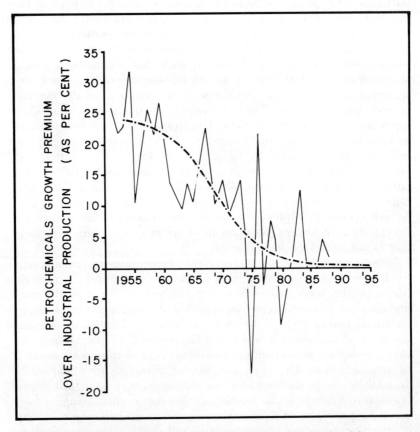

Figure 12.1 Growth of petrochemical industry relative to total industrial production in Western Europe, 1950–1995 (from data supplied by ICI Chemicals and Polymers Ltd)

strikes Western Europe) but rather demonstrates the flattening of the S-shaped growth curve. In the longer term, it is possible that the organic chemical industry will revert to the more abundant coal- and vegetable-based raw materials that were used before oil and natural gas, but this would require a huge increase in the real cost of petroleum feedstocks which seems unlikely in the foreseeable future. Thus, whatever euphemistic connotations 'maturity' may have in the context of individuals, the expression is certainly not indicative of redundancy or impending death as applied to the petrochemical industry!

There is no doubt that notions of market growth, penetration and saturation provide insights not only into the chronology but also into the geography of petrochemical investment. These are relevant at both national and international scales. For example, the rapid growth of the industry in the United States during the 1950s, and in Western Europe ten years later, attracted new entrants. This had consequences for location since new producers require new sites, which in turn raises the possibility of geographical dispersal away from initial centres of production. This effect was, however, limited because many of the later entrants into the industry were established oil and chemical companies which tended, for obvious technical reasons, to locate their first petrochemical plants adjacent to one of their existing refineries or other manufacturing facilities rather than on a greenfield site. In the United States this brought about some dispersal within the Gulf Coast region, but only served to reinforce the overall dominance of Texas and Louisiana in a national context.

The geographical effects of market factors have been less ambiguous at the international scale as the push of slackening growth in domestic markets and the pull of faster growth overseas have encouraged foreign direct investment by multinational companies. These market effects upon the location of investment have often been enhanced by political intervention in the form of barriers to trade and other import substitution measures. The influx of US companies into Western Europe during the 1960s was influenced by such considerations, and market prospects in several Pacific Rim countries are likely to attract the growing interest of the multinationals during the 1990s and beyond the turn of the century. The opportunities for these companies will partly depend upon the policies of host governments. Whatever the influence of market-related factors upon the investment strategies of the multinationals in the Third World, it is clear that the development of the industry was accelerated in many countries by state intervention. Nevertheless, this intervention was invariably motivated by these same factors. The replacement of existing imports and a belief that an indigenous petrochemical industry would both promote and sustain future economic development encouraged many countries to follow this route. This option was only available to them as a result of another aspect of the life-cycle concept associated with the diffusion of innovations.

New products and the industries they create are based on innovation. Typically, those responsible for a key innovation attempt to secure the maximum commercial advantage from their ingenuity by protecting and maintaining their monopoly of knowledge for as long possible. This strategy has both an organizational and a geographical dimension. The position of innovating firms is weakened as patents lapse or imitators develop successful alternatives. Such diffusion in an organizational sense is accompanied by a geographical diffusion which, at the international scale, is central to the issue of technology transfer between countries and, more especially, between the developed and developing world. In the case of the petrochemical industry, it is clear that such transfer was a prerequisite to its establishment in every country outside the United States[2] and that the relevant technology has steadily become more freely available. This geographical spread has not only occurred through the medium of multinational corporations based in the United States and Western Europe, but also been accelerated by the activities of other agencies such as chemical engineering contractors and consultancies.

The diffusion of innovations is only one aspect of technology-based models of industry life cycles. It was noted in section 1.2 that many efforts have been made to link locational requirements to methods of production in accounting for shifts in the distribution of specific industries at national and international scales. Most of these have concentrated upon labour as a location factor, noting how systematic changes in the nature of manufacturing processes through the industry life cycle have implications for the type of labour required and for the structure of production costs. It is argued that, as the pace of product innovation slows down, more attention is devoted to process innovation, often reflected in a trend towards larger manufacturing units and standardized or routine methods of production. Although the exploitation of economies of scale has been a feature of process innovation in a maturing petrochemical industry, the relative unimportance of labour in its cost structure has meant that the kinds of forces which have led to the redistribution of certain other industries to cheap labour locations have not affected petrochemicals. The rise of the industry in places such as Taiwan and South Korea cannot be explained in the same terms as, for example, the growth of consumer electronics and semiconductors in these countries. On the other hand, their position in the so-called new international division of labour has, of course, contributed to their rapid economic growth, which has in turn encouraged the establishment of indigenous petrochemical industries providing materials, such as plastics, to sustain this growth. Petrochemical investment in these countries is, however, fundamentally market led.

If labour, one of the key variables in classical industrial location theory, has been of minor significance in the development of the petrochemical industry, one of the other principal factors, raw materials, has been of central and continuing concern. Indeed, 'feedstock-push' may be regarded as a variation of the more familiar idea of 'technology-push' in encouraging the early development of the industry. By-product refinery gases stimulated interest in the possibility of manufacturing organic chemicals from petroleum sources in the United States before World War II, and the naphtha surplus, related to the prevailing patterns of demand for refined products, provided an initial boost to the industry in Western Europe in the late 1940s and 1950s. Viewed at a national scale, the availability of feedstock, whether from oil refineries or natural gas plants, has clearly influenced the location of the industry within individual countries. The concentration of capacity in oil refining centres has been striking, and feedstock requirements, reinforced by various other upstream and downstream linkages as well as by the impact of economies of scale, have played a major role in creating the typical agglomerations of the industry which have themselves had such profound effects upon the social and economic character of regions and communities. This tendency towards agglomeration has, if anything, been reinforced by the move towards greater feedstock flexibility related to the volatility of raw material prices. In these circumstances, location within a major complex, well served by an infrastructure of pipelines, port and storage facilities, is desirable from two points of view. On the one hand, it extends the range of feedstock options; on the other hand, it enhances the ability to deal with consequent variations in the pattern of coproducts generated by different feedstocks. In reviewing the spatial evolution of various sectors in the United States, Markusen (1985) identifies a tendency towards dispersal with the onset of maturity. The petrochemical industry reveals no such tendency. Apart from the expansion of the industry in Louisiana in the 1960s, the concentration of capacity in the Gulf Coast region has, if anything, increased through time. Similarly, the early centres of production in Western Europe have proved remarkably durable and, with the significant exception of Italy where regional development considerations influenced location strategies, agglomeration has been a persistent feature of the industry's distribution within countries. Although several factors have contributed to this pattern, it is ultimately based upon the logistics of raw material supply and cost.

These same logistics have had exactly the opposite effect when viewed at the international scale. A combination of economic calculations and political judgements following the oil price shocks led to major new petrochemical investments in certain resource-rich locations, notably in Alberta and Saudi Arabia. These developments could not have been predicted in terms of any industry life-cycle model, whether based upon some kind of internal technological momentum or upon market dynamics. They were a consequence of an external parametric shock which reoriented the industry's development path. Perhaps the most significant aspect of this reorientation was to promote a move towards the globalization of the industry.

By comparison with other important industries, a relatively small proportion of the world production of chemicals actually enters international trade directly (although a substantial proportion is embodied in the output of other industries). In the case of petrochemicals, which account for about 60 per cent by value of the total trade in chemicals (Vergara and Brown 1988, 13), this proportion is estimated to be less than 10 per cent (UNIDO 1985c). There are many reasons for this, including the technological difficulties associated with transporting certain materials such as ethylene and a wide range of organizational and institutional barriers related to the actions of both companies and governments. The relatively low level of international trade in petrochemicals suggests that the industry cannot be regarded as global in the same sense as consumer electronics, for example, in which production is organized and integrated on a worldwide basis. Nevertheless it is clear that, as with many other industries, the volume of trade in chemicals is growing more rapidly than the volume of production – a trend which implies an enhanced awareness of comparative advantage at the international scale.

The effect of the oil price shocks upon the economics of the industry certainly contributed to this awareness, causing multinational companies to evaluate critically the relative costs of individual sites within their existing production systems as well as the possibility of developing new sites in favoured locations. The internal shifts in the geography of corporate systems resulting from such evaluations were the outcome of both investment and disinvestment decisions. Indeed, in many cases disinvestment was the more important process when the combination of the oil shocks and maturing markets prompted certain companies to redirect their activities away from petrochemicals and into other branches of the chemical industry. A collective geographical consequence of such individual corporate strategies will be a continued *relative* decline in the proportion of world petrochemical capacity located in the core economies. Before 1980 this incipient trend was due to differential rates of market growth, but the effect has been reinforced since the oil price shocks by cost-based differences in comparative advantage which seem likely to favour resource-rich locations in future rounds of petrochemical investment. On the other hand, newer chemical technologies associated with sectors such as pharmaceuticals and advanced materials

will be concentrated within the core economies. As already emphasized, this is to suggest not that the petrochemical sector will rapidly
decline in these economies, but rather that its share of the total
volume and, especially, the value of the output of the chemical
industry as a whole will diminish over a long period as part of this
industry's characteristic ongoing process of self-renewal.

Figure 12.2 is a highly generalized representation of the evolution
of these petrochemical trading patterns between the major world
regions over 40 years. The diagram also provides an impression of
the principal origins and destinations of both petrochemical technology and foreign investment. These flows of information and capital
have contributed to the more tangible movements of intermediates
and products. The focal position of the United States in 1960 is clear,
but this dominance was challenged by the rise of the industry in
Western Europe and Japan which developed their own spheres of
trading influence in Africa and the Pacific Rim respectively. By
the end of the 1980s, however, investment in the Middle East and
Canada had introduced significant new sources of supply which not
only encroached upon the export markets of the core economies
in the developing world, but were also directed at their domestic
markets. The balance of trade varies from one product to another,
with the efforts of the new exporters targeted, because of their dependence upon NGL feedstocks, upon the ethylene derivatives.
Analysis of the international trade in petrochemicals is beyond the
scope of this study, but the shifting patterns evident in figure 12.2
reflect changes in the distribution of the industry which the book has
attempted to explain.

Many of these changes have been predictable to the extent that
they reflect the operation of evolutionary processes influencing the
development of markets, the nature and direction of technical change
and the spatial diffusion of the scientific and engineering capabilities
which are the foundations of the industry. To those responsible
for making the decisions shaping its development, this assertion no
doubt appears the easy platitude of a distant observer with the
arrogance of hindsight. Such a perspective is, however, valid if it
identifies general trends and patterns which are less evident in the
context of the more restricted geographical focus and shorter time
horizon within which most participants in the industry are forced to
operate. On the other hand, the development of industries, including
their spatial evolution, is not exclusively determined by some kind
of inexorable logic based upon technical and economic certainties.
Unpredictable events can have major impacts. The world was, for
example, ill-prepared for the oil price shocks which so radically
altered the business environment of the the petrochemical industry.
The very fact that it is so widely perceived as a strategic industry
has, in a sense, weakened the explanatory power of the life-cycle

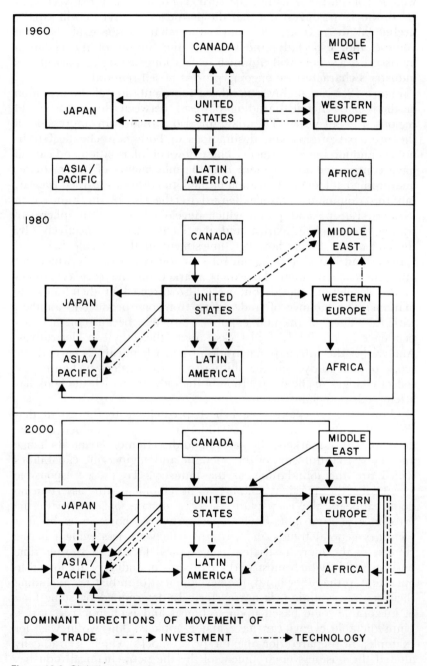

Figure 12.2 Global patterns in the petrochemical industry, 1960, 1980 and 2000

framework. Thus the timing and geographical distribution of invest-ment in petrochemicals has often been influenced, either directly or indirectly, by political circumstances and considerations. The US dominance of the industry was boosted by the damaging effect of World War II upon the European, especially the German, economy, and also by the massive federal investment poured into the synthetic rubber programme. The development of the industry has been similarly accelerated, for various reasons, by state intervention in many other countries. Such intervention emphasizes that, whilst acknowledging the value of the structural framework provided by the life-cycle model in providing a *general* understanding of the develop-ment of the petrochemical industry, a fuller understanding demands reference to the singular events of history which cannot be accom-modated within this or any other model.

Notes

1 This is a complex calculation taking account of the annual growth in the value of production relative to a chosen base year.
2 It is worth emphasizing that the United States was not the only source of technology and that the early development of the industry in the United States was facilitated by scientific advances made in Western Europe, especially in Germany. Countries such as the United Kingdom and West Germany could have established their own industries without the benefit of US technology, but this transatlantic transfer was certainly important in the immediate post-war years.

References

Abernathy, W. J. and Townsend, P. 1975: Technology, productivity and process changes. *Technological Forecasting and Social Changes*, 7, 379–98.

Abernathy, W. J., Clark K. B. and Kantrow, A. M. 1983: *Industrial Renaissance: Producing a Competitive Future for America*. New York: Basic Books.

Adelman, M. A. and Zimmerman, M. B. 1974: Prices and profits in petrochemicals: an appraisal of investment by less developed countries. *Journal of Industrial Economics*, 22, 245–54.

Adib, P. M. 1983: The petrochemical industry in Texas and Louisiana. *Texas Business Review*, 57, 165–70.

Adochi, H. and Yonaga, H. 1966: The development of Japan's petrochemical industry. In United Nations (ed.), *Studies in Petrochemicals* (vol. 2). New York: United Nations, 780–2.

Agarwal, J. P. 1980: Determinants of foreign direct investment: a survey. *Weltwirtschaftliches Archiv*, 116, 739–73.

Alberta Research Council 1957: *Papers Presented at Symposium on the Occurrence and Chemical Utilization of Light Hydrocarbons*. Circular 23, Research Council of Alberta.

Alberta Research Council 1962: *Proceedings of Symposium on Alberta Petrochemical Industry*. Information Series 39, Research Council of Alberta.

Aldcroft, D. H. 1978: *The European Economy 1914–1970*. London: Croom Helm.

Allen, J. A. 1967: *Studies in Innovation in the Steel and Chemical Industries*. Manchester: Manchester University Press.

Alonso, W. 1980: Five bell shapes in development. *Papers of the Regional Science Association*, 45, 5–16.

Al Wattari, A. 1980: *Oil Downstream: Opportunities, Limitations, Policies*. Kuwait: Organization of Arab Petroleum Exporting Countries.

Ashworth, W. 1986: *The History of the British Coal Industry. Vol. 5: 1946–1982: The Nationalized Industry*. Oxford: Clarendon Press.

Auty, R. M. 1988a: Oil-exporters' disappointing diversification into resource-based industry: the external causes. *Energy Policy*, 16, 230–42.

Auty, R. M. 1988b: The economic stimulus from resource-based industry in developing countries: Saudi Arabia and Bahrain. *Economic Geography*, 64, 209–25.

Auty, R. M. 1990: *Resource-Based Industrialization: Sowing the Oil in Eight Developing Countries*. Oxford: Clarendon.

Axtell, O. and Robertson, J. M. 1986: *Economic Evaluation in the Chemical Process Industries*. New York: Wiley.

Ayres, R. U. and Steger, W. A. 1985: Rejuvenating the life cycle concept. *Journal of Business Strategy*, 6, 66–76.

Bachetta, M. 1978: The crisis in oil refining in the European Community. *Journal of Common Market Studies*, 17, 87–119.

Baden-Fuller, C. and Longley, R. 1988: Predicting plant closures in European industry. *Long Range Planning*, 21, 90–6.

Balabkins, N. 1964: *Economic Aspects of Industrial Disarmament 1945–1948*. New Brunswick, NJ: Rutgers University Press.

Balassa, B. 1981: *The Newly Industrializing Countries in the World Economy*. New York: Pergamon.

Ballance, R. and Sinclair, S. 1983: *Collapse and Survival: Industry Strategies in a Changing World*. London: Allen and Unwin.

Beaton, K. 1957: *Enterprise in Oil: A History of Shell in the United States*. New York: Appleton-Century-Crcfts.

Beenstock, M. 1983: *The World Economy in Transition*. London: Allen and Unwin.

Beer, J. J. 1959: *The Emergence of the German Dye Industry*. Evanston, IL: Illinois University Press.

Behrman, J. N. 1972: *The Role of International Companies in Latin American Integration: Autos and Petrochemicals*. Lexington, MA: Lexington Books.

Bergsman, J. 1970: *Brazil: Industrialization and Trade Policies*. London: Oxford University Press.

Beynon, D. 1982: Rationalization: an ICI view. *Chemistry and Industry*, 16 January.

Birch, D. L. 1987: *Job Creation in America*. New York: Free Press.

Blackbourn, A. 1974: The spatial behaviour of American firms in Western Europe. In F. E. I. Hamilton (ed.), *Spatial Perspectives on Industrial Organization and Decision Making*. London: Wiley, 245–64.

Bluestone, B. and Harrison, B. 1982: *The Deindustrialization of America*. New York: Basic Books.

Boas, C. 1961: Locational patterns of American automobile assembly plants. *Economic Geography*, 37, 218–30.

Bohi, D. R. and Russell, M. 1978: *Limiting Oil Imports*. Baltimore, MD: Johns Hopkins University Press.

Borkin, J. 1979: *The Crime and Punishment of IG Farben*. London: André Deutsch.

Boston Consulting Group 1972: *Perspectives on Experience*. Technical report.

Bower, J. L. 1986: *When Markets Quake: The Management Challenge of Restructuring Industry*. Boston, MA: Harvard Business School Press.

Braber, P. 1966: Technical and economic changes in ethylene manufacture. In United Nations (ed.), *Studies in Petrochemicals* (vol. 1). New York: United Nations, 301–10.

Bradbury, J. H. 1987: Technical change and the restructuring of the North American steel industry. In K. Chapman and G. Humphrys (eds), *Technical Change and Industrial Policy*. Oxford and Cambridge, MA: Basil Blackwell, 157–75.

Brandaõ, E. O. M., de Maderios, J. B. and Peckott, O. T. 1966: The petrochemical industry in Brazil. In United Nations (ed.), *Studies in Petrochemicals* (vol. 2). New York: United Nations, 722–8.

Brown, W. C. 1973: Petrochemicals and our energy policies. In G. H. Cummings and W. B. Franklin (eds), *Declining Domestic Reserves – Effect on Petroleum and Petrochemical Industry*. American Institute of Chemical Engineers Symposium Series, 69(127), 19–22.

Brownstein, A. M. 1972: *Petrochemicals: Markets, Technology, Economics*. Tulsa, OK: Petroleum Publishing Co.

Burgess, A. R. 1983: Vertical integration in petrochemicals. *Long Range Planning*, 16(4), 55–60; 16(6), 29–34; and 1984, 17(1), 54–8.

Burgess, C. E., Dawson, J. W. and Thomas, D. M. 1988: *West Europe Petrochemicals – Stock Patterns*. London: Shell Chemicals.

Burns, A. F. 1934: *Production Trends in the United States*. New York: National Bureau of Economic Research.

Business Week 1960: Petrochemicals gurgle through maze of pipes. 3 September, 53–78.

Butler, J. D. 1953: Some economic influences on the location of oil refineries. *Journal of Industrial Economics*, 1, 187–201.

Cairncross, A. 1986: *The Price of War: British Policy on German Reparations 1941–1949*. Oxford and Cambridge, MA: Basil Blackwell.

Campbell, L. 1983: *An Assessment of the Relative Effect of Certain Federal Regulations on the International Competitiveness of the US Petrochemical Industry*. Washington, DC: US Department of Commerce, Bureau of Industrial Economics.

Carnoy, M. 1972: *Industrialization in a Latin American Common Market*. Washington, DC: Brookings Institution.

Center for Public Policy 1989: *Handbook on the Houston Economy*. Houston: University of Houston.

Chandler, A. D. Jr 1986: The evolution of modern global competition. In M. E. Porter (ed.), *Competition in Global Industries*. Boston, MA: Harvard Business School Press, 405–48.

Chapman, J. D. 1989: *Geography and Energy*. Harlow: Longman.

Chapman, K. 1970: Oil based industrial complexes in the United Kingdom. *Tijdschrift voor Economische en Sociale Geografie*, 61, 157–72.

Chapman, K. 1971: Conservative policies for the regions. *Area*, 3, 8–13.

Chapman, K. 1973: Agglomeration and linkage in the United Kingdom petrochemical industry. *Institute of British Geographers, Transactions*, 60, 33–68.

Chapman, K. 1974a: The structure and development of the oil-based industrial complex at Grangemouth. *Scottish Geographical Magazine*, 90, 98–109.

Chapman, K. 1974b: Corporate systems in the United Kingdom petrochemical industry. *Annals of the Association of American Geographers*, 64, 126–37.

Chapman, K. 1977: The utilization of North Sea hydrocarbons as raw materials for petrochemical manufacture. *Geoforum*, 8, 169–82.

Chapman, K. 1980: *Petrochemicals and Pollution in Texas and Louisiana: A Study of Trends in Pollution Control and Environmental Quality*. Department of Geography, University of Aberdeen.

Chapman, K. 1982: Petrochemicals and economic development: the implications of the Puerto Rican experience. *Professional Geographer*, 34, 405–16.

Chapman, K. 1983: The incorporation of environmental considerations into the analysis of industrial agglomerations – examples from the petrochemical industry in Texas and Louisiana. *Geoforum*, 14, 37–44.

Chapman, K. 1984: The petrochemical industry and regional development: a review of expectations and experiences. In B. M. Barr and N. M. Waters (eds), *Regional Diversification and Structural Change*. Vancouver: Tantalus, 87–98.

Chapman, K. 1985a: Raw material costs and the development of the petrochemical industry in Alberta since 1975. *Institute of British Geographers, Transactions (New Series)*, 10, 138–48.

Chapman, K. 1985b: Control of resources and the recent development of the petrochemical industry in Alberta. *Canadian Geographer*, 29, 310–26.

Chapman, K. 1988: *Public Policy and the Development of the Canadian Petrochemical Industry*. Department of Geography, University of Aberdeen.

Chapman, K. 1989: Public policy and the development of the Canadian petrochemical industry. *British Journal of Canadian Studies*, 4, 12–34.

Chapman, K. and Walker, D. 1991: *Industrial Location: Principles and Policies* (2nd edn). Oxford and Cambridge, MA: Basil Blackwell.

Chardonnet, J. 1958: *Les Grands Types de Complexes Industriels*. Paris: Editions Sirey.

Chemicals EDC 1976: *UK Chemicals 1975–1985*. London: NEDO.

Chemicals EDC 1984: *The New Petrochemical Producers and their Prospective Impact on Europe and the UK*. London: NEDO.

Chem Systems International Ltd 1983: *Restructuring the European Petrochemical Industry*. London: Chem Systems International Ltd.

Chenery, H. 1960: Patterns of industrial growth. *American Economic Review*, 50, 624–54.

Chenery, H., Robinson, S. and Syrquin, M. 1986: *Industrialization and Growth: A Comparative Study*. New York: Oxford University Press.

Chisholm, M. 1970: On the making of a myth. How capital-intensive is industry investing in the developing areas? *Urban Studies*, 3, 289–93.

Christy, C. V. and Ironside, R. G. 1987: Promoting 'high technology' industry: location factors and public policy. In K. Chapman and G. Humphrys (eds), *Technical Change and Industrial Policy*. Oxford and Cambridge, MA: Basil Blackwell, 233–52.

City of Beaumont 1986: *Economic Development Policy Plan*. Beaumont, TX.

Clair, D. R. 1984: The perils of hanging on. *Chemical Economy and Engineering Review*, 16(3), 13–18.

Clairmonte, F. F. and Cavanagh, J. H. 1985: Transnational corporations and the struggle for the global market. *Journal of Contemporary Asia*, 13, 446–80.

Clark, C., Wilson, F. and Bradley, J. 1969: Industrial location and economic potential in Western Europe. *Regional Studies*, 3, 197–212.

Clark, J. L. 1955: *The Texas Gulf Coast: Its History and Development* (vol. 2). New York: Lewis Historical Publishing.

Clarke, I. M. 1985: *The Spatial Organization of Multinational Corporations*. London: Croom Helm.

Cleveland County Council n.d.: *Cleveland Economic Strategy*. Middlesborough: Economic Development and Planning, Cleveland CC.

Cmnd 2188 1963: *Central Scotland: A Programme for Development and Growth*. London: HMSO.

Cmnd 2206 1963: *The North East: A Programme for Regional Development and Growth*. London: HMSO.

Cobb, J. C. 1982: *The Selling of the South: The Southern Crusade for Industrial Development 1936–1980*. Baton Rouge, LA: Louisiana University Press.

Comisión Petroquímica Mexicana 1986: *Medidas de Cambio Estructural y de Apoyo Para El Crecimiento de la Industria Petroquímica*. Octubre 7.

Commission of the European Communities 1981: Steel: agreement in the

298   *References*

Council. *Bulletin*, 14(6), 17–19.
CONPETRO 1978: *Petrochemical Complex of Rio Grande do Sul.* CONPETRO.
COPENE 1982: *Pólo Petroquimico do Nordeste.* COPENE.
Cornwall, J. 1977: *Modern Capitalism: Its Growth and Transformation.* London: Martin Robertson.
Cortes, M. and Bocock, P. 1984: *North–South Technology Transfer: A Case Study of Petrochemicals in Latin America.* Baltimore: Johns Hopkins University Press.
Cox, W. E. Jr 1967: Product life cycles as marketing models. *The Journal of Business*, 40, 375–84.
Czamanski, S. 1976: *Study of Spatial Industrial Complexes.* Institute of Public Affairs, Dalhousie University, Halifax, Nora Scotia.
Czamanski, S. and Ablas, L. A. de Q. 1979: Identification of industrial complexes: a comparison of methods and findings. *Urban Studies*, 16, 61–80.
Darwent, D. F. 1969: Growth poles and growth centres in regional planning: a review. *Environment and Planning*, 1, 5–32.
Davis, L. N. 1984: *The Corporate Alchemists.* Hounslow: Temple Smith.
Dedman, E. 1984: *Challenge and Response: A Modern History of Standard Oil Company (Indiana).* Chicago: Mobium Press.
De Golyer and MacNaughton 1985: *Twentieth Century Petroleum Statistics.* Dallas: De Golyer and MacNaughton.
Devine, W. W. 1983: From shafts to wires: historical perspectives on electrification. *Journal of Economic History*, 43, 347–72.
Dicken, P. 1986: *Global Shift: Industrial Change in a Turbulent World.* London: Harper and Row.
Donges, J. B. 1976: A comparative survey of industrialisation policies in fifteen semi-industrial countries. *Weltwirtschaftliches Archivs*, 112, 626–57.
Dorfman, N. S. 1983: Route 128: the development of a regional high technology economy. *Research Policy*, 12, 299–316.
Dow Chemical Co. 1989: *Annual Report.*
Doxiadis, C. A. (ed.) 1966: *Emergence and Growth of an Urban Region: The Developing Urban Detroit Area* (3 vols 1966–7). Detroit: Detroit Edison.
Duijn, J. J. van 1980: *Another Look at Industry Growth Patterns.* Faculty Working Papers 667, College of Commerce and Business Administration, University of Illinois at Urbana–Champaign.
Duijn, J. J. van 1983: *The Long Wave in Economic Life.* London: Allen and Unwin.
Dunning, J. H. 1970: United States investment and European economic growth. In C. P. Kindleberger (ed.), *The International Corporation.* Cambridge, MA: MIT Press, 141–78.
Dunning, J. H. 1986: *Japanese Participation in British Industry.* London: Croom Helm.
Dunning, J. H. 1988: *Explaining International Production.* London: Unwin Hyman.
Economic Commission for Europe 1955: *The Price of Oil in Western Europe.* Geneva: United Nations.
Ellinger, R. 1977: Industrial location behaviour and spatial evolution. *Journal of Industrial Economics*, 25, 295–312.
El Mallakh, R. and El Mallakh, D. H. 1982: *Saudi Arabia: Energy, Developmental Planning and Industrialization.* Lexington, MA: Lexington Books.
Energy Information Administration 1989: *Annual Energy Review.* Washington, DC: US Department of Energy.
Energy, Mines and Resources Canada 1976: *An Energy Strategy for Canada: Policies*

for Self-Reliance. Ottawa: Supply and Services.

Energy, Mines and Resources Canada 1980: *The National Energy Program*. Ottawa: Supply and Services.

Enos, J. L. 1962a: *Petroleum Progress and Profits: A History of Process Innovation*. Cambridge, MA: MIT Press.

Enos, J. L. 1962b: Invention and innovation in the petroleum refining industry. In National Bureau of Economic Research, *The Rate and Direction of Inventive Activity*. Princeton, NJ: Princeton University Press, 299–321.

Enos, J. L. and Park, W. H. 1988: *The Adoption and Diffusion of Imported Technology: The Case of Korea*. London: Croom Helm.

Erickson, R. A. 1976: The filtering down process: industrial location in a nonmetropolitan area. *Professional Geographer*, 28, 254–60.

Ettlinger, N. 1984: Comments on the concept of linkages from the perspective of corporate organization in the modern capitalist system. *Tijdschrift voor Economische en Sociale Geografie*, 75, 285–91.

Evans, P. 1977: Multinationals, State-owned corporations and the transformation of imperialism: a Brazilian case study. *Economic Development and Cultural Change*, 26, 43–64.

Faith, W. L., Keyes, D. B. and Clarke, R. L. 1957: *Industrial Chemicals* (2nd edn). New York: Wiley.

Fayad, M. and Motamen, H. 1986: *The Economics of the Petrochemical Industry*. London: Frances Pinter.

Feagin, J. R. 1985: The global context of metropolitan growth: Houston and the oil industry. *American Journal of Sociology*, 90, 1204–30.

Feagin, J. R. 1988: *Free Enterprise City: Houston in Political and Economic Perspective*. New Brunswick, NJ: Rutgers University Press.

Feller, I. 1971: The urban location of United States' inventions, 1860–1910. *Explorations in Economic History*, 8, 285–303.

Feller, I. 1973: Determinants of the composition of urban inventions. *Economic Geography*, 49, 47–57.

Feller, I. 1975: Invention, diffusion and industrial location. In L. Collins and D. F. Walker (eds), *Locational Dynamics of Manufacturing Activity*. London: Wiley, 83–107.

Fesharaki, F. and Isaak, D. T. 1983: *OPEC, the Gulf and the World Petroleum Market: A Study in Government Policy and Downstream Operations*. Boulder, CO: Westview Press.

Fisher, J. C. and Pry, R. H. 1971: A simple substitution model of technological change. *Technological Forecasting and Social Change*, 3, 75–88.

Forrestal, D. J. 1977: *The Monsanto Story: Faith, Hope and $5000*. New York: Simon and Schuster.

Forsyth, D. J. C. 1972: *US Investment in Scotland*. New York: Praeger.

Frank, H. J. 1966: *Crude Oil Prices in the Middle East*. New York: Praeger.

Frank, S. M. and Lambrix, J. R. 1966: Ethylene plant capacities increase as co-products' value dominates Economics. *Hydrocarbon Processing*, 45(4), 199–202.

Freeman, C. 1968: Chemical process plant: innovation and the world market. *National Institute Economic Review*, 45, 29–57.

Freeman, C. 1982: *The Economics of Industrial Innovation* (2nd edn). London: Frances Pinter.

Freeman, C. 1984: Prometheus unbound. *Futures*, 16, 494–507.

Freeman, C. 1987: Technical innovation, long cycles and regional policy. In K.

Chapman and G. Humphrys (eds), *Technical Change and Industrial Policy*. Oxford and Cambridge, MA: Basil Blackwell, 10–25.

Freeman, C., Clark, J. and Soete, L. 1982: *Unemployment and Technical Innovation*. London: Frances Pinter.

Freeman, C., Young, A. and Fuller, J. K. 1963: The plastics industry: a comparative study of research and innovation. *National Institute Economic Review*, 26, 22–62.

Gansler, J. S. 1982: *The Defence Industry*. Cambridge, MA: MIT Press.

Gatti, O., Pasquinelli, E. A. and Beltramino, R. F. 1966: The petrochemical industry in Argentina. In United Nations (ed.), *Studies in Petrochemicals* (vol. 2). New York: United Nations, 694–721.

Gibbs, D. C. 1987: Technology and the clothing industry. *Area*, 19, 313–20.

Gilbourne, D., Pocini, C. and De Blieck, J. 1978: Small ethylene plants can still be economical. *European Chemical News*, 8 December, 32, 34, 39 and 40.

Glass, D. S. 1985: The new producers, can anyone compete with them? In Chemical Marketing Research Association and European Chemical Marketing Research Association, *World Petrochemicals: A New Competitive Order*. Papers presented at meeting on 11–14 March at San Antonio, Texas.

Gold, B. 1964: Industry growth patterns: theory and empirical results. *Journal of Industrial Economics*, 13, 53–73.

Goldstein, R. F. and Waddams, A. L. 1967: *The Petroleum Chemicals Industry* (3rd edn). London: Spon.

Gordon, J. W. 1989: *The Role of the Chemical Industry in World Development*. London: Shell International Petroleum Co. Ltd.

Grant, W., Paterson, W. and Whitston, C. 1988: *Government and the Chemical Industry*. Oxford: Clarendon Press.

Groo, E. S. 1971: Choosing foreign locations: one company's experience. *Columbia Journal of World Business*, 6, 71–8.

Gross, H. T. and Vulkovic, N. 1984: *A Target Industry Identification Study for Lake Charles*. John Gray Institute, Lamar University, Baumont, TX.

Grubb, H. W. 1973: *The Structure of the Texas Economy* (2 vols). Austin, TX: Office of the Governor.

Grunwald, J. and Flamm, K. 1985: *The Global Factory*. Washington, DC: Brookings Institution.

Gudgin, G. 1978: *Industrial Location Processes and Regional Employment Growth*. Farnborough: Saxon House.

Haber, L. F. 1958: *The Chemical Industry during the Nineteenth Century*. Oxford: Clarendon Press.

Haber, L. F. 1971: *The Chemical Industry 1900–1930: International Growth and Technological Change*. Oxford: Clarendon Press.

Hall, P. and Markusen, A. (eds) 1985: *Silicon Landscapes*. Boston: Allen and Unwin.

Hamilton, F. E. I. 1976: Multinational enterprise in the EEC. *Tijdschrift voor Economische en Sociale Geografie*, 67, 258–78.

Hamilton, F. E. I and Linge, G. J. R. (eds) 1981: *Spatial Analysis, Industry and the Industrial Environment. Vol. II: International Industrial Systems*. Chichester: Wiley.

Hansen, F. H. 1975: Trends in the cost of ethylene production. *Chemistry and Industry*, 6 December, 1005–8.

Hardach, G. 1977: *The First World War 1914–1918*. London: Allen Lane.

Harrington, J. W. Jr 1985: Intraindustry structural change and location change:

US semiconductor manufacturing, 1958–1980. *Regional Studies*, 19, 343–52.

Harvey-Jones, J. 1988: *Making it Happen*. London: Collins.

Hatch, L. F. and Matar, S. 1981: *From Hydrocarbons to Petrochemicals*. Houston: Gulf Publishing Co.

Hayes, P. 1987: *Industry and Ideology: IG Farben in the Nazi Era*. Cambridge: Cambridge University Press.

Haynes, W. 1948: *American Chemical Industry: A History. Vol. 4: The Merger Era 1923–1929*. New York: Van Nostrand.

Haynes, W. 1954: *American Chemical Industry: A History. Vol. 5: Decade of New Products 1930–1939*. New York: Van Nostrand.

Hayter, R. 1987: Innovation policy and mature industries: the forest product sector in British Columbia. In K. Chapman and G. Humphrys (eds), *Technical Change and Industrial Policy*. Oxford and Cambridge, MA: Basil Blackwell, 215–32.

Hekman, J. S. 1978: An analysis of the changing location of iron and steel production in the twentieth century. *American Economic Review*, 68, 123–33.

Hekman, J. S. 1980a: The product cycle and New England textiles. *Quarterly Journal of Economics*, 94, 699–717.

Hekman, J. S. 1980b: The future of high technology industry in New England: a case study of computers. *New England Economic Review*. January/February, 5–17.

Herbert, V. and Bisio, A. 1985: *Synthetic Rubber: A Project That Had to Succeed*. Westport, CT: Greenwood Press.

Hirsch, S. 1967: *Location of Industry and International Competitiveness*. Oxford: Clarendon, Press.

Hirschman, A. O. 1958: *The Strategy of Economic Development*. New Haven, CT: Yale University Press.

Hirschman, W. B. 1964: Profit from the learning curve. *Harvard Business Review*, 42, 125–39.

Hodge, H. P. 1961: Britain's petrochemicals boom. *World Petroleum*, 301–6.

Hogan, W. T. 1983: *World Steel in the 1980s: A Case of Survival*. Lexington, MA: D. C. Heath.

Hohenberg, P. M. 1967: *Chemicals in Western Europe 1850–1914*. Chicago: Rand McNally.

Hollander, S. 1965: *The Sources of Increased Efficiency: A study of Du Pont Rayon Plants*. Cambridge, MA: MIT Press.

Holmes, J. 1987: Technical change and the restructuring of the North American automobile industry. In K. Chapman and G. Humphrys (eds), *Technical Change and Industrial Policy*. Oxford and Cambridge, MA: Basil Blackwell, 121–56.

Holroyd, R. 1967: Ultra large single stream chemical plants: their advantages and disadvantages. *Chemistry and Industry*, 5 August, 1310–15.

Hounshell, D. A. and Smith, J. K. Jr 1988: *Science and Corporate Strategy: Du Pont R and D*. Cambridge: Cambridge University Press.

Howard, F. N. 1947: *Buna Rubber: The Birth of an Industry*. New York: Van Nostrand.

Howells, J. R. L. 1984: The location of research and development: some observations and evidence from Britain. *Regional Studies*, 18, 13–29.

Howes, D. A. 1968: Raw material supplies for heavy organic chemicals manufacture. *Chemistry and Industry*, 30 March, 407–10.

Hubbard, M. E. 1967: *The Economics of Transporting Oil to and within Europe.* London: Maclaren.

Hudson, R. 1983: Capital accumulation and chemicals production in Western Europe in the postwar period. *Environment and Planning A,* 15, 105–22.

Hudson, R. 1988: Uneven development in capitalist societies: changing spatial divisions of labour, forms of spatial organization of production and service provision, and their impacts on localities, *Institute of British Geographers, Transactions* (new series), 13, 484–96.

Hufbauer, G. 1966: *Synthetic Materials and the Theory of International Trade.* London: Duckworth.

Hughes, T. P. 1969: Technological momentum in history: hydrogenation in Germany 1898–1933. *Past and Present,* 44, 106–32.

Hulten, J. R. 1973: *A Plan for the Development of an Intermediate and Downstream Petrochemical Industry in Puerto Rico.* Unpublished report of Economic Development Administration (FOMENTO), San Juan, Puerto Rico.

Hurter, A. P. and Rubinstein, A. H. 1978: Market pentration by new innovations: a review of the literature. *Technological Forecasting and Social Change,* 11, 197–221.

Hymer, S. H. 1979: *The Multinational Corporation: A Radical Critique.* Cambridge: Cambridge University Press.

ICI 1989: *ICI World Data.* London: Imperial Chemical Industries PLC.

Industrial Bank of Japan 1978: The petrochemical industry in East Asia. *Japanese Finance and Industry Quarterly Survey,* 37, 1–39.

International Petroleum Encyclopedia 1989: Tulsa, OK: Pennwell Publishing.

Isard, W., Schooler, E. W. and Vietorisz, T. 1959: *Industrial Complex Analysis and Regional Development.* Cambridge, MA: MIT Press.

Isting, C. 1970: Pipelines now play important role in petrochemical transport. *World Petroleum,* April, 38–44; May, 36–44.

James, M. 1953: *The Texaco Story.* New York: Texas Co.

Jensen, W. G. 1967: *Energy in Europe 1945–1980.* London: Foulis.

John Gray Institute 1989: *A Strategic Economic Development Plan for Southeast Texas.* Lamar University, Beaumont, TX.

Johnson, A. M. 1983: *The Challenge of Change: The Sun Oil Company 1945–1977.* Columbus, OH: Ohio State University Press.

Kaldor, M. 1981: *The Baroque Arsenal.* London: Macmillan.

Kidder, Peabody and Co. 1980: *US Chemical Companies in Europe.* London: André Deutsch.

King, R. 1977: Recent industrialization in Sardinia: rebirth or neo-colonialism? *Erdkunde,* 31, 87–102.

Kinsey, J. 1979: Industrial location and industrial development in the Aire Métropolitaine Marseillaise. *Tijdschrift voor Economische en Sociale Geografie,* 70, 272–85.

Kirby, A. M. Jr 1970: The chemical industry and the oil-import program. In A. M. Brownstein (ed.), *US Petrochemicals: Technology, Economics and Markets.* Tulsa, OK: Petroleum Press.

Kleinknecht, A. 1987: *Innovation Patterns in Crisis and Prosperity.* London: Macmillan.

Kline, S. J. and Rosenberg, N. 1986: An overview of innovation. In R. Landau and N. Rosenberg (eds), *The Positive Sum Strategy.* Washington, DC: National Academy Press, 275–305.

Kluyver, C. A. de 1977: Innovation and industrial product life cycles. *California Management Review*, 20, 21–33.

Knickerbocker, F. T. 1973: *Oligopolistic Reaction and Multinational Enterprises.* Boston, MA: Harvard Business School Press.

Krammer, A. 1978: Fueling the Third Reich. *Technology and Culture*, 19, 394–422.

Krammer, A. 1981: Technology transfer as war booty: the US Technical Oil Mission to Europe, 1945. *Technology and Culture*, 22, 68–103.

Kravis, I. B. and Lipsey, R. E. 1982: The location of overseas production and production for export by US multinational firms. *Journal of International Economics*, 12, 201–23.

Krumme, G. and Hayter, R. 1975: Implications of corporate strategies and product cycle adjustments for regional employment changes. In L. Collins and D. F. Walker (eds), *Locational Dynamics of Manufacturing Activity.* London: Wiley, 325–56.

Kuznets, S. 1930: *Secular Movements in Production and Prices.* Boston: Houghton Mifflin.

Kuznets, S. 1966: *Modern Economic Growth: Rate Structure and Spread.* New Haven, CT: Yale University Press.

Landau, R. 1981: Process innovation. *Chemistry and Industry*, 2 May, 321–7.

Landes, D. S. 1968: *Unbound Prometheus: Technology Change and Industrial Development in Western Europe from 1750 to the Present.* Cambridge: Cambridge University Press.

Langston, V. C. 1983: *An Investment Model for the US Gulf Coast Refining/Petrochemical Complex.* Unpublished PhD thesis, University of Texas at Austin.

Larson, H. M., Knowlton, E. H. and Popple, C. S. 1971: *A History of Standard Oil Co. (New Jersey): New Horizons 1927–1950.* London: Harper and Row.

Larson, H. M. and Porter, K. W. 1959: *A History of Humble Oil and Refining Company.* New York: Harper.

Leeman, W. A. 1962: *The Price of Middle East Oil.* Ithaca, NY: Cornell University Press.

Lever, W. F. 1980: Manufacturing linkages, industrial dynamics and the transmission of growth. *Regional Science and Urban Economics*, 10, 491–502.

Levitt, T. 1965: Exploit the product life cycle. *Harvard Business Review*, 43, 81–94.

Liebermann, M. B. 1984: The learning curve and pricing in the chemical processing industries. *Rand Journal of Economics*, 15, 213–28.

Liebermann, M. B. 1987: Patents, learning by doing, and market structure in the chemical processing industries. *International Journal of Industrial Organization*, 5, 257–76.

Lindberg, O. 1953: An economic geographic study of the localisation of the Swedish paper industry, *Geografiska Annaler*, 35, 28–40.

List, H. C. 1986: *Petrochemical Technology.* Englewood Cliffs, NJ: Prentice-Hall.

Little, A. D. Inc. 1978: *The Petrochemical Industry and the US Economy: A Report to The Petrochemical Energy Group.* Cambridge, MA: Arthur D. Little Inc.

Lubove, R. 1969: *Twentieth Century Pittsburgh: Government, Business and Environmental Change.* New York: Wiley.

Maddison, A. 1982: *Phases of Capitalist Development.* Oxford: Oxford University Press.

Magee, S. P. 1977: Multinational corporations, the industry technology cycle and development. *Journal of World Trade Law*, 11, 297–321.

Malecki, E. J. 1979: Locational trends in R and D by large US corporations

1965–1977. *Economic Geography*, 55, 309–23.

Malecki, E. J. 1980: Corporate organization of R and D and the location of technological activities. *Regional Studies*, 14, 219–34.

Malecki, E. J. 1983: Technology and regional development: a survey. *International Regional Science Review*, 8, 89–125.

Manners, G. 1971: *The Geography of Energy* (2nd edn). London: Hutchinson.

Mansfield, E. 1985: How rapidly does new industrial technology leak out? *Journal of Industrial Economics*, 34, 217–23.

Mansfield, E. and Romeo, A. 1980: Technology transfer to overseas subsidiaries by US-based firms. *Quarterly Journal of Economics*, 95, 737–50.

Mansfield, E., Romeo, A. and Wagner, S. 1979: Foreign trade and US research and development. *Review of Economics and Statistics*, 61, 49–57.

Mantoux, P. 1928: *The Industrial Revolution in the Eighteenth Century*. London: Jonathan Cape.

Markusen, A. R. 1985: *Profit Cycles, Oligopoly and Regional Development*. Cambridge, MA: MIT Press.

Markusen, A. R. 1987: *Regions: The Economics and Politics of Territory*. Totowa, NJ: Rowman and Littlefield.

Mason, C. M. 1987: The small firm sector. In W. F. Lever (ed.), *Industrial Change in the United Kingdom*. Harlow: Longman, 125–48.

Mason, C. M. and Harrison, R. T. 1985: The geography of small firms in the United Kingdom: towards a research agenda. *Progress in Human Geography*, 9, 1–37.

Massey, D. 1979: In what sense a regional problem? *Regional Studies*, 13, 233–43.

Massey, D. 1984: *Spatial Divisions of Labour*. London: Macmillan.

Massey, D. and Meegan, R. 1978: Industrial restructuring versus the cities. *Urban Studies*, 15, 273–88.

Massey, D. and Meegan, R. 1979: The geography of industrial re-organisation: the spatial effects of the restructuring of the electrical engineering sector under the Industrial Reorganisation Corporation, *Progress in Planning*, 10, 155–237.

McGowan, Lord 1946: Chairman's annual statement. ICI.

Melamid, A. 1955: Geographical distribution of petroleum refining capacities: a study of the European refining programme. *Economic Geography*, 31, 168–78.

Mensch, G. 1979: *Stalemate in Technology*. Cambridge, MA: Ballinger.

Mercier, C. 1966: *Petrochemical Industry and the Possibilities of its Establishment in the Developing Countries*. Paris: Editions Technip.

Milward, A. S. 1977: *War, Economy and Society, 1939–1945*. London: Allen Lane.

Milward, A. S. 1984: *The Reconstruction of Western Europe 1945–1951*. London: Methuen.

Mirow, K. R. and Maurer, H. 1982: *Webs of Power: International Cartels and the World Economy*. Boston, MA: Houghton Mifflin.

MIT Commission on Industrial Productivity 1989: The transformation of the US chemicals industry. In *Working Papers* (vol. 1). Cambridge, MA: MIT Press.

Mittmann, D. 1974: Die chemische industrie in Nordwestlichen Mitteleuropa in ihrem strukturwandel. *Kolner Forschunger zur Wirtschafts- and Sozialgeographie*, 22, Köln.

Molle, W. and Wever, E. 1984: *Oil Refineries and Petrochemical Industries in Western Europe*. Aldershot: Gower.

Moran, T. H. 1979: Foreign expansion as an institutional necessity for US corporate capitalism. In A. Mack, D. Plant and U. Doyle (eds), *Imperialism, Intervention and Economic Development*. London: Croom Helm, 160–78.

Morner, A. L. 1977: Dow's strategy for an unfriendly new era. *Fortune*, May, 312–24.

Moroney, J. R. 1972: *The Structure of Production in American Manufacturing*. Chapel Hill: University of North Carolina Press.

Moseley, M. J. 1974: *Growth Centres in Regional Planning*. Oxford: Pergamon.

Mueller, W. F. 1962: The origins of the basic inventions underlying Du Pont's major product and process innovations, 1920 to 1950. In National Bureau of Economic Research, *The Rate and Direction of Inventive Activity*. Princeton, NJ: Princeton University Press, 323–46.

Nash, G. D. 1968: *United States Oil Policy 1890–1964*. Pittsburgh, PA: University of Pittsburgh Press.

Nelson, R. R. and Winter, S. G. 1977: In search of a useful theory of innovation. *Research Policy*, 6, 36–76.

Norcliffe, G. B. 1979: Identifying local industrial complexes. *Canadian Journal of Regional Science*, 2, 25–36.

Norcliffe, G. B. and Kotseff, L. E. 1980: Local industrial complexes in Ontario. *Annals of the Association of American Geographers*, 70, 68–79.

North, D. C. 1981: *Structure and Change in Economic History*. New York: Norton.

Norton, R. D. and Rees, J. 1979: The product cycle and the spatial decentralisation of American manufacturing. *Regional Studies*, 13, 141–51.

Oakey, R. P., Thwaites, A. T. and Nash, P. A. 1980: The regional distribution of innovative manufacturing establishments in Britain. *Regional Studies*, 14, 235–54.

Odell, P. R. 1968: The British gas industry. *Geographical Journal*, 134, 81–6.

OEEC 1949: *First Report on Co-ordination of Oil Refinery Expansion in the OEEC Countries*. Paris: Oil Committee OEEC.

OEEC 1955: *The Chemical Industry in Europe*. Paris: OEEC.

OEEC 1956: *Oil: The Outlook for Europe*. Paris: Oil Committee OEEC.

OECD 1962: *The Chemical Industry 1961–1962*. Paris: OECD.

OECD 1963a: *The Chemical Industry 1962–1963*. Paris: OECD.

OECD 1963b: *The Chemical Industry in the European Member Countries 1953–1962*. Paris: OECD.

OECD 1968: *The Chemical Industry 1967–1968*. Paris: OECD.

OECD 1981: *North–South Technology Transfer: The Way Ahead*. Paris: OECD.

OECD 1985: *Petrochemical Industry: Energy Aspects of Structural Change*. Paris: OECD.

Office of Technology Assessment 1984: *Technology Transfer to the Middle East*. Washington, DC: US Congress.

Papageorgiou, G. T. 1985: *The Transfer of Technology to the Algerian Hydrocarbons and Petrochemical Industry*. Unpublished MA thesis, Norman Paterson School of International Affairs, Carleton University, Ottawa.

Penrose, E. T. 1959: *The Theory of the Growth of the Firm*. Oxford and Cambridge, MA: Basil Blackwell.

Penrose, E. T. 1960: The growth of the firm. A case study: the Hercules Powder Company. *Business History Review*, 34 (winter), 1–23.

Perroux, F. 1950: Economic space: theory and applications. *Quarterly Journal of Economics*, 64, 89–104.

Peters, E. H. 1966: New breed of ethylene plants cuts manufacturing costs. *Oil and Gas Journal*, 21 March, 94–7.

Petrochemical Energy Group 1974: *Ethane and the US Petrochemical Industry*. Washington, DC: Petrochemical Energy Group.

Petrochemical Industry Task Force 1984: *Report to Minister of Energy, Mines and Resources and to Minister of Regional Industrial Expansion*.

Petróleos Mexicanos 1966: The Mexican government and the petrochemical industry in Mexico. In United Nations (ed.), *Studies in Petrochemicals* (vol. 2). New York: United Nations, 794–801.

Pettigrew, A. 1985: *The Awakening Giant: Continuity and Change in ICI*. Oxford and Cambridge, MA: Basil Blackwell.

Pfann, H. 1979: *Petrochemicals: Their Economic Significance in the Domestic Economy*. Washington, DC: US Industry and Trade Administration.

Piore, M. J. and Sabel, C. F. 1985: *The Second Industrial Divide*. New York: Basic Books.

Podbielski, G. 1978: *Twenty Five Years of Special Action for the Development of Southern Italy*. Rome: SVIMEZ.

Porter, M. E. 1980: *Competitive Strategy*. New York: The free Press.

Pratt, J. A. 1980: *The Growth of a Refining Region*. Greenwich, CT: JAI Press.

Pratten, C. F. 1971: *Economies of Scale in Manufacturing Industry*. Cambridge: Cambridge University Press.

Pred, A. R. 1965: Industrialization, initial advantage and American metropolitan growth. *Geographical Review*, 55, 158–85.

Pred, A. R. 1966: *The Spatial Dynamics of US Urban-Industrial Growth, 1800–1914*. Cambridge, MA: MIT Press.

Rajana, C. 1975: *The Chemical and Petrochemical Industries of Russia and Eastern Europe 1960–1980*. London: Sussex University Press.

Reader, W. J. 1975: *Imperial Chemical Industries: A History* (vol. 2). London: Oxford University Press.

Rees, J. 1974: Decision making, the growth of the firm and the business environment. In F. E. I. Hamilton (ed.), *Spatial Perspectives on Industrial Organization and Decision Making*. London: Wiley, 189–212.

Rees, J. 1978: On the spatial spread and oligopolistic behaviour of large rubber companies. *Geoforum*, 9, 319–30.

Rees, J. 1984: *Oil Mergers, External Control and the Outlook for the Gulf Coast Economy*. John Gray Institute, Lamar University, Beaumont, TX.

Reuben, B. G. and Burstall, M. L. 1973: *The Chemical Economy*. London: Longman.

Rice, G. R. and Scott, L. C. 1974: *Economic Analysis of the Chemical Industry in Louisiana*. College of Business Administration, Louisiana State University, Baton Rouge.

Richter, H., Lohr, B. and Koenig, H. J. 1978: Feedstock flexibility in ethylene plants. *Chemical Economy and Engineering Review*, 10(3), 13–18.

Riddell, K. and Feagin, J. R. 1987: Houston and government: the growth of the petrochemical industry and the War Production Board. Unpublished paper presented at Southwestern Sociological Association Conference, Dallas, 20 March.

Rimmer, P. J. 1968: The Australian petrochemical industry. *Economic Geography*, 44, 351–63.

Robertson, K. N. 1986: World olefins outlook: lessons from history. Paper presented at World Chemical Congress of Marketing and Business Research, Newport Beach, CA, 10 September.

Rodgers, A. 1979: *Economic Development in Retrospect: The Italian Model and its Significance for Regional Planning in Market-Oriented Economies*. Washington, DC: V. H. Winston.

Roepke, H., Adams, D. and Wiseman, R. 1974: A new approach to the identification of industrial complexes using input–output data. *Journal of Regional Science*, 14, 15–29.

Rosenberg, N. 1963: Technical change in the machine tool industry 1840–1910. *Journal of Economic History*, 23, 414–43.

Rosenberg, N. 1972: *Technology and American Economic Growth*. New York: Harper and Row.

Rosenberg, N. 1976: *Perspectives on Technology*. Cambridge: Cambridge University Press.

Rosenberg, N. 1979: Technological interdependence in the American economy. *Technology and Culture*, 20, 25–50.

Rosenberg, N. 1986: The impact of technological innovation: a historical view. In R. Landau and N. Rosenberg (eds), *The Positive Sum Strategy*. Washington, DC: National Academy Press, 17–32.

Rostow, W. W. 1960: *The Stages of Economic Growth*. Cambridge: Cambridge University Press.

Rostow, W. W. 1978: *The World Economy: History and Prospect*. London: Macmillan.

Rothwell, R. 1982: The role of technology in industrial change: implications for regional policy. *Regional Studies*, 16, 361–9.

Rothwell, R. and Zegweld, W. 1981: *Industrial Innovation and Public Policy: Preparing for the 1980s and 1990s*. London: Frances Pinter.

Rudd, D. F., Fathi-Afshar, S., Trevino, A. A. and Stadtherr, M. A. 1981: *Petrochemical Technology Assessment*. New York: Wiley.

Saxenian, A. 1985: The genesis of Silicon Valley. In P. Hall and A. Markusen (eds), *Silicon Landscapes*. Boston: Allen and Unwin, 20–34.

Scammell, W. M. 1980: *The International Economy since 1945*. London: Macmillan.

Scherer, F. M. 1982: Interindustry technology flows in the United States. *Research Policy*, 11, 227–45.

Scherer, F. M. 1984: *Innovation and Growth: Schumpeterian Perspectives*. Cambridge, MA: MIT Press.

Schmookler, J. 1966: *Invention and Economic Growth*. Cambridge MA: Harvard University Press.

Schoenberger, E. 1987: Technological and organisational change in automobile production: spatial implications. *Regional Studies*, 21, 199–214.

Schumpeter, J. A. 1934: *The Theory of Economic Development*. Cambridge, MA: Harvard University Press.

Schumpeter, J. A. 1939: *Business Cycles*. New York: McGraw-Hill.

Seifried, N. R. M. 1984: Recent growth of the petrochemical industry in Alberta: its role in industrial diversification and decentralization. In B. M. Barr and N. M. Waters (eds), *Regional Diversification and Structural Change*. Vancouver: Tantalus, 99–110.

Seifried, N. R. M. 1989: Restructuring the Canadian petrochemical industry: an intranational problem. *Canadian Geographer*, 33, 168–78.

Sercovich, F. C. 1980: *State-Owned Enterprises and Dynamic Comparative Advantage in the World Petrochemical Industry: The Case of Commodity Olefins in Brazil.* Development Discussion Paper 96, Harvard Institute for International Development, Cambridge, MA.

Servan-Schreiber, J. J. 1968: *The American Challenge.* New York: Atheneum.

Shanafelt, R. E. 1977: *The Baton Rouge–New Orleans Petrochemical Industrial Region: A Functional Region Study.* Unpublished PhD thesis, Louisiana State University.

Shaw, R. N. and Shaw, S. A. 1983: Excess capacity and rationalization in the West European synthetic fibres industry. *Journal of Industrial Economies,* 32, 149–66.

Shell International Chemical Co. 1979: *Substitution Revisited: A Study on Petrochemical Growth.* London: Chemical Planning and Economics, Shell International Chemical Co. Ltd.

Shell International Chemical Co. 1988: *Chemicals Information Handbook.* London: Shell.

Shell International Petroleum Co. 1966: *The Petroleum Handbook* (5th edn). London: Shell.

Shell International Petroleum Co. 1990: *Petrochemicals.* London: Shell.

Shell Oil Co. of Canada (Chemical Division) 1956: *The Canadian Petrochemical Industry.* Toronto: Ryerson Press.

Sherwood Taylor, F. 1957: *A History of Industrial Chemistry.* London: Heinemann.

Smith, D. M. 1981: *Industrial Location: An Economic Geographical Analysis* (2nd edn). Chichester: Wiley.

Smith, J. K. 1985: The ten year invention: Neoprene and Du Pont research 1930–1939. *Technology and Culture,* 26, 34–55.

Solomou, S. 1989: *Phases of Economic Growth 1850–1973: Kondratieff Waves and Kuznets Swings.* Cambridge: Cambridge University Press.

Sorey, G. K. 1980: *The Foreign Policy of a Multinational Enterprise.* New York: Arno Press.

Spitz, P. H. 1988: *Petrochemicals: The Rise of an Industry.* New York: Wiley.

SRI International: *Chemical Economics Handbook* (various dates). Palo Alto, CA: SRI International.

Stauffer, T. R. 1988: Energy-intensive industrialization in the Middle East. *Industry and Development,* 14, 1–35.

Steed, G. P. F. 1978: Global industrial systems: a case study of the clothing industry. *Geoforum,* 9, 35–47.

Steinbaum, C. A. and Rothman, S. N. 1984: The Canadian petrochemical industry: reaction to policy. *Chemical Economy and Engineering Review,* 16(4), 14–20

Steiner, M. 1985: Old industrial areas: a theoretical approach. *Urban Studies,* 22, 387–98.

Stobaugh, R. B. 1970: The neotechnology account of international trade: the case of petrochemicals. *Journal of International Business Studies,* 2(2), 41–60.

Stobaugh, R. B. 1971: *The International Transfer of Technology in the Establishment of the Petrochemical Industry in Developing Countries.* UNITAR Research Report 12, United Nations, New York.

Stobaugh, R. B. 1984: Channels for technology transfer: the petrochemical industry. In R. Stobaugh and L. T. Wells (eds), *Technology Crossing Borders.* Boston, MA: Harvard Business School Press.

Stobaugh, R. B. 1988: *Innovation and Competition: The Global Management of Petrochemical Products.* Boston, MA: Harvard Business School Press.

Stobaugh, R. B. and Townsend, P.L. 1975: Price forecasting and strategic planning: the case of petrochemicals. *Journal of Marketing Research*, 12, 19–29.

Stolper, G. 1967: *The German Economy 1870 to the Present*. London: Weidenfeld and Nicolson.

Storck, W. J. 1986: US chemical industry in midst of major restructuring. *Chemical and Engineering News*, 7 April, 8–10.

Storper, M. 1985: Oligopoly and the product cycle: essentialism in economic geography. *Economic Geography*, 61, 260–82.

Storper, M. and Walker, R. 1989: *The Capitalist Imperative: Territory, Technology and Industrial Growth*. Oxford and Cambridge, MA: Basil Blackwell.

Strange, S. 1986: *Casino Capitalism*. Oxford and Cambridge, MA: Basil Blackwell.

Stranges, A. N. 1984: Friedrich Bergius and the rise of the German synthetic fuel industry. *Isis*, 75, 649–67.

Strategic Economic Policy Commission 1989: *A Strategic Economic Plan for Texas*. Submitted to the 71st Session of the Texas Legislature, Austin, TX.

Summers, R. and Heston, A. 1988: A new set of international comparisons of real product and prices estimates for 130 countries, 1950–1985. *Review of Income and Wealth*, 34, 1–26.

Sutton, A. C. 1973: *Western Technology and Soviet Economic Development 1945–1965*. Stanford, CA: Hoover Institution Press.

Suzuki, E. 1982: Japanese chemical industry and its future course. *Chemical Economy and Engineering Review*, January/February, 7–14.

Tandy, H. 1986: *Petrochemicals in the Middle East*. London: Middle East Economic Digest.

Taylor, G. D. and Sudnik, P. E. 1984: *Du Pont and the International Chemical Industry*. Boston MA: G. K. Hall.

Taylor, M. 1986: The product cycle model: a critique. *Environment and Planning A*, 18, 751–61.

Teesplan 1969: *Teeside Survey and Plan* (2 vols, 1969, 1971). London: HMSO.

Texas Department of Water Resources 1983: *The Texas Input–Output Model*. Austin, TX: Texas Department of Water Resources.

Thomas. M. D. 1981: Industry perspectives on growth and change. In J. Rees, G. J. D. Hewings and H. A. Stafford (eds), *Industrial Location and Regional Systems*. New York: J. F. Bergin, 41–58.

Thomas, M. D. 1985: Regional economic development and the role of innovation and technological change. In A. T. Thwaites and R. P. Oakey (eds), *The Regional Economic Impact of Technological Change*. London: Frances Pinter, 13–35.

Todd, D. 1985: *The World Shipbuilding Industry*. London: Croom Helm.

Toyne, B., Arpon, J. S., Barnett, A. H., Ricks, D. A. and Shimp, R. A. 1984: *The Global Textile Industry*. London: Allen and Unwin.

Trevino, A. A. and Rudd, D. F. 1980: On planning an integrated Mexican petrochemical industry. *Engineering Costs and Production Economics*, 5, 129–42.

Turner, L. and Bedore, J. M. 1979: *Middle East Industrialization: A Study of Saudi and Iranian Downstream Investments*. Farnborough: Saxon House.

Tuttle, W. M. Jr 1981: The birth of an industry: the synthetic rubber 'mess' in World War II. *Technology and Culture*, 22, 35–67.

United Nations 1966: *Studies in Petrochemicals* (2 vols). New York: United Nations.

UN Conference on Trade and Development 1979: *The Structure and Behaviour of Enterprises in the Chemical Industry and their Effects on the Trade and Development of Developing Countries*. New York: UNCTAD.

UNIDO 1969a: *Chemical Industry*. Monographs on Industrial Development 8, New York: United Nations.

UNIDO 1969b: *Selection of Projects and Production Processes for Basic and Intermediate Petrochemicals in Developing Countries*. Petrochemical Industry Series Monograph 2, New York: United Nations.

UNIDO 1969c: *The Brazilian Synthetic Polymer Industry*. Petrochemical Industry Series Monograph 1, New York: United Nations.

UNIDO 1970a: *Development of Plastics Industries in Developing Countries*. New York: United Nations.

UNIDO 1970b: *Petrochemical Industries in Developing Countries*. New York: United Nations.

UNIDO 1973: *The Petrochemical Industry*. New York: United Nations.

UNIDO 1978: *First World-Wide Study on the Petrochemical industry 1975–2000*. Sectoral Studies Section, International Centre for Industrial Studies, Vienna: UNIDO.

UNIDO 1981: *Long Term Arrangements for the Development of the Petrochemical Industry in Developing Countries Including Arrangements for Marketing Petrochemicals Produced in Developing Countries*. ID/WG 336.2, Turkey: UNIDO.

UNIDO 1982: *A Basic Technological Disaggregation Model. (i) The Petrochemical Industry*. New York: UNIDO.

UNIDO 1983a: *Opportunities for Co-operation Among the Developing Countries for the Establishment of the Petrochemical Industry*. Sectoral Working Paper Series 1, Vienna: UNIDO.

UNIDO 1983b: *World Demand for Petrochemical Products and the Emergence of New Producers from the Hydrocarbon Rich Developing Countries*. Sectoral Studies Series 9, Sectoral Studies Branch, Division for Industrial Studies, Vienna: UNIDO.

UNIDO 1985a: *The Petrochemical Industry in the Developing ESCAP Region: Past Review and Future Prospects*. Sectoral Working Paper Series 41, Sectoral Studies Branch, Division for Industrial Studies, Vienna: UNIDO.

UNIDO 1985b: *Development of Downstream Petrochemical Industries in Developing Countries*. Issue 2, Vienna: UNIDO.

UNIDO 1985c: *Petrochemical Industry in Developing Countries: Prospects and Strategies*. Sectoral Studies Series 20, vol. 1, Vienna: UNIDO.

UNIDO 1985d: *World Changes in the Structure of the Petrochemical Industry 1980–1983*. Vienna: UNIDO.

US Department of Commerce 1982: *A Competitive Assessment of the US Petrochemical Industry*. Washington, DC: International Trade Administration.

US Department of Commerce 1985: *The US Plastics and Synthetic Materials Industry Since 1958*. Washington, DC: Economic Affairs, Office of Business Analysis.

US Department of Commerce 1986: *A Competitive Assessment of the US Ethylene Industry*. Washington, DC: International Trade Administration.

US Department of Commerce 1988: *US Industrial Outlook, 1988*. Washington, DC.

US International Trade Commission 1983: *The Probable Impact on the US Petrochemical Industry of the Expanding Petrochemical Industries in the Conventional-Energy-Rich Nations*. US ITC Publication 1370, Washington, DC: US ITC.

US International Trade Commission 1985a: *Chemical Industry Growth in Developing Countries and Changing US Trade Patterns*. US ITC Publication 1780, Washington, DC: US ITC.

US International Trade Commission 1985b: *The Shift from US Production of Commodity Petrochemicals to Value-Added Speciality Chemical Products and the Possible Impact on US Trade*. US ITC Publication 1677, Washington, DC: US ITC.

US International Trade Commission 1985c: *Potential Effects of Foreign Government's Policies of Pricing Natural Resources.* US ITC Publication 1696, Washington, DC: US ITC.

US International Trade Commission 1987: *US Global Competitiveness: Building Block Petrochemicals and Competitive Implications for Construction, Automobiles and Other Major Consuming Industries.* US ITC Publication 2005, Washington, DC: US ITC.

US International Trade Commission 1989: *Foreign Investment Barriers or Other Restrictions that Prevent Foreign Capital from Claiming the Benefits of Foreign Government Programs.* US ITC Publication 2212, Washington, DC: US ITC.

Utterback, J. M. and Abernathy, W. J. 1975: A dynamic model of product and process innovation. *Omega*, 3, 639–56.

Van der Wee, H. 1986: *Prosperity and Upheaval: The World Economy 1945–1980.* New York: Viking.

Vergara, W. and Brown, D. 1988: *The New Face of the World Petrochemical Sector: Implications for Developing Countries.* World Bank Technical Paper 84, Washington, DC.

Vernon, R. 1966: International investment and international trade in the product cycle. *Quarterly Journal of Economics*, 80, 190–207.

Vernon, R. 1971: *Sovereignty at Bay: The Multinational Spread of US Enterprises.* New York: Basic Books.

Vernon, R. 1979: The product cycle hypothesis in a new international environment. *Oxford Bulletin of Economics and Statistics*, 41, 255–68.

Vernon, R. and Wells, L. T. Jr 1985: *Manager in the International Economy* (5th edn). Englewood Cliffs, NJ: Prentice-Hall.

Walker, R. A. 1985: Technological determination and determinism: industrial growth and location. In M. Castells (ed.), *High Technology, Space and Society*. Berkeley, CA: Sage, 226–64.

Walley, K. H. and Robinson, S. J. Q. 1972: Effects of scale upon the economics of olefin production – theory and reality. *Petroleum Review*, 26, 328–32.

Walsh, V. 1984: Invention and innovation in the chemical industry: demand-pull or discovery-push? *Research Policy*, 13, 211–34.

Walsh, V., Townsend, J., Achilladelis, B. and Freeman, C. 1979: *Trends in Invention and Innovation in the Chemical Industry.* Unpublished report to Social Science Research Council.

Warren, K. 1971: Growth, technical change and planning problems in heavy industry with special reference to the chemical industry. In M. Chisholm and G. Manners (eds), *Spatial Policy Problems of the British Economy*, Cambridge: Cambridge University Press, 180–212.

Watts, H. D. and Stafford, H. A. 1986: Plant closure and the multiplant firm: some conceptual issues. *Progress in Human Geography*, 10, 206–27.

Weinstein, B. L. and Gross, H. T. 1983: *Industrial Development Opportunities for the Golden Triangle in the 1980s.* John Gray Institute, Lamar University, Beaumont, TX.

Weinstein, B. L. and Gross, H. T. 1987: Spatial and structural consequences of industrial change: the American Gulf Coast Petrocrescent. In F. E. I. Hamilton (ed.), *Industrial Change in the Advanced Economies*. London: Croom Helm, 161–78.

Weinstein, B. L., Hoyte, D. R., Adamson, P. E., Gross, H. T. and Rees, J. 1985: *Structural Change in the Oil Industry and its Impact on the Gulf Coast Economy.* A report prepared for the Subcommittee on Economic Goals and Intergovernmental Policy of the Joint Economic Committee, Congress of the United States, Washington, DC: US Government Printing Office.

Wells, L. T. Jr (ed.) 1972: *The Product Life Cycle and International Trade.* Boston: Harvard Business School Press.

Wever, E. 1966: Pernis-Botlek-Europoort. Un complexe à base de pétrole? *Tijdschrift voor Economische en Sociale Geographie*, 57, 131–41.

White, R. L. and Watts, H. D. 1977: The spatial evolution of an industry: the example of broiler production. *Institute of British Geographers, Transactions (New Series)*, 2, 175–91.

Whitehead, D. 1968: *The Dow Story.* New York: McGraw-Hill.

Whitehorn, N. C. 1973: *Economic Analysis of the Petrochemical Industry in Texas.* Texas A and M University, College Station, TX.

Wijetilleke, L, and Ody, O. J. 1984: *World Refinery Industry: Need for Restructuring.* World Bank Technical Paper 32, Washington, DC.

Williams, L. H. 1960: The future of chemicals from petroleum. *Chemistry and Industry* 6 August, 1006–16.

Williams-Merz 1976: *A Study of Gas Gathering Pipeline Systems in the North Sea.* London: Department of Energy.

Williamson, H. F., Andreano, R. L. Daum, A. R. and Klose, G. C. 1963: *The American Petroleum Industry: The Age of Energy 1899–1959.* Northwestern University, Evanston, IL.

Wilson, R. 1977: International Licensing of technology: empirical evidence *Research Policy*, 6, 114–26.

Wiseman, P. 1986: *Petrochemicals.* Chichester: Ellis Horwood.

Witcoff, H. A. and Reuben, B. G. 1980: *Industrial Organic Chemicals in Perspective.* New York: Wiley.

Wood, D. E. 1986: Restructuring the Eastern Canadian basic petrochemical industry. *Hydrocarbon Processing*, August, 102G–102M.

Index

314

316

Index

export-oriented production 19,
152–3, 178–86, 193
external control 10, 274
external economies 136
Exxon 128–9, 217, 221, 224, 250; *see
also* Esso; Standard Oil (New
Jersey)

Fawley (UK) 216
Feagin, J. R. 78, 269–70, 275, 279
feedstock flexibility 29–31, 135–6,
171, 289
feedstock push 289
fertilizers 40–1, 179
Fiberloid Corporation 47
fixed costs 126, 176
flexibility *see* feedstock flexibility
follow-the-leader behaviour *see*
oligopolistic reaction
forecasting errors 230
foreign direct investment 154–6,
159–61, 202–26, 291
foreign participation 156–9, 162,
185–6
Formosa Plastic Corporation 162
forward integration 103, 164–6,
271–6
forward linkages *see* forward
integration
fractionation plants 129–30
France 40, 114, 214, 219, 245–6,
250–1, 254, 270
Freeman, C. 3, 100
Freeport (Texas) 66, 133, 216, 220,
264
functional linkages *see* backward
integration; forward integration;
linkages

gasoline 30–1, 53–4, 72–5
geographical inertia *see* inertia
Germany 39–45, 49–50, 66–8,
78–82, 111–15, 127, 139–41, 254
global corporations 31–4, 105, 144,
202–26
globalization (of industry) 290
Golden Triangle, the 130, 262,
277–8; *see also* South East Texas
government intervention (in industry)
11–12, 34, 45, 50, 64–89,

144–201, 207–9, 245–6
Grangemouth (UK) 132, 136, 216,
268
Grant, W. H. 244, 248, 249
greenfield sites 56–7, 264
gross domestic product (GDP)
106–10, 116, 153
gross national product (GNP) 91
growth centres 11, 261, 268–75
growth poles 11, 261
Gulf Oil 139, 254
Gulf Coast region (US) 60–2, 76–8,
102–3, 128–30, 139, 220, 261–8,
275–84
Gulf Co-operation Council 152

Haber-Bosch process 41–2, 65
Heavy Liquids Program 191
Hekman, J. S. 9–10
high octane gasoline 72
high-tech industry 11, 37–9, 64, 280
Hoechst 32–3, 81, 250
Hollander, S. 119, 121
Houdry, E. 53
Houston 78, 262–4, 266, 276
Houston Ship Channel 130, 164
Hufbauer, G. 48, 107
hydrogenation 50–2, 54–5

ICI
foreign investment by 213–14, 238
innovation in 47, 60, 99, 234
raw material policies 83–4, 133,
219
on Teesside 50–1, 133, 268–9, 280
IG Farben 42–5, 49–52, 60, 67–9
IJmuiden (Netherlands) 56
imitation lag 48, 107, 146
import substitution 19, 151, 154–67,
208–9
India 156
industrial development strategies
7–8, 149–68, 178–86, 209
industrial disarmament 80–1
Industrial Revolution, the 3
industrial structure
of countries 7–8
of regions 10, 275–81
industry associations 248
inertia

318   *Index*

market area extension   8–9, 204–7,
   209–18
market development   96–7, 229–40
market penetration   184, 287
market saturation   6, 96–7, 229
market share   138, 192, 207, 210, 228
market size   106–10, 150–4, 204
market threshold   110, 205
Markusen, A. R.   4–6, 227, 259, 289
Marshall Plan   82–3, 85, 88, 90
Martinez (California)   55–6
Massey, D.   278
maturity
   of industries   2–13
   of markets   6, 91–101, 228–30
   of products   6–7, 96–7
Mellon Institute of Industrial
   Research (Pittsburgh)   56
Mensch, G.   3
merchant market   136, 245
mergers   6, 247–8, 250, 255
Merseburg (Germany)   41, 80
methane   25–6
methanol   179, 234
methyl rubber   66; *see also* synthetic
   rubber
Mexico   155–7, 159–62, 271
mezzogiorno (Italy)   270, 272–3, 274
Middle East   151–2, 154, 178–86,
   237, 289–92
Midland (Michigan)   46
minimum efficient size   110
Ministry of International Trade and
   Industry (MITI)   149, 248,
   251–2
Mississippi corridor   262–4
MIT Commission on Industrial
   Productivity   249
model complex   130–2, 134, 271–2
modular construction   182
Monsanto   49, 57, 100, 101–2, 209,
   211, 216, 249
Mont Belvieu (Texas)   129, 173
Montecatini   44, 86, 105, 113, 135
Montreal   194, 198
Morgenthau Plan   81
Mossmorran (UK)   223, 250
motor vehicle industry   11, 25,
   118–19, 228
multinational corporations   8–9,

32–3, 144–7, 154–6, 159–67,
   185–6, 202–6, 287–8
multi-plant companies   8–11, 85–6,
   101–6, 138–9, 250–7, 278
multiplier effect   261, 266–75

naphtha, as petrochemical feedstock
   29–31, 55, 85–6, 96, 126, 130,
   171, 173–4, 178
   price of   31, 126, 149, 159, 173–4,
   178, 191–3, 220
   surplus of   85–6, 96, 130
National Coal Board   101
National Distillers Products   101
National Energy Program (NEP)
   (Canada)   196–9
natural gas   25–31, 50, 54–5, 56, 57,
   66, 111, 128–9, 154, 179–84,
   190–1, 196–7
natural gas liquids (NGLs)   25–31,
   129–30, 173–6, 190–1, 221, 270
Naugatuck Chemicals Company   47
Nazi Germany   50, 67–8, 81
Neoprene   46, 67, 102
Netherlands, the   56, 85, 114,
   139–41, 216–18
new firms   280–1
nitrogen fixation   41–2
Norsk Hydro   34, 222
North Sea   31, 111, 222–3
'North–South' relationships   146–9,
   166–7
Norway   111, 222–3
Nova   32, 222
nylon   4, 14, 44, 46, 82, 102

oil companies (in petrochemical
   industry)   32–3, 51–2, 54–6,
   68–9, 85–7, 103, 111–13, 185–6,
   211, 219
oil price 'shocks'   20, 33, 152,
   169–70, 189, 199–200, 221, 229,
   238, 289–90
oil refining industry
   economies of scale in   119
   as source of petrochemical feedstock
   25–31, 54, 56–7, 60–2, 66, 83–7,
   128, 130–3, 171, 219–20, 262–4
   technical change in   52–4, 72–5

322 *Index*

war
  and diffusion of German chemical
    technology   81–2
  negative impact on German
    chemical industry   78–82
  as stimulus to development of
    chemical industry   41, 43–5,
    50–1, 64–89
war damage   78–80
Wesselling (Germany)   127
Western Europe
  coal industry in   83–4
  petrochemical industry in   82–7,

  91–7, 111–15, 207, 213–18,
  222–4
  oil refining industry in   85–6
Whiting (Indiana)   54, 57, 103, 128
Wilhelmshaven (Germany)   214, 238
Wilmington-Dominguez (California)
  56
Wilton (UK)   133, 219
World War I   41–2, 45–6, 50, 57,
  64–5
World War II   48. 65–82, 87–9

xylenes   23, 27